PRAISE FOR

Tantra Yoga: Journey to Unbreakable Wholeness

"Todd Norian's new book on Tantra is destined to be a classic. It is a stunning achievement: beautifully written, crystal clear, entirely accessible to the Western reader. I could not put it down. This is the kind of book that is the fruit of a lifetime of work, and it will be speaking to readers for decades to come. In many ways, the book itself is a living embodiment of tantra. It is both profoundly embodied and profoundly mystical. It points in the gentlest and most unassuming way to the profound mysteries of ordinary life. Bravo, Todd!"

Stephen Cope, bestselling author of *The Great Work of Your Life* and many other books on yoga and the spiritual life.

"Be prepared to be rocked out of your comfort zone as you read master yoga teacher Todd Norian's spiritual memoir. The questions he asks of his own life become your own, and the answers demand change. Here is the raw and messy material of a life—the shame, the betrayals, and the achievements, wrung from life's losses. *Tantra Yoga: Journey to Unbreakable Wholeness* is more than the story of one man's spiritual journey. It is a manual of self-inquiry and practices that, as you learn to listen to your heart, may upend your life. The Nondual philosophy and practices in this book will open your heart and expand your mind. As Norian guides you to sweep away the debris of your false self, get ready to reclaim your most authentic life. If you're ready for transformation, put *Tantra Yoga: Journey to Unbreakable Wholeness* on the top of your list."

Amy Weintraub, author of *Yoga for Depression* and the novel *Temple Dancer*.

"In his book, *Tantra Yoga*, Todd does something of enormous importance. He makes tantric philosophy 'real' by taking it to the hard questions we all face in our own lives. Too often, tantric philosophy is presented in terms of feel-good generalities while skirting the hard stuff. This treatment of tantric philosophy goes straight to where we live.

By making this a deeply contemplated, deeply personal, and deeply felt journey, Todd unfolds the urgent and healing relevance of a philosophy at the heart of hatha yoga that explores the central cosmic paradox: how divine, creative consciousness willingly assumes limitation and imperfection for the sake of creation, and then must walk the difficult path of self-acceptance — reconciling with limitations, sorrows, and doubts of self-worth to fulfill the journey home to wholeness."

Doug Keller, yoga teacher trainer, author of *The Therapeutic Wisdom of Yoga*, *The Heart of the Yogi*, and *Refining the Breath*.

"A mature knowledge of yoga philosophy interlaced with touching stories of personal life and childhood innocence make this book a beautiful adventure into the wisdom of the heart that is the true essence of Tantra, so often misunderstood in the West. You will learn, laugh, and love your way through these pages and come out wiser for the adventure."

Anodea Judith, Ph.D., author of *Eastern Body-Western Mind*, *Wheels of Life*, *Chakra Yoga*.

"Todd's writing touched, captivated, and inspired me to see familiar tantric teachings in a whole new light. He skillfully weaves wisdom teachings into his personal and often very amusing life story, which has the unexpected yet welcome effect of casting a light on the reader's own shadows. Todd reminds us in his own brilliant way that suffering is not a sign of failure or weakness, but rather a natural growth process. Thank you Todd for offering this message in your way, right now."

Desiree Rumbaugh, yoga teacher, co-author of *Fearless After Fifty*

"Through decades of study, practice, and teaching yoga, Todd Norian has cultivated an extraordinary gift for sharing the treasures of his path with all those who seek self-awakening. Told masterfully with warmth, humor, and unabashed candor, Todd's story will inform, delight, and inspire you to continue your own journey back to your true self, where wisdom, love, and joy abound."

Don Stapleton, Ph.D., author of *Self-Awakening Yoga*

"This is a tender account of author Todd Norian's quest to discover the meaning of life and the role of following his heart's deepest desires. Through his journey he explores dimensions of faith and the acceptance that both the light and the dark shadows of our lives have lessons to offer us."

Sharon Salzberg, author of *Lovingkindness* and *Real Change*

"Todd Norian has written a courageous spiritual memoir that is tender, tragic, humorous, and jaw-dropping. To his great credit, he opens his heart and shares his most vulnerable secrets with great candor -- an inspirational read for spiritual seekers in any tradition."

Constantina Rhodes, Ph.D., Professor of Religion, author of *Invoking Lakshmi: The Goddess of Wealth in Song and Ceremony*

"Todd Norian has written a beautifully crafted, emotionally honest, and deeply insightful addition to the understanding of yoga and its practice. By honestly reflecting on both his challenges and triumphs, Todd provides a living example of how to practice yoga. Because his study and practice have been so wide ranging, and profound, the prescriptions offered in this book will help anyone interested in becoming happier and adding unexpected dimensions of passion and joy into everyday living."

Patton Sarley (aka **Dinabandhu**) past Chief Executive of the Kripalu Center for Yoga and Health and the Omega Institute for Holistic Studies.

"Toward the beginning of this memoir, Todd Norian says, 'Here's the quintessential Tantric attitude: everything in life is for your awakening.' By this, he really means "everything." A highly adept yogi and skilled teacher informed and inspired by the perspectives of nondual Tantra philosophy, and with remarkable candor, honesty, and clarity of self-understanding, he shares with readers engagingly written narratives of his life that express his hopes, doubts, discoveries, heart-breaking disappointments, heart-bursting joys, realizations, inner transformations, and fulfillments. Drawing on his study and understanding of important historical texts and contemporary spiritual teachers from the Tantric tradition and interwoven with passages from philosophers, poets, psychologists, therapists, and others, this fascinating book demonstrates in narrative form the quite Tantric sensibility that, as Norian says, "We are like wrapped gifts, concealed intentionally. Life then is the process of unwrapping this gift slowly over time, savoring each moment as we come to know ourselves more deeply."

William K. Mahony, Ph.D., Professor of Religious Studies Davidson College, author of *Exquisite Love* and *The Artful Universe*

"Tantra Yoga is a profound testimony to the transformative power of the practice. Todd's vulnerability and wisdom come through in his writing, making this a valuable read for any seeker, whether student or teacher."

Elena Brower, bestselling author of *Practice You.*

"Todd has been a teacher and a role model for me for over 25 years. Throughout this time, I have watched him use the practices he lays out in this beautiful book to heal his heart and to serve his community with perseverance and grace. *Tantra Yoga* is a brilliant work of inspiration and wisdom…a "must read" for anyone on the path of the heart."

Rolf Gates, yoga teacher and author of *Meditations from the Mat: Daily Reflections on the Path of Yoga*

"As an avid reader of spiritual memoirs, I can say without reservation that Todd Norian's *Tantra Yoga* is an exceptionally good read. Inspiring, instructive, and heart-wrenchingly honest, this book deftly weaves Todd's story together with bite-sized tantric teachings that invite readers to deepen their own connection to a heart-centered life. If you have an interest in yoga, meditation, or living a fulfilled and happy life, this is a book worthy of your time and attention."

Danna Faulds, author of *Go In and In* and *Into the Heart of Yoga*.

"This is the very human tale of a sincere seeker, walking the path of spiritual unfoldment. In this personal memoir, Todd's shares experiences—light and dark—to reveal some of the insights at the foundation of tantra. His humor, honesty, and humility are laced with wisdom, reminding us that everything—the sacred and the profane—exists for the purpose of awakening. In keeping with his decades-long dedication as a teacher he leads us to reflect on questions that lead to self-inquiry and self-discovery."

Rod Stryker, author of *The Four Desires*, founder of ParaYoga, creator of the app, *Sanctuary*.

"It has been said by wise teachers that one of the highest aspects of a spiritual seeker is sincerity. If that is so, a deep bow to Todd Norian. His personal practice, his artistry, and his commitment to service are deeply informed by honesty and a pure heart. This book reflects both his journey of awakening as well as invaluable lessons for us all as we seek to be more alive and awake."

Jonathan Foust, MA, CSA, Insight Meditation Community of Washington and former president of Kripalu Center

TANTRA
YOGA

JOURNEY TO UNBREAKABLE WHOLENESS

A Memoir

By Todd Norian, Internationally Acclaimed Yoga
Teacher and Founder of Ashaya Yoga®

with

Mary Poindexter McLaughlin, M.A.

Book Cover by Seesaw Design: https://www.seesawdesign.ca/
Photo of Todd by Kevin Heslin Photography:
https://kevinheslinphoto.com/

DEDICATION

To all of my teachers and students, and all heart followers seeking true happiness, freedom, and fulfillment.

CONTENTS

FOREWORD

BY SALLY KEMPTON AND DOUGLAS BROOKS

Sally Kempton

In 2017, I had the pleasure of co-teaching with Todd Norian at a yoga conference. I had never been to one of his classes before, so on Saturday afternoon I dropped by for a few minutes—and ended up staying for two hours. Todd's class was alive with chanting, humor, precise yoga instruction, and an atmosphere of friendly devotion. But what particularly struck me was how seamlessly he integrated psychological work with yogic teachings. Here was a teacher, I realized, who had done several levels of inner work. He displayed mastery of postural yoga. Fluency in yoga philosophy. The capacity to help students kindle their hearts. And a profoundly mature understanding of the psychological work that a modern yoga student requires in order to discover the depths of healing that yoga can offer.

The book you're about to read is an honest, humble, and authentic account of the journey he took to become the teacher he is today.

Tantra Yoga belongs to one of the great genres of spiritual literature. It's a Seeker's Journey tale, a classic story of personal awakening and growth, layered with Todd's nuanced explanatory essays on yoga and modern tantra. It's also a great read. The chapters on life in an American yoga ashram in the late 20th century are alone worth the price of the book. If you've ever wondered what it would be like to give yourself to an eastern monastic tradition, you'll find out in these pages. And if you've ever lived in such a place, you'll recognize yourself in his descriptions.

But what really sets Todd's journey apart from the standard story of awakening and spiritual apprenticeship is his nuanced account of his experience with two talented teachers who were the center of major scandals. He emerged from those relationships clear-eyed, but with his faith in the yogic process intact. In other words, he was able to process his anger and hurt, and use his experience to deepen his own journey. So, in these pages, Todd is able to give us something that is still quite rare in the spiritual world: an authentic testament to one of the great paradoxes of spiritual discipleship.

How is it that a spiritual teacher can be both the catalyst of your transformation and the agent of your disillusionment? How can you accept the fact that the teacher who awakened you is also the person who betrayed and disappointed you? How do you process the betrayal without losing your faith in the path itself? To give an authentic account of this subtle aspect of the modern spiritual journey, you have to have taken the trip yourself. In other words, you have to have gone through a process that few people are equipped to handle: passionate commitment to a lineage tradition, soul-wrenching betrayal, and the willingness to use your disillusionment for your own transformation. Those who watch this process from the outside, or who refuse to face the complexities that can arise in a guru-disciple relationship, cannot realize the significance of this fiery lesson. When you can accept the fact that your revered teacher is also a flawed human being, it allows you to go a step further. It allows you to accept one of the key truths on the spiritual path: that you yourself are both a ray of divine light and an imperfect human who makes dumb mistakes.

This paradox lies at the heart of eastern spiritual teachings. The great Zen teacher Shunriyu Suzuki Roshi expressed the koan of our divine humanness when he said, "You are perfect as you are—and you could use a little improvement." As practitioners, we all walk the razor's edge of Suzuki's insight, and hopefully discover for ourselves how to balance both sides of the paradox. On the one hand, we need to do our character work, to hold ourselves to high ethical standards, and to become the best people we can be. But at the same time, we need to realize that self-improvement alone will not take us to the goal—because, as countless great teachers have told us, we are *already* which we seek. In time, through trial and error, we get the message that our human flaws and failures cannot prevent us from realizing the deeper truth of our own divine nature. In my experience, though, some of us don't learn without going through the process that Todd so beautifully describes. Disillusionment with your teachers, like disillusionment with your parents, can force you to realize that in the end, the highest wisdom is the wisdom that comes from within, from the state beyond conditioning and belief. And strangely, once you learn to trust your own wisdom, you also learn to bless the pain that led you there. In other words, you discover that disillusionment is an indispensable catalyst for spiritual growth.

What does it mean to grow through a relationship with a flawed mentor? First, it asks you to recognize how you projected your own spiritual light onto another person. Second, it requires you to realize that ultimately, the light is within you. Third, it asks you to take back your power. Fourth, it requires you to let go of your feelings of victimhood and genuinely forgive the teacher. Finally, it asks you to honor your teacher's own journey, and the indispensable gifts you received from him or her – even as you take to heart the lessons of your teacher's human mistakes.

And at that point, maybe, you might get to realize that there are no mistakes. That, as Todd says in these pages, life is for our awakening.

Todd is walking this path, and his witness can clarify it for you. One of the great gifts we receive from the unfolding dialogue between Eastern wisdom and Western psychology is the understanding that spiritual life is not a journey with a final end point. It's an ongoing dance of movement and stillness, of aloneness and relationship, of effort and grace, of wisdom and silliness. It's endless. It's filled with wonder. It is life itself. Todd's book embodies that insight. Enjoy the journey!

Sally Kempton is a widely respected teacher of meditation and spiritual wisdom. A former journalist who wrote for "Esquire," "New York," and the "Village Voice," she has spent over four decades practicing, teaching, and writing on meditation and spiritual philosophy. Sally spent 20 years as a swami in a traditional Vedic order of monks. Sally is the author of the best-selling books, "Awakening Shakti: The Transformative Power of the Goddesses of Yoga," and "Meditation for the Love of It."

Douglas Brooks

When I proposed study of a living Indian Tantric tradition to my Harvard mentors some forty years ago they first wanted to know how I knew. Their concerns centered on the ethics of such learning, the disclosure of "secret" materials, and maintaining critical perspective. Among the many features that form Tantra's definition, esotericism and secrecy necessarily come first. Tantra is an insider's game played by insiders not likely to come forward or ever reveal themselves, much less discuss their ideas or practices to outsiders.

What is generally known about Tantric practices is that they seem at best wholly indifferent to social norms and are far more likely to be deliberately transgressive.

Tantra poses a double bind: since you can't study Tantra without becoming a Tantric, how can you study Tantra as a Tantric? Put simply, if it takes one to know one, wouldn't revelation disqualify the Tantric *and* disqualify the scholarship? Can *secrets* be revealed *and* form the basis for critical study? The situation is made more complicated by Tantra's unseemly notoriety and how this reputation implicates any participant, be that in matters of practice or study.

My own first strategy of explication to my mentors was to contend that Tantra was *much more* than their familiarities. Yes, I had gained access as an insider but had also received permission to discuss matters freely and critically. Yes, I was privy to ideas and behaviors that were not regarded in some circles as wholly acceptable, but I knew that there was also *more* Tantra that was nothing like these sordid traditions. To put it bluntly, Tantra was indeed about far more than sex, more than secrecy, and more than magical claims and con games foisted upon the innocent by charlatans and hucksters. As for studying one's self, well, don't we all? Why would personal experience disqualify one from critical self-reflection?

I have taught Tantra for at least 20 years now not only as an academic endeavor but in practice to those who have asked. Just what these particular "Tantric" teachings entail can be easily discovered by any internet search. But the most important teaching about any Tantric study and practice is that it must be lived. Tantra becomes as much what is assimilated and experienced as it is what one hears and receives. In whatever ways a practitioner identifies with a tradition, a lineage, a teacher, the Tantra must be defined essentially as individual understanding and personal experience. Teaching becomes the choice to express those experiences in ways that others too can learn and make *their own* experiences. We can quibble over espoused doctrines or other matters of orthopraxy but like all matters of definition, what is argued over most is likely tied as much to critics asserting their own agendas. In the end, Tantra truly is what a Tantric says is Tantra and *that* is what we might study if we have access and opportunity.

Like most of the accomplished persons I would identify as Tantrics in history, Todd Norian is a person of unremitting curiosity, creativity, and intelligence. He has studied the history of religions, music, science, and endeavored to live a life of yoga and serious spiritual contemplation. *His* story as a Tantric is one only he can tell just as *his* understandings of Tantra reveal *yet another Tantric story.* We can safely leave it to Todd to tell us what Tantra is in his own experience. Perhaps just as importantly Todd will tell us what *more* Tantra can be when it is imbibed and practiced by so accomplished a yogin. This book represents an opportunity for any reader to hear a Tantric's story not only *from the inside* but *from the heart.* Here is a story driven by learning, serious contemplation and critical thinking, *and* a willingness to lay it all on the line personally and professionally.

Todd rises to the occasion to show just how one can be a Tantric and have a lucid, honest, and critical assessment of history and practices. He solves the double bind of being one and studying because he demonstrates how Tantric secrecy and esotericism can lead us to an open heart and a transparent conscience. Todd knows Tantra from the inside because he has learned from serious and competent teachers, done the work, and brought equal amounts of passion and sobriety to the discussion of a spiritual and professional life.

This is more than a book about Tantra or about what Tantra can be. This is a work that means to show a way forward, to provide insight and example that proves how much more Tantra *will* be when it is offered by a person of such unmistakable integrity and gifts.

Douglas Brooks is Professor of Religion in the Department of Religion and Classics at the University of Rochester in Rochester, New York, where he teaches Eastern Religions, Comparative Studies, and Sanskrit. He holds degrees from Middlebury College and Harvard University and studied in India at Madurai University and for many years under his teacher, Dr. Gopala Aiyar Sundaramoorthy.

ACKNOWLEDGMENTS & AUTHOR'S NOTE

I am grateful to all those I've had the privilege to interact with during the writing of this book. I've learned that it takes a village to publish a memoir of this scope, and I would need to write another book with my gratitude for everyone who helped me. I couldn't possibly thank everyone so I will mention a few people who were instrumental in my journey and who helped make this book a reality.

First off, I want to thank my family – my dad, Sanford Norian, my mom, Sandra Norian, my stepmom, Celia Norian, and my sister, Sherri Shovers, for their love, acceptance, and support and for always giving me the space to follow my heart and be me.

I wish to acknowledge, from the bottom of my heart, my co-writer Mary Poindexter McLaughlin, without whom this book would have remained in its unreadable raw form. Her uncanny ability to hear what I was trying to say underneath it all is what pulled this work together. She was the thread and the weaver who took the Tantric teachings and wove them into the narrative of my life. Thanks for hearing me, seeing me, and saying it could be so.

I am forever grateful to all of my teachers (music and yoga) with whom I've had the good fortune of being in their presence, who have showered their love, acceptance, knowledge, and blessings upon me, including Douglas Brooks, Paul Muller-Ortega, Sally Kempton, Bill Mahony, Constantina Rhodes, Don Stapleton, Katrina and Joel Feldman, Garrett and Ila Sarley, Sam Dworkis, Bobbi Goldin, Bill Dobbins, Louis Nagel, Ruth Rus, and Ruth Hemmes.

I want to thank Sally Kempton for her amazing love and support, for her capacity to speak directly to the heart of the student, and for contributing her Foreword. Her direct feedback to me about the manuscript, especially the title, was extremely helpful and timely. Special thanks to my teacher and friend Douglas Brooks for his unabashed teachings of radical affirmation and for contributing his Foreword. For the last 20 years, his genius, scholarship, brilliant insights, love, cajoling, and humor has cracked open my heart again and again. Thanks also to my teacher Paul Muller-Ortega for his profound wisdom and powerful practices that have opened a portal of creativity within me and stabilized my sadhana. Thanks to the Blue Throat Yoga community for their dedication and companionship.

I'm forever grateful to my longtime friend, mentor, brilliant author, and colleague in crime (an old ashram buddy), Stephen Cope, whose warmth, wisdom, and encouragement spurred me on to complete this work.

Special thanks to Constantina Rhodes for her careful review of my manuscript. Her philosophical suggestions and diacritics clarification were very helpful. Her friendship and down-to-earth goddess nature have been a gift in my life. Thanks also to Hareesh, Christopher Wallis, for his simple, elegant, and distilled teachings that continue to illuminate the Tantra for me. Thanks for his support and generous permission to adapt the 36 Tattva Chart.

I'm deeply grateful to David Kuttruff for his detailed editing, clarifying several philosophical points, and for adding Sanskrit diacritics. His genius and generosity are much appreciated.

Thanks to Marianna Adams and Gerry Hebert for their generosity, caring, and meticulous editing. Their enormous contribution to this work was unparalleled and so appreciated.

Many thanks and a deep bow to Stephanie Leeds *(Kalagni Rudraya)* who did the painstaking task of line editing and, in certain sections, helped me figure out what I really wanted to say. She talked me away from the ledge many times when I was lost in my own self-doubt and wanted to give up.

So much gratitude to Brooke Semple, graphic designer, for her beautiful work on the cover. Her tireless patience and positive attitude as I requested change after change of the cover, without ever complaining once, is worthy of sainthood.

This book would have never made it down the "birth canal" without the tremendous support and "midwifery" of the Ashaya Team (A-Team): Lisa Haggis, Brooke Semple, Terry Wolfisch Cole, Aria Greenberg, and my administrative assistant, Stephanie Leeds, who has stood by my side for many years through thick and thin without wavering. I feel so lucky to be surrounded by such great and capable beings.

I wish to acknowledge and thank Danna Faulds for her generous editing, use of her poem, and for her friendship over the years. Both she and her husband, Richard, have been by my side through much of my journey. Danna's poems have accompanied me through the most difficult times and continue to shine light on the path ahead.

Thanks to all of my friends and colleagues who shared the Kripalu experience with me back in the day and who continue to dedicate themselves to transformation, as well as my colleagues and friends from Anusara; their love and wisdom continue to uplift me.

Everything I share in this book is based on my own personal experience, perception, and memory. I tried to keep all of the dialogues truthful and without hyperbole. However, I take responsibility for the occasional expansion of the dialogue in support of the narrative without obscuring the underlying intention. I ask forgiveness in advance for any errors in my memory or perceptions that may differ from those of others.

My perceptions of my family are solely my own and do not reflect fully who they are. Nor do my depictions reflect my family's perspectives of themselves or of me. I love and cherish my family for being exactly who they were for me, and for who they are for me now.

Also, I want to acknowledge that, although I value and cherish my years of yogic experience and practice, I am not a yogic scholar, and this is not a scholarly work by any means. The teachings I offer here are based on what I heard, not necessarily what was said. However, I do stand boldly in my heart behind everything I share in this book as true and real for me, including the truth and efficacy of my transformational experiences. My deepest intention is to share what was meaningful for me in order to inspire, uplift, and empower others to see their own journey as sacred.

In addition, I have made an effort to alternate gender-specific examples and pronouns throughout the book, in order to ease the flow of text. Whenever I use a gender-specific term, please know that I am referring to all genders, unless explicitly stated.

All of the characters in this book are real. Some have given me permission to use their real names while others I've assigned a pseudonym to protect their privacy.

Note About Sanskrit Terms:
We are displaying Sanskrit terms in italics using the IAST (International Alphabet of Sanskrit Transliteration). Here is an easy chart you can use in order to pronounce Sanskrit terms correctly. We have decided to use this approach as it is more accurate, honoring the beautiful tradition from which this ancient wisdom has come.

Sanskrit (IAST)	English Pronunciation
c (as in citta)	ch (like "chitta")
ś (as in Śiva)	sh (like "Shiva")
ṣ (as in Kṛṣṇa)	sh (further back in throat)
ā (as in āsana)	longer "a" as in "father"
ī (as in Īṣvara)	"ee" as in "meet"
ū (as in ūrdhva)	longer sound of "u"

INTRODUCTION

It's Not About Sex

Today, just before sliding into the water for my U.S. Masters swim practice, I stood on the pool deck, stretching my hamstrings and shooting the breeze with Sophie. A 20-something athlete, Sophie is friendly, sweet, and always conversational.

Rolling her shoulders to loosen them up, she asked, "How was your day?"

"Good!" I said, "I spent the day writing my book."

"Neat. What's your book about?"

"Tantra yoga."

Her eyes lit up, she smiled wide, and in the split second before she responded, I thought: *Here we go.* Then, sure enough, she said, "Oh, you mean sex?"

I couldn't help sighing a little internal sigh. "No. Tantra is not about sex."

I considered explaining what Tantra *is* about, but since we both had laps to swim, we parted ways instead. As I sliced through the water in my lane, I thought about our discussion. Sophie's misunderstanding of Tantra is typical, because Tantra has been given a bad rap. Today, when you enter "Tantra" into an Internet search engine, up pop numerous sex-related sites. A quick scan of the books on Amazon's lists of Tantric books reveals that nearly half are related to sex, desire, or bodily pleasures. Why is this?

There are multiple reasons. Part of the misunderstanding in the West about Tantra is a carryover from a similar misunderstanding in the East – even in India. Historically, there were multiple versions of "Tantric Philosophy" across multiple Indian religions, including Hinduism, Buddhism, and Jainism. There are wide variations in the meaning of the word "Tantra" itself. It has been described as book, text, doctrine, or scripture. It is defined as "to save or protect a soul," "to expand and contract," and the most commonly cited, "a weaver's loom."

Tantra also gained a reputation for being associated with black magic practiced by charlatans with no grounding in the actual Tantric practices and sacred texts. Add to that confusion the many warring tribes and invasions, during which many of the Tantric temples were destroyed and the texts were either lost or hidden by practitioners for protection. It is no surprise that we end up with what we have today: an esoteric, bewildering concept.

Although all of that certainly helps to explain the basic lack of understanding that surrounds Tantra, it still doesn't explain why people associate Tantra with sex. Here is an oversimplified answer, one that will have to do for now: While other religions were turning *away* from the material world in favor of transcending it, the Nondual Tantric philosophies *embraced* the material/physical world as our spiritual playground. Thus, Tantra became known as the body-and-pleasure-friendly religion.

There is much, much more to it than that. And that is why this book exists. *Nondual Śaiva-Śākta Tantra,* sometimes called *"Kashmir Śaivism,"* came into my life after a long search, and now informs every facet of my life. The old saying, "When the student is ready, the teacher appears," certainly applies in this case, though I like to say, "When the student is ready, the *teaching* appears," a subtle but important distinction I make. After reading this book, you'll understand why.

For 13 years, I lived a monastic life at the then-ashram Kripalu[1] in Massachusetts, before it became the yoga and retreat center it is today. During my time there, I thought that yoga was one all-encompassing philosophy. In addition, I lumped Buddhism into the "yoga" category as well. I had no idea that there were distinctions between yoga and Buddhism, and within yoga itself. I thought all yoga philosophies were the same.

It wasn't until later, through study with yogic scholars, that I became aware of the distinctions between types and styles of yoga, traditions, and lineages of yoga and Buddhism. My whole understanding of yoga exploded with distinctions and nuance, which ultimately led me to *Nondual Śaiva-Śākta Tantra.*

I've devoted the rest of my life to understanding, living, and teaching the *Nondual Śaiva-Śākta Tantra* philosophy. It is the basis for Ashaya Yoga, the style of yoga I founded and teach worldwide. And even though I'm still deepening my understanding of it, I want to share with you what I know. I want you to have those basic teachings that have changed my life forever for the better.

Why share them now? Simple. One day I woke up and I was 50. The stark realization that my life was likely more than half over pushed me to evaluate my contribution on this planet. After some self-reflection, I decided that my purpose, my "North Star," was to give more: more inspiration, more support, and more joy. By setting down on paper my own journey, woven together with Tantric teachings, I could perhaps give others the tools I've learned for awakening to their own North Stars – not in a scholarly way, but by bringing Tantra to life in a deeply relevant, accessible way.

Tantra is a path of heart-centric learning. One of the purposes of this book is to help you deepen your connection to your heart, where longing resides: longing for a great life, an extraordinary life, a fulfilled life. You have the potential to live your dream. In the West, the phrase, "live your dream" has become synonymous with a supersized fantasy, one that is so enormous that it is impossible to fulfill. The dream I'm describing is the simple one you carry in your own heart. It's a gift or talent you were born with, a life lived freely in pursuit of your interests, or a vision of peace and joy.

All dreams are within reach if you follow your heart. It's a choice. *Nondual Śaiva-Śākta Tantra* teaches that we are, as Sting so aptly put it, "spirits in the material world."[2] Life is the greatest gift on the planet, the greatest blessing ever bestowed, but it's our choice to view it that way.

"Spirituality is optional," says my friend and Professor of Religion at the University of Rochester, Douglas Brooks. He's right. You can still live a normal, happy life without ever believing in or opening yourself up to a bigger energy. But my question is, how will you feel at the end of your life? Will you feel fulfilled? Will you feel that you lived a life of value, evolved your consciousness, and left behind a legacy of greatness? Will the deepest questions of your soul – why am I here, what is life about, and what is my purpose? – be answered without a broader perspective? It's impossible to know the answers. But I do know that without my Tantric philosophy guiding me, I wouldn't have challenged myself to ask these questions, to go beyond my perceived limitations. I wouldn't be who I am today.

When you look at life from a Tantric perspective, you become more and more able to discover fulfillment and direction in the questions themselves. Rainer Maria Rilke[3] expressed this perspective beautifully:

> *Be patient toward all that is unsolved in your heart and try to love the questions themselves, like locked rooms and like books that are now written in a very foreign tongue. Do not now seek the answers, which cannot be given you because you would not be able to live them. And the point is, to live everything. Live the questions now. Perhaps you will then gradually, without noticing it, live along some distant day into the answer.*

Living the questions requires the courage to step again and again into the unknown, leaning in the direction of your heart. It's all the journey. If you are reading this, you are already on the journey. And if you can't *not* be on the journey, how will you choose to travel? Here's the quintessential Tantric attitude: *everything in life is for your awakening.* If you choose to embrace this belief, then you are empowered to make meaning that uplifts your life.

The alternative – that some things are for your awakening, but others are not – suggests that some things should not have happened. You must have failed in some way or made a mistake; you must have zigged when you should have zagged on your spiritual path.

But if you believe that life keeps happening *for* you, then *everything* in life is for your awakening: light and dark, "good" and "bad." This is the yogic journey of making all experiences meaningful in an empowering way, and it has seen me through every one of the dark episodes of my awakening. In *Nondual Śaiva-Śākta Tantra*, there can be no light without the dark. When the night sky is the darkest, that's when the stars shine the brightest.

Yoga, derived from the Sanskrit root *yuj*, is defined classically as "union, or yoking," the way and means of uniting your individual nature with your universal nature. I define yoga as the process by which you shine the light of consciousness into the shadows of the unknown in order to gain self-knowledge – because when you know yourself, you know the whole universe. Just as the acorn seed contains the imprint and potential to become its full expression as the adult oak tree, the whole universe of infinite possibility and vastness, unbounded freedom, joy and bliss is imprinted deep in your heart. You have the DNA of the divine hidden there. As it says in the *Chāndogya Upaniṣad*[4] 8:1:3,

> *As large as the universe outside, even so large is the universe within the lotus of the heart. Within it are heaven and earth, the sun, the moon, the lightning, and all the stars. What is in the macrocosm is in this microcosm.*

That's where you come in. An acorn doesn't automatically sprout and become a tree; plenty of acorns are buried by squirrels and become their breakfast later. You are responsible to create the right environment to grow your "seed," to grow your spirituality. It needs the right kind of soil, the right amount of water and sunlight. You create that environment by touching the longing in your heart for freedom, a longing to know yourself, a longing for health, vitality, and a balanced lifestyle. You nourish your seed through the practice of yoga or any other spiritual practice. *Nondual Śaiva-Śākta Tantra* is just one of many paths but it's the one I love and the one I want to share with you now.

BACK ON DECK

I finished my last lap, touched the wall and paused, breathing heavily. I had had plenty of time to come up with an explanation of what my book is about. But once I lifted my foggy goggles and pulled myself out of the water to sit on the pool's edge, I could see that Sophie was gone. I resolved to tell her, the next time we met on the deck, the following:

This book is about the journey of my heart as I moved from one experience to the next: from my love of classical music to jazz, from jazz to yoga, from becoming a monk to meeting the love of my life and getting married, from letting go of my spiritual fantasy of living at an ashram for the rest of my life to teaching and traveling worldwide. This is about my journey of being heartbroken and spiritually betrayed by my beloved teacher and then losing my community not once, but twice. This is about being led back to where I started to finally recognize that the one I've been seeking and searching for my entire life, is me. I just didn't know it.

> *What we call the beginning is often the end*
> *And to make an end is to make a beginning.*
> *The end is where we start from*
> *[...]*
> *We shall not cease from exploration*
> *And the end of all our exploring*
> *Will be to arrive where we started*
> *And know the place for the first time.*
>
> ~T.S. Elliot, from *Four Quartets*[5]

Yet this book is not just about my personal journey. It's about the journeys we all must take. My wish is that this book may inspire you to access your heart, to lead you from the unknown to the known, from darkness to light, from insecurity to safety, and from fear to love as you walk your own path of hope, happiness, and true transformation.

Dive in.

NOTES

[1] Find out more about Kripalu at: https://kripalu.org.

[2] **"Spirits in the Material World,"** written by Sting, performed by The Police, on the 1981 album, *Ghost in the Machine*.

[3] Rilke, Rainer M, Franz X. Kappus, and K.W. Maurer. *Letters to a Young Poet*. London: Euston Press, 1943. Print.

[4] Swami Lokeswarananda, translator. *"Chāndogya Upaniṣad,"* Verse 8:1:3. *Wisdomlib.* https://www.wisdomlib.org/hinduism/book/chandogya-upanishad-english/d/doc238708.html. Accessed 8 May 2020.

[5] Eliot, T S. *Four Quartets*. New York: Houghton Mifflin Harcourt, 1971.

CHAPTER ONE

A Call from the Heart

Allow

There is no controlling life.
Try corralling a lightning bolt,
containing a tornado. Dam a
stream, and it will create a new
channel. Resist, and the tide
will sweep you off your feet.
Allow, and grace will carry
you to higher ground. The only
safety lies in letting it all in –
the wild with the weak; fear,
fantasies, failures and success.
When loss rips off the doors of
the heart, or sadness veils your
vision with despair, practice
becomes simply bearing the truth.
In the choice to let go of your
known way of being, the whole
world is revealed to your new eyes.

Danna Faulds, "Allow," from
Go In and In. Poems from the Heart of Yoga[1]

1982

My hands shake just a little as I dial the unfamiliar number. Nerves are to blame, of course, but also a combination of excitement and lack of sleep. All night I had lain awake on my narrow bed in the converted men's dormitory, or "brother's barn," listening to the snores of my roommates and planning the move. At 3:00 am, it had dawned on me that I needed to call my parents and share the news, immediately followed at 3:01 am by the slightly sickening realization that I'd have to inform my professors, too.

A restless hour later, I had thrown off the covers to start my last day at the normal wake-up time. In the dark, no one had noticed my heightened state, and I did my 30-minute jog in the hilly fields before I joined the others in our now-accustomed morning practices: an hour of *āsana* (yoga postures), an hour of *prāṇāyāma* (breathing exercises) and sitting meditation followed by chanting. A vague uneasiness had infused all of these activities until I found myself at noon, smudgy black pay phone receiver in hand, calling California.

"Hello?" my mom answers.

After a pause, I hear the operator's standard "Will you accept a collect call from… Todd Norian?"

My mom's voice sounds anxious as she accepts the charges, and then the operator turns it over to me. "Go ahead," she intones.

I clear my throat. "Hi Mom."

"Todd! Where are you?" Her voice is urgent.

"I'm still in Pennsylvania, at the ashram."

"Are you all right? Are you safe?"

2

"Yeah! I'm…really good."

She exhales. "Oh, thank God. Your father and I have been so worried."

Thinking I can quickly allay her fears, I interrupt. "I need to talk to you, Mom," I start, and then, without thinking, I plunge ahead and tell her. All of it. It tumbles out of me like water from a ruptured dam: how the last 10 days have been like nothing I could have ever imagined for myself; how the "Quest for the Limitless You" program that I've just finished lit me up from within; how I have discovered this refuge, a place where I can live amongst other seekers in peace and harmony; how I have opened and grown and cried tears of ecstasy; and how I finally feel happy and free.

Essentially, it is the kind of outpouring that parents in the 70s dreaded hearing from their children. But this is the 80s, and I am oblivious to how I must sound. I just talk and talk, and then finish with the coup de grace:

"And I've decided that I'm not going back to school. Ever."

I don't need to explain; she is fully aware of the free-ride fellowship at the University of Miami. I am supposed to be starting my master's in jazz composition and education in three days.

"I've changed my mind. I'm going to live here in the ashram, indefinitely."

There is complete silence. In the space between us, the word "indefinitely" hangs like smoke from a fired pistol. For the briefest moment, I think the silence signals acceptance, probably because I have been surrounded for the past 10 days by people who talk, live, and breathe acceptance. But no. She is stunned into silence.

"I— I don't…" she stutters, searching for some kind of response to the bomb I just dropped. Eventually, she completes the sentence. "I don't understand," she says simply, her voice a little tremulous.

I feel lousy. I know she is dealing with problems of her own, having recently moved to California and going through a divorce. My decision to forego a master's degree, in lieu of joining what she no doubt thinks is a hippie commune, is yet another piece of difficult news.

"I know. I'm sorry," I offer with genuine sympathy.

"You seemed so happy about the teaching and composing," she says, and she's right.

"I know, Mom, but this is bigger than that. I can't explain how… how much happier I am here." Even as I say that, I realize how impossible communicating my experience is going to be. How can you describe gradations of happiness?

"Oh, Todd. Are they… are they making you think things…" She trails off. I know what she's not saying.

"I'm not being brainwashed, Mom."

"Are you sure? You don't sound like yourself."

"It's because I've never felt this happy before. Happy and free."

There is another pause before she says, with resignation, "All right, well… if you think this is the right thing, there's nothing I can do. I can't stop you. I'm sure your father will be as… as confused as I am…. But what can we do? You're old enough to make your own decisions."

Even with utter certainty in my decision, I am stung by what feels to me like patronizing disapproval. I don't know what to say, other than, "Okay."

Perhaps sensing my hurt, she tells me she loves me and to be safe. "I love you too, Mom. I will," I reply, and put the receiver back in the cradle.

I sigh deeply. I knew she would have a hard time understanding but I had thought that sharing my excitement over this new path might win her over. And if *she* had a hard time… I shudder, imagining what my professors are going to say. Before I can think too much about it and get cold feet, I pick up the receiver again and dial the operator. *Let's get this over with*, I think.

I should have known that calling a professor collect would not set the stage for a happy conversation. From that rocky start, it slides downhill. No sooner have I told him my change in plans than I hear an inhalation, similar to the whooshing sound that comes before a tornado. "You're *what?*" he says, and a barrage of phrases like "utter disappointment" and "huge inconvenience" fills my ears. Years later, I won't recall the rest of the words he used in his cyclone of anger and disapproval. Like a dog who just hears "bad dog" and slinks away deaf, I hear his disappointment and nothing else.

Nothing, that is, except his continual question, "Are you sure?" to which my response is a confident, "Yes. I'm sure. I'm sure." Finally, having no choice but to accept my decision, he utters one more last-ditch "Are you sure?" and then gives up. It is clear—to him and to me—that he is not going to change my mind. Actually, he is not going to change *my heart*.

For that is the part of me that made this decision.

ŚRADDHĀ

Following your heart means opening your heart, being vulnerable, and letting your guard down. To do that you have to be willing to trust in something bigger: a bigger energy. *Śraddhā*, the Sanskrit word for faith, means choosing to place your heart where you believe you will have the most fulfillment and do the most good. When you place your heart in something bigger, when you have *śraddhā*, you have the courage to hold to your vision when life gets tough. We all give up too soon without faith.

But what is that "something bigger," really? The bigger energy is synonymous with life itself: everything that exists, seen and unseen, physical and non-physical. It's what you understand and what you don't understand. It's the totality of all that is, ever was, and all that will be. To trust that this totality exists takes *śraddhā*, and *śraddhā* is an exercise of personal choice. You choose to place your heart in a good place – in success, in hope, in love, in happiness, in peace – in the belief that grace abounds, that life has your back, and that life is intrinsically good.

Faith, then, is not a passive experience; it's an active choice. True faith comes from believing because you want to believe. This is different from blind faith. In her book *Faith: Trusting Your Own Deepest Experience*,[2] meditation teacher Sharon Salzberg defines three different kinds of faith: blind faith, verifiable faith, and wisdom.

1. Blind faith is acceptance without knowing why, without examination and without understanding. Because the hunger for approval or the need to be liked may drive blind faith, this type of unquestioning belief lays you wide open to manipulation.

2. Verifiable faith is faith that has been tested. You know something is true because you've experienced it. You understand the reason and you have evidence from trusted sources, but most importantly, your own experience dispels all doubt. You don't have to take someone's word for it. You felt it. You know it.

3. Wisdom is faith that is so ingrained in you that it is undeniable. You might say that wisdom is verifiable faith that has been time-tested. Over years of listening to your heart, experiencing how life works, and seeing your faith in action, you now have the deepest level of faith; you have wisdom that no one can shake. You have *śraddhā*.

To get to that place of wisdom you have to first make a choice. You must choose faith over doubt, the face of fear. Doubt diminishes faith and if left unchecked, will kill it. Making the choice to believe – in yourself, in positive outcomes – kicks off a chain reaction; faith leads to more faith. Like a muscle, faith can be strengthened, and it gets stronger with practice. Just as a strong-willed individual doesn't give up easily, "strong-faithed" people don't allow doubt to sabotage what they know in their heart to be true.

HṚDAYA

When I talk about the heart, I'm not referring to the physical organ located slightly left of center in the chest. I'm talking about *hṛdaya*, the spiritual heart of the human being, the center of the Self, located along the midline of the spine. (There is an important central energy channel located along the front of the spine known as the *suṣumna nāḍī*. For more about the body's energy channels – the *nāḍīs* – and instructions for clearing them, see Appendix A.) *Hṛdaya* represents the "middle of the middle," and it corresponds to the fourth *cakra* (energy vortex) called *anāhata*, which means unstruck silence, or the sound that is always resonating without force, like unconditional love, like grace. It just *is*.

There are three cakras below *anāhata*, representing our worldly cakras, and three cakras above, representing our spiritual cakras. The heart sits in the middle between spirit and the world, between heaven and earth. (It is symbolized by two interlacing triangles that make up a six-pointed star – a symbol that from my earliest memories of attending synagogue always stood for Judaism. I was surprised when I learned that the "Star of David" had other connotations, as well.)

Within the *anāhata* symbol, one triangle points downward and represents the manifestation current or embodiment. This is the descent of energy into matter, the unmanifest into the manifest, and the universal into the individual. The other triangle points upward, representing the current of liberation and the longing for freedom through transcendence. This is the movement of matter into spirit, the manifest into the unmanifest, and the individual into the universal. The heart is known as the "cave of the yogi" where the divine paradox that we are both matter and spirit resides; we are both limited and unlimited, finite and infinite. The heart holds our humanity and our divinity all at the same time.

Throughout the history of yoga, the heart is considered the location of our connection to the entire universe. The Self, the goal of all spiritual paths, dwells in the heart of the individual – just like the acorn that carries the adult oak tree's full potential for expression. Quantum physics, latecomer to the energy conversation, has determined that there is a unified field of cosmic consciousness that interpenetrates everything, and string theory suggests that we are all connected as if by threads of energy. Tantra figured that out a long time ago, adding that not only are we connected to divine energy and to each other, we are the expression of that divine energy.

> *In the city of Brahman is a secret dwelling, the lotus of the heart. Within this dwelling is a space and within that space is the fulfillment of our desires. What is within that space should be longed for and realized. As great as the infinite space beyond is the space within the lotus of the heart. Both heaven and earth are contained in that inner space, both fire and air, sun and moon, lightning and stars. Whether we know it in this world or know it not, everything is contained in that inner space.*
>
> ~from *Chāndogya Upaniṣad,* 8:1:1, 2 [3]

The importance of the heart rings throughout many of the ancient yogic scriptures: the *Vedas, Upaniṣads, Bhagavad Gītā, Bhakti Sūtras,* and more. The goal of all yogic realization and practice is to awaken and know your heart. In particular, the *Upaniṣads* are explicit about the home of the Self in the heart:

> *Bright but hidden, the Self dwells in the heart. The shining Self dwells deep in the heart. Everything that moves, breathes, opens, and closes lives in the Self. The Lord of Love is the source of life and truth. And may be known through love but not through thought. The Lord of Love is the goal for our lives. Walk this spiritual path and find him.*
>
> ~from *Muṇḍāka Upaniṣad,* 2.2.1 [4]

So why should you want to live through your heart? Because the heart is the doorway to the infinite, the passport to happiness. It's the home of your true nature, which is joy. When you go to your heart, you align with the bigger energy *and* awaken what's already written in your cells. Remember, you are human and divine. As Hafiz[5] says, "You are the sun in drag. You are God hiding from yourself." When you awaken your heart, you tap into your own infinite source of knowledge and facilitate the progression of your own unique path.

YOGA OF THE HEART

Why can't we see into the heart? Why can't we easily access the heart experience? Two reasons. The first is that many of us are out of practice. Distracted by the mind and constantly triggered into fight-or-flight survival strategies, we never have the time to truly let go. Accessing the heart means clearing off our mental screen by allowing all the software programs of the mind to sleep or shut down. Only then can the soft, accepting, sensitive, high-powered listening part of ourselves kick into gear. As poet William Blake put it, "If the doors of perception were cleansed, everything would appear as it is, infinite."[6]

The second reason is that even though the universe is in constant dialogue with us, many of us are usually asleep to it. Starting from the place of *śraddhā*, you must learn how to listen. There is a subtlety here: You must commit to *listen to your listening*. As in meditation, when the mind becomes still enough to recognize that there is a deeper "you" behind the thoughts, the listening must come from that place, that deeper you. For this, you need to back off and create some space between you and your reactions. If you can stay calm, breathe, and relax as you listen for the whisper of the universe, then you can begin to trust what you hear.

The next step, if you have tuned into the subtle voice of your heart, is to pay attention to what you are hearing. It's easy to write that inner voice off, to override it in favor of other, more pressing needs. When that voice speaks up, the tendency is to deny it, reject it, doubt it, judge it, and push it down. "Leave my stressful relationship? Play more? Let go of judgement? Nah, that can't be what my heart is saying." We are quite good at ignoring the messages from within, usually because those messages conflict with the status quo.

But with practice, you will get better and better at allowing that voice to come forward and inform your everyday life. Your heart will become your compass. You will begin to weigh the messages of your heart against your feelings and your interpretations of those feelings. At that stage, you will be able to discern whether or not you want to follow your heart; there may be times when there are good reasons not to. Then, at least, you know you are making a conscious choice, not a reactionary or habitual one.

Ultimately, when you begin to operate within the realm of your heart, your whole life becomes a flow and a journey of joy. When that happens, you reunite with the essence of all that is you. This is yoga.

Most yoga systems and traditions describe the heart as the final destination or resting place of the soul. I like to think of the heart as a plateau or "pit stop of love" along the journey of the soul, a place you can always return to again and again. Is the journey ever finished? From my perspective after more than four decades of yoga practice, and from the perspective of *Nondual Śaiva-Śākta Tantra*, the answer is no, the journey is never finished. The spiritual journey is about penetrating the layers of the heart to gain experience and knowledge of the self, during every lifetime. It's an arduous journey that requires courage and takes no less than all of you. It's not for the faint of heart, surely, but since you're here anyway, why not make the effort?

DISAPPOINTING OTHERS

When you follow your heart, you will inevitably disappoint others. It's a fact, and there's no way to get around it. Choices that emanate from deep inside you are often ones that take you in a direction that others don't expect and often don't like. Choices like that make others uncomfortable, because they shake up the status quo. They disrupt the narrative others have created for you and for themselves.

Individuals will go to great lengths to keep the calm. Consider this: how many of us choose to ignore the quiet promptings of the heart, to avoid those inevitable disappointments? You may not even be consciously aware that you are making choices based on the imagined reactions of others. It becomes habitual, this tuning in to others' needs before you honor your own. I always like to say that if you don't disappoint others regularly, who might you be regularly disappointing?

I am a huge proponent of taking care of your own needs first, and *then* supporting others. When you take care of yourself and nourish yourself, you will have an overflow of energy that allows you to give even more fully to those whom you love.

The airline industry got it right. The now-iconic speech of the flight attendant who tells us to put on our own oxygen mask first before putting them on others is self-care genius. Yes, it's okay to help yourself first, even in an emergency. In fact, it's particularly crucial during life's most chaotic times—those times when we are most likely to ignore our own needs. (Though I don't recommend this, I have to admit that the suggestion made by one Southwest airlines attendant, "If you're traveling with two children, after you put the mask on yourself first, then put the mask on the child you love most next" – made me laugh.)

On that day in August 1982, I knew that every cell of my body was in agreement with moving to the ashram. I had to put on my oxygen mask first. Even though I knew that by doing so I was now the source of deep disappointment and inconvenience for my professors and parents, I was able to hold firm and, at the same time, let go of what they wanted for me. My certainty, my *śraddhā*, gave me strength.

Having spent my entire young life seeking self-worth by never disappointing or angering others, I needed that strength.

EXERCISE: Deep Heart Listening

Take a few minutes now to sit quietly with yourself. Have your journal and pen ready. Close your eyes and take a few deep breaths. Soften your skin. Relax and allow yourself to reflect within. Look into your heart with an open mind, a curious mind, a nonjudgmental mind. When you're ready, either have a friend read the questions to you or softly open your eyes and read the questions to yourself. After each question, jot down whatever first comes into your mind. What are you feeling in your heart?

1. Where in your life do you feel as though you might be disappointing yourself?
2. What's in the way of following your heart?
3. Who are you afraid you will disappoint if you follow your heart?
4. If you disappoint someone, what will the cost of that be to you emotionally?
5. What will be the payoff or benefit to you for following your heart anyway?

NOTES

[1] Faulds, Danna. *Go In and In. Poems from the Heart of Yoga.* Peaceable Kingdom Books. 2002.

[2] Sharon Salzberg, *Faith: Trusting Your Own Deepest Experience.* New York: Riverhead of Penguin. Reissue 2003. Print.

[3] Swami Lokeswarananda, translator. "Chāndogya Upaniṣhad," Verse 8:1:1,2. *Wisdomlib.* https://www.wisdomlib.org/hinduism/book/chandogya-upanishad-english/d/doc238708.html. Accessed 8 May 2020.

[4] Swami Sitarama Sastri. "Muṇḍaka Upaniṣhad with Shankara's Commentary," Part 2, 2:1. *Wisdomlib.* https://www.wisdomlib.org/hinduism/book/mundaka-upanishad-shankara-bhashya. Accessed 8 May 2020.

[5] Ḥāfiẓ. "The Sun in Drag," *The Gift: Poems by Hafiz the Great Sufi Master.* Purported to be translated from the original Persian (Farsi) by Daniel Ladinsky. New York: Penguin, 1999. Print.

[6] Blake, William. *The Marriage of Heaven and Hell.* London: Camden Hotten, 1868. Print.

CHAPTER TWO

The Shame Game

Shame is a soul eating emotion.

Carl Jung[1]

NORMAL, U.S.A

In the 1960s and 70s, I grew up in the epicenter of normalcy, East Grand Rapids, Michigan. I lived in a standard brick-and-wood colonial in a quiet suburban neighborhood, surrounded by undeveloped fields and connected backyards. My sister and I played the typical games with our neighborhood friends: kick the can, capture the flag, red rover. I did flips on our trampoline, built forts in every possible location, and ate Rice Krispy treats at Fourth of July potlucks. Like many boys my age, I loved reptiles. I kept turtles and I caught frogs to feed my pet snakes.

Unlike the rest of the kids on the block, I was Jewish. Judaism wasn't a huge deal in our household. But my father was brought up extremely Conservative, almost Orthodox, so our family went to a Conservative, just-short-of-Orthodox synagogue and celebrated all of the major holidays, not just Yom Kippur and Rosh Hashanah. Our family went to services on most Saturday mornings, to Sunday school on Sunday morning, and to many Friday night services.

East Grand Rapids was primarily made up of Dutch Reformed Christians, and all of my neighbors growing up were non-Jewish. The Jewish community was tiny, but close-knit; almost all my parent's friends were Jewish. Their kids were my friends too, and we did everything together as families: holiday celebrations, cookouts, vacations to Lake Michigan, or skiing up north. They were our tribe.

I was allowed to have non-Jewish friends as well, which was lucky since only a handful of classmates at my elementary school were Jewish. I loved my non-Jewish friends, particularly my next-door neighbor, who moved in when he was three and I was four. On the day he arrived, I went over to his house and introduced myself. We became close friends, but it became clear to me that his family was different. They said grace before meals, which I really liked. And they celebrated Christmas.

Now don't get me wrong. I loved getting one present every night for the eight nights of Hanukkah, particularly when the presents included

14

matchbox cars. I had tracks set up all over the house and would play with matchbox cars for hours on end.

But that paled in comparison to Christmas morning, when my friend received about 20 different presents all at once. I always made a point to invite myself over to his house on Christmas morning or the day after, so we could play with all of his new toys and games. I think I looked forward to his Christmas more than my Hanukkah.

Growing up with a mix of friends from different traditions, I felt like I had the best of both worlds. In photographs from every birthday of my young life, there we all are: my entire Jewish "family," a few non-Jewish buddies, and me, sitting around the table waiting for me to blow out the candles.

On the outside, I portrayed the image of a normal American Jewish kid in the early 70s. Ironically, because I was taught in Sunday school from the time I was very young that the Jews were God's chosen people, I even pretended for a short time that I was something special because I was chosen and my non-Jewish friends weren't. But I couldn't fully buy into that concept. On the inside, I did not feel normal. I did not feel special. I felt unworthy.

> *Shame is the intensely painful feeling or experience of believing that we are flawed and therefore unworthy of love and belonging. We are hard-wired for love and belonging: hard-wired for connection. It's what gives purpose and meaning to our lives. The fear is we are unworthy of love and belonging. Wherever love and belonging are absent, there is suffering.*
>
> ~Brené Brown: *Men, Women, and Worthiness*[2]

When I look back, although I see much beauty and grace, I also see a string of darkness originating long ago. I know I'm not alone in having had feelings of unworthiness. As I now travel around the country teaching yoga, I encounter so many adults who still carry the same kind of darkness from an early age. The lucky ones find their way through to the other side; the unlucky ones carry their burden for a long time, some throughout their entire lifetimes.

Research professor and author Brené Brown does groundbreaking and enlightening research on the topic of shame. According to her:

> *Many of us will spend our entire lives trying to slog through the* <u>*shame swampland*</u> *[emphasis mine] to get to a place where we can give ourselves permission to both be imperfect and to believe we are enough.*

Although the circumstances are different, I know for sure that all of us have had experiences as children that shaped our fundamental beliefs about ourselves, beliefs that we are somehow "less than." Mine started with a nightmare.

PARALYZED

Everything is dark. Blackness surrounds and suffuses me. I can't see out. There is no light, only darkness, and the sensation of a great pressure bearing down on me. A thick, dull weight compresses my head and body as if space itself is closing in on me, as though I'm inside a coal mine that is slowly collapsing. I sense imminent danger, but I can't escape, I can't run. At my feet there's some gruesome, reptilian creature opening its wide, dark mouth to swallow me whole. I am shaking. Cold sweat covers me and I scream for my life but there is no one to help me. No one hears me. I am alone, utterly alone. The darkness closes in on me. I'm suffocating. I'm trapped. Doomed. Dense space tightens around my neck and body. I can't breathe. Helpless. *Help me.*

"Help!"

I feel a stinging blow across my cheek. The pain pulls me into my bedroom, my bed, reality. There are more blows. My dad slaps me again and again until, gasping, I open my eyes. The light from the bedside lamp blinds me, but I can see the outline of my mom standing nearby. I am breathing hard and crying in jagged bursts. My eyes adjust. I hear my dad murmur, "Don't cry. You're okay. You're safe. We're here. You were having a nightmare, Todd. Calm down and try to go back to sleep." My mom looks scared. They both do. I nod, confused still, but exhausted. My dad rubs my back in slow circles, and eventually, I melt back into sleep.

CONCEALMENT

This nightmare recurred from ages two to five. My memories of it are blurry, but its impact on my life is clear. Even though my parents dismissed it as unimportant, saying, "It's normal for children at that age to have nightmares," I can see that those horrifying dreams had a purpose. I outgrew the dreams themselves, but the feelings of anxiety, fear, and ultimate doom that they evoked accompanied me into adulthood, into those times of my life when my path forward was unclear or difficult.

I've interpreted the nightmares in many ways and have come to understand them as both a representation of my survival instinct and an imprint of the primordial experience of the universe becoming me, of infinite freedom becoming finite. This is one of the most fundamental themes of Tantric teachings, so let me take a moment to explain it.

The main premise of *Nondual Śaiva-Śākta Tantra* is that the transcendental Absolute, which is beyond attributes, paradoxically forms the essence of all that is. What does that mean? It means that the infinite *chooses* to become finite, by limiting itself...as you, and as everything around you. It limits itself and conceals itself in the world in order to be revealed and experienced as *pūrṇa*, fullness in the infinitude of form. It has to limit itself in order to experience its limitless nature.

> *Grace, the blessing of the God/Goddess, is nothing but an act of remembering, or self-revealing, that cancels out the previous act of forgetting or self-concealing.*
>
> ~Christopher Wallis, *Tantra Illuminated* [3]

Your life, then, is the expression of the infinite. Your physical being and the manifest reality around you are not illusions, nor are they inferior to the Absolute. Rather, they are real, and they exist as the living embodiment of the great Absolute in limited form.

The Big Bang can be seen as the moment the vast universe of oneness exploded and broke apart into a multiplicity of finite forms in order to experience its own existence in myriad ways. The "uni-verse," one song, chooses to become the "multi-verse," many songs, taking the form of you and me and everything that exists. It's as if the Absolute leaves its home to have an adventure in the relative in order to experience yet another facet of itself. Keep in mind that the relative is not merely a contracted form of the universe and therefore inferior; instead, it is the exalted crystallization of the divine's desire to know itself. You are the embodiment of wonder itself.

Another way of saying this is that "earth is sky, condensed." Earth contains all of the qualities of the vast and unlimited sky but in limited form. In the process of the contraction of the Absolute, no amount of its fullness is lost. The form changes, but the essence remains unaltered.

When the Absolute limits itself through the vehicle of embodiment, it invariably experiences cosmic amnesia. It forgets who it is and where it came from.

The purpose of the practice of yoga, then, is to help us reawaken and realize that the Absolute is hidden deep within our own hearts. It's as close to us as our own breath. It's the life force that has always been here, has never left, and will always be here. The Absolute is contained within the marrow of everything that is.

This idea of cosmic amnesia sets the stage for *Nondual Śaiva-Śākta Tantra*'s unique understanding of suffering. It's the only philosophy I know that holds a positive view for why suffering and limitation exist in the world. Suffering or *saṃsāra* (the disease of worldliness) is real; it is not an illusion. But the cause of suffering, while also being created by negative *karma* (action due to laws of cause and effect), is the play of

Śiva, the great light of consciousness. Basically, *Śiva*, out of his own delight, chooses to limit himself in order to experience the revelation of his true unlimited nature again. It is *Śiva* who self-conceals (*sva pracodana*) for the thrill of self-revelation (*sva prakāśa*). *Śiva* causes himself to forget – the origin of suffering – so he can delight in remembering again.

The main point here is that without concealment (forgetting) there can be no revelation of our limitless nature (remembering). You need one to experience the other. If you never forget who you are, you never have the joy of remembering again.

In Tantra, limitation is an essential facet of the dance of creation. The one infinite, unbounded universe chose to limit itself by becoming you for the sake of its own delight. Ultimately, the purpose of limitation of any kind is to help you awaken to your unlimited, joyful nature.

To be clear, my recurring nightmare was not one of joy or bliss. I was scared to death! I can only place this in the category of concealment. By experiencing the contractive pressure within the nightmare, I was embodying the great universe's contraction. Later, I did find the other half of that equation, the delight in the revelation of remembering my true nature – though it took a long, long time. It's a paradox, but Tantra is filled with them. Instead of trying to fix the problem, Tantra is about embracing the paradox. Only in paradox does this life make any sense.

I know now that my father's slaps were loving and that they came from a sincere desire to help me. Yet at the time I felt I was being hit for something I couldn't control, and I interpreted them to mean that I was flawed. The unconscious message I took away was, "Stop crying. Big boys don't cry. There must be something wrong with you."

BANANA NOSE

My transition from kindergarten to first grade is my first conscious memory of feeling unworthy. Breton Downs Elementary School kindergarten was a sweet, safe place. During recess outside, when boys chased girls and girls chased boys, I was overjoyed to find myself always pursued by the cutest girls. After letting them catch me, we would disappear into barrels on the playground, kiss each other's cheeks, and pull each other's hair. I was deliriously happy to feel so connected and loved.

Inside, we sat in clusters in the warm, comforting presence of our teacher, singing songs and finger painting. It was a cocoon. Suddenly, on the first day of first grade, all that warmth and connection evaporated. Seated in uniform rows, we were given mimeographed sheets and assignments. It was as though I was expected to be an adult, overnight. I was totally disoriented. To make matters worse, I also found myself the target of unwelcome attention from a few other boys in the class.

"Hey! Banana nose!"
"Bird face, bird face, Todd's got a bird face!"
"Can you smell better with that big nose, huh?"

I never let on to the other kids how hurt I was; I just laughed off their insults. Yet every morning for about six months, I had a stomach ache. Sometimes it was so intense I would call my mom from school to come take me home. I never let on to my mom my true feelings. Once home, I would disappear into the four goldenrod-colored walls of my bedroom and stare with disgust at the reflection of my large nose in the mirror. I hated it. I hated myself for having it. I was so ugly.

As siblings often do, my sister Sherri found a way to compound my misery. She was three years older than I, and to tease me, she drew the ugliest pictures of me she could, with a purposefully misshapen head and lopsided features, distorted and hairy. To make sure there was no mistake, she always added an arrow pointing from her title of the piece, "This is Todd," to the picture. Waving the work of art in front of me was like waving a red cape in front of a bull. Every time I reacted instantly, chasing her around the house, flinging insults and angry threats that I would beat her up when I caught her, which I never did. The three-year head start she had on me ensured she was bigger and could outrun me. I always eventually gave up, feeling exhausted, diminished, and hurt.

20

I'm certain she had no idea that her preferred instrument of teasing me pushed the exact button of shame that was perpetually pressed by my classmates in school. And yet, it was one more instance where I felt flawed for something outside my control. I'm embarrassed to admit I took some comfort when I found out later that Sherri suffered in the same way over her own oversized nose. Ultimately, however, whatever schadenfreude I felt at her misery didn't last.

Around this same time, I was interested in exploring the differences between boys and girls – as many children are at that age. There was a neighborhood girl I knew, who traded rides on our backyard merry-go-round for showing me her privates. One summer afternoon we were in the midst of that enterprise when my mom appeared.

She took one look at us and said immediately, her voice low and disapproving, "Todd, you come inside right now."

I felt embarrassment wash over me, a sick, hot tide. I knew I had done something terribly wrong. Mom sent me up to my room, where I hunkered down like a criminal awaiting sentence.

Later that day, when my father came home, I heard them discussing in hushed, urgent tones. They called me from my room and sat me down in the olive-green striped chairs in the living room. My dad sat across from me with pursed lips and sullen eyes. He spoke with a forced calm that belied anger underneath.

"We don't do these things, Todd. Don't ever do that again."

I considered asking "why?" but the severity of his face shut me down. I nodded, and that was the end of it. Except that it wasn't. I still was curious, and my neighbor friend was still willing, so we found ways to hide our exploration, driving it – and my guilt – underground. Shame embedded itself in me way, way down, like an invasive plant that had found fertile soil.

My parents told me we don't do these things, yet I was still doing them. *There must be something wrong with me.*

WHAT IS SHAME?

In order to gain a deeper understanding of shame, it's useful to compare shame with guilt. According to Brown, guilt is initiated by action and can be expressed as, "I did something wrong." Shame, on the other hand, is experienced as a state of being and can be expressed as, "I am wrong." Guilt is easier to overcome since an apology for unskillful action caused by poor judgment can often make things right again. When you feel guilty, you usually want to do better next time. There's a sense of hope and perhaps a learned lesson. Shame is demoralizing and destructive because it belies a deeper belief that your intrinsic flaws are permanent.

You will never get it right. Brown claims that people with unresolved shame take one of three approaches to life: fight, flight, or freeze. They fight against life by becoming defensive, bullying others, or forcing their beliefs on others in order to get their way (anger is often a smokescreen for shame); they flee by disappearing, shrinking, or going underground (think of a caged animal trying to escape); or they freeze by becoming immobilized and holding shameful feelings inside ("If I can keep it a secret, it might just go away"). This last mechanism is similar to fighting, but it's directed inward and can cause deeper issues such as depression, addiction, even suicide.

Our susceptibility to shame has provided fertile ground for many religious traditions that say:
- "You are not perfect, and therefore you must return to earth to suffer until you finally get your act together."
  or
- "I've been trying to teach you to shape up, but you don't listen. You continue to follow your desires and choose lust over me. Therefore, I will punish you. You're a sinner."
  or even,
- "You came into this world already a sinner."

I call this the Santa Claus philosophy: *"You better watch out, you better not cry/ Better not pout, I'm telling you why/Santa Claus is comin' to town… He knows if you've been bad or good/So be good for goodness sake."* [4] Life then becomes a measuring process with God holding the yardstick. It's basically a tradition that makes God something *other* than you.

It is this philosophical ethos from which the notion of self-torture arises. There are numerous examples of adepts and saints who seek to inspire believers to transcend human desires in order to gain divine favor. The Buddha starved himself and tortured his body in the name of enlightenment. At one point, he sat under the Bodhi Tree and didn't get up until he had achieved it. Christ carried the cross and died for our sins. Clearly, martyrdom is not new.

But how do you gain enlightenment by punishing yourself? Tantra takes a different approach. Here the view of the world is not a test of perfection, with a prize of immortality at the end of the assessment. It's not win or lose, heaven or hell. No one is watching to evaluate whether you prayed hard enough, suffered enough, tortured your body enough, or repented enough to be "saved." Suffering is not a sign of failure and weakness; rather, it's a natural process of growth.

Within the Tantric paradigm, yes, there is karma and when you misalign, you have to take responsibility for the consequences. But there is no moral judgment of shame hovering over your imperfections. Your imperfections – your limitations – are caused by the universe itself, and therefore your smallness (or sins, in punitive parlance) is for good reason. The Tantra teaches you to view your limitations as guideposts, markers set there by the universe to draw you back to the experience of your vast universal nature.

The most common yogic teaching from the Classical Yoga and early Buddhist traditions is that life is suffering. Incarnating in a body that gets old, decays, and finally dies, is the epitome of suffering. I agree that suffering is real; we do get old and die. But isn't there more to life than

23

suffering? Must suffering be the ground of our being? Tantra provides an answer.

Tantra does not deny that there is suffering, but its approach turns the traditional yogic philosophy *uttānita* (upside down). In Tantra, suffering is seen as a misalignment with nature. You are already free. You just don't know it. Your suffering isn't because you've been bad and you need to repent for your sins and you didn't come here because you failed last time. Earth is the place to come to wake up to who you really are.

Rather than waiting until you die to achieve your salvation, you can have enlightenment while you are still here in your body. Instead of using yoga to transcend the physical in favor of the spiritual, the goal is to get more into your body, more into life, more into your role and relationships because God is in you as you. You, and everything around you, are the embodiment of the universe. That universe is a much more forgiving, compassionate, purposeful, and positive place.

As a kid, though, I was still mired in shame. Day after day of unhappiness at school sent me searching for relief. Of my available choices – flight, flight, or freeze – I chose flight. I disappeared into music.

PIANO

You know what a gift is by the way it makes you feel when you do it. For me, clearly, it was the piano. Before I ever touched the keys, I loved listening to the piano. Sherri started taking piano lessons when I was in kindergarten. I would lean against the brown Cable console piano when she played songs like "Happiness Is" from *You're a Good Man, Charlie Brown* or "Love is Blue" and just melt into the sounds.

Music transported me beyond the bullying of my classmates to a place that felt secure and joyful. I wanted to play, too, but my parents made me wait until I turned eight to take lessons. I still don't know why. When I finally started lessons after those interminable two years it felt like I had come home. I played for the sheer joy of it and within a year I surpassed Sherri's skill level. Sitting on the cushioned bench covered with my grandmother's light green floral crochet, I got lost in the sounds. Sometimes just touching the smooth ivory keys could take me to that place of security and ease.

My father was a trumpet player-turned-insurance salesman who had played in the marching band while studying at the University of Michigan. He used to practice every day, a habit that continued into his child-rearing years, so I'm certain I heard music in utero. Growing up, I listened to my father for hours as he practiced scales and drills on the trumpet, and when I began to play the piano, I adopted his work ethic. I, too, practiced for hours – only this time it was my grandfather who listened.

My maternal grandfather, Aaron Stolorow, lived with my grandmother Ida on the other side of town. The sharpest dressed man in Grand Rapids, Grampa always wore perfectly fitted clothes over his deep brown tan. When I visited, he always picked me up, the spicy aroma of his aftershave lotion (mixed with freshly washed and scented clothes) enveloping me. He held me suspended in a strong bear hug and gave me a big kiss on my little cheek to say hello. I grew to love his smell because it forever reminded me of those warm greetings.

As I grew, I spent more time at his house. In the summer, he hailed me from the front porch where he sat in a chair with his shirt off, drinking his morning coffee and reading the newspaper. With a big grin, he ushered me into the living room. "She's been waiting for you," he'd say, gesturing toward the rickety old baby grand Grinnell piano sitting in the corner. "She" was faded and always slightly out of tune, and more than a few of her ivory keys had cracked and turned grey. None of that mattered to me.

What mattered was that Grampa would refill his coffee, settle himself into his favorite chair at the other end of the living room, and close his eyes – the better to hear me. He sat there the entire time I practiced, listening and drinking his coffee. For hours I worked on classical pieces and popular pieces, as well as scales and technical drills. He couldn't possibly have enjoyed listening to what I was playing, because let's be honest: who can stand listening to hours of *Hannon: The Virtuoso Pianist*? But Grampa didn't listen for entertainment; he listened because he loved me.

TANTRA: FROM EAR TO EAR

In the study of yoga, the teachings are transmitted from teacher to student. However, it's not exactly what the teacher says that transmits the knowledge; it's what the student *hears*. It is said that the esoteric teachings of Tantra are not transmitted from mouth to ear only. They are transmitted from ear to ear. What's important is *how* you listen. What is the meaning you assign to the teaching? What is touched inside of you? What's waking up inside? How do you feel listening to this teaching? What do you hear in it and what does it make you think about? How does that teaching make sense to you?

Being a musician, I loved this idea when I first heard it. Developing a good ear was an integral part of my musical training. I spent hours listening to music, training my ears to hear notes, chords, particular keys, and especially intervals (the distance between two notes). Later in my jazz studies, I learned that to improvise, I had to hone my ability to listen deep within myself. What music I played spontaneously came from what I heard inside myself, blended with my knowledge of the idiom, my technical skills, and my emotions.

Since its inception, jazz has had myriad practitioners and, therefore, multitudes of interpretations, each one as unique and beautiful as panes of a stained-glass window. Yoga philosophy encompasses that same kind of gorgeous diversity; there are as many different interpretations of yoga philosophy as there are authors, teachers, and students who study it. Every time I pick up another book on yoga philosophy, I discover a slightly different commentary. This is the beauty of yoga philosophy. Like jazz, it is creative, always expanding, and infinite. In teaching yoga, I always say there are no mistakes, only learning. The same is true for jazz: there are no mistakes, only solos!

I am not a scholar and never pretend to be. Rather than put forth teachings in a scholarly way, I share what I heard my teachers say, blended with my own experience. I offer those teachings that have made the biggest difference to me in terms of my capacity to embrace life and find its deepest joy and fulfillment. Given that the Tantric teachings are transmitted from ear to ear, I trust that what I share with my students inspires deeper listening inside themselves. And then I invite them, like good improvisers, to synthesize the transmitted teachings into their own beautiful melodies.

I'll never know for sure what Grampa took away from his hours of listening to my piano practice. Occasionally, however, I would come to the end of a piece and hear a grunt of approval from the other side of the room, something like "boychik, boychik, boychik," or "yessiree, yessiree, yessiree," or "yowza, yowza, yowza." Meaningless Yiddish-sounding words that were either made-up or authentic, I never knew which. It didn't matter. When he uttered these sounds, I heard them as the greatest trio of compliments a grandson could receive.

COMPETING FOR LOVE

Piano became my go-to activity. I practiced for hours after school, on weekends, and during vacations. I was so enthusiastic that in third grade, my piano teacher Ruth Kuipers entered me in a local competition. I was excited. I had played recitals at her house with all her students and their families, as well as in downtown Grand Rapids at the St. Cecilia Music Center. Those were difficult experiences but manageable. How different could a competition be from a recital? When the day came, I showed up at St. Cecilia's nervous but ready to do my best.

The grand auditorium filled slowly with overwrought piano students and their parents or teachers. I took my seat next to Mrs. Kuipers and clung to my sheet music like a safety blanket, my sweaty palms leaving damp imprints on the paper. The lights lowered and one by one, each student was called to the stage to perform. I watched as each boy and girl played, bowed, and excited to warm applause. Then it was my turn.

I don't remember how I found my way to the piano bench or what went through my head before I began to play. All I remember is a complete inability to play what was on the page in front of me, what I had practiced for weeks leading up to that moment. I lurched through "Fur Elise," my frozen clammy fingers butchering Beethoven's familiar notes, until it was over, mercifully, and I half-bowed to polite applause and collapsed in my seat. Mrs. Kuipers kindly patted my knee and said, "Beginner's nerves, that's all. Next time will be fine."

In retrospect, I can see that this competition was an entirely different league of stress. My own natural shyness, combined with the underlying fear of disappointing my teacher and parents, created a maelstrom of anxiety and partial paralysis. Even though I was a talented pianist and thought I knew the music cold, when I sat down to play, panic took over. I clutched.

The competition ended and a skinny girl with her blonde hair pulled back in a big bow-clip walked onstage to accept the award for my age group. Even in my dazed state, her calm, clean performance had stood out among the others. But I had missed her name. "Who's that?" I whispered to Mrs. Kuipers. "That's Karen Kleinhuizen," she whispered back. "Comes from a musical family of pianists." In that moment, Karen seemed to me as exalted as Beethoven himself. And I, in contrast, felt like the lowest of the low. Little did I know, I could get lower.

In school, things were looking up. As I grew, I had become one of the fastest runners in the school and I had a "girlfriend," Martha Major. That term really only meant that she liked me, I liked her, and when it was time to square dance in gym class, we were automatically partners. Yet in grade school in the 70s, having a girlfriend was enough to raise my status above that of Banana Nose.

Until Bobby Lorr came to town: a short, skinny kid with brown hair that fell into his eyes and a raft of freckles across the bridge of his nose. He was all legs and no hesitancy, and when he heard I was the fastest in the school, he bee-lined over to me at recess and challenged me to a race.

Bobby and I lined up next to the kickball first base. "Let's see how fast you really are," sneered one of the boys who had taunted me about my looks. "On your mark… get set… go!"

The dust went flying as we took off across the kickball diamond. Within seconds I knew this wasn't going to end well for me, and it didn't. By the end of the day, I had lost the race, and with it, whatever popularity I had had. Even worse, I had lost Martha, too. She and Bobby "liked" each other now. Although I can look back and recognize a childlike silliness in this life event, at the time I was utterly crushed. Losing the race – and consequently losing her – meant I was a failure, unworthy of love.

Competition at the piano, on the playground… it didn't seem to matter what the circumstances were. Any time I measured myself against others and fell short, I believed even more strongly in my own unworthiness – which just perpetuated more "failure." Like most kids, I just wanted to be liked by everyone. I orchestrated my life around pleasing others so I could feel like I was enough, so I could be loved. Even the piano became an "instrument" of validation. I adored playing it for my own enjoyment, but I also received lots of praise for playing well. Because I was good at it, or at least showed some competency in music beyond the norm, piano was my ace in the hole. The love, connection with others, and sense of self-esteem it brought me, even if it came from outside in, carried me through my childhood. Most of the time, it worked.

But not at the dining room table one night.

I was unusually quiet. My mom had made Sloppy Joes, the staple of Midwestern fare in the 70s. The conversation drifted; I paid no attention. Instead, I focused on my food. While Sherri complained yet again to our parents about her excessively thick and wavy hair, I grew more and more frustrated by my inability to keep the meat and tomato mixture inside the bun. I kept changing my grip, shifting my fingers to shore it up, but no matter what I did, the slop kept sliding out. Suddenly, I snapped. In a fury, I squeezed the bun as hard as I could. Meat sauce shot out of the bun in all directions, landing on the tablecloth, my sister's plate, and my lap. It was a tomato-red mess.

"That's the end of it! GO. TO. YOUR. ROOM," my mother yelled, "You're grounded!" I threw my stained napkin onto the table and pushed myself back from the table. I stomped across the white living room carpet, all the way up the stairs, marched into my room and slammed the door, shaking the "Todd's Wolf Den: Keep Out" sign and the slimy plastic creatures that hung next to it to scare my sister away. Once inside, I tore my room apart, knocking over my orange plastic and wood hourglass chair, pulling all of my drawers out and throwing my clothes everywhere, making a huge mess. Afterwards, I collapsed on my bunk bed and sobbed hot angry tears all over the ships and cannons of my pirate sheets. I think I may have cried myself to sleep.

In the days and weeks that followed, I never talked with my parents about my outburst, its cause, or their reaction. We all just went about our lives. Parenting norms were different then. In fact, I think parenting has come a long way towards the appropriate management of difficult emotions. Back when I was growing up, however, not talking about your feelings was routine. My parents were no worse than others. They were just doing what they thought was best and what other parents around them did.

NAME YOUR SHAME

We are not born with shame; we acquire it along the way. My parents' silence reinforced my mistaken belief that there was something wrong with me, that I was unlovable. We all carry shame caused by our own false beliefs, but according to Brown, the real problem arises when we're not aware of our shame. Unacknowledged shame resides in the darkest region of your subconscious mind where it festers and grows, fed by silence, secrecy, and judgment.

Naming your shame is one of the ways to "cut shame off at the knees." As Brown says, "If you don't claim your shame, it will claim you." If you recognize it, expose it to the light, and seek to understand it without judging yourself, then it shrivels and dies. If you don't, it will control your behaviors and emotions in negative ways. Empathy, your capacity to have compassion for your "lesser" self and your suffering, heals and diminishes shame. There's no shortcut: no mantra or herbal remedy. Only by bringing your darkness into the light of self-acceptance and self-compassion will you overcome your shame and evolve yourself.

Yoga is the practice of peeling away the layers of shame that veil the true capacity of your heart to shine. Only when you fully embrace your shadow, comprised of your imperfections, will your light be authentic. This is the true work.

The Tantrika (one who practices Tantra) wants to engage with life because only through engaging with life, in responsible ways, can you truly experience your freedom. The more you duck, dodge, and deny facing your life and your relationships, the less free you are. Freedom is found only when you choose to walk through the fires of your life and not avoid the problems. Your problems, when faced square on, are what shifts your consciousness and awakens you to higher octaves of existence. I like to say that "you have to go through it in order to get to it."

Although it has been my personal experience that these limits or *saṃskāras* (imprints, grooves, or deeply rooted patterns in your subconscious mind) gradually become less intense through the daily practice of yoga, the negative patterns don't necessarily ever go away. Instead, these patterns become more subtle and new patterns emerge to be dealt with. Sometimes these new *saṃskāras* are more intense, but your skill in working through them grows commensurately. Overall, it does get easier, but the work is never completely finished.

As Brooks said, "The journey of yoga is like walking down the path always with a pebble in one shoe." We are like oysters. A grain of sand or a parasite works its way into the oyster and creates so much irritation and discomfort that the oyster coats the intruder with a protective fluid called "nacre." Layer after layer is laid down, hardening into a beautiful pearl. The lesson?

There's value and beauty when, rather than turning away from suffering, you embrace it, integrate it, and learn from it. It's nature's way of producing something of value: a stronger, more lustrous, and more beautiful you.

I WILL BE PERFECT

My sister Sherri was like that grain of sand in my parents' (particularly my dad's) oyster, though I don't think they ever thought of her that way. She tested their tolerance in the most dramatic ways. Creative, defiant, and unattached to order, she routinely ignored Dad's constant reminders to clean her room. She didn't seem to care in the least. One day, a few months after the now-famous Sloppy Joe Incident, my father had had it with her. It had been two weeks since she had made her bed, and there were stuffed animals everywhere. Homework papers, dirty socks, magazines, and her "This is Todd" drawings littered the floor of her room. You couldn't walk to the bed without stepping on mounds of clutter.

"Sherri," he said, with studied restraint, "your room needs attention."

Glancing up from the cartoon section of the *Grand Rapids Press*, she murmured, "Mm-hmm... after I get back from the sleepover tomorrow," and went back to reading.

"No, you'll do it now."

She bristled. "I don't have time, Dad."

"Sherri," he demanded, "You will clean up your room *right now*."

I watched from the sidelines as they went back and forth, each one getting louder and louder, until they were both hollering and my dad's face was the picture of pure rage: angry, pained eyes, red face, neck veins popping out. All of this upset was making me uneasy and I looked for a way to exit. Just as I was sidling out of the room, I heard the loud BANG of something heavy hitting the floor. The house shook. I scurried like a frightened mouse and curled up in the corner of the room. I was convinced I was going to die.

Sherri ran up the stairs with Dad tromping after her, roaring at the top of his lungs. I had never heard him yell like that before. Terrified, I curled up tighter into a ball and listened to her footsteps as she ran into her room and slammed the door. I heard the lock turn just as my dad reached her door. He pounded with his fists, bellowing, "OPEN THIS DOOR! OPEN IT! RIGHT NOW!" But Sherri didn't. She stayed in her room while the pounding and shouting continued and then finally died down. After what felt to me like hours, my dad eventually gave up. I waited for someone to come find me, to check on me, but no one ever did.

At breakfast the next morning, there was silence. Sherri was grounded, that was clear. Internally, I assessed the situation. With the logic of a young mind, I formed the following equation: when my parents yell or otherwise express their anger, they are not punished. When my sister and I are angry, we get sent to our rooms or are grounded. My parents' anger must be acceptable; mine is not. My anger is bad, and therefore, I am bad. In that moment, I remember making a decision that has endured to this day: I will always clean my room. I will be perfect.

My perception of my childhood was that no matter what I did, I was never good enough, so I became a perfectionist in everything I did to try to win my Dad's approval. This is a normal part of childhood development; we will do whatever it takes to fulfill the primal need for love and belonging. Brown contends that the human need for love and belonging has an important evolutionary history. To be ostracized by the tribe meant being left outside the cave at night and potentially eaten by wolves. Belonging was *serious*.

In order to stay in the cave, we adapt our personalities to become the person we believe others need us to be, to be lovable. I call this our "core-wounded identity." We all have at least one, usually several. Core-wounded identities, like the good little boy or girl, the cry baby, the performer, the victim, the rescuer, the pleaser, the bully, or the caretaker, give us the love and attention we need. Unfortunately, the love that comes our way often is conditional, and though it helps us survive our childhood, ultimately it can't satisfy our deep longing for acceptance.

Most psychologists will tell you that we form our sense of self or ego identifications between the ages of one and six. Therapist Shelley Klammer, in her blog, "Understanding Your Core Wound and False Self," [5] writes:

> *We first experience our core wound when we realize we are separate from unconditional love. In psychological terms this is called the 'narcissistic wound.' Psychology points to the first time a child is shamed as the cause of the narcissistic wound, which is our deepest, darkest belief about ourselves. From a transpersonal perspective, we actually organize our entire being around a particular feeling of lack much earlier in infancy – when we first feel the vulnerability of being separate from the unconditional love of our mother or primary caregiver.*

If we never consciously come to grips with our core-wounded identity, if we never change those patterns that are so ingrained within us, we don't realize what's driving us. We can find ourselves in our 20's, 30's, and 40's, saying, "I better not complain," "I better not cry," or maybe, "I need to cry louder." For me, it was, "I'd better be perfect."

It is no coincidence to me that around this time, I became nearsighted, started wearing glasses, and developed hay fever allergies. The body is never separate from our emotions; on the contrary, the body is the expression of our emotional signature. Aristotle[6] took it a step further when he said, "We must no more ask whether the soul and body are one than ask whether the wax and the figure impressed on it are one."

I became convinced that there was something terribly wrong with me. I was irredeemably imperfect. If what you experience in your soul is imprinted in the body, then it seems likely that I manifested in a physical way the "proof" of that conviction.

I became neat and tidy from that moment on. In all fairness, being neat isn't a terrible habit to cultivate. When my external environment is orderly, my mind is orderly. I have to admit I even enjoy cleaning. But I now know that when I find myself obsessively cleaning instead of completing a task, I am revisiting an old wound. I am trying to be perfect to avoid my father's wrath.

PERFECTLY IMPERFECT

Perfectionism squelches worthiness. Perfectionism sets an unreachable standard for yourself, one that guarantees you can only fall short and fail. This constant "failure" then confirms the inner belief of not being enough and the vicious circle is complete. Instead of my worth coming from deep inside my own heart, it was based on externals: the admiration of my peers, the love of a grade-school girlfriend, the results of a piano competition. Both perfectionism and unworthiness have their roots in that deep bog of shame.

Worthiness is not something that you attain by deeds or experience; worthiness is your birthright. It comes along with the gift of life. What is a gift? Brooks' definition of a true gift is something you don't "deserve," you can't earn, and you never have to pay back. That is worthiness: the recognition of your intrinsic goodness. Because you are alive, you are worthy. Congratulations, you made the cut!

If worthiness is the recognition of your intrinsic goodness, then what is perfection? I'll never forget the freedom I felt years later, when I first heard Brooks say that I was "perfectly imperfect" just the way I was. It was September of 1999, I was in an Anusara teacher training in Park City, UT, and Douglas was teaching the philosophy segment.

"Really?" I said. "Does this mean that we are already perfect?"

He said, "Yes."

"Even with our flaws, we are perfect?"
"Yes. Imperfectly perfect."

"So, we can't really screw up?"

"Well, not really. When you screw up, you get to learn something and realign yourself."

"We are already free?"

"Yes."

"So… we're not trying to be good so we can get off the cycle of birth, death, and rebirth?"
"You got it."

"Wow," I said. "I just want to celebrate."

"Yes!" he exclaimed. "That's the idea. If we're not here to solve a problem, then there's no problem to be solved."

Then why are we here? We are here for the fun of it. To play, to delight, to savor, to sing, to dance, to learn, to love, to serve. Tantra teaches that the highest expression of the spirit is embodied in you as you, and that nature is the expression of spirit. Therefore, what's natural, what's happening right now, is the highest because it's *what is*.

This means that who you are, exactly as you are right now, is perfect. This is not license to give up on your own evolution but it is permission to be yourself. In your essence, with all of your unique idiosyncrasies, you are the way the universe has made you to be. When I first heard this teaching from Brooks, every cell in my body relaxed. It was as if a great burden had been lifted from my shoulders. I was somehow previously holding onto that childhood notion that I was imperfect and flawed and that I needed to remain vigilant at all times in order to improve myself. As you'll see, this notion stayed with me for decades.

Can the highest get even better? Can perfection become even more perfect? Yes, it can. Perfection can become even more perfect because the universe is not fixed. The universe is expanding and accelerating, as is life, as is knowledge... and as is perfection. It's not an end-stop game; it constantly evolves and gets better.

Since we live in a perfectly unfinished universe of becoming, there is no "there" at which to arrive. Can "here" ever be good enough? The answer is another resounding Yes! That's where the spiritual journey begins.

I've worked with all of my core wounds extensively throughout my spiritual journey but it's an ongoing process of refinement. Now when I catch myself saying "I'm a perfectionist," I try to remember to reframe it, and say instead, "I'm having a moment of perfectionism" as a way to "undo" my old identification pattern with perfectionism. Naming it that way allows me to re-engage with a more empowering vision for myself, one that acknowledges my continual evolution.

RAT MAN TO THE RESCUE

In third grade, I didn't know any of this yet. I was just desperate to find a way back to the good graces of my peers. That feeling of social acceptance that I had known during my brief tenure as king of the running hill was seductive, and I was determined to get it back. Thus I found myself following in the footsteps of the countless other bullied youth of the world: I resorted to comedy.

From as far back as my days in a highchair, my father and I had entertained each other by twisting our faces into ridiculous contortions. "Funny face!" he would prompt, and we'd square off, each outdoing the other in grotesquery until one of us would "give up" by breaking into laughter.

I had no intention of using that skill in the classroom but on one particular day it emerged. Our teacher asked us to open our desks and take out a pencil and sheet of paper for an impromptu math quiz. My good friend, Greg Beckett, who sat on the other side of the aisle and was no fan of the times tables, lifted up his desk lid and stuck out his tongue at me from behind that barrier. In solidarity, I returned the salute with the most hideous face I could muster, all squinty-eyed and buck-toothed and puckered. Trying to stay quiet, he snorted, then erupted into full-blown laughter.

Our teacher was quick to address him: "Greg! Would you like to share with the class what you find so funny?"

I knew he wouldn't rat me out, so I spoke up. I didn't want him to be punished for something I did.

"It was me," I admitted.

She looked surprised. "You?"

I nodded.

"What did you do, Todd?"

I hesitated. *Well, she asked...*

"This." And I made the face again. This time, the whole class snorted and giggled. Greg shouted, "Rat Man!" either because my face really did look like a rat, or because Greg knew I raised rats to feed my cousin's boa constrictor, or both. Fresh peals of laughter erupted at that, and my teacher had to clap her hands to restore order.

> *At the height of laughter, the universe is flung into a kaleidoscope of new possibilities.*
>
> ~Jean Houston[7]

Rat Man was born. Desperate for friends, or at least the kind of attention that felt like friendship, I trotted out Rat Man – and an increasingly varied collection of warped faces – on call. He also became my go-to deflection weapon, useful in any gnarly social situation. I took my Achilles heel and turned it into a karate kick, debilitating my attackers with their own laughter.

I also, without conscious awareness, embraced my "imperfection" and found its perfect outlet. I gave myself permission to be myself, just as the universe gives all of us that same permission. When we allow ourselves that gift, when we celebrate our uniqueness, we find the power that resides in "imperfection."

THREE YOGIC WORLD VIEWS, IN A NUTSHELL

Within Christianity there exists Catholicism, Protestantism, Lutheranism, and Christian Mysticism, to name a few, and within Judaism there exists Hasidism, Orthodox, Conservative, Reformed, Reconstructionist, and Kabbalah. In that same way, the broad term "yoga philosophy" encompasses a number of different religious paths, including Buddhism. Although it's true that all yoga and Buddhist philosophies overlap in some ways, and that superficially they might seem like they are basically the same philosophy, on a deeper level there are differences – crucial ones.

Before we go any further, I want to give you a little background (just a little, I promise) about the two major philosophical strains that preceded *Nondual Śaiva-Śākta Tantra*: Classical Yoga and *Advaita Vedānta*. If you know the broad brushstrokes of these views, you'll get a lot more out of some references I make later. You also might find, as I did, that learning the distinction of all three yogic worldviews clarifies your yogic path of study. It might allow you to place various teachings and practices into categories, making the yogic journey a little easier.

One disclaimer: although I now consider myself a Tantric yogi at heart, I embrace both Classical and *Advaita Vedānta* as well. Distinguishing these three schools is not a critique or judgment of non-Tantric thought; rather, it describes the evolution of consciousness that led up to Tantric thought. If it were not for Patañjali[8] (the purported author of the *Yoga Sūtras*) and his dualist colleagues, there would be no Tantra.

The Three Yogic World Views are:

1. Classical Yoga (300-500 CE)
    a. Important scripture of that period: *Yoga Sūtras*, by Patañjali
    b. Main teacher: Patañjali
2. *Advaita Vedānta* (300-820 CE)
    a. Important scripture of that period: *Upaniṣads*
    b. Main teacher: Shankara (788-820 CE)

3. *Nondual Śaiva-Śākta Tantra* (400-1300 CE)
   a. Important scriptures of that period: *Tantrāloka* by Abhinavagupta, *Śiva Sūtras* by Vasugupta, *Vijñāna Bhairava Tantra* and *Pratyabhijñā Hṛdayam* by Ksmeraja (student of Abhinavagupta)
   b. Main teacher: Abhinavagupta (975-1025)

1. Classical Yoga (Patañjali's Yoga)

Classical yoga is a "dualistic" view of the world, which means that it sees the universe as irreducible down to two elements having two separate realities: spirit (*puruṣa*) and nature (*prakṛti*). *Puruṣa* is considered superior to *prakṛti*. The whole spiritual journey is about learning how to subdue nature – which includes body, mind, and all of our human desires – in favor of spirit, our end goal. *prakṛti* is that imperfect stuff that's in the way and must be overcome in order to reach enlightenment.

This view is steeped in the notion that life is synonymous with suffering and that you are here today in this incarnation because you failed to get enlightened last time. Because of your negative karmic ties, you have returned to try again. The Classical journey is about getting off the karmic wheel of *saṃsāra* (suffering caused by identification with the world of *prakṛti*). Thus, the Classical view is that life is a problem to be solved and yoga is the solution.

2. *Advaita Vedānta*: Nondualism

The second yogic worldview, nondual in nature (the universe is irreducible down to one element), is *Advaita Vedānta*. *Advaita* means not two. *Vedānta* means the "end of the *Vedas*" – *Vedas* being the oldest known Hindu scripture, approximately 1800 B.C.E. One might ask, why not just refer to "unity" rather than "nonduality?" In both *Advaita Vedānta* and *Nondual Śaiva-Śākta Tantra*, there is a recognition that we must deal with the fact that duality does, in fact, *appear* in life. It would be naive or irresponsible to attempt to argue otherwise. But how then do we avoid dualism? *Avaita Vedānta* emphasizes that we should focus on the differences as a problem to overcome and treats differences primarily as illusory. *Nondual Śaiva-Śākta Tantra* treats duality differently, as you'll see soon.

The leading proponent and teacher of *Advaita Vedānta* was Shankara, who said there are two levels of the self: the small "s" self, which is how we identify ourselves in this lifetime; and the large "S" Self, which is eternal, infinite, and essential. Small "s" selves are like waves on the ocean of being, momentary differentiations that are still the ocean itself. Your essence and the essence of the universe are one. Oneness is all there is. Only the eternal is real. All sense of difference is an illusion and doesn't really exist. Through our ignorance, we have mistaken the small self for the unchanging eternal Self.

Like Classical Yoga, *Vedānta* views life as a problem to be solved. The answer, according to *Vedānta*, lies practicing *"neti, neti, neti:"* "not this, not this, not this." Enlightenment comes when you dis-identify with the world in which we live and identify only with spirit. A common *Vedānta* teaching is, "I am not my body. I am not my mind. I am the eternal spirit."

3. Nondual *Śaiva-Śākta* Tantra: Nondualism 2.0

Emerging around 400 CE in Kashmir of Northern India, and flourishing between the 9th and 12th centuries CE, *Nondual Śaiva-Śākta Tantra* assimilated much of the previous yogic philosophies into its system, much like the Borg in Star Trek, who mechanically intoned, *"Resistance is futile. You will be assimilated."* "*Śaiva*" refers to *Śiva*, which is understood in the conventional Hindu religion as the name of the Hindu God. The deeper, esoteric understanding, though, is that *Śiva* refers to the Absolute – beyond space and time, infinite, filled with freedom, bliss, and love. Nondual *Śaiva-Śākta* Tantra is a nondual path that takes the view that spirit is infused in all things.

Where *Advaita Vedānta* says *"neti, neti, neti:"* "I'm not this, not this, not this," Tantra says *"Tat Tvam Asi,"* "I'm this too, this too, this too." You are all of this. Tantra bases identity on a model of inclusion rather than exclusion, embracing all of your forms: divine unlimited *and* divine limited.

The main premise of *Nondual Śaiva-Śākta Tantra* is the notion that the Absolute – one, unified energy – becomes many energies and forms, you and me and everything around us. Yes, the Absolute is transcendental and beyond attributes. Yet it also, paradoxically, forms the essence of all that is. All of the different forms, forces, and experiences in life are *manifestations* of the nondual source from which they come. They are variegated *expressions* of that non-differentiated source.

In this model, reality is not an illusion (as thought by the *Advaita Vedāntists*), nor inferior to the Absolute (as stated by Classical yogis), but rather, the living embodiment of the Absolute, in limited form. Therefore, rather than considering the expressions of the nondual source as *problems*, we can nourish life by means of that perfect state of freedom and bliss, just as white light brings power and translucence to the various colors of the rainbow.

Another idea that sets *Nondual Śaiva-Śākta Tantra* apart from *Advaita Vedānta* is the concept of dynamism. In the *Advaita Vedānta* universe, where only oneness is real and diversity is an illusion, there's a kind of static, unchanging, and non-dynamic quality to reality.

In the *Nondual Śaiva-Śākta Tantra* universe, however, *Śakti* is the very essence of dynamism. As the expression of *Śiva,* she is the living diversity and dynamic throb of life. Through this lens, *Advaita Vedānta* can be viewed as *Śakti* -less and static, while *Nondual Śaiva-Śākta Tantra* can be seen as just the opposite. The one undifferentiated energy of *Śiva* expresses itself in an infinite array of diversity and dynamism, just as light refracts into a rainbow when it passes through a prism. The light that creates the rainbow is divine, as is the resulting diversity. *Nondual Śaiva-Śākta Tantra* teaches that it's all divine, it's all beautiful, whereas *Advaita Vedānta*'s version of nonduality is a kind of qualified oneness that sees diversity as a mistake in identity, an illusion, and not real.

Taking this concept to a more human level, any refusal of diversity has the potential to lead to oppression of others. At its extreme, exclusion in any form can justify racism and other types of discrimination. *Nondual Saiva-Śākta Tantra,* with its dynamic inclusion, is a relevant, welcome view today. By embracing diversity in all forms – gender, race, sexual orientation, and all other shapes reality takes – *Nondual Śaiva-Śākta Tantra* can help humanity achieve a greater sense of unity.

In Tantra, the human experience is valued as the highest form of consciousness since each one of us is the crystallization of the Divine's desire to know itself. In other words, the essence of the entire universe exists in seed form in the heart of every human being. Just as a star shines its light outward due to a powerful contractive nuclear fusion in its center, Tantra is the practice of moving deeper into life – experiencing it, savoring it, and integrating it – in order to grow and expand consciousness.

Unlike the Classical model, in Tantra, life is not a problem. It's a gift. You can't get off the karmic wheel since in a nondual worldview there is no "other" place to go. The focus, then, is on how to get *into* life more fully. Rather than trying to get off the waves of life, you want to learn how to surf.

Through integrating the notion of both the dual and nondual views, Tantra found a way to create a unified vision of transformation that has both its source and final destination in the heart – the place in the middle. The spiritual heart is the threshold between worlds that pulses with the highest joy and is the home for the realization of our full potential. The heart is the abode of the great paradox of life where all polarities find their resolution, where the dual touches the nondual, where human touches spirit and awakens to the possibility of its own ever-expanding consciousness.

Yes, *Nondual Śaiva-Śākta Tantra* is an esoteric, mystical, and deeply philosophical path of initiatory yogic practices and yogic thought. But it's also a simple yet profound philosophy, the spiritual lovechild of

Classical and *Advaita Vedānta,* who took the best genetics of his/her parents and became something magnificent and unique.

UNDERWATER BASKET WEAVING

There is much disagreement about the meaning of the word "tantra." It has been defined as the Sanskrit word for book, text, or scripture, and as a system of spiritual practices, yet the most common understanding is that of a weaver's loom. This points to the paradoxical teaching of Tantra that in order for you to experience freedom, you must create healthy self-boundaries; you must "loom" yourself in order to expand yourself. (More on this later.) Just as we are both human and divine, limited and unlimited, Tantra weaves back together the dispersed parts of yourself into an integrated, meaningful matrix of relationship – where *all* parts of you are welcome and needed, not just the "spiritual" parts.

This is an important distinction and it brings us back to shame and imperfection. It's tempting to ignore those parts that you don't like, those darker, "baser" aspects, in favor of the happy stuff. Tantra teaches you how to weave underwater; it teaches you how to embrace and move through your shadowy parts, like walking through Brown's "swampland of shame," in order to get to the other side.

EXERCISE: Name Your Shame

Find a quiet place and sit in silence for a few minutes. Allow the natural rhythm of your breath to soothe and calm you. Breathe into your heart and open to a bigger energy. Allow yourself to just be as you are. Offer yourself acceptance and compassion for whatever you might be experiencing right now. When you're ready, open your eyes and write out the answers to the reflections below.

1. When was your first experience of shame? How old were you?
2. Who shamed you? What were the circumstances? How did you feel?
3. What decisions did you make in order to get through that time in your life?
4. What behaviors did you adopt to help you get through it?
5. Knowing what you know now, what wisdom can you offer your younger, less evolved self?

NOTES

[1] Quote is attributed to Carl Gustav Jung but source cannot be verified.

[2] Brown, Brené. *Men, Women, and Worthiness*. Louisville, Colorado: Sounds True. 2012. Audiobook. Learn more about Dr. Brown's amazing work on her website: https://brenebrown.com. Accessed May9, 2020.

[3] Wallis, Christopher D. *Tantra Illuminated: The Philosophy, History, and Practice of a Timeless Tradition*. Boulder, CO: Mattamayura, 2nd ed. 2013. Print.

[4] Coots, J. Fred and Gillespie, Haven, *Santa Claus Is Comin' To Town*. Vocal Popular Sheet Music Collection. Score 2997, 1934.

[5] Shelley Klammer article, "Understanding Your Core Wound and False Self," *Shelly Klammer Expressive Art Inspirations*. https://intuitivecreativity.typepad.com/expressiveartinspirations/2014/07/understanding-your-core-pain-and-false-self.html. 2014. Blogsite.

[6] Aristotle. Hugh Lawson-Tancred (Translator). *De Anima (On the Soul)*. New York: Penguin Classics. 1987. Print.

[7] Quote attributed to Jean Houston but original source is unknown.

[8] There are many translations of the *Yoga Sūtras of Patañjali*. Two I like are: Bryant, Edwin F. *The Yoga Sūtras of Patañjali*. New York: North Point Press. 2009. Print. & Iyengar, B.K.S. *Light on the Yoga Sūtras of Patañjali*. New York: Thorsons. 1993. Print.

CHAPTER THREE

Good Boy, Bad Boy

Out beyond ideas
of wrongdoing or rightdoing
there is a field.
I'll meet you there.

Rumi, *The Essential Rumi*[1]

When I was nine years old my father let me sit in with his band, the Sandy Norian Orchestra. This was a big-band jazz and pop style group that played at local events in our hometown of Grand Rapids, but it might as well have been the Beatles, as thrilled as I was. I had just learned a few pop songs and couldn't wait to try them out with the band.

I counted the days until rehearsal. When the musicians finally showed up at our house on a cool September evening, I hopped from one foot to the other in excited anticipation. I watched each one arrive, shake hands with my dad, and carry his instrument into our living room to set up. Normally, my dad practiced in the basement, between the wet bar and the pinball machine, but there wasn't enough room for the whole band down there.

Finally, after what seemed to me an eternity, they were all squeezed in together: the drummer, Gene Cohen, who took up the most space with a complete drum set; the bass player, whose huge stand-up acoustic bass seemed three times my size; a guitar player; the piano player; a sax man; and a few other horn players, my dad among them.

I watched in fascination as they warmed up, cracking jokes I didn't understand but laughed at anyway. They were big and jovial and seemed to enjoy my excitement; the heavy-set bass player kept smiling at me under his enormous mustache. After much trilling and honking and thrumming, they were ready to play.

"All right, fellas." My dad directed them to the music folders on their red-and-white Sandy Norian Orchestra music stands. "Let's start with 'In the Mood.'" Papers shuffled, then there was quiet.

He lifted his baton, counted out the beat, and POW! The horns came to life, swinging into the rhythm with sass and verve. The bass rumbled underneath the steady rhythmic strumming of the guitar, the piano meandered in clear, bright tones, and the drums sashayed with cool precision. I was in heaven.

Sitting in the same room and listening to these professionals, play was thrilling. So penetrating was the richness of the sound that I could feel the music deep in my bones, especially the bass and drums. The rhythm and groove of the jazz beat was palpable; my whole body vibrated. I had never been that close to the sound before! It was as though I was sitting inside the music itself.

I watched each musician carefully. Not one of them was really following the notes on the paper. They all seemed to improvise and play off the sheet music in such a way that was perfectly orchestrated with the other musicians. It seemed like magic! How did they do that? How did they know what to play, and when? It wasn't until later in my life that I fully understood that particular brand of magic.

They finished "In the Mood" and went on to play a few more numbers. I sat in the corner, happily lost in the music, until my dad's voice cut through my dreamy fog.

"Hey Butch, you ready to play?" he asked, using the nickname he had given me years ago when I was a tiny person with a white-blond buzz cut.

"Yes!" I yelped and leaped to my feet. The musicians laughed and I'm sure I blushed all the way to the roots of my now-grown-out hair.

His piano player moved over and I slid onto the familiar bench. I addressed the group with as much nonchalance as I could muster. "Do you know "You Are the Sunshine of My Life? By Stevie Wonder?" A chorus of recognition arose.

"What key? C?" asked the bass player.

"Yes," I said coolly, about to bust.

Gene said calmly, "Hit it." My dad counted off, "A-one, two, three, four," and off we went.

That moment, that first experience of playing with a group, sits with me even decades later. I remember the bass and drums supporting me, lifting me up musically, gently nudging me forward, while also surrounding me with kindness and appreciation. I remember feeling high and free. I remember smiling so hard with joy that my face ached, and then laughing with pure, 9-year-old delight. My laughter threw off my rhythm a few times and I had to stop. But they kept on playing, allowing me to jump back in when I found my way. They followed *me*.

After I finished, they were so kind. "Great job, kid!" and "You were killing it, Butch!" filled my ears, and I blushed again. I have no idea what I sounded like, and I imagine that my timing must have been all over the place. They didn't seem to care. They just followed me and played whatever I played. They made me feel and sound like I was part of the band. In retrospect, they were probably planting the seeds of jazz in my soul, but at the time, I just felt *full*.

PŪRNATVA: THE PRINCIPLE OF FULLNESS

Pūrṇa, mentioned earlier in the context of concealment, means fullness or perfection. (*Tva* means "principle," or "quality of.") The mantra *Pūrṇamadaḥ Pūrṇamidam* (*Īsha Upaniṣad*)[2], can be translated to mean, "from fullness, only fullness arises." *Adaḥ* means "that," "outer world," or "over there." *Idam* means "this," "inner world," or "closer to home." Fullness is yonder over there and fullness is also here, closer to me. Even when you take fullness away from fullness, in fact, only fullness remains. There is no exhausting the fullness of the Absolute. It's simply not possible.

The Absolute is not like a fuel gauge that registers less than full when fuel is used. There is no depletion. There is no capacity to diminish that abundance, that richness, that wealth of unboundedness, and have it in any way be made less. It is finished in the sense of accomplished, perfectly made, perfectly constructed, perfectly concluded. It is replete. It is filled, satisfied, and contented.

Even if what arises from the Absolute seems to show itself as fragmented, incomplete, contracted, small, limited, or bound, in truth, what is arising is the radiance and perfection of the Absolute moving in expression, articulation, and shaping of itself. In its perfect movement of fullness from fullness, it is eternal and perennial. In the Tantric view, the universe is *pūrṇa,* full and lacks nothing. It is not a mistake that we need to correct.

As I've said before, the universe is perfect, yet always evolving. It's so full that it includes everything: imperfection, incompleteness, growth. *Pūrṇa* for someone who is lying sick in a hospital bed might mean just trying to sit up. Fullness is doing the very best you can from where you are. It's using no more than what's needed to get the job done.

Pūrṇatva can be lived through what I call the three L's – named after the goddess Lakshmi, who represents fullness, prosperity, abundance, and beauty. She is the crest of the wave, the peak expression of life.

- **LOVE fully**: Express your love now. Don't wait. Life is short. You never know when you'll lose a loved one. Allow love in. Give it. Fall in love with yourself, with your life, with beauty. Love the little things in life, love what's ordinary. The ordinary seen with eyes of love becomes extraordinary.

- **LIVE fully**: Be present. Pursue your dreams. Don't wait, don't hold back. Express yourself. Follow your heart. Be full, be outrageous, be enthusiastic about life and learning.

- **LAUGH fully**: Smile, play, have fun. Don't take life too seriously. Look for the lighter side of things. Life is an adventure, not a penance. Life is good.

Every time you see, hear, smell, touch, or taste something, you have an opportunity to penetrate the moment, to experience it fully. We experience *pūrṇa* through the forms the universe takes: a perfect sunrise, a first kiss, a field of mature corn stalks.

To wake up each morning and live fully requires a kind of longing for *pūrṇa*, a fire for completion. Striving for pūrṇa means telling yourself you are divine and that today will be your best day yet. It means facing challenges with an open heart and without closing down, releasing your fears: of others, of failure, of success, of being big. It means stepping forward fearlessly and shining your light as brightly as you can.

Playing "You Are the Sunshine of My Life" with my father's band initiated me into a glorious introduction to *pūrṇa*. My performance, as inexperienced and flawed as it was, swept me up in the totality of lush musical fulfillment. I felt free, sunny, and utterly complete. I felt perfect.

IF YOU'LL BE MY BODYGUARD

During the summer between second and third grade, Payton Holdenberry moved into our neighborhood. He and his family lived two blocks away, next to a huge undeveloped field that I played in with other neighborhood kids. His father was a musician too and we became friends, spending time at each other's houses.

Payton was my physical opposite. Tall and strong, he had already developed the exterior toughness required to survive in a family with two older brothers. His mother loved that I played the piano and I can remember entertaining her by playing Scott Joplin music from the movie "The Sting." Perhaps it was her desire to protect this skinny, sensitive musician that influenced her son, or perhaps he took it upon himself, but for whatever reason, Payton became a kind of bodyguard for me. During school at recess, after school in the neighborhood, he was always by my side, looking out for me. He didn't have to resort to violence very often, because when he did, he was very good at it. When confronted with Payton's intimidating presence next to me, the boys who had made my life miserable in the two years prior suddenly left me alone in third and fourth grade.

My gratitude for Payton's protection led to a deep friendship. We spent more and more time together, which meant I also spent more and more time with his circle of friends, a group I would now affectionately call "the wrong crowd." By the end of fourth grade, I could often be found after school in forts we built in the field next to the Holdenberry's house, smoking stolen Salem menthols. This group of rebels gave me a sense of value and belonging, something I had been craving ever since I could remember.

In fifth grade, I found that same kind of belonging in a band I started, inspired by my dad. We were called The Pee Wees. The guitar player was eight, the drummer was nine, and I was our elder statesman at 10. Our first gig was at my neighbor's Dental Hygienists Auxiliary Luncheon. We practiced daily for weeks and on the appointed day we wobbled through three songs: two from "Jesus Christ Superstar," and "Lonely Days," by the Bee Gees. We played for 15 minutes and each of us walked away with five whole dollars. I felt like a millionaire!

By the time I reached junior high, I was living a split existence. On the outside, I looked like I had it all together: a pack of friends, a band (renamed The Todd Norian Trio), growing musical skills, and social acceptance. On the inside, I was still the same little boy who felt unloved and unworthy. My relatively harmless behavior with my gang of pals began to slide into other exploits, such as sneaking out at night, smoking pot, and drinking. I looked for any way I could to rebel against the "good boy" image I had presented all my life. What more perfect way than to act out against my family's religion?

BAR MITZVAH DROP OUT

In Grand Rapids there were primarily two Jewish congregations: Conservative (who went to synagogue) and Reformed (who went to temple). I had friends at both congregations, but for us kids, the temple was "where it was at." Reformed temple services and ceremonies were mostly in English, rather than Hebrew, and the rabbi – who played guitar and told jokes – was one cool dude. All in all, the temple was much more relatable and fun. More importantly, Tanner Radner was a member there with his family.

Tan (short for Tanner) was four years older than I, so our age disparity meant we weren't close friends, but he was my hero. When he was in high school, he started a band that played Beatles and Monkeys cover songs for all of the elementary schools in the region. He was a role model for me as a musician and the Pee Wees were born partly out of that admiration. At the temple, he and his cousin, Mort, often played music during the services.

But the temple's biggest draw for me was that there was *no Hebrew school at all.*

I hated Hebrew school. In third grade, in anticipation of my impending bar mitzvah at 13 years old, my parents forced me to go to Hebrew school every Tuesday and Thursday for two hours after school. I resisted studying Hebrew, I resented that it caused me to quit the basketball team because I missed so many practices, and I despised that it was on top of the hours and hours already spent at synagogue, listening to services in Hebrew. I especially hated that it didn't answer any of the big questions I had, like, "Who am I? Why am I here? What is my purpose?" Since I had no choice but to attend, I expressed my dissatisfaction in other ways.

My friends and I acted like delinquents. We either paid no attention or made fun of our teachers: a sweet married couple, Israeli by birth, who spoke broken English with heavy, almost unintelligible accents. The husband, a bald, narrow-faced man with sharp features, droned on endlessly in his English that sounded like more Hebrew. He and his wife, dressed respectively in a black suit and frumpy dress, seemed like relics from some dusty old time.

To alleviate our boredom, we frequently blew spit wads at one another behind their backs. These were saliva-soaked little pieces of paper rolled into small, tight, explosive missiles, blown through plastic straws. The wads weren't necessarily dangerous, but they stung when they hit skin. We also sometimes used clay pellets, "high-tech" ammo, that sailed through the air with more power, speed, and a more predictable arc, increasing accuracy and sniper-ability.

As infuriated as our teachers were by our surreptitious projectiles, nothing irritated them more than our blatant conversations, held right in the middle of their lesson plans. The more upset they became, the louder and ruder we became. This usually escalated until the teachers totally lost control and angrily shouted over and over at the top of their lungs, "Sheket Bevakasha! Sheket Bevakasha! Sheket Bevakasha!" which means, in triplicate, "Shut up, please!" Sadly, this is the only Hebrew phrase I remember from those lessons. I still feel bad about how poorly we treated them. Clearly, I was an obnoxious kid in Hebrew school.

However, a year before my bar mitzvah I got serious about learning Hebrew – probably to avoid a disastrous showing on that day. At that time, my dad started going to the synagogue on Saturday mornings for the *minyan*, a traditional religious gathering requiring ten Jewish adult men. (In the more traditional Judaic streams only men can participate but in more modern streams women are included.) He took me along with him several times during my year of determined Hebrew study. During the minyan was a special prayer for the dead, the Kaddish, which my dad recited in memory of his mother, who died when I was six years old. Much as I detested Hebrew school, I loved this communal worship experience. Inexplicably, it spoke to me on a deep, visceral level.

After my uneventful bar mitzvah, I dropped out of Hebrew school as soon as humanly possible and proceeded to find other ways to rebel against my forced involvement with the Jewish community. In 8th grade, I joined the local chapter of B'nai B'rith, which was an extra-curricular Jewish youth group for boys that held monthly meetings and social gatherings. Rather than conjugating Hebrew, we sold cookies to fundraise and got high; this particular local chapter was filled with pot smokers who couldn't get through a meeting unless they were high. Most of the kids were from the much-cooler Reformed temple, not the stuffy old synagogue.

We attended annual State and Regional B'nai B'rith conferences in Detroit, MI, where hundreds of Jewish high schoolers gathered to participate in discussions about anti-Semitism, the Holocaust, and the role of Judaism in the world. In ninth grade we went to a huge conference in Gross Point. To kick off the meeting, all of the chapters were invited to offer something for a talent show.

When it was our turn, the curtain drew back and we stepped forward to sing our "theme song." Although I mercifully can't remember the exact lyrics, they started with something like: "We're the boys from EGR. We drink, smoke, and screw…" and ended with "…and cordially we say f**k you." The curtain couldn't close fast enough on us as the boos resounded in our ears. But in our stoned state, none of it registered. I thought these conferences were just an excuse for overachieving Jewish kids, most likely prompted by their parents, to show off their intelligence and Jewish action in the world. Our performance felt to me like some kind of hip, cool protest. We had no concept of how undignified we were or what kind of reputation we garnered from that kind of display.

Even if I had known, I wouldn't have cared. I just wanted to have fun and party, to live outside the rules and be free. So that's what I continued to do.

BOUNDARY & FREEDOM

What is freedom? Although the three yogic worldviews all agree that freedom is freedom from suffering, they have three different approaches to attaining it.

- **Classical**: Freedom is attained by separating spirit (*puruṣa*) from the material world, including the body and mind (*prakṛti*). You are free once you identify completely with spirit and transcend material reality.

- *Advaita Vedānta*: Freedom comes by changing the way you see the world. You are free once you can see the one spirit within everything, and you recognize that all difference within the world is an illusion.

- **Tantra**: Freedom is experienced and maintained by setting healthy self-boundaries.

Classical Yoga and *Advaita Vedānta* start from the assumption that we are bound beings; therefore, their goal is "freedom *from*." But because Tantra maintains we are already free, it emphasizes "freedom *to*."

In Tantra, we gain freedom through setting healthy self-boundaries. Here's a mundane but real example: I love organic dark chocolate, but my body doesn't. If I eat a whole bar, I'm destined for two or three days of intense migraine pain. Yet I derive so much pleasure from the taste that year after year, I kept testing it – and suffering the consequences. Eventually, I aligned with the truth – too much chocolate makes me sick – and created a boundary for myself: three squares only. By setting this boundary, I'm now able to enjoy the freedom of eating chocolate. I know how to savor it within the limit that's right for my body. Paradoxically, setting this boundary has set me free.

In Tantra, the question is not, "How do you become free?" but rather, "What do you want to bind yourself to?" Because if you don't bind yourself to what you truly desire, something else will bind itself to you, and it probably won't be what you truly want. The only impediments to sustaining and creating greater and greater levels of freedom are your own self-created limitations.

Whether you realize it or not, you are already bound by the unconscious thoughts and habits that you've assimilated into your life. Those boundaries limit and define you, bringing pain and suffering. The trick is to choose your boundaries consciously, to determine which boundaries expand your light, and which ones dim you down. You have *svātantrya* (one's own freedom, or self-looming), which allows you to create a future of your own making. You weave your own web. Boundary is needed in order to maintain your good health; you need to bind yourself in order to unbind yourself. Freedom without any boundaries leads to a bondage of another sort.

The Tantra path will always point you toward the *madhya*, the "space in the middle," because living within a rigid set of rules only creates additional stress. Yet living without any rules at all will also lead to stress – the stress of being lost and ungrounded, of being too wild. In

56

Tantra, we seek the place in the middle where we don't abstain but also don't indulge to excess.

Yoga is not about becoming free; it's about recognizing you are already free and then living in the threshold of healthy self-boundaries. It's about making good judgments and binding yourself to knowledge that awakens you to your inherent freedom. This may not be easy, but it is, in fact, aligned with the highest intention of the universe. After all, that's what the universe did by becoming you – it put a limitation on its formless nature to become you with a form. As Brooks has said, "Freedom has freely created freedom with boundaries – you." For integration and healing to happen, you learn how to embrace your limitations and then lean in the direction of your heart to the best of your ability with acceptance and compassion. When asked what his definition of freedom was, poet Robert Frost replied, "It's being easy in your harness." [3]

When I went to Israel to teach yoga, I taught the principles of Tantra. Surprisingly, when I taught the topic of freedom, I was met with strong opposition, voiced loudly and harshly. At first, I perceived this as a rude response. The Israelis in my classes seemed to have a sense of confidence bordering on arrogance, which intimidated me – yet also felt oddly familiar. Then it dawned: they weren't trying to be rude; they just communicate the way my family always did! When they talk, they yell!

Perhaps this is because the endless fighting in Israel has put everyone on their guard, particularly young people. It's mandatory for all teenagers to enlist in the army for two years; that alone could explain the protective barrier surrounding their hearts. Getting through that wall seemed monumental.

Once I identified this cultural phenomenon, I fully embraced it. I started yelling back, "Freedom is definitely your true nature! We were all born free! Yoga is the discovery of that freedom deep inside!" The more I yelled at them to drive home my point, the more they liked me. By the end of the course, we were all speaking the same energetic language.

They softened and came to understand what I was trying to say: there is a longing deep in everyone's heart for peace, understanding, and love.

Unlike these Israeli students, when I was in high school, outwardly, I gave the impression of being easy in the harness. But inwardly, I was just like them. I chafed against any and all externally imposed limitations, and I wasn't capable of creating healthy boundaries for myself. I was far, far away from understanding Frost's reply, or the Tantric paradox of freedom and boundary. To me, freedom meant busting out of any restrictions whatsoever.

THE STREAK, PART I

In February of 1975 I invited Payton and another friend since grade school, Andrew Paisano, to sleep over at my house since my parents were out for the evening. The three of us created one of our signature forts under the ping pong table in the basement, stole a bottle of vodka from my parents' liquor cabinet behind the wet bar, and hung out together in the fort, smoking joints and drinking, long after my mom and dad had gone to bed.

It was after midnight when I emerged from our hazy den and peered through heavy lids at the world outside. Snow blanketed the yard. In the pitch black I could just see the snow falling in the light of the new moon. I was seized with what seemed to me the perfect idea.

"Let's streak!"

This was the 70s when the phenomenon of streaking was at its peak. The novelty song "The Streak" played regularly on the radio, even after topping the charts less than a year before. Payton was half asleep already and barely responded, but Andrew grinned, and I knew he was in.

We stripped down to just our shoes. Andrew said, "Come on, let's take off our shoes too."

As energized as I was about the idea of streaking, this did not seem appealing.

"No way. My feet will freeze off. How about if we just leave our shoes on?"

"Okay," he agreed. "Shoes on. But that's all we're wearing."

Naked but for sneakers, we tiptoed up the stairs from the basement. We paused for a moment, listening for any motion upstairs, but my parents and sister were sound asleep. Giggling quietly, we made our way toward the sliding glass door to the backyard.

"I can't believe we're doing this."

"Yeah, this is a rush. It's crazy," said Andrew.

"Okay," I said, sliding back the door and shivering in the blast of cold, "When I say go, we'll run around the house two times."

Andrew nodded, hugging himself tightly.

"Go."

We took off into the night. I have vivid memories of the sensations that surrounded me within the first few steps: the fresh, chilling air; the snowflakes that clung to my skin for just a moment before turning warm and liquid; my breath that hung in the air, visible, like my own personal cloud. I felt awake and alert. Adrenalin flowed.

No one was up. No cars. It was totally still. I felt perfectly safe in a strange way. As I turned the corner into the front yard, I felt free, utterly free of all inhibitions: natural man in his natural habitat...plus shoes. I jumped and leaped and pranced like a deer. I looked over and saw that Andrew was grinning ear to ear just as I was. I couldn't believe we were doing this. It was so much fun.

Feeling confident and exhilarated, I decided to show off and slide across the snowy cement driveway. Halfway through my slide, I realized that underneath the thin layer of fresh powder was black ice. My feet flew out from under me, and I catapulted forward, landing hard. I lay there dazed and naked on the snowy driveway, not really sure what had just happened. My jaw ached.

I looked up and saw Andrew above me, doubled over with laughter. I touched my chin, and it felt warm and wet; my hand came back bloody. Apparently, I had hit my chin just perfectly on a crack in the cement and split it wide open.

Andrew could not stop laughing hysterically. I was seriously hurt but the sight of me lying naked on the driveway all covered with snow, compounded with the effects of illicit substances, was enough to keep him convulsed. I stood up carefully. My chin throbbed and the pain was sobering me up quickly.

"Oh my God. What am I going to do? I have to tell my parents."

We looked at each other in a moment of shared panic. Almost simultaneously, we said, "Oh shit!" and Andrew started laughing uncontrollably again. Later, he told me it was the snow angel imprint that my body left in the snow that made him laugh. Apparently, my glasses landed intact, perfectly placed on the bridge of the angel's nose.

"Shut up, Andrew. This isn't funny." The cold slap of my words hit him, and he pulled himself together.

We made our way back into the house and snuck back down into the basement. On the way, I concocted the story that I had had a nightmare and hit my chin on the corner of the ping pong table. After deciding to leave Payton snoring heavily, Andrew and I got dressed, woke up my parents, and spun the tale. Miraculously, my parents bought it. They drove me in the dark to the emergency room.

The doctor on call took me into the treatment room. He examined my chin, and prepped it for stitches, saying with a wry smile, "Looks like you won't need much Novocain tonight." I smiled back, pretending I didn't know what he was talking about, while internally saying *thank you thank you thank you* for not telling my parents what he obviously deduced. I got stitched up, went home, and tried to sleep.

The next morning, Andrew and Payton went home, and no one mentioned anything about what happened. No questions were asked. I somehow stole a bottle of liquor, got drunk and high, streaked, broke open my chin, and went to the emergency room – without getting caught. I never told my parents the truth about what happened. I still have the scar: my souvenir of the wild and free within me.

DOWNHILL

Emboldened by my unpunished misdeeds, I continued on my path of dual existence. In the spring of that same year, the Jewish youth group took a weekend ski trip to Boyne Mountain in Northern Michigan. After the first day of ski runs, my buddies and I tramped into the ski shop, ruddy with cold and tracking wet snow. We wandered around a bit and quickly got bored.

"Hey Todd, you comin'?" someone said.

"In a sec," I replied. They left noisily, and I wandered over to the clothing section, filled with cold-weather gear. I was attracted to a beautiful white ski hat with Swiss-patterned markings in rainbow colors. Inexplicably, I lifted it from the display, looked around, and shoved it under my parka. Keeping my hand under the coat and lowering my gaze, I hurried out the door. I had made it only ten paces or so before I felt a hand on my shoulder.

A stern voice said, "Excuse me."

I knew before I turned around that the jig was up. To this day, I don't know what the security guard looked like, because I kept my eyes fixed on the snowy ground as I faced him. I couldn't look him in the eyes.

"Yeah?" I said, with forced calm. My heart was racing.

"Let's see your hands," he said.
For a moment, I thought I was going to get away with it. I removed my hand, and the hat stayed hidden. I found the courage to challenge him: "What."

But he'd seen this all before. "Open your jacket, please."

Heat filled my face, and I did as he asked. The hat, colorful and bright, peeled away from my middle and fell to the ground, like the last maple leaf of the season. Neither of us said anything. We both knew.

During the three-hour car ride back to Grand Rapids, my parents kept asking me why. "I don't know," was all I could say, and I meant it. I truly did not know. They grounded me, adding to the deep humiliation I already felt at their disappointment, and they gave up asking "why?" when it became clear that I had no explanation whatsoever for my actions. They chalked it up to adolescent anomalies, since as far as they knew, I was the model child and student.

They never brought the incident up again. I found I could forget about it easily when I drank or smoked, which I began to do every weekend. I believed that I only drank and smoked socially. I didn't realize it was becoming a habit.

WELCOME TO MORE SWAMPLAND

It may have been my impaired decision-making skills that led me to try out for the high school football team during the summer before my freshman year. I had loved playing tag football with my neighborhood friends when I was younger. We never played rough and we enjoyed competing against each other – and sometimes even our moms or dads

– for fun. In retrospect, I can see that as a 120-pound scrawny musician, I really had no business trying out for the team. But since I was good enough at running and handling the ball to play fullback on the junior high school team, and since I possessed the bravado of a burgeoning teen alcoholic, I signed up.

I thought it would be fun. I was wrong.

I knew our school had a strong and competitive team with a "terrific" coach, George Barcheski. What I didn't know was that team practices started in August and lasted all day, every day of the week, for three weeks. In the blistering, humid Midwestern late-summer, we lined up over and over again in two lines facing each other, awaiting the signal. The coach blew the whistle and we thundered toward each other with the sole purpose of crashing into and taking down the person opposite. I hated it. The coach yelled at us if we shied away from hitting as hard as we could. Then he matched me up with a human refrigerator. Not only did I get yelled at because I hesitated before hitting the 200-pound sophomore, but I also got the crap rammed out of me every single time.

The forearm and shin pads did almost nothing to protect me, and at that time there were no precautions taken to prevent concussions as there are today. By the end of the first week I was black and blue from head to toe. I taped up my bruises and limped back to practice every day. I sweated, hit head-to-head, and got knocked down, over and over, but kept coming back for more. I was dedicated.

At the end of the three weeks, the coach lined us all up in a row. Battered and weary, I held my helmet in my hand and shielded my eyes from the late afternoon sun.

"All right, listen up!" he shouted. "I'm calling out names. If your name is called, you can start running laps around the field. You made the team."

He fixed his eyes on his clipboard and didn't look up. "Biggs. Ellis. Jones. Murphy…" I watched as one by one, the kids whose names were called took off across the field. More names, more kids running. "O'Brien. Parini. Poinsetto. Swartz." He had reached the end of the list. No Norian.

The coach affixed the paper to the top of the clipboard, adjusted his cap, and turned his back on me and the two other hapless players who had not made the team. We stood there, forlorn and awkward, waiting for some… something. Acknowledgment of our efforts? A "try again next year" or "too bad"? Even just some kind of recognition of our very existence? None came. With his back to us, he blew the whistle for the new team to assemble in a huddle, and never looked at us again.

My jaw hung open as I stood there.

My first thought was, I can't believe I didn't make the team. And almost immediately following, I'm a failure and I'll never succeed. I'm not good enough. I held my head down and walked home through that proverbial Shame Swampland.

Once there, I did what I had been doing ever since I was a child: I escaped into the comforting world of music. I sat down at the piano, still in my grubby, sweaty practice pants, and played Beethoven.

Over the next few years, I settled into a comfort zone that included marijuana, alcohol, and playing keyboard with The Todd Norian Trio, all the while maintaining my "good boy" image. No one knew that I was engaging in unlawful and verging-on-unlawful hijinks. I never shoplifted again but I did find creative ways to act out, like sneaking out late at night with my friends after New Year's Day, dragging discarded Christmas trees into the street to create huge tree-barricades, and, in the morning, watching from hiding spots as frustrated drivers shook their fists.

The glee I took in such activities did nothing to compensate for the black hole of unworthiness that grew darker and deeper. If anything, it made the hole worse, though I didn't know it at the time.

MALAS: DUST ON THE SURFACE OF CONSCIOUSNESS

Dust is a naturally occurring phenomenon. It accumulates on surfaces regularly, no matter how meticulously they are cleaned. Dust appears particularly in empty, abandoned places; just go up into the attic and notice how much dust has accumulated. In Tantra, this dust is called *malas* (impurities) – not to be confused with *mālās*, or garlands, or mālā beads used in japa mantra practice.

The *malas* are "dust on the surface of consciousness," and all darkness or sense of limitation is caused by this "dust." Every time you forget how miraculous you are, more dust bunnies appear. *Malas* are the self-limiting thoughts that the infinite universe has placed on itself in order to become a finite being. As this finite being, we can release this limitation at any time we wish.

In Tantra, there are three kinds of *malas* – *āṇava mala*, *māyīya mala*, and *karma mala*.

1. *Āṇava Mala*: The feeling of "not enough," or lack of fullness. This type of dust makes you feel as though you are missing something, that there is an absence of fulfillment. *Āṇava* is considered the "universal *mala*," because everyone experiences this feeling of insufficiency and because the *āṇava* forms the basis of the other two *malas*.

Āṇava is the cloak of low self-esteem, insecurity, and a deep feeling of unworthiness. It also describes a complete preoccupation with self – like the person who assumes that everyone around him must be as obsessed by the zit on his face as he is. It's the experience of having too much subject. When this *mala* is more pronounced, you become so focused on yourself that you rarely consider the consequences of your actions, especially as they relate to others. You end up engaging in damaging behaviors, like cheating, lying, or stealing, without noticing that you are hurting others. By the time you wake up to what you're doing, you've completely trashed your life and the lives of those closest to you.

The roots of this *mala*, as well as the roots of the other two *malas*, trace back to shame – which we now know can dissolve through self-love. Fortunately, *āṇava* can give rise to a longing for fullness again; consciously recognizing our feelings of lack often causes us to reach higher. For example, I caught a cold recently that just wouldn't go away. For weeks I soldiered on with a head full of goo, and just when I thought I was over it, it came back. My longing for health was never greater! This longing is what eventually healed me, since it forced me to slow down, take better care of myself, and get much more rest.

2. *Māyīya Mala*: Being caught up in distinctions and difference; the feeling of being separate and different. This is the condition of worrying about what everyone else thinks all of the time. It's the experience of having too much object. *Māyīya* invariably leads to comparison to others, which often gives rise to jealousy, since it is rooted in the fear that you are somehow not good enough and that others are better than you.

This *mala* finds its healing in practicing gratitude. When you appreciate yourself and your own uniqueness, you attract more appreciation – even from others. It takes courage, but sharing your authentic self attracts many more than it repels. Most people want to hang out with someone who is genuine and comfortable in her own skin – foibles and all.

3. *Karma Mala*: Being caught up in identification with your actions. This *mala* is steeped in over-identification with doing and "the doer." *Karma mala* is what happens when you either try too hard or don't try hard enough, ultimately manifesting in workaholism, drug and alcohol addiction, adultery, over- or under-eating, over- or under-exercising, gambling, or excessive spending. It's all about functioning at the extremes, often turning to substances or other people for immediate gratification of your imbalanced desires.

Karma mala is also a feeling of apathy or the feeling that you have no agency or power to act. It can be the result of the other two *malas* operating; for example, we sometimes go into denial as the world is falling apart around us. Rather than step up to deal with the circumstances in front of us, or the unsavory consequences of our actions, we bury our heads in the sand. The good news about *karma mala*? When you finally lift your weary self out of the ditch and allow yourself (and the mess all around you) to be seen, accepted, and forgiven, you can begin to rebuild your life.

The *mala*s, although painful, are gifts in disguise that allow you to re-frame your experience and beliefs about yourself. Once you see these conditions of the mind for what they are – dust on the mirror of consciousness, a normal byproduct of human existence – then you have a chance to question your choices and realize you are the creator, not the victim of your reality. No matter what life is presenting, you always have a choice.

Not that I grasped any of this growing up. It's clear to me now that from grade school into high school, I was operating under the steady influence of all three *mala*s – like most adolescents. I was perennially preoccupied with self, others, and how my accomplishments stacked up. Yet if you had asked me then how I felt about my life, I would have said it was great, except for one glitch. Her name? Karen Kleinhuizen.

EXERCISE: What is Your Primary *Mala*?

All three *mala*s are present in all of us. But usually there's one *mala* that is most prominent. Take a few minutes to sit quietly, reflecting on the three kinds of "dust" above. Then answer the following questions:

1. If you had to identify your blind spot (self-limiting tendency), what would that be?
2. How does that tendency play itself out in your life?
3. Which *mala* does it most closely relate to? Try to clearly articulate your particular version of this *mala*. We each have our own "brand" of *mala*. What's yours?
4. Reflecting on the solutions to the *mala*s above, what quality of heart could you give yourself to help change, reduce, or dissolve this *mala*? (For example, self-empathy, accepting yourself more fully, etc.)
5. What is the benefit or value of your *mala*? What lesson is your *mala* trying to give you?

NOTES

[1] Barks, Coleman with John Moyne, translators. *The Essential Rumi*. New York: Harper Collins. 1995. Print.

[2] Swami Nirvikarananda, translator. *Isha Upaniṣhad*, Verse 1. https://www.wisdomlib.org/hinduism/book/isha-upanishad/d/doc122460.html.

[3] "Frost, Poet, Is Honored On Birthday: New Englander, 80, Views World as Too Crowded and Hurried" *The Hartford Courant*, 26 March 1954. p. 14, Column 1. Hartford, Connecticut.

CHAPTER FOUR

A New Way

Quietness

Inside this new love, die.
Your way begins on the other side.
Become the sky.
Take an axe to the prison wall.
Escape.
Walk out like someone suddenly born into color.
Do it now.
You're covered with a thick cloud.
Slide out the side. Die,
and be quiet. Quietness is the surest sign
that you've died.
Your old life was a frantic running
from silence.

The speechless full moon
comes out now.

Rumi, *The Essential Rumi*[3]

As a junior in high school, I found myself slumped yet again in the 500-seat auditorium at the St. Cecilia Center, watching my nemesis, now tall and lanky, play flawlessly. For years now, Karen had been regularly humiliating me in local, regional, and state competitions. So it was with a creeping sense of déjà vu that I knew, with perfect clarity, what would happen next: she would finish, the judges would confer, and she would step forward to receive the award. Indeed, I was right. Karen Kleinhuizen, the girl who lived on the other side of town and was surrounded by musical excellence her whole life, triumphed again.

At that moment, an image flashed through my mind. I saw myself on the football field, getting the crap knocked out of me over and over and over. Suddenly, I couldn't stand losing to her any longer.

My daily mantra became: *how can I beat Karen*? Not a particularly yogic mantra, for sure, but that's where I was at age 16. I thought about winning, all day long. This intense longing ignited a fire of concentration and one-pointedness that I had never experienced before. It was so pure and passionate that it superseded the long-standing *I'm not worthy* mantra that had looped in my head constantly, from the lost footrace in elementary school through mortifying football tryouts and beyond.

DESIRE: THE SOURCE OF THE SOLUTION

As I mentioned earlier, in Tantra, the question is not, "How do you become free?" but rather, "What do you want to bind yourself to?" Desire is not seen as something to be avoided; it's seen as the essential nature of the universe. Remember, the infinite desired to become finite as you in order to delight in yet another perspective of itself. The universe desired to be known by you by becoming you. Nothing happens without desire, even existence itself.

Desire, then, becomes the source of the solution. The problem is not that you desire; the problem is that you don't desire enough. You don't want it badly enough to make the sacrifice to release what no longer serves you. The day you have no desires is a dreadful day – it's the day you don't get out of bed due to lack of motivation. Since your desires fuel your life, having none of them can be a key component of depression. Aligning with your highest desires, those desires deep in your heart, is the key to freedom.

The key to following your heart is to develop the skill of discerning which desires are good for you and which are not. After being beaten by Karen over and over, I was inspired to reach deeper into my own desires, to ask myself, "How badly do I want it?" The response that came back was, "I want it more than anything else."

The Tantra tells us that we are born free. If that is true, then there are only three questions you need to ask yourself, according to Brooks:

1. What do you most deeply desire?
2. What value is it for you?
3. What are you willing to do about it?

In order to examine all three questions more thoroughly, we first need to understand how the universe is ordered, according to Tantra.

ICCHĀ ŚAKTI, JÑĀNA ŚAKTI, & KRIYĀ ŚAKTI

Within the cosmology of *Nondual Śaiva-Śākta Tantra* is a series of 36 principles of existence called *"tattvas"* (literally "that-ness-es"). Organized into seven sets of five, plus one, the *tattvas* explain the Tantric view of how the universe came into being. The top five *tattvas*, known as the five *śaktis* (the divine feminine) or the Absolute *tattvas*, are the most esoteric and subtle. They represent the attributes of the one Absolute in its journey from the formless into form. The five *śaktis* are: *cit śakti* (the power of consciousness), *ānanda śakti* (the power of bliss), *icchā śakti* (the power of intention or desire), *jñāna śakti* (the power of knowledge), and *kriyā śakti* (the power of spontaneous action). Let's take a closer look at three of them. (See Appendix B for a diagram of the 36 Tattvas and more information.)

What you most deeply desire has its roots in the Sanskrit. *Icchā* means having the will to be, to exist. Since *śakti* describes the fullest expression of universal power, *Icchā śakti* is our deepest will to be. It describes the nature of the universe in its most primordial form that has, at its essence, the will to exist. *Icchā śakti* is your longing for what's possible, and desire then becomes the driver of all experience. I'm not talking about desire for sensory pleasure, though that could be part of it. I'm talking about a profound desire connected to your purpose, an intention of your heart that wishes to be expressed. It's a desire for long-term fulfillment versus short-term gratification.

"What value is it for you?" relates to the importance and urgency you give to your desire. To discern its value, you must be able to know and interpret your experience. The Sanskrit for that is *jñāna śakti*, the power to know. *Jñāna* is the Sanskrit word for knowledge which comes from the root *jñā*, related to the modern English word "to know." *Jñā* is also related to the Greek noun, *gnosis*, knowledge, and Gnosticism, which refers to ancient religions that embraced the spiritual world of mysticism. To know yourself requires inner reflection, awareness, and the ability to distinguish levels of subtlety. You need to know what you need, understand whether your level of desire is superficial or deep, survival-oriented or life vision-oriented, and then decide whether it needs to be satisfied right now or can wait.

Value signifies the importance you give something and not all desires are equally valuable. Take hunger, for example. If you are ravenous, then your desire for food increases in value, and continues to do so the hungrier you become. Other considerations related to food – What food is available? Do you like it? Can you afford it? – take a backseat if your hunger is strong enough. In certain circumstances you might eat anything anywhere. Just getting food, any kind of food, takes precedence over everything, even your desires related to your life purpose and spiritual journey. What we value is all relative and contextual; determining value is dependent on *jñāna śakti*.

"What are you willing to do about it?" requires an action; it requires *kriyā śakti,* the power to act. In this context, *kriyā śakti* refers to agency or the power to act on the physical level to change your life. To manifest your desire and see it take shape in the world, you must either take action yourself or arrange for someone else to do the action for you. Either way, action is needed.

So, what was my *icchā śakti*? My desire was to beat Karen. Using *jñāna śakti,* I placed that desire above all else and then, finally, I employed the power of *kriyā śakti* to manipulate my world in order to produce my desired result.

I planned out a strategy to beat Karen, starting with switching piano teachers. I knew that Karen was taught by the best piano teachers in Grand Rapids and that if I had any shot at beating her, I'd have to make a change. Much as I loved Mrs. Kuipers, I was ready for the next level. I contacted Ruth Russ, a professor of music at the local Calvin College. She didn't often accept high school students, but made an exception for me, perhaps because I had gone to kindergarten with her son, another shy musician like me.

At our first lesson I played a Mozart sonata for her and she nodded, saying, "Well, okay. That was nice. Let's go back to the beginning." She turned the pages back, picked up her pencil, and in her own patient, clear, and calm way, she proceeded to mark every single note with an instruction teaching me how to play with more nuance and sensitivity. There were so many pencil markings that I could hardly see the musical notes. Apparently, I had been playing everything wrong. Yet instead of feeling shame, I felt encouraged.

I could sense I was in the presence of a true virtuoso teacher. Mrs. Russ, for whom I had great respect, was a consummate musician with deep humility. She knew my goal: to improve my playing and win the competition. Therefore, she poured out an immense amount of feedback, but she did it with so much love that it melted any defensiveness I might have had. I was receptive and wanted to hear everything she had to tell me. I was open to trying anything.

After two hours, the lesson was over. During that time, I tapped into a deep hunger within to learn and grow, to understand the art of making music for the love of music itself. I was completely inspired; she ignited my passion to excel and become the best I could be. I felt an incredible surge of energy. I was on fire.

I began practicing earnestly four to six hours every day. My parents, acknowledging my renewed fervor, offered to purchase a new piano – a black Baldwin baby grand – and I chipped in what I could afford from my modest earnings from The Todd Norian Trio. I practiced during all of my free time after school, and without ever making a conscious decision to do so, gave up all smoking and drinking. By the time I arrived at the next competition six months later, I was clean... and I was ready.

I watched Karen play as perfectly as always, in front of the judges. But for the first time in my entire young life, I felt that I could compete at her level. What I had to offer was just as valuable.

I sat down in front of the gleaming instrument. All was quiet. In the moment before my hands touched the keys, I sensed a familiar nervousness: my cold, clammy hands, my irregular heartbeat. At the same time, I was aware of a different feeling – a passion for the music itself. This feeling was buoyed by the love and support of my teacher, the confidence that grew out of the hours I had poured into my preparation, and the clarity of my one-pointed focus. I was primed and determined.

Focusing on that passion, I felt my anxiety diminish. *Full speed ahead.* I took a deep breath and began to play. From start to finish, the notes flowed out of me effortlessly; the music and I were one. I played my heart out and, to my surprise and delight, I won the competition. I finally beat Karen Kleinhuizen.

It had taken me my entire childhood up through my junior year in high school to generate enough self-esteem to have the courage to apply myself with total commitment toward a goal. Until that time, I was

74

impaired by that potent concoction of unworthiness and self-doubt. Because I believed that I was "not enough," I was therefore filled with fear, which in turn prevented me from living fully. I was unable to own the right to show up, the right to create, the right to fail and succeed and, ultimately, the right to be. I couldn't comprehend that I was worthy to be here *just as I am* because it was my birthright.

My triumph over Karen was a small victory in the self-esteem department but it also had another salutary effect on me: I never went back to drinking or smoking pot. Though I still struggled with believing in my own inherent worthiness, drinking and smoking no longer felt like a viable solution. I simply felt too good when I took better care of myself. Plus, I had gotten to the point of feeling burned out most of the time. Partying just wasn't fun anymore. By consciously binding myself to my desire for success, I freed myself from the unconscious attachment I had created to those mood-altering substances.

TAPAS

Not to be confused with small savory Spanish appetizers, *tapas* is a Sanskrit word that means heat, austerity, or fiery discipline. According to the Classical yogis, *tapas* is needed to burn away impurities and anything that's no longer needed: the old *saṃskāras*, imprints, or habits of behavior or thinking that keep you stuck in your patterns of smallness. There was certainly an element of that fiery discipline present in me as I prepared relentlessly for the competition.

Yet there is another way of viewing *tapas*. In the Tantric view, *tapas* is the longing for freedom or the longing for god – any longing for something greater than oneself. My desire to win the competition and the disciplined effort I put forth to do so, provided me with my first true experience of *tapas*. My longing for success, added to my disgust with losing, catapulted me to the winner's seat. I did not know then that the concepts of Classical as well as Tantric *tapas* would return to play a major role in my life.

HAVE STEAK, WILL TRAVEL

Because I had taken my piano playing to this new, accomplished level, I decided to pursue it further. I applied to all of the major music schools around the country to study classical piano performance and was accepted at all of them. I chose the University of Michigan School of Music since both of my parents went to U of M. My parents and I were delighted, and I enrolled in the fall of 1978. I had no idea what I was in for. At the university level everything was different. The level of intensity was high and everyone around me was cut-throat serious about their music careers. I practiced and worked continuously, so it was a relief when the first year was over and I returned home.

During that summer break, Tanner Radner called to invite me to spend the day water skiing with his extended family at their summer cottage on Whitefish Lake. I was delighted. I still looked up to Tan as someone who had followed his heart and manifested his dream by playing in a band. He mentioned that they were all vegetarians and would be serving tofu – a new word in my vocabulary – but that I could bring meat if I wanted. Since I certainly wasn't a vegetarian, I agreed to come only if I could bring a steak.

I arrived with my beef in tow and spent the day skimming over the clear blue lake with Tan and his cousin Mort. We came to the dinner table with damp hair and rosy faces, happy and relaxed.

"Here you go, Todd," said Tan's aunt, as she handed me a plate with my steak, still hot from the oven.

"Thanks so much for cooking it," I said, gratefully. "It smells delicious." I looked around at the other plates piled with vegetables and something that looked like cubes of roasted potato. *Must be that "tofu."* I ventured a question.

"Um… what actually IS tofu?"

The group laughed. "It's made from soybeans," Tan answered congenially. "Wanna try some?"

I was curious. Growing up in my solid Midwestern household, I had never seen or heard of eating soybeans; wild rice was about the most exotic plant we ever ate. Never one to turn down a new opportunity, I nodded. Tan held out his plate, I forked a cube, and ate it.

"So?" Tan asked.

It was better than I had anticipated. "Pretty good, actually. Not as good as my steak, but..." I gestured apologetically for the tofu.

Tan guffawed and the table joined in. The conversation turned to other pressing matters: Who had the best water-skiing technique? The worst wipeout? Who was developing the most painful sunburn? We chatted and laughed, and all the while, I kept finding myself staring at Tan. He looked, for lack of a better word, clear. His skin, his eyes – I thought I saw a kind of light or brightness exuding from him, a vitality that radiated. Finally, I had to say something.

"You're so... bright, Tanner. You look so healthy! What are you doing?"

He smiled. "I was studying dance in college but that's probably not it. It's probably the yoga."

I leaned in. "Yoga? Really?" Here was yet another unfamiliar word for my vocabulary. "Tell me more."

Tan explained the derivation of the term yoga, that it meant union or uniting our individual nature with our universal nature – the process of yoking yourself to spirit. Years later, I learned that the Tantric perspective envisions the yoke as both the concept of joining together *while also separating*. Like a chicken's egg, which is simultaneously both a whole entity and two separate entities (the yolk and the whites), yoga means both to unite, join, or bring together, but also to separate.

"Yoga" is an oxymoron, just like the term Tantra, which means both to weave and to expand.

Tan's understanding of the word yoga was more in line with the Classical tradition. He went on to explain that after graduation he had discovered a "yoga community" in Pennsylvania and that he was living there now. He didn't say much else, other than to tell me that he was happy there and that I could visit him any time I wanted. I didn't press him for more details. But the imprint of certain aspects of that experience stayed with me: his glowing good health, yoga, the community in Pennsylvania, and of course, tofu.

PRELUDE IN C-MINUS

I returned in the fall to U of M. I was working harder than ever, but the hours and hours I spent playing in tiny practice rooms, with virtuosos practicing on either side of me, made me realize that while I was talented in high school, I was no prodigy.

In case I had any doubt, my professor drove the point home. "You're not doing well," he said curtly. "I'm being generous by giving you a C minus in piano performance. This can't continue. You need to figure out if you want to be here or not." After the initial shock, I just felt numb. Clearly, I had lost interest in classical piano performance. My heart wasn't into it anymore.

I left his office and went for a walk, heading toward the Arb (Nichols Arboretum) nearby. I felt defeated. The old familiar "you are a failure" mantra started up, unbidden, and accompanied me like an unwelcome friend as I walked. My professor's words came back: "You need to figure out if you want to be here or not." Did I want to be here? I knew I was working at full capacity. If my best wasn't good enough, then what? Everything I had worked so hard for up until this moment now felt meaningless.

MEANING-MAKING MACHINES

*Ever more people today have the means to
live, but no meaning to live for.*

~Viktor Frankl[2]

One of Tantra's most surprising teachings is that life is meaningless. This is not to say that life doesn't have meaning. Rather, life invites you to bring meaning to it. It's *up to you to assign meaning to your life experiences.* You create the meaning that life has for you. Like a musician, you compose the song of life onto the blank score paper of the universe, using your own thoughts, feelings, and longings. You get to interpret everything that happens to you through your own belief system.

Not everything that happens in life is good and you certainly can't stop the bad things from happening. But you can always choose your response; in fact, your ability to respond is the definition of responsibility. In any situation, you have two basic choices: disempowerment or empowerment. When you choose to blame others and respond negatively, when you play the victim role and view everything in life as working against you, then you miss your opportunity to learn and rise higher. Conversely, when you abandon the temptation to blame, and instead respond positively, you step more fully into your power to shift the experience to your advantage. Choosing to see that everything in life is for your awakening places you in the driver's seat and accelerates your growth.

The bottom line is that whatever you choose to believe, the universe will support you. When you look for signs from the universe to support your positive *or* negative view, you will find them. It will always provide the evidence you are seeking, so why not choose an empowered life by giving positive meaning to events?

Christopher Reeve, the actor and director who became universally known from his title role in *Superman*, was paralyzed from the neck down in a horseback riding accident. He had a choice: to become bitter, depressed, and broken, or to rise up and overcome his challenges. He chose to thrive and became an inspiration to others. Even though he was confined to a wheelchair and needed a respirator for the rest of his life, he founded the Christopher & Dana Reeve Paralysis Foundation to promote research into spinal cord injuries and lobby for federal funding for stem cell research. He even went back to acting a few years later. Could there be any better example to show us that how you view your life makes all the difference?

We live in a universe of power, not a universe of morality, of right and wrong. It's up to you to bring that power into your life, by creating meaning. As human beings, we are hardwired to be meaning-making machines. That's what we do.

Right now, you're making meaning of these words. You made meaning of your experience yesterday, today, and you'll do it again tomorrow. Ultimately, you become the meaning you make of your experiences. If you fill your days with regret, guilt, and blame, rather than adventure, learning, and gratitude, then, at the end of your life, that's what you'll have and who you'll be. It's up to you.

EVERYTHING IN LIFE IS FOR MY AWAKENING

To bring meaning to my life, I return again and again to the belief that everything in life is for my awakening. This belief supports the natural resiliency of the human heart, by creating the right environment for this to happen. You need a "bounce-back mentality" as Pastor Joel Osteen says, in order to rise up. This belief is also the corollary to "Life is happening *for* me," rather than "Life is happening *to* me."

Obviously, when things are going well, this belief is far easier to employ. The real trick is to be able to say it – and mean it – when life is dishing out the hard stuff: pain, illness, betrayal, separation, loss… to name just a few. You must be willing to say to yourself, "No matter how bad this experience feels right now, it is still for my awakening." With this perspective, every experience in life can be used to your advantage. Nothing gets you down, at least not for long, because if everything is for your awakening, then whatever hurts or doesn't go your way has a deeper purpose of supporting you in the long run.

Tantra's gift of a "meaningless" life allows us the freedom to adopt and apply this empowering belief, which I call the "yogi's belief" because it is so essential to living a yogic life of fulfillment, insight, and true happiness. If everything in life is for your awakening, then you literally can't fail. It's the "no-mistake" theory of life.

NOW WHAT?

I walked deeper and deeper into the woods, ruminating on the conversation with my professor. I stopped and closed my eyes. I took a deep breath and smelled the sharp warm scent of the pines. In that moment, in that pause, I knew I had to make a change. I *didn't* want to be here. Not playing classical music, anyway.

My eyes still closed, I began to see something: an image of myself at age 13, with Robert Cassard, the guitar and bass player for the Todd Norian Trio. I saw us in his living room, lying on the shag carpet and listening to a jazz album that we bought with earnings from the band. After school every week, we spent hours listening to the Manhattan Transfer, Kenny Clarke/Francy Boland Big Band, Charlie Parker, Dizzy Gillespie, and John Coltrane. Robert had an insatiable appetite for jazz and his enthusiasm was contagious. Those hours spent with him, soaking up every riff, every dissonance, and every syncopation made me passionate about jazz.

Standing there with my eyes closed, I saw the smile on my young face and suddenly knew: Classical wasn't a mistake; it just wasn't bringing me joy anymore. What *was* bringing me joy was moonlighting with an avant-garde jazz band called Antares, playing gigs at Mr. Flood's Party, a popular jazz bar in Ann Arbor, Michigan. Within six months, I had researched the top jazz programs in the country and had transferred to the University of Miami (Florida), which had the top jazz bands and one of the best programs for piano.

JAZZ

At Miami, I majored in Studio Music and Jazz, which included the art of jazz performance and composition. As a sophomore, I was further behind than some of the other students who had been studying jazz all along, but I was thrilled to be there. I threw myself into the program and my studies with gusto.

Playing jazz was a far cry from classical. It was like the difference between delivering a musical *monologue* and having a musical *conversation* with a friend. I loved it! Jazz musicians who listened to each other could communicate in a completely spontaneous way, improvising lines that passed back and forth between players with surprising twists and turns, inventing creative sequencing of notes, scales, rhythms, and chords. Improvising together was a thrill.

It was also a new experience of collaboration. Being the pianist, I often had the role of accompanying the singer or "comping" for the soloist. My focus was on making the soloist sound his or her best. Having played alone for years, jazz was a welcome change. I loved serving and uplifting the other musicians, as well as being supported by others when it was my time to solo.

"Studies" for a jazz studies major did not mean poring over books in cubicles at the library. Instead, my fellow majors and I regularly piled into a 5' by 9' practice room together with a piano and lost all concept of time, jamming for hours. We would emerge in the wee morning hours, disoriented, hungry, and euphoric.

One evening, a saxophone player who was new to the school joined us for one of our jam sessions. Since none of us had played with him before, we had no idea what to expect. After some introductions and a few warm-up notes, we launched. Within minutes, it was apparent that this guy was something special. I had never played before with someone whose musical phrasing was that artistic, intelligent, and beautiful – so much so that it inspired me to dig deeper and find a more creative way to express myself.

I took a deep breath and let go completely to the pull of the music. What came out of me was totally surprising: beautiful notes and chord progressions that originated from such a deep place, I could almost taste them. I was enchanted. It's as if this new, brilliant sax player opened me to a bigger energy and a potential I didn't know I had. I expanded beyond all previously held limits, beyond what I thought I could do. During those precious few moments, the impossible became possible for me.

I wasn't the only one in that session who was inspired. The drummer, too, seemed to open up to his untapped potential, playing such profound, complex jazz rhythms that it launched me into an uncontrollable laughing fit. (I've since determined that when I reach a certain creative limit, my body gives way to uncontrollable laughter. The joy is so immense, it's uncontainable.) As the beat lifted me up metaphorically and carried me across countless bar lines, it gently placed me down on the downbeat where the rest of the band rhythmically caught up. What a ride!

What I experienced that night stayed with me and became a guiding principle in my artistic life. I continued to play jazz with the goal of inspiring others and finding inspiration in their brilliance, always reaching for a higher, more creative way to express ourselves, our feelings, our passions, and our hearts. The most memorable jam sessions for me were those in which we all pushed the boundaries of what's possible, to try something new. One of my favorite jam sessions took place every Monday night at the Unitarian Church in South Miami, hosted by the famous jazz trumpeter, Ira Sullivan.

I began to see jazz as a necessary blend of science and art, where the best technicians (science) were not always the best improvisers (art). Although I was still impressed with virtuoso technique, I noticed that sometimes the overly technical musicians weren't really saying that much musically. They liked to impress others, perhaps using technique to prove themselves worthy or cover up other deficiencies. I decided that using technique to entertain is like talking constantly, using a big vocabulary, without saying anything meaningful.

For musicians to move me, they had to play from the heart – that's the highest expression of jazz. In the best and most satisfying jazz, players express what's inside them: sometimes, joy and humor; other times, deep grief and sadness. When my fellow musicians expressed their deepest feelings through the music, I felt it inside me. It moved me and opened something up within me.

YOGA

In 1980, I was deep into my studies. I loved it, but I was also struggling. When I looked in the mirror, a haggard, washed-out version of myself stared back. Remembering the day on the lake and my friend Tan's radiant glow, I decided to try yoga. The closest studio was the Iyengar Yoga Institute of South Miami, just two blocks from campus. When I called, I was told that before I could join the general level class, I was required to take three private lessons with Sam Dworkis, the director, so that I could be familiar with the basics.

At my first lesson Sam greeted me with a huge smile beaming out from under his dark eyes and black curly hair. As this was Iyengar yoga, precision was important, so he started by walking me through some alignment principles. I watched as he moved his strong, very tan, rail-thin body with smooth fluidity into perfect versions of beginning *āsanas* (postures): mountain, down dog, forward fold. I followed as best I could but found that even the simplest stretches challenged me. Even after three sessions, I was still so stiff I couldn't touch my toes, but I was "ready" for the general classes now.

For just over an hour, Sam led me and the rest of the class through a simple sequence of *āsanas*. Bobbi Goldin, who was one of the students he was training to become a yoga teacher, assisted him during the class by doing hands-on adjustments. She was incredibly detailed and serious about alignment, but she also laughed with a lightness that made her seem almost childlike. She and Sam focused much of their attention on me that day, as I was still so brand new. Every single pose was difficult and I hurt all over. As was the case in Hebrew class, I was a terrible student, but fortunately for my teachers, this time I complained silently

84

to myself the whole time. I endured what seemed like an endless torture session and couldn't wait to get to *śavāsana* (corpse pose) for the final relaxation.

Finally, achy and sore, I stretched out on my back on my mat. Bobbi turned down the lights and lit candles as the sweet scent of sandalwood incense wafted about. The room felt cozy and safe. I closed my eyes and took a deep breath. With my eyes closed, I tuned in to the beautiful flute music playing, "Inside the Taj Mahal" by Paul Horn. The long notes of the flute inside the cathedral of the Taj Mahal in India echoed with a distinct spiritual overtone. Paul seemed to be playing on the overtones, which correspond to jazz harmonies. The overtones are what give the sound its warmth and timbre.

As I lay on my back, I gave myself over to the whole experience. I began to feel what I can only describe as a melting sensation in my heart – somewhat uncomfortable and somewhat pleasurable. I made a conscious decision to accept it and breathed more deeply into the sensation. Suddenly tears flowed from my eyes for no apparent reason. I wasn't sad; in fact, I was extraordinarily happy. I felt deeply moved by something much bigger and more powerful than anything I had ever experienced before. These were tears of joy.

It was the most extraordinary experience, difficult to put into words. I felt as though a blanket of grace was draped over my previously aching body. All my pain was now released, and I felt open and spacious. I felt free inside, as though I was floating. I felt complete acceptance of myself as if for the first time, with no pressure to become anyone special or accomplish anything. I was okay just being me. I had come home to myself. Later, I realized that this was my very first experience of pure worthiness for no reason at all. As the tears continued to stream down my cheeks, pools of water began to form in my ears. I laughed out loud because it was so absurd, and then for the next few minutes I alternated between laughing and crying. I couldn't control what was happening, but the experience was so pleasurable that I didn't want it to stop.

After the class, Sam pulled me aside and Bobbi handed me a tissue. They had seen my outpouring of extreme emotions in *śavāsana* and wanted to make sure I was all right. Sam asked how the class went, then chuckled at my response: "I think I relaxed for the first time in my life."

Between the two of them, they created an environment for me that was the perfect balance of discipline and humor, strength and softness. In time, I became more limber. I found myself calmer and more relaxed in life situations that previously felt stressful, including the intense atmosphere of the Jazz Studies program. I also consistently experienced a heightened awareness of everything around me. I found that between the surface of my eyes and the center of my brain there was a space that was non-reactive, calm, and serene. I felt as though I could almost stand outside my experience, witnessing what was happening outside of me, around me, and inside of me in terms of my thoughts, emotions, and body sensations. I noticed that for the first time in my life, my body no longer craved meat. I felt lighter.

Bobbi and Sam eventually asked me to substitute teach for them at the Institute, which I did, even though I wasn't a trained teacher yet. They said I was "a natural."

BLUE MAN CUBE

Connecting with the Iyengar community opened my eyes to the rich diversity of culture, race, religion, and lifestyle that existed in Miami. Coming from Michigan, I found it to be a real culture shock. Miami was much more open and progressive. I was exposed to all kinds of people, beliefs, and spiritual traditions, especially at the Institute, where Sam and Bobbi hosted senior teachers several times a year from the Iyengar tradition and other spiritual paths.

Given that my focus was primarily on jazz, and very secondarily on yoga, I had little time to devote to other spiritual endeavors. However, I attended a few Sufi (Islamic mysticism) lectures and workshops, including one in which we learned whirling, a form of dancing meditation, and one with a Sufi teacher on meditation practices. I vaguely remember the instruction for a practice known as Zikr (which means remember), that involved extremely slow circular movements with the head and neck, coordinated with breath and mantra. After practicing this for about 20 minutes we were guided to sit in stillness and breathe.

The teacher then asked us to visualize blue transparent cubes moving slowly in the center of the heart. We were instructed to not only see the cubes but also to allow them to move and flow as if they were a waterfall of blue cubes. I easily fell into a curious and deep state of "blue cubeness" until I could feel the cubes as three-dimensional objects and see deep into the space inside them. They grew and grew, becoming large enough to contain me. *Should I? Why not?* I stepped inside one of the cubes.

The hair on my scalp stood on end and my skin prickled with goosebumps as the cool, clear, deep blue cube took off with me inside it. To steady myself, I reached my hand out to touch the glass-like walls of the cube, and as I did so, I had a moment of shock. I had disappeared and merged with the blueness of the cube. I became it. My whole body tensed, and my mind told me to scream and cry out for help. But something deep down inside of me encouraged me to stay present and keep going. I deepened my breath and relaxed, allowing the oneness. Suddenly I felt a wave of calm. My fear completely dissolved, and I explored this new blend of feelings: unity with the blue cube, awareness of the cube, and awareness of myself experiencing the cube.

I lost all sense of time. When the soft meditation bell rang and I heard the teacher's velvety voice guiding us to return and open our eyes, I had no idea what had just happened. When I shared my experience with the circle of practitioners, the teacher confirmed that, indeed, I had taken a unique spiritual sojourn. I felt that something had shifted for me and, for the rest of that day, I was lit up from inside with warm blue light.

A NEW LONGING

Yoga helped me navigate my final year at Miami. All along I had been devoted to playing jazz but I never made it into the top jazz band. In fact,

I didn't make it into *any* of the jazz bands. As my time there came to a close, I reflected on the reasons for my lack of success, and determined that although I was enthusiastic about jazz, I wasn't as gifted as some of the other players. Also, I resisted commercial music, electronics, and synthesizers. The keyboard players of all the top bands didn't just play the acoustic piano; they knew how to play several electronic keyboards at once. I was a traditionalist, and in terms of popularity, a dying breed.

And unlike my experience beating Karen K., I had no Mrs. Russ this time, no coach who could help me strategize and work on my weaknesses. Back then, I had proved to myself that I could be successful if I got the right support and put my mind to it. Now, I couldn't do it on my own.

What I did not yet understand was that much of my reaction to competition was shaped by the burden of shame that I still carried.

Because I held the deep, unconscious conviction that I wasn't good enough, I invited all the experiences from the universe to prove my belief. I had no idea that I was bringing that upon myself. I was more comfortable staying small than motivated to reach outside myself to get the help I needed. I didn't have the uber-incentive I had had in high school, the desire to win that overrode all my "I am unworthy" programming.

For years I couldn't figure out why I didn't have that incentive. Today, I believe that the yoga and spiritual explorations I had embarked upon had planted a new incentive: a longing for self-knowledge, for freedom within, for the divine. Somewhere beneath my conscious mind, I believe I knew that music alone wasn't enough for me. I was meant to follow a different path.

In 1982, before I graduated with my bachelor's degree in Studio Music and Jazz Studies, I applied to the master's program in Jazz Composition and Education at the University of Miami with the idea that I would shift my focus from performance to composing and teaching. I was accepted and awarded a full ride fellowship – a welcome surprise, which made me reconsider my previous ideas about my lack of success. Maybe I was

88

cut out to be a teacher, not a performer.

After graduation, I took a summer Jazz Studies course at Eastman School of Music in Rochester, NY. When it ended, I started the long drive back to Miami. When I reached the Pennsylvania border, I thought again of Tan. He had been right about yoga; my regular yoga classes had brought vitality back into my body and spirit. I pulled over at a rest stop, got out, and stretched. I unfolded my travel atlas and discovered that the yoga community he had described years ago was not that far out of my way. Was he still there? Could I stop in for a weekend visit since my master's program didn't start for a little more than two weeks? A phone call later, I was back on the road, headed for Summit Station, PA.

EXERCISE: Everything in Life is for Your Awakening

Bring your journal and pen to a quiet place where you can be reflective and still. Find a comfortable, upright seat. Take a few deep breaths. Soften your face. Allow the light of the universe to fill you. Lengthen your side ribs from your hips to your shoulders. Allow your collar bones to smile upwards, with the head of your arm bones back. Release your hips to the earth and extend the top of your head toward the sky. Reflect on the following contemplations:

1. Become aware of any challenges in your life, now or in the recent or distant past. Take a few moments to find a specific issue, challenge, or difficulty you've been dealing with. Soften yourself around the challenge and see if you can just let it be there, resting in your heart freely.

2. How has this challenge changed you for the better? Underneath all of the suffering and hardship, how has this challenge benefitted you?

3. In what ways has it strengthened you?

4. What insights has it given you?

5. If everything in life is truly for your awakening, how has this challenge awakened your heart?

6. What lessons has it offered you?

Once you've finished responding to the questions above, make a list of 10 things you're grateful for. Writing out a gratitude list is helpful in resetting the tone of your heart. Gratitude is the chalice for grace.

NOTES

[1] Barks, Coleman with John Moyne, translators. *The Essential Rumi*. New York: Harper Collins. 1995. Print.

[2] Frankl, Viktor E. "The Unheard Cry for Meaning," *Psychotherapy and Humanism*. p. 21. New York: Washington Square Press. 1984.

CHAPTER FIVE

Ascending the Summit

And the day came when the risk to remain tight in a bud was more painful than the risk it took to blossom.

Elizabeth Appell[1]

"ASHRAM"

I drove for what seemed like forever, through rolling hills and farms. I finally turned in at a dirt road, bumped along it through a canopy of trees, and arrived at a cluster of clapboard buildings and a few stone homes that appeared to be an old farm. Parking in front of the largest building, I turned off the ignition and heard the engine of my old brown Chevette cough a few times before it settled to rest. I opened the car door and swung my feet out. No sooner had I stood up than two apparitions in white floated toward me. I blinked. For a moment, I believed I had arrived in heaven and was being greeted by angels. How else to describe the two men dressed head-to-toe in white, their pure, clear eyes lit up, their countenances so beautiful and peaceful?

"Welcome!" they said, in unison. Hearing them speak was almost a disappointment; they were human, after all.

"Thanks," I said.

"What's your name?" asked one. "Where do you live?" asked the other.

I told them, and before I could ask anything in return, they offered to help carry my bags. I thanked them again, then rummaged in the back of my car. I pulled out the luggage I needed, exposing the rusted-out hole in the floor of the Chevette. I hoped they didn't see it. If they did, they made no sign. They remained…angelic. I handed over a few bags, then gripped my own suitcase nervously. *What have I gotten myself into?*

As I followed them toward the house, I scoped out the compound. Everyone was wearing white. Some wore loose *punjabi* (a long kurta or loose, collarless shirt) like my two escorts, while others wore similarly flowing white garb. Everyone I saw also seemed to have the same ethereal yet grounded quality and the same joyful glow that Tan had radiated years before. I found their demeanor comforting and even oddly familiar – as though I recognized them as my tribe. With great warmth and kindness, they checked me into my room in the "brothers' barn," and as I signed my name, I noticed that my hands had relaxed their death-grip.

"Todd!"

I turned around to see Tanner striding toward me, arms extended. We hugged, and after catching up a bit, he toured me around the buildings and grounds. It was clear he was excited to share all of it with me: the books he was reading, the people he loved, and the philosophy he was learning. He even offered to give me a Shiatsu healing massage, which he said would help balance my energy channels. I'd never heard of Shiatsu and I'd never had a massage, but I was game. We planned it for the following day.

So much was new for me. I tried to take it all in but something basic wasn't computing. I had to ask.

"Tan... what *is* this place?"

He threw his head back and laughed. "I know, it's a lot. I felt that way, too, when I first arrived."

I was relieved. But I still need to know. "So?"

"It's a yoga ashram, called Kripalu."

Being with Tan always seemed to bring new words. "Ashram? Kripalu?"

"Right. So, an ashram is a community that focuses on spiritual practices, studying and living a yogic lifestyle," he explained. "It's a sacred space, secluded from the world, where the higher values like peace, love, devotion, and service are practiced."

"Like a monastery?"

"Yeah, except without the Christianity, and there are men and women here." I had already noticed that difference.

"And what does 'Kripalu' mean?"

"Kripalu means 'compassion', 'merciful one', or 'divine grace.' It's the name of the ashram founder's teacher: Kripalvanandaji, from India. Some call him 'Bapuji,' which means 'beloved father.'"

I sat with all of that for a moment. I had many more questions, but it was time for dinner. I followed Tan into the dining room, which was set up with long tables. Food was served family-style and this time I was not surprised to see tofu among the trays of vegetables. Some of the members of the ashram served the meal; others took away our dishes and washed them. I learned that still others helped in the large garden to grow the food and worked in the kitchen to prepare it. All of this service seemed to come straight from the heart. It was highly appealing.

For the next two days, I fell into the rhythm of the ashram. In the mornings, I woke up early and practiced yoga, breathing, meditation, and chanting with the rest of the community. During the day, I took long walks in the surrounding hills or helped out with the hands-on work that kept the ashram running: picking lettuce and rinsing off its muddy roots, chopping onions, fixing a broken fence. In the evening I chanted and listened to *satsanga* (being in the company of truth) where senior teachers discussed all manner of yogic philosophy, such as how to be more fully present in the world or the nature of reality. This was all new to me and I drank it in.

On Thursday, after the morning practices, I reluctantly went back to my room to gather up my belongings. I opened up my suitcase and had started tossing in some socks when Tan poked his head into the room.

"Hey, how's it going?"

I couldn't tell if his question was an offhand greeting or a real inquiry, but I chose to answer it honestly.

"I don't know, actually. I'm kinda bummed." I half-heartedly chucked in another pair of socks.

He nodded. He seemed to know exactly why. "You know, you could stay."

I paused, staring at him. *Is he joking?* "Really?"

"Yeah. Starting tomorrow, there's a 10-day course here. You could do that and then still make it to Florida, right? When do you have to be there?"

"Two weeks."

"You'd have three days to drive..." he trailed off. We looked at each other in silence and then he backpedaled, probably wanting to take any pressure off. "But it's totally up to you."

In what felt like forever but was probably only three seconds at most, my mental train took off:

> *I love that it's surrounded by nature, how kind everyone is, how they talk about healing and serving from the heart. I love the regular yoga practice. I love that everyone works together in harmony, that they share a vision of acceptance, compassion, and tolerance. I love that it's the complete opposite of the dog-eat-dog world of competition and comparison, where no one has compassion for anyone. And even though I can't explain it, I love that everyone here seems to glow. I have no idea whether I'm crazy or if this place is for real, but I resonate with it and I want more of it.*

I looked at Tan and said, "I'll stay." I gleefully unpacked my socks, put away my suitcase, and registered for the 10-day course, called "The Quest for the Limitless You."

FEEL IT TO HEAL IT

I had no idea what to expect other than more of what I had already experienced: yoga and its philosophy, breathing exercises, simple vegetarian fare. The 10-day course, with 120 participants of all ages, included all those things. Within a few days I noticed changes in myself. I had more energy. I felt lighter, more youthful – as though I had dug down into an unknown, infinite wellspring of life force. My mind was clear, and I noticed a happiness inside me that I hadn't realized was missing from my life.

What I didn't anticipate was the deep psychological work that we engaged in every single day. If I had known that we would drill down daily into the nerve endings of some of our most painful life memories, I might have packed up my Chevette, waved goodbye, and motored south. But the glimpse of happiness and clarity that the weekend provided me was enough for me to trust that the program would be good for me. It was. Like a deep-tissue massage or a much-needed visit to the dentist, the next 10 days were painful, but transformative.

Much of the work we did focused on acceptance and having compassion for our journey to this point, all parts of it. Perhaps not surprisingly, one of the most excruciating exercises for me centered on competition. One of the co-directors, Don Stapleton, Ph.D., (known as Samadarshan at the ashram, whom we called Sam for short) set up a game called "bombardment," which was actually just a variation on the old grade school horror show: dodgeball. As the red rubber balls started flying, I time-traveled back to recess at Breton Downs Elementary, where the older boys had ganged up on me: threatening, shoving, and knocking me down. I was overcome with a nauseating combination of anxiety, defeat, and resignation. I stopped playing.

I ran into the corner of the room and curled up into a ball. I cried. Sam joined me there, gently laying a hand on my shoulder. When psychological content like this surfaced, which was one of the intended goals of the exercise, we were encouraged not to change anything, but simply to feel.

"Be with your feelings. Breathe into them," counseled Sam. I did, and I cried harder. He stayed next to me until the worst of it subsided and then, lovingly, he invited me back to the game.

I looked at the floor. "I can't. I don't want to get hurt." I felt my lip quiver. *What a baby.*

"Okay. That's fine," he reassured me. "You can stay here."
I felt a wave of relief. I nodded.

"Do you need anything?"

"No, thanks," I said, and I looked up for the first time into his eyes. There I saw confirmation that, even in my diminished state, I was still okay just as I was. I didn't have to join the group. I could just be myself and feel sorry for myself.

So that is what I did. I hunched in the corner, watching the rest of the game and occasionally shedding a few more tears of bygone humiliations. When the game ended, I left my nest and rejoined the group for the next activity. Without skillful facilitation during the game and afterwards, this might have been an exercise in masochism; instead, in Sam's hands, I came out of the session feeling as though I had molted. Gone was a skin of fear I didn't even know I had.

EVOLUTIONARY JOURNEY

The most profound exercise we did was adapted from visionary futurist Jean Houston's *The Possible Human*, [2] a book that was on the leading edge of psycho-spiritual awakening at the time. In the book, Houston describes an experience of evolutionary integration, in which "in order to go forward we must recover the past." With masterful guidance from Gita, the program leader, and accompanied by a variety of musical soundtracks and live drumming, we retraced the evolutionary roots stored within our energy field and muscle memory. Gita led us through a movement journey – from the beginning of cosmic time before life on the planet to human existence today. What that means is that we undulated on the oceanic floor as one-celled organisms, swam as fish, wriggled out of the oceans on our bellies, grew arms and legs until we could crawl and climb, became Tyrannosaurus Rexes and attacked and ate each other, swung our arms like monkeys, and then finally formed tribes as early hominids.

It was inevitably chaotic and disorganized, with 120 people all moving and dancing through the room having individual experiences – some shouting, others sobbing, some expressing rage, others exhibiting a kind of primordial intimidation and power. Still others cowered in fear in the corner, as I had in the bombardment exercise. During all of this mayhem, I somehow felt a profound sense of excitement and longing, almost driven by a deeper aboriginal instinct to survive. This inner drive felt ancient, as if it had been there since the beginning of time.

As fun as this was, it was the next levels of evolution that were the most interesting to me. Gita asked us to shift from unconscious instinctual human beings, staging wars and sacrificial ceremonies, to become conscious human beings with intelligence and vision for the future. We moved from a world of repressive autocratic government where conflict and authoritarian power reigned, to one of unified, collaborative, and peaceful governance from the heart. But it didn't end there. The music became sweeter, more lyrical, and we evolved yet again.

This time we transcended human form and became angels full of compassion and love. Ethereal and free, we moved above the earth, offering blessings to each other and to the world below. To finish, we sat in silent meditation on the floor, merging with the life force itself and returning to the greater universe from which we came.

I found I now had access to a deeper freedom, a broader perspective. All of my personal problems seemed to recede into the vast experience of life itself. At the end of the experience, we took time to process our feelings and share insights. During that exercise something deep within me broke loose.

Each day I went deeper and deeper into cleansing my body and my psyche. This world I had entered was so foreign to me, yet I felt as though it was delivering exactly what I needed. I cried heaving sobs at least once every day while Sam held me and encouraged me to release my buckets of tears. Sam became my angel, always appearing somehow at the perfect time when I needed to be hugged or held. There was something so soft yet strong about his presence. He became a combination mother-and-father to me, and his unconditional love allowed me to grow and evolve unimpeded, without judgment or shame. I'm certain those tears swept away what I no longer needed to fear, because within even a few days, I felt better and better, lighter and lighter. Like the quality of lushness left behind after a torrential storm, my life was swiftly becoming brighter and more meaningful.

SAVOR YOUR EXPERIENCE

Rasa becomes the delectable savoring of the Self by the Self.

~Abhinavagupta, from *Locana,* and *Abhinavabharati*[3]

After many years of exploration, I've boiled it down to two main reasons why we're here:

1. To gain lessons that our soul needs in order to become more of ourselves and fulfill the bigger purpose of our existence; and
2. to savor the experience of life itself.

What does savor your experience mean? For a deeper perspective, I turn to the Tantric term, *rasa,* which means to savor. It also means divine taste, full of juice, essence, nectar, and liquid. The nine *rasas* describe a wheel of nine different emotions or "flavors of life" that represent all of the various feelings and emotions we can have: *śānta* (peace), *śṛṅgāra* (eros or passion), *hāsya* (humor), *karuṇā* (compassion), *raudra* (fury or anger), *vīra* (heroism), *bhayānaka* (fear), *bībhatsa* (disgust), and *adbhuta* (wonder and awe). (See Appendix C for the *Rasa* Mandala and more information on the *Rasas.*)

The *rasas* teach us that every human emotion we have is divine and that our experience of life is to be savored. Our passion, our "juice," our purpose for living, are inextricably linked to our capacity to experience

99

our embodied humanity. As Ayurvedic teacher Dr. Robert Svoboda says, "Existence without juice is dry and tasteless." [4]

The term *dhvani,* which means sound, echo, or resonance, when combined with *rasa,* describes the full experience of a taste, emotion, or even a work of art. Savoring any one *rasa* includes the initial impression of it, as well as the ensuing vibration of its presence. In terms of emotions, you not only feel it, you attune to it. When you resonate with what you are feeling, you achieve vibrational harmony with it – allowing you to more readily make sense of it, integrate it, and take the lesson from it.

Rasa dhvani is the optimization of *rasa,* the choosing to embrace it. Resonating with an emotion doesn't mean you have to like it; for instance, *bībhatsa,* disgust, is something we generally resist. But there's a way to experience disgust, by letting it in, recognizing it, feeling the disgust in your body, then releasing it. This is *dhvani.*

When I was little, we used to have dinner at grandpa Aaron and grandma Ida's house every Sunday night. Grandma always made enough food for an army, usually consisting of matzo ball soup, salad, bread, gefilte fish, brisket, chicken, potatoes, green beans, and then sweet lokshen kugel (baked noodle pudding or casserole) and some type of pie and ice cream for dessert. I loved it! I was always a little skinny and I think Grandma was secretly trying to fatten me up.

My favorite part of the meal, however, was Ida's matzo ball soup. Not because it was the best on the planet, which I'm certain it was, but because the accompanying family ritual never failed to disappoint. Every Sunday, Sherri and I silently grinned at each other as Ida served the soup to the table as the first course. Let the show begin!

My mom always started.

"Be careful, dear," she warned my dad, "the soup is hot."

Without fail, he ignored her admonition, diving into his bowl with gusto

100

and spooning the piping-hot liquid into his mouth, then emitting a cry that practically shattered the water glasses, shrieking:

"Oye, Ma???!!!! This soup is too hot! Why did you make it so hot? I could kill myself!"

Even though we knew he had probably burned his tongue, we couldn't help laughing at his predictable predicament and the transformation of his face that went along with it: first, as the hot soup scalded his mouth, his eyes grew huge and white while his face turned red. But then, as he yelled at Grandma, his eyes narrowed into red slits and his face turned white. It was a dramatic display.

Ida, razor-sharp and nobody's fool, always defended herself by saying, "Oyoyoi, Sandford, it's not that hot. You have to develop an asbestos tongue like me, that's all." While Sherri and I giggled, Grandma and my father went back and forth, arguing about how hot or not the soup was. Once the argument stopped, the soup had cooled enough for us all to eat it safely.

As crazy as it seemed to my sister and me, my dad's behavior was, in some ways, *dhvani*. He most certainly felt his feelings unabashedly and unapologetically, achieved vibrational harmony with the experience, and then released it fully and completely. The only part he missed was taking the lesson from it, though it would have been far less entertaining for the rest of us if he had.

FEEL YOUR FEELINGS

People tend to push away negative or difficult emotions like grief, anger, sadness, fear, or disgust, and get attached to the "good" emotions like joy, passion, peace, humor, or compassion. In her book, *My Stroke of Insight: A Brain Scientist's Personal Journey*,[5] Jill Bolte Taylor states that all emotions last fewer than 90 seconds. The brain, responding to an initial triggering incident, releases chemicals that dissipate in less than a minute and a half. During those 90 seconds, the goal is to just stay within the experience fully without reacting to it. If you can do this and keep your breath moving naturally – ideally, holding yourself with acceptance and compassion throughout the process – then, after that time, you can choose whether or not you want to add more story to it.

Feeling fully is a key to healing our bodymind. *What You Can Feel You Can Heal: A Guide to Enriching Relationships*[6] by Dr. John Gray, describes the experience of the healing benefit of feeling your feelings. So often, we resist difficult feelings, thinking or hoping they will just go away. But they don't. Undigested feelings and emotions build up energetically and wreak havoc on the tissues of the body. They reinforce patterns of denial, which strengthen the walls we build for protection around our heart.

When you resonate with what you are feeling, you achieve vibrational harmony with it – allowing you to more readily make sense of it, integrate it, and take the lesson from it. You are always left with a feeling of deep release and calm. You find yourself more insightful and connected to yourself, others, and to life itself.

If you accept the concept I described earlier – that the Absolute chooses to limit itself through the vehicle of embodiment – then the bodymind is also a contracted form of divine embodiment. What you view as its limitations are actually portals to discover your boundless true nature. Likewise, your emotions are not obstacles to spiritual awakening to be avoided, repressed, or transcended. Instead, they are the God-given means to understand and expand your experience of life. Ultimately, the bodymind is a divine gift to help you recognize and understand the Absolute within your own heart and to then serve others from this higher dimension of consciousness.

My emotional catharsis in the arms of Sam helped me begin to break down the patterns of resistance to my own feelings. I was becoming more and more capable of moving through emotions freely; I was becoming *dhvani*.

GURU IN THE HOUSE

About halfway through the course, I was seated next to Tan at breakfast, eating in silence as was the practice. We finished and he eagerly motioned for me to follow him. When we reached the hallway, he didn't have to hold back any longer. He burst out:

"The guru is back! He'll be teaching *satsaṅga* this evening!"

I'm sure my blank look was highly disappointing. "What's a guru?"
He exhaled, exasperated. "Guru means teacher, Todd. He's the founder of this place." I could see how excited Tan was, but I was not impressed. I had had plenty of teachers; why was this one so special?

"Great," I declared, hoping that I didn't sound as detached as I felt. Apparently, I didn't.

"Isn't it?" he gushed, then he squeezed my shoulder before he hurried away.

Later, I learned that the word "guru" literally means the "weighty one," or "the heavy one." It describes an individual whose powerful connection to his or her center creates a force of gravity, rock-solid and unmovable like a cast-iron cauldron. Dedicated to follow the heart and stay connected to a bigger energy, the guru is someone with the capacity to hold space for the full spectrum of life, light and dark, without getting knocked off balance. Another definition of guru is based on Sanskrit etymology: *gu* means "dark," *ru* means "light." Therefore, a guru is one who reveals the light and leads you out of darkness. If Tan believed the guru could do all that, it was no wonder he was so excited.

As the day wore on, I saw evidence of that same excitement throughout the ashram. It fairly buzzed with anticipation. The staff doubled their efforts to clean the rooms and scrub the floors and bathrooms. Everything smelled fresh, and a hint of sandalwood incense filled the air. Late in the afternoon, all of the residents donned their best whites. A double line formed out the front door of the building along the path,

103

dotted with flower petals, to welcome the guru home. I wasn't present when he arrived; I decided I could wait until that evening's *satsaṅga*.

After dinner, we all gathered together in the sanctuary. There were musicians on harmonium and guitars, and several drummers – one of whom I found out later had been a jazz major at Berklee College of Music in Boston – playing beautifully complex rhythms. Hundreds of voices joined in devotional chanting that filled the room, and the energy of the space was palpable. Between the chanting, the rhythm of the drums, and the ecstatic dancing going on all around me, I was uneasy. What *was* this place? But I gave up my resistance and allowed the music and the rhythm to carry me, much as I did when playing jazz. This was no place for intellect; this was all about heart. Soon I felt an inner knowing: Everything was okay. I was okay. All was well. I could relax.

That was it! I flashed back to the feeling I had had at the end of my first yoga class. Tears instantly began to flow again, but why? The only reason I could find was gratitude. I had found my soul group. I was surrounded by beautiful beings, seekers like myself, all envisioning a world of peace and love. I knew that what I was telling myself sounded like the peace movement of the 1960s, but it didn't matter. It was here, and now, and real. I had found my purpose and my place in the world, and it felt as though everything had led me to this moment of pure perfection.

I was conscious of how the universe orchestrated my entire life – every person, every experience, each response – for better or for worse, culminating right here, right now. Everything *was* happening for my awakening. I felt a depth of gratitude that penetrated through to the essence of life itself.

Suddenly the music stopped. Everyone stood up. A deafening blast from a conch shell sounded, and I covered my ears. A single voice, pure and clear, called us to an invocation to the guru, *"Bolo Śri Sadguru,"* and everyone echoed in unison. Then silence. All 200 people stood in absolute stillness, barely breathing. Time stood still. I don't know if it was five seconds or five minutes before the most beautiful being I had

104

ever seen entered the room from the side door. It was the guru, Amrit Desai.

He was Eastern Indian, of dark complexion, with long flowing black hair down to his shoulders. His tan robe hung gracefully from his thin, regal frame, and as he moved, the fabric seemed to merge seamlessly with the air around it. Was he walking or floating? I couldn't tell. His gait was perfectly smooth, his posture upright but not stiff.

As he glided to the platform, he turned to everyone, hands in *añjali mudrā* (palms together in front of the heart). With the deepest marble brown eyes I've ever seen, he connected with every single person in the room. His smile was broad and his eyes, still and deep, sparkled. The joy he radiated was returned by everyone in the room, including me. I felt my heart jump out of my chest with longing to be seen by him. When our eyes finally met, a current of bliss flowed from his eyes to mine and my heart raced. I was almost giddy. I didn't know why, but it didn't matter. I just was.

He bowed his head to us, turned to the altar, and knelt down to offer his respect to the picture of his teacher. He then sat down in his enormous magenta chair, the size of a double throne, and began to teach. I'm not even sure what he said, because I was so transfixed by his form that his words were inconsequential. The evening concluded with *ārati,* a ceremony of light performed with candles, ghee wicks, and mantras. It was all so beautiful; it was almost surreal.

During the morning and evening sessions for the next few days, the guru repeatedly visited those of us in the 10-day program. He spoke passionately about different topics, such as love, awareness, or consciousness. Each time I was in his presence, I felt myself trusting more and more – not only trusting him but also trusting the growing feeling of freedom deep inside me. It was almost like a game.

I discovered that when I let all my doubts go, I felt bliss. The more I let go, the more bliss I felt. As soon as I followed some fear or negative thought, I got distracted and the bliss dissipated. It was very much like meditation. I kept bringing my awareness back to the present moment to see if I could melt any lingering fears or doubts.

The last few days of the program felt like a crucible in which my life purpose was clarified and refined. There was a quickening within me, an urgency to wake up and move forward in my life. This was not a conscious, rational thought; rather, it was an instinctive one. It was as though all of the emotional purging burned away all the flotsam and jetsam, leaving a capacious space for my heart to shout its desires through the rooftop. The message was bright and clear and resounding: I wanted knowledge, union, joy. I wanted to honor and serve the light within me and within everyone else. I wanted to change my life.

WHAT'S IN A CONTRACT?

After each talk, the guru opened it up for individual questions. This was my favorite part of *satsaṅga*, probably because I loved the surprise, the spontaneity of the interactions between the guru and student. Like good jazz, it was a mesmerizing dance of energy, and I delighted in both the questions and the answers. I wanted to participate, too, but I couldn't get past my own nervousness.

On the last night of the program, the guru took a sip of water, rearranged his robe, and said, "Time for one last question." I watched, amazed, as my hand lifted into the air, as though some invisible puppeteer had just pulled the string connected to my wrist. The guru looked directly at me. "Yes, come here," he said kindly, and I clambered to my feet. I lurched toward the altar, trembling with each step. You would have thought I was approaching the Great and Powerful Oz. I sat down, and there was a moment of silence. He smiled. For the first time, I saw the charming space between his front teeth. *Is he missing a tooth?* He seemed so human, so warm… I felt completely accepted and held by him, a feeling of love like never before. It was all-encompassing.

I finally spoke.

"My name is Todd Norian and I'm here in the Quest for the Limitless You program. I'm loving it so much. I love being here. I feel like I've found my family… and I want to move in."

Some part of the back of my mind was shouting, *Hey! Who said that? Who authorized that? Who's in charge, here?* Yet it was exactly how I felt. Until that moment, I hadn't known that I really did want to move in. I was in love with the community, the lifestyle, the yoga, and now the guru.

"Yes," he said, "go on."

"There's only one problem. I signed a contract to do a fellowship for two years in a master's degree program in music that starts in three days. I wouldn't be able to come back for two years."

He smiled even wider now. As I gazed at his form, I saw the unfamiliar Indian figure in front of me, an individual who was a complete stranger to me until one week ago. But I also saw his smile, his warmth… and his nose. *His nose is as big as my grandfather's,* I thought. *I'm in good company.* Then he said, with a lilt that verged on a classic Jewish grandfather accent, "What's in a contract? Two years is too long for me to wait."

That was all I needed. It was almost as if he knew what I needed to hear, and how I needed to hear it. Elated, I felt that the dream I had in my heart was heard and encouraged. My sense of kinship with him, bundled with the love and compassion I heard in his voice, pushed me into certainty. His response gave me permission to change my destiny.

So that is what I did, when I picked up the phone the next day in August of 1982 and called my parents and then my professors. Was I sure? they had asked. Yes, I was. I was never so sure of anything.

And I had no idea how to handle what happened next.

107

EXERCISE: You Can Heal What You Feel

1. Find a comfortable place in which you can lie down on your back, a quiet place where you won't be disturbed, and preferably, where you are free to make sounds. As you become comfortable, deepen your breath. Relax your body and release any strain or stress. Allow all tension to drain out of you.

2. When you inhale, invite the light of the universe to fill you. When you exhale, release anything in the way of your capacity to let go. Release any fear or anxiety and just let yourself be. Allow the universe to be with you.

3. Breathe into your heart. Feel the state of your heart. Sense, without any judgment, if your heart is open or closed, tight or constricted. Just notice. There's no need to change anything about how you are.

4. Allow your awareness to penetrate just beneath the surface of your heart. Breathe into any feelings or experiences. See if you can allow yourself to feel what's there. Feelings are as natural as the sky is blue, and the grass is green. It's all okay.

5. If you begin to tense up, slow it down. There's no rush to feel. Tensions respond to softness and gentleness. Allow your breath to be soft and gentle. When your heart is ready, it will let you go deeper. Don't force it.

6. See if you can allow your feelings to touch you. Perhaps there's sadness, grief, anxiety, or doubt. Perhaps there's confusion, fear, numbness, or feelings of anger or betrayal. Bring your breath to whatever it is you're feeling and allow it to be. If there are tears, allow the tears. If there's laughter, allow the laughter.

7. Alternatively, you might experience joy, peace, gratitude, or a kind of vastness. Whatever is there, allow yourself to be with it nonjudgmentally.

8. Once you are in touch with your feelings, explore them. Breathe more deeply and allow your loving attention to go deeper as if you could go beneath the feelings.

9. What's behind the feeling? Continue to penetrate the depths of your heart until you find the center – your heart of hearts. Dwell there for a few moments or longer.

10. When you're ready, slowly begin to return. Open your eyes and find your journal.

11. Take a few minutes to reflect on what you felt. Remember: what you can feel you can heal. Often, when you allow yourself to simply be with your feelings in a loving way, insight arises and your inborn wisdom offers you an experience of beauty, a moment of clarity, where you gain a broader perspective. Stay with your experience and see what arises.

NOTES

[1] The quote is widely attributed to Anais Nin but scholars have not been able to locate the source in any of Nin's work. It appears the quote was written by Elizabeth Appell in 1979. Consult these blogs that address the mis-attribution: http://anaisninblog.skybluepress.com/2013/03/who-wrote-risk-is-the-mystery-solved/ and https://www.wildmind.org/blogs/quote-of-the-month/anais-nin-getting-unstuck.

[2] Houston, Jean. *The Possible Human: A Course in Enhancing your Physical, Mental, & Creative Abilities.* Los Angeles: TarcherPerigee of The Penquin Group: 1997. Print.

[3] Ingalls, Daniel Henry Holmes. Translator. *The Dhvanyāloka of Ānandavardhana with the Locana of Abhinavagupta.* Vol49 of Harvard Oriental series. Cambridge: Harvard University. 1990. Print.

[4] Quote is attributed to Dr. Robert Svoboda but original source is not known. Find out more about Dr. Svoboda at http://www.drsvoboda.com.

[5] Taylor, Jill Bolte. *My Stroke of Insight: a Brain Scientist's Personal Journey.* New York: Viking, 2008. Print.

[6] Gray, John. *What You Can Feel You Can Heal: A Guide to Enriching Relationships.* John Gray's Mars Venus LLC: 1993. Print.

CHAPTER SIX

Icarus

"We are no longer linear beings having a linear experience. We are dimensional beings having a dimensional experience."

Dr. Joe Dispenza, *Breaking the Habit of Being Yourself: How to Lose Your Mind and Create a New One*[1]

"Take your left hand and place it over your beautiful heart to bless your body as your temple... To bless your life that it be an extension of your mind, your kingdom... To bless your soul that it speak to you in infinite ways... To bless your past that it turn to wisdom... To bless your future that it be filled with opportunity and adventure... To bless the adversity in your life that it may initiate you into greatness... To bless the divine in you, the power within you, that it move in you and through you... That it move all around you and show evidence in your life that it is real."

"To sum up the meditative process, you have to break the habit of being yourself and reinvent a new self; lose your mind and create a new one; prune synaptic connections and nurture new ones; unmemorize past emotions and recondition the body to a new mind and emotions; and let go of the past and create a new future."

THE LIMITLESS ME

I was on top of the world: thrilled about moving into the ashram, connected to everyone around me, and riding the euphoric high of my momentous decision to change my life. It had all happened so fast, and I was still flying. But because I didn't have time to think it out clearly, I didn't anticipate how I would feel when my "real life" at the ashram began. I also didn't expect what my decision to follow my heart fully and completely would bring.

The program ended. All of the guests with whom I had grown close packed up, and I waved goodbye as each one drove away. I watched as Sam, Gita, other course leaders, and the guru left town too, headed for another seminar. The energy of the ashram dropped like the end of a Broadway run and mine with it. I signed up for "*seva*-exchange," which was their work/study program. This now made me one of the staff. I didn't mind that so much, but I felt my happiness drain away. I no longer had that excited feeling of love and support that was so obvious and all-pervasive during the last few days of the program. I felt flat.

Nevertheless, I showed up for work in the kitchen, and within minutes, was chopping vegetables and washing dishes. I had bought several books from the bookstore, as well as about a dozen cassette tapes of lectures by the guru, including an endless loop of "*Om Namo Bhagavate Vasudevāya*," a mantra that was handed down from the guru's guru, to the guru, to all of us. A program leader had told us that Swami Kripalu translated the mantra to mean "thy will be done." The leader had also said that it had special powers in that lineage and encouraged us to repeat it as often as we could throughout the day. Ever the conscientious student, I popped the tape into my portable cassette player, the one I had used to transcribe Herbie Hancock's piano solos and those of other jazz greats, and slid on my headphones. I loved this mantra and found it calming, so I listened to it nonstop while I prepped food.

Another recommended practice was *trāṭak* (to gaze or look at), a meditation practice of focusing your awareness on a single point, or a photograph of a spiritual being or guru. We were told that when you

111

practice *trāṭak* with a photo of the guru, you take on all of the divine qualities of the guru. It seemed far-fetched, but I was game. After lunch, I searched in the store for one particular photo that resonated with me – a copy of the large framed portrait that was placed on the guru's chair when he wasn't in residence. Students often gathered to meditate in front of that photo, practicing *trāṭak*. I found it, bought it, and set it on a small table in the brothers' barn.

Eager to test-drive it, I sat down cross-legged in front of the photo and closed my eyes. Once I felt perfectly still and centered, I opened my eyes and softly gazed at the photo. As I watched, the two-dimensionality of it fell away, and the guru's face became real. His skin breathed and moved, and his eyes twinkled. I started. *This couldn't be happening*, I thought. *The photo is a photo. It's not real.* I shook my head, but nothing changed. In a panic, I squeezed my eyes shut.

I took a few deep, calming breaths, and told myself that I was just hallucinating. Reassured, I opened my eyes again… and sure enough, the picture came alive again. I stared in amazement. This time, I set aside my doubt and resistance and just allowed it to move. My fear vanished and was replaced by a peaceful benevolence.

As I watched the subtle actions of the guru's face, I felt a sweet and steady energy flowing from the photo into my heart. I felt held by this energy. I felt whole and complete. I sensed the presence of grace and began to experience the bliss of being in the guru's actual presence, similar to what I had felt in *satsaṅga* a day or two ago, though not as strong. The moving image seemed to invite me into an internal, hypnotic state of joy. After several minutes of this meditation, I lay down in *śavāsana*. When I arose, I felt completely refreshed, as though I had just taken a nap.

DARK NIGHT OF THE SOUL

That night I couldn't sleep. I lay in bed, staring wide-eyed into the darkness. I finally got up quietly, threw on my long white kirtan shirt and cotton jacket, and left the brother's barn. Barefoot, I headed in the vague direction of the sanctuary, where we had the program and all our *satsaṅgas*. Carrying no light with me, I strained my eyes to see the path in front of me in the misty darkness. Suddenly, movement shimmered in my periphery, and my heart quickened. I picked up my pace. I looked directly off to the side and saw several black cats chasing one another in the brush.

Rather than feeling relieved, however, I believed that their antics confirmed something more sinister. I slipped into a state of paranoia. I was convinced that I had seen someone or something treacherous, and that an evil entity was sneaking up on me. My body began to shake uncontrollably, and my mind raced; I couldn't stop myself from thinking I was being followed by some murderous dark force. My instinct was to run and hide.

I took off along the path, stumbling in the dark. *They are closing in on me.* The fear I felt merged with my memory of my childhood nightmares and became one engulfing, palpable terror. *There is nowhere to hide. I will be swallowed whole.* I was in a true state of panic. In the dark up ahead, I saw the sanctuary. I reached the door, breathing hard, and flung it open. I ran inside and closed the door behind me, my fingers fumbling with the latch.

Inside, there was more darkness. I longed for light. Without thinking, I grabbed a white sheet that I found in the back of the sanctuary and wrapped myself in it. I just wanted to feel safe. I wanted the light. Tired and afraid, I pulled the sheet around me tighter and then curled up on the altar next to the guru's chair, empty but for the large black and white photo. Swaddled in white, comforted by the picture next to me, I managed to drift into a restless sleep for a few hours before morning practices started.

The next day, I did the usual yoga, meditation, breathing, and chanting, but I noticed that I felt different. Something had shifted inside. Just before breakfast, I asked our kitchen manager, "Do you want me to check the water jugs?"

She smiled. "That's okay, they're all full."

There was nothing in her demeanor to suggest it, but somehow I knew: *she's angry*. I had to know if I was correct.

"Are you okay?" I ventured.

"Why?" she asked, narrowing her eyes. "I'm fine." But then she took a breath. "Actually, no, I'm pissed. Almost everyone showed up late today, and I had to totally scramble to get the food out on time."

"I'm sorry," was all I could think of to say.

"Thanks. You were on time." She looked at me carefully. "How did you know?"

I was stumped. I had no idea why I could feel what she was feeling. I just shrugged and shook my head.

All morning, it kept happening. Every interaction I had, no matter how brief, left me with a clear impression of that individual's emotional state. Sadness, embarrassment, delight, grief, longing… over and over, I was spot on. Each person was always amazed that I could name what they were feeling. As the day progressed, however, my newfound ability began to scare me. I couldn't turn it off. I also couldn't slow down its progression. By lunchtime, I had become so attuned, so empathic, that I began to hear the thoughts forming in people's heads before they spoke. It was getting creepy. *How is this happening?* I needed to get away from people for a while, perhaps re-center myself and get more grounded. I excused myself, headed out the door, and started walking briskly toward the pond.

My mind was racing. A storm of thoughts converged on me, none of them distinct. I looked up and saw the faint silhouette of the moon fading into the daylight sky. Somehow, that image became a portal of sorts, a two-way funnel to distill the chaos in my mind and return it as one pure transmission. A stream of vibration poured into my brain, lighting it up with insight and knowledge, as if the moon and the stars were sharing their wisdom with me. I was awestruck. I resonated so fully with the universe that it seemed as though the entire mystery of the universe was downloaded into my brain, like a cosmic data dump.

I felt as though I *became* the point where the infinite touches the finite, where time and space interconnect, where the mortal and immortal merge. I was the threshold, the space in the middle between the physical and the non-physical, and from there, I had the perspective of both sides. I saw evidence of the life force all around me and I sensed the oneness of it all. I could see into the energetic structure, the atomic architecture of everything around me. I had a kind of laser vision that infused a deeper knowing within. I was on the inside of the universe looking out, and all I wanted to do was to stay there and keep witnessing it.

This heightened state came on gradually but powerfully, and it demanded my full surrender and trust. To this day, it was the deepest and most profound experience of cosmic consciousness that I have ever felt. The universe was at play inside my body and mind, and there was nothing I could do about it... except ride it out.

The pond was just on the other side of a copse of trees. I began to walk but stopped short with a pebble in my sandal. I reached down and slid off the back strap to free the stone, and noticed that the middle of the sole of my foot was sore. In fact, the same spot on my other foot was sore, too. As were the center of my palms. *The stigmata.* I had read about it, and now it was happening to me, out of nowhere. I could explain away the sores on my feet – I walked barefoot a lot to soak up earth energy – but I had no idea how I could develop them on my hands so quickly. I stared at my palms, intrigued, then kept walking.

I paused at the edge of the pond. In the reeds, a family of ducks made their way out of the water and walked toward me. In my state of complete oneness with all that is, I had a Dr. Doolittle moment: I understood their quacks. I swore I heard them talking to me. I felt their energy and sensed they were communicating with me and I with them. It was magnificent! The family passed by me, and I walked along the edge of the pond, stopping at the shadow cast by a picket fence around a bed of flowers.

During the 10-day course, I had read about healing different parts of the body, including eyesight, and I was intrigued. Since 2nd grade I had been wearing glasses, and later, contacts, to correct my considerable nearsightedness. As I gazed at the picket fence, I heard a voice deep inside me telling me to trace the slats of the fence with my eyes, moving them in a particular sequence along the edges of each slat, slowly, one by one. The voice coached me to breathe deeply, adjust my head, neck, and shoulders into alignment, and keep my eyes soft as they traced. I must have stood there for 20 minutes, following the voice's directions. Then I realized what this "workout" was doing: the universe was guiding me to heal my vision. I was enthralled.

I eventually made my way back to the main building, in a place of deep calm. The joy I had felt at the end of the program reappeared and multiplied exponentially. I had no appetite. Food seemed superfluous. All I wanted was to listen to the mantra and bask in the wisdom pouring down from the universe. I floated through the next few hours in a bubble of my own making, lost in the separate reality of an endless looping mantra. Whether this was a spiritual breakthrough or a psychotic breakdown, I wasn't aware of anything being wrong. I was simply in a state of pure being.

I headed to the brother's bathroom to take a shower. I started to undress, but when my eye caught sight of the showerhead, the hairs stood up on the back of my neck. Suddenly, the words "ashram" and "Auschwitz" scrambled together in my mind, and I was flooded with fear. I had the terrifying thought that maybe I was going to be gassed in these showers. Gone was the state of loving, peaceful presence I had felt just minutes before, replaced with paranoia and horror. *Is this place Auschwitz? Am I going to die here?* I refused to take a shower. I turned around and "escaped" from the bathroom in a mild hysteria. Unable to trust anyone, I kept my fears to myself.

THE STREAK, PART II

Later that day, things got worse. Much worse. I returned to the headphones for solace. The mantra continued to envelop me, and no one asked me to take the headphones off, probably because acceptance and non-judgment were held in such high regard. There was no one around to advise me or help me stay grounded; the program directors, my program friends, the guru – they were all gone. So when I heard the voice from deep within again, I followed it unquestioningly. Who else was there to listen to?

I heard that I needed to purify my body. The voice told me to hike up the hill behind the ashram. It guided me to a particular area, indicating that I should stop, sit down, and meditate – all of which I did. I closed my eyes and in time, sank down into a deep, deep state of consciousness. To my surprise, an image of Christ as a yogi came into my awareness. I had never worshipped Christ before; I was raised Jewish! I don't know how or why this image came to me, but it did. Christ asked me to surrender and to do exactly as he said. As I believed this was a direct transmission from God, I listened carefully.

I was directed to return to my primordial being, my natural being, and was told that I had nothing to hide. To remove any barriers between me and the universe, I proceeded to take off all of my clothes; they were just a cover-up, an agreed-upon socialization. I even removed my contact lenses and flung them into the bushes, thinking that I was banishing every last degree of separation. All of this made perfect sense to me. Every last shred of cultural and social discrimination or propriety had fled, leaving behind a happy, naked, unselfconscious being who viewed the world around him with awe and wonder. I was Adam.

I left my backpack in a pile with my cassette player, glasses, notepads, and all of my clothes, and sauntered blithely back to the ashram to be my primordial self. Not that the ashram was ready for me, however. This place – where celibacy was strictly enforced, men and women lived separately and were encouraged not to intermingle or even socialize – was not the place to try out primordial living. But I had no inkling of

117

that. Deep in a dazed state of meditative awareness, unaware of my nakedness, I walked in the bright August late-afternoon sunshine from the top of the hill, across a country road, through someone's yard, past their private home, and onto the ashram property.

Luckily, Mahadev, the administrator of the ashram, saw me just as I stepped onto the property. He quickly whisked me into the brother's barn and threw a blanket over me.

"What on earth are you doing?" he asked, and I just looked at him, dumbfounded.

I was nowhere near being able to comprehend what he was saying or what was happening. He asked me again; again, I had no words. I felt as though something or someone else inside of me was running the show, and I was just the message-less messenger. In short, I was in a state of complete intoxication with the divine. The administrator eventually realized what was happening to me, but he had no idea how to deal with this type of crisis, this state of consciousness. Those who might have known – the program directors or the guru – had left the day earlier. I was considered a liability to the ashram, so he began planning my removal from the premises, starting with a call to my parents to pick me up.

Thus it was that only two days after I had spoken to my mother and told her that I was the happiest I had ever been, she received a call from the ashram telling her I had gone off the deep end. I believe they deemed it a "spiritual emergency." Whatever it was, I was in need of help. I found out later that my crisis forced my parents, who were not speaking to each other at the time, to communicate. My mom called her brother-in-law, Bob, who lived in Philadelphia, and he and Aunt Dede and my cousin Laurie drove to Kripalu within 90 minutes.

Uncle Bob had a calming, steady presence, and my aunt radiated sincerity. I felt safe enough with my extended family to agree to leave with them. They packed up the few belongings I had in my room and put my bags in their car. Laurie was planning to drive my old Chevette,

as I was clearly in no shape to drive. They looked to me for the keys…
but they were nowhere. Even after they searched my backpack (one of
the brothers had found it and my clothes up on the hill) we still came up
empty. The ashram called a locksmith. While we waited for him to open
my car and get it started, I sat on a fallen log and felt the setting sun
warm my face. I watched all of the activity with a contented, detached
curiosity, and then, just before the sun sank behind the Pennsylvania
hills, I got in the backseat of Bob and Dede's car and waved goodbye to
Kripalu.

By this time, I was almost delirious. I was conscious, but I was in my
own world, a world where oneness was everywhere, a world where there
was no difference between my thoughts and reality. In fact, it seemed as
though whatever I thought about would come to pass instantly.

From the backseat, I heard Uncle Bob switch on the radio, and within
moments, I was certain that the music I heard was the Todd Norian Trio.
There were the bass lines of our bass player, the beats of our drummer,
and piano notes… by me! I was fascinated. *How could my band be on
the radio in the middle of nowhere, PA?* But there it was. I heard it. As
freaky as this was, I accepted this as the reality of my evolving
consciousness, and I sat back and enjoyed the music.

I also accepted the synchronicity of my urges and the actions of the car.
I had to go to the bathroom and without thinking, I just opened the car
door. At that exact moment, timed to the second, we stopped at a stop
sign. It happened again and again, exactly the same way. Whenever I
felt the urge to get out of the car, the car would mysteriously stop. Each
time, my uncle got out and closed my door.

At one point the car rolled to a four-way stop on a country road and I
got out. Uncle Bob called me to come back to the car, but I was
determined. More than determined, I was being called from a higher
source: I had to pee. Across the road I saw a farmer, covered in grease
and dirt, working on his tractor in his yard, so I crossed the road without
a second thought. The farm was a disaster: an unkempt yard, a

dilapidated house, a few rusted-out cars in the front yard. But nothing stopped me.

"Could I use your bathroom, please?"

The farmer stopped what he was doing and stared at me, wiping his hands on a grease rag. I'm sure I was the first person ever to make that request of him. He pointed one blackened finger toward the shed. "Go down them steps. Bathroom's at the bottom in the cellar. Help yourself."

I heard myself thank him, and carefully walked down the few filthy steps to the basement. There was just one rickety door in front of me. I opened it and was greeted by a radiant light from inside. It was a perfectly new bathroom, immaculately clean, with state-of-the-art, gleaming white fixtures. I smiled to myself with secret certitude: this was just another sign that the universe was with me, a confirmation that everything that was happening was part of the process. *Just enjoy the ride.* I finished up, strolled back to the car, and we continued.

SPONTANEOUS *KRIYĀS*: UNLEASHED POWER OF GRACE

We arrived at the Philadelphia State Psychiatric Hospital. I sat with my aunt and uncle in the overflowing waiting room. I don't remember much about it, but I do know I must have become unruly because some hospital workers tried to subdue me with a shot of heavy medication. It didn't seem to have much effect. I still had fits of rage, fear, and grief, and I lashed out at the hospital workers for what seemed to be no reason. What they didn't comprehend was that, even now, I was in an empathic state and was therefore still taking on the thoughts and feelings of others – and the room was filled with seriously desperate individuals.

Uncle Bob and Aunt Dede made sure that one of them was constantly by my side, and they did what they could to keep me calm while we waited for a room to become available. Late in the day, my parents finally arrived from California. I barely recognized them, and I'm sure they couldn't believe that the psychotic-seeming catastrophe in front of them was their son.

There was still no space in the hospital for me, so I spent the night in a hotel room with my dad. All I remember is sitting on the bed and exhaling. And exhaling. And exhaling. My breath just left my body and kept going, so much so that I couldn't breathe in. At the end of the exhalation, I was without breath. I panicked. I became hysterical. Dad had no idea what was happening to me. I eventually took a slow breath in, but it never felt like enough, and it was quickly followed by another intensely slow exhalation that kept going and going and going. Again, fear and panic ensued: I felt my *and* my dad's fear. This uncontrollable cycle kept repeating, always leaving my lungs empty and my mind spinning with panic.

I later recognized this as a *prāṇāyāma kriyā* (spontaneous action of yogic purification) with *bāhya kumbhaka* (holding the breath out at the end of the exhalation), an exercise that can be therapeutic when done in moderation and with care. But in that hotel room, it was just a frightening, recurring episode that was happening unconsciously and spontaneously. There was no control, only terror. Finally, during yet another spell of airless hysteria, Dad slapped me. Hard. My childhood nightmare came flooding back, except this time, my eyes were wide open. I saw his open hand pull back, then felt the sharp sting on my cheek again. And again. And again.

I don't have much memory after that. There are only two disconnected scenes, events strung together only by the thinnest thread of recollection:

> I'm on an examination table in the hospital. *Why do these doctors keep pricking me?* Aunt Dede is standing by my side, lovingly trying to reassure and comfort me. *She is beautiful. I love her. I want to kiss her.* I follow my impulse instantly, with no thought of moral or social propriety. She politely resists, extricating herself from my embrace, and the doctors restrain me. *Why must they control me?* I have no control over what I'm doing.

121

I'm locked in a padded cell. *I am fire!* My whole body ignites into frenzied dance. I leap, thrash, roar, gyrate... *I am the wind!* I shriek, moan, howl, laugh. I utter mantras that I have never studied, in a language I don't recognize. *I am the sea!* I float, spin, dive, sink. I pour myself forth into a spontaneous flow of *prāṇāyāma*s, *kriyā*s, and movements. *I am free!* I lose control of my bladder. I am a mess.

Throughout this torrent of disembodied chaos, a ray of consciousness flickered deep in the background. This consciousness allowed everything to happen as it did. As paradoxical as it may seem, some essential part of me was riding out the storm while the rest of me was completely out of control on all levels. Though I couldn't have imagined it, the day in solitary confinement allowed me to act all of this out. My body gradually exhausted itself.

I don't know if I fully settled down on my own, or if they medicated me, but I eventually stabilized. Over the next few days, my "normal" way of being returned. As though awakened from a coma, I soon recognized the world around me, and was able to see myself as a separate entity. I knew my parents. I could understand ideas, communicate effectively, and act appropriately. My mom cried tears of joy and relief; her son was back.

She and my father were less than thrilled, however, that my first request was to listen to the mantra tape again. They might have given in to my entreaties, but the doctors were adamant. No mantra. Instead, they let me listen to all of the lectures by the guru and read the books I had bought at the ashram store on the last day of my program. After about a week, I felt stronger and more centered. By day 10, I was deemed well enough to leave the hospital. It wasn't until much later that I saw the synchronicity: 10 days in the Quest for the Limitless You program; 10 days in the hospital.

I spent the next week or so recuperating at my aunt and uncle's beautiful home in the suburbs of Philadelphia. I took slow walks on the tree-lined streets, increasing the duration daily. I also ate voraciously. After being on a strict vegetarian diet at the ashram and then not eating for several days, I had lost about 15 pounds. Aunt Dede fed me chicken soup, roasted chicken, chicken in every way imaginable. Though I had happily adopted vegetarianism at the ashram, eating animal protein again helped ground me and bring me back into balance.

PORTAL OF THE HEART

Meditation takes you to the dynamic still point within your heart, the *madhya* (place in the middle). The heart is a kind of threshold, a portal to the "other side." It's the interstitial space between the Absolute and the Relative, between the universal and the individual, between sky and earth. It's the place where the wave touches the ocean.

The heart represents the middle of the middle since it holds the center position of the cakras, with the three spiritual cakras above and the three worldly cakras below. The heart has the daunting task of integrating the unseen with the seen, spirit with matter, human nature with divine nature. The truth is, we are both the Absolute and the Relative at the same time; we are, paradoxically, both *Śiva* and *Śakti* in such a way that they are one and separate at the same time.

When you meditate, your purpose is to find that paradox within the *madhya* and dwell there. You intentionally journey into the unknown and linger there, in a place that requires you to let go of all expectations, even your past identity. You have to access the most subtle aspect of your being, essentially becoming what may feel like "nobody" in order to cross to the other side. Once you relinquish your to-do list, the need to accomplish anything, the need to understand, and even the need to touch the *madhya* space, then you effortlessly go into the place in the middle.

That place is like the space between your breaths: the pause at the top of your inhalation or the bottom of your exhalation, where breathing ceases. A third thing happens in that gap between breaths – the threshold of a greater reality. A window opens to the mystery, the unbounded, the limitless place of the Absolute. In this place, as Dr. Joe Dispenza says, "we are no longer linear beings having a linear experience. We are dimensional beings having a dimensional experience."

In Tantra, the goal is not to access subtler and subtler levels of consciousness in order to depart from this world – the way I did during my "spiritual emergency." Rather, you enter into the subtle experience in order to bring that heightened sense of awareness down to earth and live day-to-day from that state of vast perspective.

NYĀYA: DYEING THE CLOTH

A *nyāya* is a teaching, concept, or principle often told through story, myth, or metaphor. The "dyeing the cloth" *nyāya* is an excellent example of the Tantric view of the purpose of meditation. In India, the traditional way to dye cloth is to soak a clean white cloth in a bucket of dye. Once the cloth is thoroughly saturated with color, it is put in the sun to dry. Under the hot sun, the dye fades, and the cloth becomes lighter. The next day, the cloth is dipped in the bucket of dye and again, the cloth becomes saturated and dark with color. Once more, the cloth dries out in the hot sun and fades, but not as much this time. This process repeats over and over until the cloth becomes colorfast and no longer fades as it dries in the sun. The color is now permanent.

In the same way, through continual practice, we meditate and go deep into the silence, dyeing our cloth of consciousness as we become absorbed in the Absolute. As we come out of meditation and go about our day-to-day responsibilities and activities, the feeling and memory of absorption diminishes naturally. Our "dye" begins to fade. The next day we practice and go deep again, only to come out of it and enter back into the world, managing tasks and engaging in relationships, our depth of connection to source fading again. After many weeks, months, and years of dyeing the cloth through practice, we become what I call "spirit-fast." You remain in touch with the Absolute even as you carry out your responsibilities in the world.

The alternating rhythm of going deep within and coming back out assists the overall process of growing your consciousness because it provides the necessary contrast. It also strengthens the "muscle of consciousness" which needs to be worked and toned, like any physical muscle. When I first started to meditate, it would take me about 15 minutes to drop into a deeper state of stillness. But once I had a more established meditation practice, I could access that inner depth in just two or three breaths.

SAMARASYA: OPEN-EYED *SAMĀDHI*

Samarasya is the Sanskrit term that describes this kind of consciousness where you live in the world yet retain the perspective of the Absolute. Within this state of consciousness, you maintain your "spirit-fastness" even as you go through the normal ups and downs of life. *Samarasya* is another word for open-eyed *samādhi* – the experience of absorptive consciousness with your eyes open as you carry on in everyday life. *Samādhi* is the eighth and highest limb of Patañjali's *Aṣṭāṅga* Yoga (*aṣṭa* is eight, *aṅga* is limb) and is traditionally experienced with your eyes closed while in a deep state of meditation. *Samādhi* comes from two words: *sama* (equal, even) and *dhi* (mind or intellect); therefore, it means even-minded or equal-minded. In this closed-eye meditative state, your mind is balanced and you are undisturbed by the outside or inside world of distractions. You are centered and grounded within yourself, content, complete, and wholly at peace.

Samarasya is similar to *samādhi,* except with your eyes open. It's the capacity to act in the world of duality from the perspective of the nondual or Absolute. In other words, in the state of *samarasya* you're fully aware of your intentions, thoughts, feelings, and emotions while you do what you do. The waves of life can be raging and even as you rise and fall with the waves, you never lose touch with the stillness of the ocean deep down. It's a place of deep inner contentment regardless of what's going on.

You may find the following analogy helpful to distinguish *samādhi* from *samarasya.* Classical Yoga maintains that the eight limbs are like sequential rungs of a ladder, steps to take along a hierarchical path that leads to full enlightenment. Tantra views those same eight limbs as the legs of a spider, where each leg plays an important role to move our consciousness into deeper and deeper states of *samādhi*. The eight limbs all work independently and together to establish Absolute consciousness while being balanced in the world.

After my experience of losing myself completely, I became a little wary of disappearing into consciousness without reserve. Yet at that stage of my spiritual development, I was unaware of any other way to meditate. I still believed that the goal of meditation was to merge with the Absolute: to climb as high as possible to the summit of consciousness, stay there, and never come back. It wasn't until much later that I found *samarasya*, the Tantric concept of going in and out of deep states of *samādhi*: climbing to the summit, then coming back down to the village. Then going up again, perhaps climbing a new summit – maybe higher, maybe lower – and returning to the village.

Tantra taught me that it's all about rhythm and balance.

Once you stabilize the recognition of the Absolute in your consciousness, you can merge with the divine *and* maintain your individuality. You *know* you are merging and therefore sometimes allow yourself to let go and be temporarily absorbed by the Absolute consciousness without any self-awareness. Sometimes you hold yourself back to pause at the edge of merging, just shy of the place of no return, in the space in the middle, the threshold, where the primordial creative energy of *śakti* flows.

EXERCISE: Become the Flame

1. Sit in a comfortable position for meditation. Light a candle and place it in front of you. Be sure the candle is safe and protected. Close your eyes and take deep breaths. Inhale fully. Exhale fully.
2. Focus on your breath and become aware of the flow of the breath at the nostrils. Sense or feel the light touch of the breath at the tip of the nostrils and bring all of your awareness there.

3. Slowly open your eyes halfway and gaze at the flame. Take in the light, the movement, the shape of the flame. Watch with curiosity and awe.

4. Close your eyes and envision the flame inside your heart. See or sense the flame glowing inside your heart. Watch it dance and flicker within.

5. Open your eyes again and gaze at the flame in front of you. Soften your gaze and breathe. As you relax more deeply, allow yourself to enter into the flame as though you could merge with it.

6. Now close your eyes and again, allow yourself to merge with the flame, this time internally.

7. Continue alternating your gaze between the flame in front of you and the flame within you for a minute or two.

8. After several repetitions, close your eyes and settle deep inside yourself. Sit in deep meditation as long as you wish.

9. After your seated meditation, lie down on your back and rest for a few minutes.

10. When you're ready, slowly return. Draw your knees into your chest and roll to the right side.

11. Slowly make your way back up to sitting and find your pen. Write in your journal on the following questions:
    - What was that experience like for you?
    - How was the experience different when gazing on the external flame versus gazing on the internal flame? Was one easier or more difficult?
    - What insights arose for you?
    - What would the possibility be for your life if you could maintain your connection to the Absolute (universal energy) in your day-to-day life?

NOTES

---

[1] Dispenza, Joe. *Breaking the Habit of Being Yourself: How to Lose Your Mind and Create a New One.* Carlsbad, CA: Hay House. 2012. Print.

CHAPTER SEVEN

Miami

You are not an encapsulated bag of skin dragging around a dreary little ego. You are an evolutionary wonder, a trillion cells singing together in a vast chorale, an organism- environment, a symbiosis of cell and soul.

Jean Houston[1]

HELLO, GOD?

When my family and I decided I was fully recovered, I gratefully embraced Aunt Dede and Uncle Bob, and got back in the brown Chevette. The leaves were just starting to turn as I drove south, heading for Miami and my old apartment. I made the drive in two days, only to find that my dad had moved all of my belongings into storage, since no one, including my landlord, had known when I would return. Miraculously, I got my apartment back and retrieved my belongings. Slowly, I settled back into the Miami community.

No longer interested in pursuing a master's degree, I cobbled together a new life. I went back to yoga classes with Bobbi and Sam, taught my own yoga classes at a church in Coconut Grove, and played piano with a band through Music Associates, a company that booked us gigs at large parties, weddings, and bar mitzvahs up and down Miami Beach and Ft. Lauderdale. I was surprised to discover that I couldn't play jazz in the way I had before my awakening experience at Kripalu. I just didn't have the same drive or intensity. My heart was set on spiritual exploration. I was constantly reading, seeking, studying, and attending lectures and workshops. When my jazz buddies started raving about their spiritual teacher, I was eager to check her out at a *satsaṅga* in Coconut Grove.

I walked into the dimly lit room to find a handful of people all meditating, sitting cross-legged in silence. Incense wafted through the air and soft ethereal music played in the background. I noticed a radiant and beautiful woman meditating at the front, facing out to the group. *This must be the teacher*, I thought to myself: Malila Saint Duval. I knew very little about her except that she was an actress from Hollywood, CA and a relative of Antoine de Saint-Exupery, author of *The Little Prince*. In fact, though I didn't know it at the time, her real name was Ysatis De Saint-Simone; Malila was her stage name. [2]

Out of the silence, Malila began speaking in a voice that was soft and soothing, yet emphatic. With a slight Spanish accent, she spoke of the deepest spiritual truths and about having the experience of spirit, not just reading about it. At first, I was uncomfortable as she spoke about things

129

I had never heard of before, like the Aquarian Gospel and the Essene Gospels of Jesus. And then she used the name Jesus and "Yogi" in the same sentence, referring to Jesus as the ultimate yogi. *Whoa.* I leaned in. My Jewish upbringing had made me perpetually curious about this Jesus dude. She followed it up with the concept that during the "lost years of Christ" it was rumored that Jesus the yogi traveled throughout India studying with various adept yogis. I sat up even straighter. *This is fascinating.*

After my recent spiritual awakening, my mind and heart were now so open that many of my previous walls of belief were now permeable. I could hear the truth of any teachings, beyond cultural or formal religious delineations of Jewish, Christian, or Hindu. As Malila brought forth these teachings generally accepted as Christian, my heart began to glow with the light of recognition: "Live from your heart"; "Love thy neighbor as thyself"; "Knowing yourself is knowing God"; "Seek the kingdom of heaven within."

I enjoyed *satsaṅga* so much, I asked to come back the next time. Over the next several months Malila became a spiritual teacher for me. I put a picture of the sacred heart of Jesus on my altar and began practicing meditation regularly, praying to see Christ. Malila's teaching that depth of faith and belief would result in Jesus revealing himself to me in the flesh, inspired me to meditate for increasingly longer periods. Sometimes I sat for a few hours, praying, meditating, and waiting for Christ to appear.

Because I was so caught up in thinking I could see God outside of myself or thinking that God was a separate, particular personality, I ignored the living God already inside myself and in all those around me.

This is one of the distinctions in Tantra: the living God takes the form of all beings. You don't need to see a particular form of God as the image you think God is, although that's fine, too. There is only one spirit or one God – universal energy – and that one God expresses itself in the many. In this way, Christ's admonition to love your neighbor is the way to love God.

God is not "out there," existing somewhere else or dwelling in certain people but not others. God is everywhere. God is here. Right here, right now, in you, as you. God is also made manifest in *all things*. To love yourself and your surroundings is yet another way to love God. It's a much larger perspective that sees the one God energy in everyone and everything. As quantum physics teaches us, everything pulsates with one energy. This is the nondual concept of Tantra. Swami Muktananda, a great *Nondual Śaiva-Śākta Tantra* guru, said, "*Love yourself, honor yourself, meditate on yourself, for God lives in you as you.*"

Within nonduality's oneness is the embrace of all duality. How? Because the nondual can only be realized through duality: through reflection and relationship. To understand that fully, it's helpful to first explore what "God" means, according to *Nondual Śaiva-Śākta Tantra* philosophy.

THE ABSOLUTE

I've already mentioned the Absolute, and *Nondual Śaiva-Śākta Tantra*'s definition of it: the unmanifest reality from which all possibility and manifestation springs forth. It can also be called God, but it's not the conventional idea of God many of us know, with an accompanying story, personality, and particular path of teachings.

Instead, this God represents the vast intelligence of the universe without distinction, beyond all paths and all religions, a luminous yet empty space without boundaries, that exists as pure transcendental being. It is the spiritual essence that infuses the foundation of all traditions and all paths.

This supreme consciousness simultaneously comprises the Absolute world of pure spirit and the relative world of the physical. It encompasses the full spectrum of everything, all at once – the worlds of the unmanifest and the manifest, the unlimited and the limited, the immeasurable and the measurable. The Absolute is the transcendent, supreme, and highest state of consciousness. It is the quality of "beingness" itself and is the source of everything that is. Likewise, it is intelligence itself and is omnipresent, omnipotent, and exists beyond all limitations.

Another name for the Absolute, from the Buddhist teachings, is *śunya*, or "emptiness, the great void." It is a wonderful paradox, for though it's empty, it's also full of the unbounded nature of existence itself. The void is without dimensionality, without locality, and is beyond time and all sequence of time. It is infinite and eternal. At the same time, it is full of light, potentiality, auspiciousness, bliss, and ultimate freedom. It holds within it the full spectrum of vibration, both positive and negative, light and dark. It encompasses the totality of everything.

ATTRIBUTES OF THE ABSOLUTE

The qualities of the Absolute are infinite. Any attempt to quantify or name the Absolute is, in a sense, limiting the Absolute. But for us to understand, study, and talk about the Absolute, we need words and language to describe it. There are eight primary attributes of the Absolute that give a basic sense of the vastness of its qualities, some of which we've already discussed:

- *Sat*: truth, "is"-ness, existence itself
- *Cit*: consciousness, intelligence
- *Ānanda*: bliss, joy, expansion
- *Pūrṇatva*: fullness that is so full it includes lack; perfection so vast it includes imperfection
- *Śrī*: auspiciousness, goodness, divine beauty
- *Prakāśa/Vimarṣa*: *prakāśa* is the capacity to radiate light outward. *Vimarṣa* is the capacity to reflect the light inwardly, as in consciousness that can reflect on itself and see itself
- *Spanda*: pulsation, vibration, the throb of life
- *Svātantrya*: supreme freedom, one's own freedom

These eight attributes point us toward a limited understanding of the Absolute, because it's virtually impossible to see or experience the Absolute directly. This brings us back to the earlier statement: "the nondual can only be realized through duality: through reflection and relationship." What does that really mean?

YOU ARE THE REFLECTION OF THE ABSOLUTE

You may not have realized this, but your eyes have never seen your own face. Unless you have shrimp eyes or an extremely large nose like mine, the only way you've seen your own face is through reflection, be it literal (a mirror or a photograph), or metaphorical (through the eyes of others). Those images are not you, however. They are only reflections of you. If you try to look at the sun, you will burn your eyes. We cannot perceive the "one" directly. We must gaze at the moon, which reflects the sun's light. In the same way, you can only truly see yourself and know yourself through reflection, through relationship.

I often tell my students, half in jest: if you really want to see yourself, get married. After I was married, I saw more than I ever cared to about myself! (More on that later.) In the same way, the Absolute needs the reflection of you to see itself, and thus chooses to limit itself *in you as you* in order to experience its limitless nature.

LENT

At that point in my spiritual evolution, however, I was still stuck in a dualistic paradigm: looking for God outside myself, praying for a visitation from Jesus. After several months of practice, Malila invited us to join her in fasting for Lent (the 40 days before Easter) in honor of Christ. I decided to do it. The first week I ate only fruit; the second, only juices. By the end of the second week I floated into yoga class, emaciated and spacy. Sam and Bobbi took one look at me and said, "Are you okay?"

"Yeah," I said, "I'm just a little light-headed. It's probably the fasting."

"Fasting? For how long?" asked Sam. Bobbi looked worried.

"Forty days. Well, 26 more," I said, then added proudly, "I've already done two weeks."

At that, they both erupted, talking over each other. "What?" "40 days?" "No!"

I nodded, surprised at their outburst. I hadn't looked in the mirror. I was so focused on fasting in order to see Jesus in the flesh that I blocked everything else out, including my own swiftly diminishing flesh.

"You have to get grounded. You must begin eating more food," said Bobbi sternly. She was rarely this adamant. "Okay?" she asked, and I nodded. "Promise?"

"Yes," I reassured her. "I promise."

In retrospect, I seriously tested the limits of being an extreme fundamentalist – holding a belief so strongly that I ignored everyone around me, including myself. I did slowly begin to eat more food and I ultimately gave up the fast.

I continued studying with Malila, eventually discovering that her teachings were sourced from a spiritual movement called the Great White Brotherhood (a mystical/spiritual practice from the 19th century that is not related to any contemporary racist organizations or philosophies). She was preparing us for initiation, which would supposedly enable us to finally see Jesus. I still don't know if she was officially "ordained" or not, but my desire for a visitation by Jesus blinded me to such details.

On the appointed day at 6:00am, my friends and I headed for the beach at the end of Key Biscayne, stopping along the way for bagels – a detour that amuses me to this day – to sit in meditation facing the ocean. Finishing the last few bites, we sat down on the cool sand and closed our eyes. A few minutes later, we caught the intermittent wafts of incense on the ocean breeze; Malila had arrived and was meditating with us. She recited a few prayers, read some passages from the Essene Books, and gently rested her hand on the top of our heads to bestow a blessing. We followed her meditation instructions, practicing on the beach for an hour, and then opened our eyes. At that, she pronounced us initiated into the White Brotherhood.

EASTER CARDS

Malila was not only a spiritual teacher, she was a painter as well. She made beautiful greeting cards with Christian themes, and during the year of my fast, she created Easter cards depicting Christ's resurrection. Their messages – rising up, living the life of your dreams, bringing the light of your heart to the world in service to others – spoke to me, so I decided to buy several of them to send to my family. *My very Jewish family.* Apparently, the alarm system inside my brain had been disconnected, because this idea should have produced an immediate flashing red light of caution across the screen of my mind. But no. My one-pointed, narrow, fundamentalist frame of mind made it all too easy to see the logic in my motivation: everyone should get over their cultural disagreements and accept Christ as a universal yogi and role model.

Sending an explicit Christian card with a picture of Jesus rolling back the stone to my Jewish relatives is probably one of the most insensitive insults on the planet. What was I thinking? Looking back, I know I just wanted my family to experience the same joy and bliss that I was experiencing in my newfound open spirituality.

Even though the whole point of the White Brotherhood was to spread the message of Jesus, to me, it was all god. I was like a Jewish born-again Christian, convinced that I could convert my family to worship Christ. Instead, I discovered the quickest way to create disillusionment, confusion, and separation. Those well-intentioned cards did considerable damage to my relationship with my family and sealed the deal: in their mind, I was crazy and lost. How could I blame them?

MACROBIOTICS: THE GREAT LIFE

Since my body was so detoxified from the fast, someone recommended that I do colonic therapy to really take the trash out. So I did. I couldn't believe what came out of me: the buildup from 22 years of eating the "Standard American Diet" – mostly junk food, meat, white sugar, and white bread. Afterwards, I felt amazingly healthy and vital, and was drawn to take a job at the Oak Feed Health Food store in Coconut Grove, FL. Working there was perfect for me. The owner of the store was deeply into macrobiotics (a Japanese-based philosophy of eating and way of life), and I enjoyed being around people who were as interested as I was in all areas of health. I met a vast array of spiritual seekers who strolled into the store, asking me questions about diet and various foods. To better answer their questions, I took every opportunity to read up on healthy eating.

I met Louis Solana and his wife Flora, who often came into the store to buy "macro" supplies. Louis's smile and friendly demeanor lit up the entire space, and Flora's radiant glow was mesmerizing. *They must be doing something right. I want that, too.* I attended Louis's macro lectures and Flora's macro cooking classes, throwing myself headlong into the whole package. I must have bought and studied every macrobiotic book on the market during that time. For 15 months, I took on a strict macro diet and followed the philosophical teachings as best I could. I even attended a macro summer camp in Chico, CA, called the French Meadows Macrobiotic Camp. It was so extreme.

There, I had a private consultation with the senior teacher. After a careful reading of my entire body and face, he looked at me and said, "Todd, your nose is so big because you've eaten so much chicken in your lifetime." I stared at him, waiting. Was he serious? Yes, he was deadly serious, and he was the top dog. So I believed him and walked out of his office with a spring in my step. *Finally, the answer! I can blame it on something! Chicken!*

I returned from French Meadow camp, as gung-ho macro as ever. A few days later, my mom arrived in Miami for a visit, and I could hardly wait to show her around Miami and share all my newfound knowledge. Almost as soon as her luggage was stowed in the back of my car, I blurted, "Mom! I finally know why my nose is so big!" And I proceeded to tell her why.

I don't remember exactly how she responded, but I do remember her uncomfortable laugh and the concern I detected underneath it. Given that I had been recently institutionalized, I suspect she wasn't judging me too harshly. Still, I look back on that moment with embarrassment. Like a kid with all kinds of new toys, I wanted to share my pride and my enthusiasm with her about *everything*.

MORE THAN THE FIVE SENSES

Science has already proved that there is more to our world than what meets the eye – the microscope, telescope, and X-ray are instruments of that proof. Quantum physicists will tell you that, at the level of your subatomic particles, you are flashing in and out of existence even as you read this. Your senses (smelling, tasting, seeing, feeling, and hearing) are only the puny measuring tools of consciousness, the constrained external expression of the power of your infinite mind to discern your reality.

Animals prove this to us every day. Dogs have a heightened sense of smell; robins can hear and sense the movement of worms under the ground; deer have a heightened sense of radar, like a sixth sense, that can detect your electromagnetic field long before they see you or you see them. Clearly, there is more to life than what your five physical senses experience.

If seeing is not necessarily believing, then what about the opposite? Is believing seeing? Tantra supports the notion that what you believe on the inside influences what you see on the outside. In other words, belief can create your reality. As author Mike Dooley[3] says, "Thoughts are things. Choose the good ones. "Beliefs are powerful and "believing is seeing" is a more empowered philosophy, because it requires that you take responsibility for what you see around you. It also encourages you to hone your beliefs, to bring forth the dreams in your heart, even though those dreams may be far from happening in reality. But it has its limits, as well – as the above "chicken nose" story illustrates.

"Believing is seeing" can be taken to an extreme, beyond what's healthy and safe. Having faith that you can fly and then testing your faith by jumping off the roof, is stupidity. That's blind faith. For me, there's validity in both "seeing is believing" and "believing is seeing." By using both my faith and my senses, I stay grounded in reality while not giving up my dream of bringing heaven on earth. Remember *śraddhā*? Where you place your heart? That's it. As I keep discovering, freedom is the place in the middle, the place of the heart.

My mom might not have been able to articulate that particular truth, but she probably knew that I was living at the edges of extremism. During her visit I cooked her a macrobiotic meal: wakame salad, miso soup with tofu, brown rice with gomasio seasoning, and umeboshi plums. She ate it politely, and graciously acted excited for me, but I could see she was struggling with it. I recognize now that because Mom loved me so much, she always made a heroic attempt to try the things I was into, at least once.

AWARENESS LIST

Living in Miami was an expansive, educational time for me, but I knew I didn't want to remain there. Nestled in the back of my mind during this whole period, was the clear intention to return to Kripalu. The "Miami" period was a time to regroup, rebuild my connection to my inner strength, and make the move back to the ashram consciously and carefully. By March I felt completely ready. It never dawned on me that the ashram, however, was not ready for me.

Excitedly, I called to let the staff at Kripalu know I was returning. The voice on the other end of the line put me on hold, then another voice came on. Kindly but firmly, it stated that I was on the Kripalu "awareness" list. I asked what that meant, half-hoping it was a good thing; after all, weren't we all seeking awareness? The answer I got was unequivocal: legally, I wasn't allowed to visit the ashram because I was a "psychological liability." Dejected, I hung up.

I understood how allowing me to return as a resident could be an unacceptable risk for the community. But surely that didn't apply to satellite programs! I perked up. I knew that the guru was offering a workshop in Leesburg, FL, so two weeks later I drove over four hours to get there and showed up unannounced. Krishnapriya, the head administrator and personal assistant to the guru, recognized me and pulled me into an office.

"What are you doing here?" she demanded.

"I didn't know that satellite courses were barred," I said. I must have seemed completely calm and rational compared to the stories she had heard about my "spiritual emergency." She hesitated for a moment, watching me closely, and then spoke.

"Well... I suppose... if I can get verbal permission from a guardian – your mother or father, say – then it would be all right."

I was so pleased. I thanked her and dialed my dad. There was a three-hour time difference; he might not be home. The phone rang three times, four times...*Please let him be home. Please let him pick up.*

"Hello?"

"Dad!" I fairly shouted. "Dad, it's me. I'm at a yoga program in Leesburg and the person who runs it needs to get your permission so I can participate. Can I put her on?"

"Well, I guess. But why do they need my permission?"

"They think I'm still a liability."

"Oh," he said, and then fell silent. I knew we were both remembering Philadelphia.

"So…" I said, trailing into hope.

I could hear him take a deep breath before he said, "Put her on." I handed the phone over to her and listened closely to her side of the conversation. I couldn't tell which way this was going to go. I closed my eyes. *Please let him say yes. Please let him say yes.*

"Okay, thank you, Mr. Norian. You, too." She hung up and turned toward me. "You can stay."
My heart swelled. He was my hero. After all the heartache I had caused, he still found trust in me.

I was happy to stay at the workshop, but before it started, I felt I needed to speak with the guru first. I asked if I could meet with the guru one-on-one, a request he rarely honored. But he granted my wish. The two of us sat together in a room all alone, and although I felt nervous to speak with him, I was far more grounded this time. I told him what had happened to me – the spiritual crisis, my hospitalization, the upset I caused my parents – and he listened carefully. Then he said, simply, "Always love your parents. Just give them love. It will all work out."

I thanked him and bowed my head. Very lovingly, he touched me on my shoulders and when I raised my head, he looked into my eyes and smiled that big gapped-tooth smile. The Jewish grandfather in him moved me yet again. I grinned and he left the room. I have followed his simple, wise words to this day.

In May, I made another attempt to stay at Kripalu as a guest. This time, they agreed to a trial period. If I successfully managed my energy for a weekend, they would allow me to come for a week. No issues arose during my weekend on probation. I returned in July for a weeklong visit, which was also non-eventful, and in September, the ashram consented to let me participate in the *seva*-exchange program for a month. By that time, I was restless. I was ready to move back in. Without telling them, I let go of my apartment and either sold or gave away all of my belongings – except for what would fit into my trusty Chevette. It was easy enough to let it all go. The only pangs I felt were in dispersing my music equipment: amplifiers, speakers, two electric pianos, and my treasured collection of over 500 vinyl jazz records. Yet giving them to my cousin Gary, an accomplished jazz pianist who went to the University of Miami right after I graduated, made it feel right.

I rolled the dice and headed for Pennsylvania once again.

NOTES

[1] Jean Houston, FaceBook Post. 8 March 2014.
https://www.facebook.com/jean.houston.page/posts/please-know-this-you-are-not-an-encapsulated-bag-of-skin-dragging-around-a-drear/613495762059895/

[2] For more information see: https://ysatisdesaintsimone.com.

[3] Quote is attributed to Mike Dooley but original source is unknown. See more about Mike Dooley at www.tut.com.

CHAPTER EIGHT

All In

To experience oneness directly, to know it for
certain, we need the grace of the one from
whose energy it is made. Any experience of
awakening arrives spontaneously on its own –
no matter how much we have worked for it, it
comes when it will.

Sally Kempton[1]

It wasn't until I had been there a few weeks that the memories flooded me. I stood in the shower one evening, letting the warm water pour onto my face, when a queasy feeling descended on me. I recalled being at the peak of my fear, and confusing "ashram" with "Auschwitz." I remembered other disturbed thoughts, too.

As I stood under the stream of warm water, I made a conscious decision to let the water wash away any residual doubts I had about all that had transpired during that period: the psychotic thoughts, intense fear, darkness, and loss of control, as well as the cosmic awareness, amazing bliss, and the open portal I seemed to have accessed with the universe. Watching the water drain away, I let it all go and stepped out of the shower refreshed and renewed in my relationship with Kripalu. I was ready to create a different, deeply grounded life here.

On a break from my kitchen work, I navigated back to the spot on the hill where I had disrobed almost a year prior. Standing in that place I took in the view: the entirety of the ashram; beyond it, farms and wooded hills; above, the immense sky. Much had happened in the past year, yet I still had a close connection to this place. I felt drawn to meditate there again, so I sat cross-legged on the grassy slope, closed my eyes, and tuned in.

As I sank deeper and deeper, I became part of a bigger energy again…and again I heard it call me, urging me to be a servant of the light, to be an instrument, a conduit. Everything in my being wanted to say yes, but there was another voice inside that I would not ignore, one that was strong and clear: *be careful this time*. I wasn't willing to just surrender and let grace do her thing inside of me. I wanted to serve, but in a way that was healthy for me. Without naming it as such, I was desiring a more Tantric relationship with *samādhi*, a balance between universal and individual consciousness.

I offered up a proposal: *I agree to go with you again. But I have to do it on my terms. I have to be in control.* Instantly, the universe replied, "Okay. You can do it your way. I support you. Know that I will always be in your heart if you need me." Just like the response from the guru, it was exactly what I needed to hear. And in retrospect, that the universe agreed to meet me in my heart couldn't have been more appropriate.

When my month of *seva* came to an end, I was permitted to stay at the ashram permanently. I was thrilled. My parents, however, were not. They were confused and angry with me, but they were also hurt and angry with each other, having just finalized their bitter divorce. They communicated with me infrequently, leaving me with the impression that they had renounced me – which made my decision to join the ashram all the easier. Little did I realize this community would be my chosen family for the next 13 years.

A DAY IN THE LIFE

I quickly settled into a daily routine. Right after I moved into the ashram, the guru and residents took up jogging as part of the spiritual practices, so my day started at 3:30am with a two-to-three-mile jog. Either by myself or with others, I ran in utter darkness through the woods on dirt paths that became so familiar I could almost traverse them blindfolded. At 4:30am I met up with another *seva*-exchange student who happened to be trained in Iyengar Yoga, for half an hour of our own *āsana* practice. Having learned that style of yoga in Miami, I was pleased to find someone else who eschewed the softer Kripalu-type yoga in favor of the more focused, alignment-based Iyengar techniques.

At 5:00am, I participated in the Kripalu hour-long guided yoga class for guests, and then Lila Osterman took over. Lila, in her loud, emphatic German accent, led us all in *prāṇāyāma*, *kriyās* (acts of purification), meditation, and mantra chanting. In her 60s, Lila was one of the oldest teachers at Kripalu, but she fired out instructions with the force of a young drill sergeant. At first her incessant yelling felt inappropriate and scary, but over time I came to appreciate her intense dedication to the practices, her love of the spirit, and her devotion to the guru. All of this came through her in a sharp and unique way that made me sit up tall and pay attention. In fact, I believe I have her to thank for the one-pointed focus and calm alertness in *prāṇāyāma* and meditation that I have today.

Breakfast was at 6:30am, then we all dispersed to our various *sevas* at 7:15am. As I had come to the ashram as a 22-year-old music graduate with very little in the way of practical skills, I was assigned more kitchen duty. I didn't mind; after all I had gone through, I was just happy to be allowed to be part of the community. I chopped vegetables until noon, took a short break for lunch, and continued working until dinner at 5:30pm. Evening *satsaṅga* was at 7:15pm, often following a period of meditation. We ended each night with *ārati*, the devotional offering of light, to offer back the gifts of the day with gratitude. At the end of *ārati*, we sat in total silence for several minutes while we meditated with the guru and the entire community. Often, this silence was the most profound. To be bathed with blessings of goodness and love in the presence of a loving teacher and community of great beings was a splendidly integrated way to end the day. By the time 8:30pm rolled along, I fell into bed and was asleep in seconds. My bones sank down so fully into the foam pad, I felt I genuinely became part of the earth. I slept, motionless, until 3:30am the next day.

Every day was the same except for Sundays, when our afternoons were free. I usually did laundry that day, exchanged a massage with another brother, hiked, or slept. Essentially, I lived the life of a monk. The daily schedule left little room for socializing or creative pursuits, but I still found both, through music. Happily, I regularly got together with some musician friends to improvise beautiful, blissful soundscapes and original songs.

This fusion of styles played spontaneously from the heart was the early beginning of my band, *Shakti Fusion*, that became the eight-piece Kripalu "house band" many years later, combining jazz, rock, fusion, Afro-Cuban rhythms, and Sanskrit chanting. Mark Kelso, a pianist who later became a recording artist and engineer, taught me how to play the harmonium, and another musician wrote some astounding hybrid jazz, rock, Sanskrit chanting songs, which we learned and performed at *satsaṅga*. I loved playing with this band because we all had a deep spiritual practice paired with a passion for music. We even made a few recordings in a makeshift sound studio, which was great fun. I found that my relationship to music was no longer competitive; I had returned to my original love of it. I was now able to enjoy it for the delight that it was, separate from making a living or proving myself.

Just as I was feeling like I had found my forever home, it was announced that Kripalu was moving. Having outgrown its Summit Station compound (the ashram population had nearly doubled, from 120 residents in 1982 to approximately 220 at the end of 1983), the ashram bought a Jesuit Seminary building and its surrounding 450-acre property in Stockbridge, Massachusetts – an enormous place that hadn't been inhabited for over ten years. I was transferred from kitchen duty to an ad hoc moving crew. Within a few months of finally finding my home here, I packed up again and moved to our new home in the Berkshires.

I stayed on the moving crew for a few months as we began the laborious task of renovating the entire building. During that time, I bunked in a small dorm room with five other yogis. The rooms were spartan with only a sink, bunk beds, dresser, and a hall bathroom. After several more months, I was assigned a double room. Then after two years, I earned the privilege to have my own room. Even though it measured only nine feet by nine feet, when I looked out at the surrounding mountains and the lake below, I felt like a king in a castle.

SEVA

I was always tight with my money. I loved to hoard it. When Grampa Aaron visited us as kids, he would hold out two fistfuls of quarters from his parking lot business, saying, "Choose a hand." Sherri and I tapped the hand we wanted and then squealed with delight to see the wealth of quarters there. Sherri almost always found things to spend it on, but I always locked mine away in my little pirates' chest bank. Knowing it was full gave me immense joy; I remember feeling smugly rich. At the same time, I had an almost visceral aversion to anything worldly. I didn't read the paper or follow the stock market. In spite of all this, or perhaps because of it, I was assigned a new *seva*: the purchasing department.

I knew nothing about purchasing and processing invoices, I had no idea how to keep books or do accounting, and although I was in Advanced

Placement Calculus in high school, I was a slow thinker. I struggled with math. In short, I'm not the person you'd want in a purchasing department. My supervisor there, Michael Penny (whom we called Balaram), was always patient with me, even when it took me months to understand the fundamentals of finance. Our department was in charge of all of the purchasing at the ashram, which grew to become a multi-million-dollar organization. It took me a long time, but I gradually learned how to purchase and account for things.

Once I had gotten the hang of it, I found that the job was not tremendously interesting. In fact, it was downright boring. The brightest spot of my day was the impromptu performances of one of my purchasing colleagues, Tom Jackman, a.k.a. Bharat. He had been a weightlifter for years, and he maintained his strong, bulky form with running, cross-country skiing, and biking. He was the last person you'd expect to break into song, but that's exactly what he did.

On random days, but always in the midafternoon when we were all fading away from exhaustion, Bharat would jump up on his desk and start belting out some Broadway tune, like "Consider Yourself" from *Oliver!*, "New York, New York," or the title song from *Oklahoma*. He was animated and theatrical – he sang it like he owned it – and he never failed to break us all up. After a few lines, he would sit back down at his desk, deadpan, as if nothing had happened. He was hilarious.

Balaram would just shake his head, a wry smile on his lips, and tell us to get back to work. Not only was Balaram a tolerant guy, but he was a solid, smart family man. He had tremendous people-skills and loads of common sense, and I looked up to him as a mentor and friend. He knew I loved yoga and that I taught some in Florida before moving into Kripalu, so when he learned that the ashram was in need of resident yoga teachers, he encouraged me to teach. I wasn't interested. I was so shy and insecure I couldn't imagine handling the pressure of standing up in front of people I didn't know to teach yoga. I was convinced I'd make a fool of myself.

After months of his encouragement being met with my consistent, flat-out "no," Balaram grew less and less accommodating and more and more assertive. Finally, exasperated, he ordered me to "get out there and teach." I had no choice but to do it.

MY FIRST CLASS

In 1984, the guru decided that all residents should do a morning *sādhanā* (regular spiritual practice) together, including *āsanas*. Yet not everyone at the ashram enjoyed *āsana* practice. Many residents connected with the Kripalu path through *Bhakti Yoga* (devotion) to the guru, or *Raja Yoga* (meditation), or *Karma Yoga (seva* or selfless service). Others were there because they were lost, depressed, and had no other place to go. Then there were other residents who were called "Perms," short for "Permanents," who had been with the guru since the very beginning in 1972. They had infinitely more knowledge and experience than I, and I looked up to them. As I saw it then, my yoga class audience was filled with a mixture of experienced yogis and resistant residents forced to wake up early. Not the ideal set-up for a nervous newbie.

I showed up at 4:45am, dry-mouthed and breathless. In the dim light, I rolled out my mat on a raised platform in front of the large room and took my place. It was too dark to see clearly, but I could still make out the shapes of the residents entering one by one. My heart pounded and I tried to focus on my breathing to calm myself as the room filled slowly over the next 15 minutes with close to 80 people. At 5:01am, I couldn't put it off any longer. I commenced my class with a quavery, "Good morning."

My anxiety grew worse as I began instructing the group. I remember little about my class, except that the residents seemed to just do their own thing, regardless of what I said. Mercifully, the room was so dark I couldn't see anyone clearly. In fact, I didn't pay that much attention to my students, as I was doing and teaching all of the poses simultaneously. It was all I could do to stay with my own breath and in my own body, and to cross the finish line with a final "om." With my eyes closed, I heard a few half-hearted "oms" scattered around the room. *At least it's over.*

I opened my eyes to see a stampede to the door. Even though I had no idea why they were all rushing, my interpretation was that they couldn't wait to flee from such a terrible teacher. Later, I surmised that everyone wanted to hurry to the main hall to get a choice seat in front of the guru for the 6:00am *prāṇāyāma*, meditation and chanting with him. Or perhaps they wanted to go back to bed. In either case, I stayed on the stage, waiting, as the room emptied. I wasn't even sure what I was waiting for.

I gave it a few more moments, then sighed and rolled up my mat. I heard a muffled cough from the back of the room and looked up; someone was waiting for me. It was Indra, a dedicated yogi and recent friend. Indra ran the retail store at Kripalu, so we had a connection through *seva*. We didn't know each other that well, but a few days earlier I had shared with him how nervous I was about teaching this class. I stepped off the stage with my mat and approached him with a hangdog look. He smiled warmly, opened his arms, and bear-hugged me.

"Thank you for this class, Todd. It was wonderful."

I was instantly overjoyed. That was all I needed to hear. Because of my chronic insecurity and low self-esteem, it made all the difference that someone, anyone, liked my class. I hugged him back. This seemingly small interaction at the end of my class gave me the courage to teach again.

FEAR

Fear is our instinctive reaction to the unknown, a knee-jerk response that overrides our intelligence. It's an immediate recoil that switches the body into high-gear survival mode. Everything else takes a back seat, including any dream of a consciously satisfying and fulfilling life. Fear is the strongest emotion with the greatest amount of power, and it generally drives all other negative emotions, including shame and anger.

Furthermore, fear contracts the field of consciousness. It can render an individual's awareness almost entirely inoperative. Fear freezes us, making the body rigid and the brain numb. It instills a false sense of being limited, without the capacity to act, think, or pull ourselves out of a hole.

Running in the woods once, I learned a significant lesson about fear. It was a sunny fall day in the Berkshires and the leaves had already begun to turn a beautiful array of colors. I was enjoying the fresh smell of earth and decaying leaves, and filling my lungs with the cool, sweet autumn air. It was wonderful. All of a sudden, I heard a rustling in the bushes behind me. I slowed up a bit, turned to look, but saw nothing. I kept going. Then I heard it again, louder. Just as I flashed back to a comment I had heard earlier in the week about black bear sightings, I saw something black streak into the periphery of my sight.

My heartbeat exploded; I took off running at top speed. It was a bear, I was certain, and it was chasing me. I hadn't taken more than ten panicked strides when my foot snagged a root under the leaves, launching my whole body into the air. I landed with a thud and felt a sharp pain in my right ankle. My mind raced. "Oh no! I broke my ankle and I can't move," I thought in terror, hearing the animal's approach. "I'm going to be someone's dinner! I'm a goner!" Just then, I felt the wet tongue of a black Labrador licking my face. It was wagging its tail, eager to play.

Fear is rarely as big as it seems. But when it kicks in, there's no ability or time to stop, pause, and consider your options. Instead, an instantaneous reaction occurs, similar to the involuntary jerk of your foot when you tap your knee with a rubber hammer to test your reflexes. The difference with fear, though, is that through deeper understanding and practice, you *can* delay your reaction time. You can learn to hold your fear at bay while you take a moment to consider the larger perspective. Had I been able to slow everything down and assess the situation calmly, from a place of consciousness, I might have seen what was actually rustling the bushes. Had I been mindful, I would have avoided the suffering of a sprained ankle. As it was, I limped all the way

150

home, determined to gain some insights about fear and the role it plays in our lives. Here are some of them:

- Don't ignore fear; it's there for a good reason. It teaches respect, and it's there for your survival.

- Fear, like any other emotion, is just energy.

- All energy is vibration, and all vibrations – since they are manifestations of the Absolute – are actually love in a different form.

- Fear, then, is love not yet brought into consciousness. Therefore, fear is not to be avoided; it's meant to be felt. Fully.

In doing so, it doesn't have to run the show. I like the acronym:

Feel
Energy
And
Release.

If you allow yourself to feel fear fully, rather than fight it, it will take you into your heart where it integrates and dissolves into love and kindness. Fear secures your limits. Love secures your possibilities.

After my first teaching experience at Kripalu, Balaram thanked me and told me to get on the regular schedule, which I did. In time, my confidence grew, and more and more residents expressed their gratitude for my teaching. I hadn't found a way to get rid of fear, but I settled into some sort of uneasy coexistence with it. A yoga teacher was launched.

TAPAS RETURNS

Life at Kripalu was steady, predictable, and virtually worry-free. All of my basic needs were met – plenty of home-grown food, a massive roof over my head, stipends of $35 per month to buy toiletries or other necessities and $250 per year for clothing, use of a bicycle or car when

I needed it, a caring community – so I could focus completely on service, which I did with zeal. Service, we were told, was the highest expression of the practice, and therefore I worked from before dawn to after dusk, as hard as I could, until I was totally exhausted. After evening *satsaṅga*, I dropped dead into bed only to do it all over again the next day. I lived most of my days in bliss, working my proverbial ass off in selfless service.

Just as I threw myself into service, I threw myself into *all* my practices with the same fire, believing that this was the path to true enlightenment. Since my initial spiritual awakening had been full of many unexplainable experiences, I was open to the fantasies and mysteries that surrounded yoga.

One such mystery presented itself in the form of the "Bates Method." [2] A dear friend of mine, Sudhir (Jonathan Foust) and I, became obsessed with healing our vision problems using the method devised by William Bates. Every morning, in the slim time gap after practices and before breakfast, we stood on the front terrace and did our eye exercises as the morning sun rose. After several days of this activity, the head administrator at that time, Krishnapriya, called us into her office. She had noticed our mysterious movements and practices and wanted to make sure we were not practicing another style of yoga. Once we told her what we were up to, she laughed and told us not to practice in public if we could help it.

After a few months of this work I noticed little improvement to my eyesight so I dropped the practice. Part of the practice involved wearing my glasses as little as possible, and I became frustrated with fumbling through my day half-blind. Although I believe the method has merit, the amount of time and effort needed was more than I was willing to put into it. More importantly, because there were so many practices in the spiritual community, I decided to focus on those that brought me the most benefit.

For example, I believed the practices of austerity and abstention from self-destructive habits would free me from my karmic ties, and therefore, I dove into *tapas* with complete devotion. Didn't beating Karen Kleinhuizen prove to me that with discipline, anything is possible – even enlightenment? At that time, I didn't fully grasp the very different philosophies behind the classical understanding of *tapas* (austerity, discipline, and the abandonment of desires) and the Tantric understanding of tapas (longing for God). Later, I understood that winning the piano competition was the perfect experience of Tantric *tapas*. For now, I was solidly in the Classical *tapas* camp.

WE GOTTA GET OUTTA THIS PLACE

Patañjali is credited as the author, or one of a group of authors, who wrote the *Yoga Sūtras*, a collection of 196 aphorisms on the art and science of yoga. This collection was the first written codification of yogic teachings and is widely considered to be one of the foundational texts of yogic philosophy. The Sanskrit word *sūtra,* which can be translated to mean many things, including "rule" or "sew together," also is the origin of the English word "suture." The *sūtras* are a body of interwoven teachings intended to instruct the practitioner on how to unite the individual with the universal. Scholars disagree on the timeline, but one of my teachers believes the *sūtras* were written around 450 CE, close to the beginning of Tantra in approximately 400 CE.

The *Yoga Sūtra*, the primary root text of Classical Yoga, provides an important foundation for the later refinement and reinterpretation by the various schools of Tantra. The *sūtras* are unquestionably filled with great wisdom and genius. For over three decades I have enjoyed studying them, and each time I delve into their teachings, I emerge with fresh understandings and deepened perspectives. Without the *sūtras*, we wouldn't have the Tantra we have today.

Sūtra 2.29 delineates the eight-limbed path of yoga, or *Aṣṭāṅga* yoga. Although some scholars think *Sūtra* 2.29 may have been added to the work later and might not actually be attributable to Patañjali, the eight limbs or paths have become the backbone or infrastructure of the full Classical yogic journey of enlightenment.

Patanjali's Aṣṭāṅga Yoga: The Eight Limbs or Steps to Enlightenment

1. *Yama:* your relationship with others

- The five *yamas* are ethical guidelines of restraint or control that support you in your interactions with the *external* world and the world of relationship.

- They circumscribe behavior towards yourself and others on all levels: actions, words, and thoughts.

- The *yamas* include: nonviolence, truthfulness, moderation and celibacy, non-stealing, and non-possessiveness.

2. *Niyama:* your relationship with yourself

- Five observances or practices that support your relationship with yourself and your *inner* world.

- The *niyamas* include: purity, contentment, austerity, self-study, and surrender to God.

Together, these first two limbs constitute the totality of respectful, moral, and devotional behavioral guidelines to support your practices. They are meant to increase vitality and bring you more and more inner freedom. Without these clear boundaries of morality, the increased energy and power you gain through your spiritual practices can be easily dissipated, or worse, used to harm yourself or others.

3. *Āsana:* seat or posture

- *As* means "to sit or be," "to take your seat," or "take the seat of your heart."

- An alternative definition is formed by *as* (to be), *san* (united with), *na* (the eternal cosmic vibration). *Āsana* thus means "to be united or one with the eternal cosmic vibration."

154

4. *Prāṇāyāma:* the practice of breathing

- *Prāṇāyāma* fosters expansion of the life force.

- *Prāṇāyāma* comes from joining two words, *prāṇa* (life force) and *yama* (to control). The word *prāṇa* can also be split in two: *pra* means "to bring forth," and *na* is "the eternal cosmic vibration." *Prāṇa* means to bring forth the eternal cosmic vibration, the life force.

- *Prāṇa* can be described as the energy flow that permeates all things. It's in food, water, and sunlight. When the *prāṇa* of the body is disturbed, you feel sick or off-centered, and at the time of death, *prāṇa* leaves behind the empty shell of your body.

5. *Pratyāhāra:* withdrawal of the senses, focusing inwards

- This marks the pivoting of awareness from outside to inside. The senses turn inside out and withdraw their normal function of receiving stimuli from the external world in favor of receiving stimuli and sensation from the deep, mystical inner world.

6. *Dhāraṇā:* concentration described as putting a "concentric ring" of awareness around an area of focus.

- The process of limiting your field of awareness to a single point of focus, usually for a short time. The mind becomes one-pointed, then wanders, over and over again.

- A metaphor for *dhāraṇā* is pouring water out of a pitcher, one drop at a time.

7. *Dhyāna:* meditation described as sustained concentration on one object over a longer period of time.

- When you string together several points of concentration in succession.
- A metaphor for dhyāna is pouring oil from a pitcher – it flows out as one continuous, unbroken stream.

8. *Samādhi:* sustained meditation over a longer time where the practitioner dissolves into the object of awareness. Eventually both the meditator and the object of awareness merge and dissolve.

- A mystical state of consciousness described as absorption in source, or a state of indescribable ecstatic union with all that is.

- There are several stages of *samādhi* that describe the increasingly more subtle experiences of being.

The path outlined by Patañjali is that of Classical Yoga, geared toward the renunciate lifestyle. It was created for those in the elite Brahmin caste who could reject the world and live as monks. It's one of the traditions that Kripalu embraced and taught: a renunciate path in which *prakṛti* (everything material in the world) is inferior to *puruṣa* (consciousness, spirit.) In fact, *Puruṣa* literally means "conscious person." The goal of this tradition, simply put, is to "get out."

Patañjali's yoga is a rejection of the world, a turning away from *prakṛti* and its world of desires, pain, and pleasure, toward your true self as *puruṣa,* pure spirit. *Prakṛti* is what's in the way. It's what keeps you from realizing your true nature, which is *puruṣa*. Patañjali's yoga provides you with a one-way ticket to transcendence – up and out.

In contrast, Tantra teaches how to get more *into* the world, how to master the art of living, no matter your gender, caste, or creed. It's a householder path, meaning you don't have to renounce your life in order to practice. Instead it's a path of refinement. You can find freedom *through* the body, rather than finding freedom *from* the body. As householders we pay bills, raise families, hold down jobs, and do all of the mundane things "normal" people do. You no longer have to run away to an ashram, live in a cave, or escape to the deep forest in order to

156

achieve enlightenment. You can do it in the center of the life you are living now.

In that way, Tantra is a round-trip ticket. You touch the deepest depths of source energy within you and then return to yourself and to your life. Expanded by a bigger vision, you see the sacredness of all things as the embodiment of the universal energy itself in limited form.

To help demonstrate the contrast between the Classical and Tantric traditions, let's take a brief look at the two different ways *prāṇāyāma* is defined and practiced. As you saw above, the Classical tradition defines *prāṇāyāma* as control over *prāṇa*. There's a sense of the subjugation of the life force, an attempt to somehow triumph over or tame nature. But we all know that trying to control *śakti*, is like trying to contain a hurricane. It's impossible.

The Tantric tradition reinterprets the definition and practice of *prāṇāyāma*. Instead of splitting the word up into *prāṇa* and *yama*, they split it into *pran* and *ayama*. This changes the meaning of *prāṇāyāma* in a big way. As in English, in Sanskrit the "a" in front of a word often means the opposite of that word. *Ayama*, from this perspective, means "to release control," or "to go with the flow." *Ayama* also means "to extend, stretch, or expand." Therefore, *prāṇāyāma* means to extend the life force or to flow and expand with the life force.

Prāṇāyāma is not the control over *prāṇa*, but rather the co-participation with the life force as the divine. We align our individual self with the universal self in the form of the breath. The breath, being both voluntary and involuntary, is the perfect metaphor of co-participation with the divine.

But at Kripalu, I didn't know all this yet.

It seems that for Patañjali's Classical yoga, finding yourself in a body here on this planet is some kind of punishment. If you are unfortunate enough to be here, you can look forward to a "life sentence" of suffering. If you want out, according to Patañjali, yoga is the answer. You must turn away from the world to achieve true freedom. The renunciate path was considered superior to all other paths because of a particular interpretation and worldview at the time of Patañjali regarding *saṃsāra*, the "disease of worldliness," which leads to suffering.

Let's look closer at the Sanskrit term *"saṃsāra." Saṃ* is to be held back, stuck, or limited, and *sāra* is the essence, the spirit, the current, or the flow. *Saṃsāra* is the state of being bound by the flow, held back by the current. To be human, and to participate in the cycle of birth, death, and rebirth (the flow) is to be imprisoned. You must get off the karmic wheel of *saṃsāra* to be liberated. The only way to do that, says Patañjali, is to reject desire.

Classical Yoga insists that *prakṛti* is limited and bound by the constant cycles of pleasure and pain. Desire is seen to be the root cause of suffering because desire can never be satisfied on the material level. Since everything on the material plane is impermanent and changing, we must reject all yearnings for everything worldly to be more heaven-like. *If we cling to what is constantly changing, we will suffer.* This is Classical *saṃsāra*.

Furthermore, in Classical Yoga, all pleasure is actually hidden pain, suffering in disguise. We have an unquenchable thirst for pleasure, which throws us into the painful cycle of life, death, and rebirth again and again. In the Bible's Old Testament, Adam and Eve follow their desires, eat the forbidden fruit, and are punished by being ejected from the Garden of Eden. Classical Yoga is focused on transcending the karmic wheel of all pain to attain pure spirit, or *kaivalya*.

Kaivalya, meaning "pure isolation or separation," is the title of the fourth and last chapter of the Yoga *Sūtra*. This state of consciousness is the highest state achievable and is the end game, so to speak, of the practice: the liberation of the soul. In *kaivalya*, there are no distractions, no desires, and no worldly pulls; aspirants finally identify so fully with *puruṣa* (spirit) that they are completely and thoroughly isolated from *prakṛti* (material self which harbors their suffering, attachment, and worldliness, *saṃsāra*). In other words, they have overcome their "lower" desires and dwell continuously in a state of transcendence.

This can only be attained through the austerities of practice over a long period of time and through non-attachment, self-study, and surrender to God. Patañjali defines his yoga in *Sūtra* 2.1 as *kriyā* yoga, the yoga of action: "*Tapas, svādhyāya, īśvara pranidhāna, kriyā yoga.*" Translation: "Burning zeal in practice, self-study and study of scriptures, and surrender to God are the acts of yoga." In my opinion, this *Sūtra* is the distinguishing tenet of Patañjali's yoga.

In the Classical Yoga world view, you are born into this world because you botched it last time. You failed to transcend, so you have to come back and suffer all over again in order to learn your lessons. Eventually, at some point if and when you practice hard enough and are pure enough, you will not have to come back. Within this view, there is a kind of frantic push toward transcendence. Hurry! Practice yoga to get into your body! Now get out of it and transcend it! Why? Because your body is in the way of transcendence. The body is *samsāra*.

It's part of nature, and since nature is constantly and uncontrollably changing, your body is against you. Furthermore, it's full of unquenchable desires and distractions. It's messy and uncontrollable. Bottom line? It must be disciplined. Quickly.

This is where *tapas* comes in. At Kripalu, this underlying philosophy suffused everything we did, but particularly the intense focus on *tapas*. What might seem like an idealistic spiritual fantasy of enlightenment was presented to us as attainable in this lifetime. All we had to do was look to the recent history of the Kripalu lineage: our great-granddaddy guru, the guru of the guru of the guru, named "Dadaji" or Lord Lakulish, who was supposedly the 28th incarnation of Lord Śiva (which in my mind, is more myth than fact, since it's unverifiable). How would you confirm that anyone was a reincarnation of anyone else? If it's true, then who was the 27th reincarnation of Śiva? or the 26th?

I'm not dismissing this as entirely false, since yogic philosophy and Hindu lore is vast beyond measure. But in my opinion, this further perpetuated the mystique of the Kripalu lineage to somehow give it more power and credence by telling us that Dadaji was a direct descendent of *Śiva*. Whether it's true or untrue, I prefer to leave it as myth that people can choose to believe or not. Dadaji apparently achieved the "divine body," the highest state of consciousness in which your body becomes immortal, is free of disease, and never dies.

The concept of divine body is quite common, having roots in almost every spiritual tradition. From *Divine Body Through Yoga,*[3] by Swami Rajarshi Muni, a disciple of Swami Kripalvanandji:

> *Through the ages the concept of the Divine Body has resurfaced again and again, not only in the great religious traditions of the world, but also in the realm of myth and legend, from the "philosopher's stone" of medieval alchemy to modern science fiction. In the western world the resurrection of Jesus Christ and his ascendance into heaven is the best known example of the divine body, but the author includes the stories of many other great saints who have tested the principle of the divine body on the anvil of practical experience and achieved the ultimate goal of human existence. These include Kabir, Mirabai, Milarepa, Moses, and Elijah, among others. The author asserts, therefore, that the divine body is neither a myth nor is its achievement limited to one particular individual or faith. On the contrary, it is both real and attainable, and from the time that the seers and sages of ancient India demonstrated the scriptural truth of this phenomenon, it has been witnessed in the traditions of most of the major religions of the world including the Vedic tradition, Christianity, Buddhism, Jainism, and Zoroastrianism.*

There is an entire myth that explains how Dadaji achieved his divine body, including various purifying practices and an unbroken *samādhi* for 12 days. At the end of his life (is there an end if you have the divine body?) he merged his form with a *linga* (obelisk) made from a mysterious, unearthly material: a meteorite, perfectly carved to resemble his likeness. We were told that it wasn't carved by anyone. Dadaji merged into it, meaning that the likeness was, in fact, his real face. Hmmmm. I never questioned that. I took it as truth based on faith.

160

The divine body concept was never described in any great detail, perhaps to better retain its veil of mystique. I so wanted to believe in the story that I never thought to question its veracity. Whether truth or myth, it was a beautiful fantasy that kept me on the straight and narrow: *I will practice so intensely that I will outlive death.*

As exhausting as they were, I loved my practices. They were my path to free *puruṣa*, transcend *prakṛti*, and eventually attain the fantasy of becoming "supernatural."

I continue to be curious about what happens to us after we die. Aren't we all? My greatest fear used to be that when I die, I will cease to be. This is a universal fear; Patañjali's *Yoga Sūtra* describes the fifth *kleśa* (affliction) as *abhiniveśa* (clinging to life or fear of death). The idea that I will just disappear always made my heart sink. *After all this life and all this work, the payoff is death? That's a bummer. That can't be why we're here. That can't be the game plan, can it?* Nondual Śaiva-Śākta *Tantra* would say, no. That's not the game plan.

From the Śaiva perspective, at the time of death, your physical body returns to the five elements (also known as the *pañca mahābhūtas*) at the bottom of the *Tattva* chart (Appendix B). Earth, water, fire, air, and sky are considered the densest part of our material being and when you die, all of what makes up your physical incarnation returns to those elements. Your muscles, bones, and organs dissolve into the earth; your fluids, like blood and lymph, return to the water element; your breath releases into the air element; the space that your body takes up returns to the sky element; and when your body becomes cold after death, that's your heat returning to the fire element.

On the gross plane, then, yes – the body ceases to be. But *Nondual Śaiva-Śākta Tantra* goes on to describe what happens to the subtle body, as represented by the 31 *Tattvas* above the five elements: it lives on and continues its journey. When I first heard that teaching, I felt such comfort. *Phew! Okay, so I don't have to worry any more about ceasing to exist.* I relaxed, knowing that I will continue to live on, even though

161

I'll be in a different form. I may not know how that will roll out, but I accept the idea that life continues on a subtle level infinitely.

Although the fear of death is natural and predictable, the more I meditate and touch the power of the Absolute within, the more familiar I become with this part of me. And the more I can connect with my "subtle me," the more prepared I believe I'll be when it's time to die and let go of my physical body – that's the hope, at least. Perhaps the "divine body," then, is not the attainment of physical immortality. It's achieved when one becomes finely attuned and absorbed in their subtle body *even while going through normal activities on earth*. In fact, that's another way of describing open-eyed *samādhi* (discussed in Chapter 6), one of the goals of the *Nondual Śaiva-Śākta Tantra* path. *What a relief.*

As I reflect on my state of consciousness at the ashram, however, it makes sense that I wanted to conquer death, the ultimate sign of failure. Of course, a perfectionist would choose a path with perfection as its goal. I say now, "Get real, Todd!" but at the time, I was completely inspired. I threw myself into every practice with total commitment. Just as a few years prior I wanted to see the body of Christ, now I wanted to become the body of Christ, the body of consciousness, the divine body. My "spiritual transformation" of a few months ago, where I experienced the power of *śakti*, offered me incontrovertible proof that the esoteric was real and that, as human beings, we had access to a reality beyond the senses. That proof spurred me on.

REFRAIN

Without a doubt, the most controversial *tapas* practice – and probably the most difficult for many people – was the third *yama* of the *Yoga Sūtras*: *brahmacarya*. Translated as "walking in the footsteps of God" or "moderation in all things," *brahmacarya* is most often interpreted as sexual abstinence. This moral code was the pillar of yogic practices at Kripalu during my residence there and the word "*brahmacarya*" became synonymous with celibacy. To reinforce the practice, men and women lived separately, on opposite sides of the massive building, and we were discouraged from socializing or even making eye contact with the opposite sex. Moreover, we ate on opposite sides of the dining room and sat on opposite sides of the Main Hall for *satsaṅga*.

The goal of celibacy at Kripalu, through meditation and practices of austerity, was to conserve and reverse the flow of sexual fluid, to move it up the spine rather than down and out of the body. Supposedly, the fluid would energetically flow up through your cerebral-spinal fluid to bathe your brain in *ojas* (essence, the most potent form of *prāṇa*, the life force), increasing your inner light and vitality, and awakening your higher centers of consciousness. This practice had a name, *ūrdhvareta*, which means the transmutation or sublimation of sexual energy to achieve greater consciousness.

Ūrdhvareta also fed the fantasy of doing yoga to escape the inevitable: death. Swami Kripalvanandji was preoccupied with the divine body because *his* guru had achieved it and had told him that Bapuji too would achieve it in this lifetime. Although rumor has it that Bapuji died before achieving the divine body, *our* guru taught us that our main goal should be to transcend and escape the suffering of life through Classical Yoga practices such as *ūrdhvareta*, among many others.

I was totally impressed and starry-eyed with the notion of achieving the divine body, so I resolved to practice celibacy as best I could for as long as I could. Like some sort of "spiritual scientist" using my own body as the laboratory, I became completely absorbed in experimenting with the idea of creating a divine body. As diligent as I was, I was never able to maintain the practice longer than about six months.

There are many physical, mental, and spiritual benefits to this practice that are not understood by most people, including yogis, and I will say that attempting *ūrdhvareta* had its benefits. I felt amazingly energetic, focused, and happy. However, that could also have been a result of the stress-free life the ashram provided, where I could focus purely on spirituality and attending to my practices. My bet is that anyone who lived that way would feel the way I did. My chief stressor was the worry that I was not able to transcend my base, inferior desires; I was still attracted to beautiful women and secretly wanted to have sex with all of them! I resisted that natural attraction, thinking that I was not yet fully evolved.

In the Classical tradition, since the spiritual is considered superior, the lower cakras (below *anāhata*, the heart cakra) are seen as inferior to the upper cakras. We were told that we must overcome the lower three cakras – which include materiality, sex, and egoism – in order to live a spiritual life of purity. Therefore, all of the body's natural needs and desires were shunned and repressed, even as they were, ironically, given lofty names like "sublimation" and "*ūrdhvareta*."

In Tantra, all cakras are needed, and all are spiritually based. There's nothing inherently wrong with any of them. Imbalances can occur in any of the cakras, not just the lower ones, and these imbalances are seen as opportunities for lessons, necessary to the healthy development of being a fully actualized human being. On the contrary, each cakra is a divine step and stage of power, "on schedule to evolve," as Carolyn Myss says, as we experience the journey of life.

At the ashram, this particular kind of *tapas* perfectly fostered my core-wounded identity of perfectionism and unworthiness. Since I kept giving in to my "lower" desires, I always had something to shame myself with – and it dovetailed perfectly with my experience as a young, curious boy.

Today when I look back, I have such compassion for what I was trying to achieve: sublimating my sexual energy in the name of trying to achieve immortality. During my twenties and thirties when my physical body and sexual hormones were at their peak? Really? But at that time, I fully believed that by following the specific yogic teachings of certain paths, and by strict adherence to abstemious practices, I could conquer my desires and rise above and beyond nature.

In addition to celibacy, we engaged in many *tapas* practices that revolved around food, or the lack thereof. I once fasted for 10 days on just brown rice and water alone, nothing else. During another period of time – several months in a row – I fasted on Thursdays (in Sanskrit and other modern Indian languages, *Guruvār* means Thursday, or guru day) on just brown rice in honor of the guru. Another fast required me to eat only two meals per day, which I did for weeks.

My most dramatic diet-related *tapas* was based on the book, *Power Eating Program: You Are How You Eat* by Lino Stanchich, a survivor of a communist concentration camp, who claims to have survived by drinking his food and chewing his drink. All of us adopted the "power eating" techniques, chewing our food 150 times per bite. I think part of the psychology was that the pain of chewing dissuaded us from eating more. It took me over an hour to finish just one bowl of food, and my jaw was so sore after the first few meals that I totally lost interest in eating. There was, however, a distinctly powerful meditative aspect to this way of eating. By chewing the food so thoroughly into its liquid form, it mixes with the digestive enzymes in the mouth, which eases the work of the stomach once you finally swallow. I found that my entire digestive system relaxed and my whole being slowed down.

This method was intended to increase the powers of digestion and calm the appetite. It worked. After 30 days, I dropped from my normal weight of 140 pounds to 122 pounds. I was skin and bones. The worried ashram directors advised me to abandon the chewing program immediately and start eating lots more, including some fish to increase my protein intake.

The ashram was strictly vegetarian, as was I. Even though I was given an order from the administration, my guilt over eating animal protein was tremendous, matched only by my embarrassment. The only way to add fish to my diet was to get it outside the ashram. Instead of going into local Lenox for it, I drove to the next town over to wolf down some haddock – in order to lower my chances of being seen by a fellow "ashram-ite." My body clearly loved the protein, but my mind constantly flipped back to worry: *Am I not committed enough? Will others think I'm cheating?*

Here was more Classical *tapas* – denying the body to transcend its inherent impediment – and, like celibacy, it dovetailed with my childhood pattern of shame. Having never felt "good enough," I completely bought into the idea that I showed up on this planet having already failed.

Although self-acceptance and loving yourself just as you are were taught at the ashram, these teachings were always countered with the practice of *tapas*, and with the idea that natural desires of the body were bad and to be transcended: a confusing and paralyzing set of teachings. Looking back, I can see that we were taught to strive for something that was unobtainable, such that I always remained feeling slightly less than my full potential.

I believe a more sustainable and perhaps more mature definition of the *yama brahmacarya*, is moderation. Over the years of experimentation, often exploring the extremes, I've come to recognize the power of moderation and the place in the middle, or *madhya*. Moderation is not necessarily easy. Just try to find the place in the middle and stay there. You'll soon find out it's harder than you think. A good example of this is fasting. Most people find it easier to fast and stay within a particular regimen than to simply eat moderately. Fasts are often followed by a binge phase: the body's natural response to being deprived and its attempt to return to *madhya*.

RENOUNCE

After living at the ashram for a year, I was invited to become initiated, which was a sacred ritual that I understood would deepen my commitment not only to austerities and *tapas*, but to the guru and ashram itself. Also, initiation promised a faster path to spiritual growth, hugely alluring to an impatient go-getter like me. I was flattered and excited; initiation seemed like the passport into the secret club of seekers, and I wanted to be on the inside. I accepted the invitation. For 10 days prior to the ceremony, I studied and practiced with my initiate group in retreat, fasting and preparing body, mind, and soul for this highly anticipated increase in *śakti*.

Initiation also included receiving a spiritual name in Sanskrit, which was optional, but encouraged. The new name signified rebirth, a

166

manifestation of this newly commenced spiritual journey. The Sanskrit name offered me an opportunity to start over with a new identity and to leave the old life behind, to sever all ties to what kept me bound and limited – including my former world and family of origin. I had to give my heart completely to the guru in order to receive his full blessing – which is also why celibacy was so essential to life at Kripalu, as it kept my heart focused on him. As a disciple, and for me especially as a monk in training, the relationship with the guru was primary, even more important than my relationship with my family, who at this point in my life seemed very, very far away.

Since most of my friends who were previously initiated had Sanskrit names, I was excited to receive mine. I was given the name, "*Manu*," which means "lawgiver of the human race," "wise," or "soul." Like Adam, the first human in Christian belief, Manu is the name of the progenitor of the human race in Hindu belief. There's a scripture called the *Manusmṛti*, "The Laws of Manu,"[4] which is an ancient esoteric text of rules, guidelines, social responsibilities and interactions, and maps for enlightenment. Manu felt like the perfect name for me. Whether it was the power of suggestion, community support, or the potency of yogic rituals and lineages, it all worked. I found a new identity in Manu and was happy to answer to that name for over 13 years. When I went home to visit family, however, I had to go back to Todd. As weird and uncomfortable as that felt, I just couldn't ask my parents to use my new name.

As part of our initiation preparation, we each received the guru mantra, "*Om Namo Bhagavate Vasudevāya*," which was the mantra passed down to our guru from his guru. This mantra has a special *śakti* (energy) signature of the Kripalu lineage. By repeating this mantra, you gained direct access to the lineage of blessings and spiritual powers. Instantly, I remembered this mantra, which was the auspicious catalyst for my spiritual emergency two years prior. We were told to practice it constantly.

To do so, we were also given a *mālā* bead necklace: a prayer necklace consisting of 108-plus-one *rudrākṣa* beads, which are seeds from the

167

rudrākṣa tree in India. It produces a hard, blue seed that turns black when it dries. The extra bead is called the *meru* (mountain) bead, *bindu* (the whole universe condensed down into a point), or guru bead. There is a meditation technique called *japa*, from the Sanskrit word *jap*, which means to mumble or repeat quietly moving your mouth, lips, or tongue. In *japa*, you hold a bead in your fingers and say a mantra, continuing along the strand and repeating the mantra with each bead until your fingers touch the meru bead. Then you flip the strand over and go the other way so that you never "cross the guru."

One round of *japa* is 108 repetitions of the mantra, and a *lakh* (the number 100,000) of *Mala*s is 100,000 rounds of *japa*. Once I was initiated, I joined others in doing one *lakh* at a time. After each practice, I kept a running tally of how many rounds of *japa* I did; over the several years when this practice was "in vogue" at the ashram, I completed several *lakhs*.

After many years of practice as an initiate, there came an opportunity to go even deeper by joining the renunciate order. The "renunciate" model of turning away from the world – a monastic path common within many spiritual traditions, including the Kripalu lineage – was about releasing your attachments to the world, including your family, job, and all responsibilities outside the ashram in favor of a life dedicated to spirituality and service. Many of my close friends who were a few years older than I had just taken their vows and shaved their heads. I looked up to them. The renunciates had many privileges, including sitting up close to the guru for every *satsaṅga*, helping out in all of the ceremonies and rituals, and having private *darśans* (being in the presence of the guru). Becoming a renunciate meant wearing the saffron-colored clothing that attracted honor and respect from others in the community; it was the ultimate sign of spiritual ascension.

Saffron, the color orange, has been worn by swamis in India for hundreds of years and represents the highest level of sacrifice. The three primary colors associated with Hindu worship – red, yellow, and orange – were chosen because of their sacred connection to nature in the forms of the sunrise, sunset, and fire. The sunrise and sunset meet in *sandhyā* (twilight), the mystical transition between two opposites.

Fire, *agni*, represents the ultimate sacrifice and renunciation of the ego and is the power that transforms one substance into the next higher state (earth into heat and light, water into steam). Fire is also known for its power to dissolve everything back into dust or ash, signifying the perpetual cycle of nature to which all life is bound – birth, life, death, rebirth.

In fire, red is the color towards the bottom of the flame and signifies worship; married women wear *kumkum* (red powder) on their forehead and a red sari during weddings and rituals. Yellow, the color in the middle of fire, is worn by priests who are not renunciates. Orange, or saffron, is at the top of the flame and is reserved for the highest aspirants, the renunciates, those who have renounced everything.

At Kripalu, we were taught that the renunciate model, the highest path you could choose, was closer to God. And though no one ever said it aloud, the underlying message I sensed was that anything "less" than this path – getting married, creating a family, being a responsible citizen, pursuing a vocation – was, in a sense, a cop-out and a failure. I joined a group of brothers and sisters who intended to become renunciates; we called ourselves renunciates-in-training. We met every week for a year to study scriptures and share the spiritual teachings and our intentions. I was entirely committed. I saw becoming a renunciate as the fulfillment of my spiritual path.

In many ways, the clear-cut path of renunciation was easier for me. Because I felt much shame around relationships, my desires, and especially sex, I found it easier to reject those parts of myself rather than confront them head-on. I also felt soothed by the structured and predictable nature of monastic life. It was inward-focused and controlled – perfect for a shy introvert like me – and you didn't have to make many decisions, because all the "dos and don'ts" were already spelled out. I was already excellent at following directions, and I learned at a young age how to be the "good boy." All in all, it played to my strengths since all I had to do was follow the path laid out before me and surrender. Yes, withdrawing from life appealed to me greatly.

Whether or not all of this was a ploy to control disciples, to train them to be submissive to the guru and give him everything they owned – including possessions, money, and soul – can't be verified. From my experience, I would say that less-than-noble intentions were at play, as were the purest intentions for our higher evolution. Regardless, renunciation can be a fine path for many, and while I was on it, I loved it.

REGRESS

Not only was Kripalu strictly vegetarian, but it was also sugar-free. They served fruit, muffins, and granola during breakfast, but nothing in the evening that would even remotely satisfy anyone's longing for something sweet. However, soon after my initiation, they started serving desserts on Wednesday nights – our one "fun night" off from *tapas*, when we were allowed to watch a movie, chosen by the administration, and eat popcorn, too. This was the only night where enjoyment was "legal" and sanctioned by the ashram governance.

After lunch on the first Wednesday the "fun night" began, I sat at my purchasing office desk after lunch. My hand was poised over a box, cutter in hand, to slice open the tape. Suddenly, a rich, buttery, long-forgotten but unmistakable aroma enveloped me: *fresh popcorn*. My hand fell limp, and I almost whimpered with longing. All I could think of was the old Popeye cartoons, when Blimpy smelled hamburgers and the aroma floated him, led by his nose, to the source of the smell. Bharat and I, along with the rest of the purchasing group, could barely keep it together for the rest of the afternoon, as wave after wave of sweet, mouth-watering smells wafted up from the kitchen. Plus, the prospect of not working or doing anything healthy – *we're going to watch a movie!* – made the last few hours of paper-pushing and box-unpacking interminable. It felt like sitting in a high school classroom, hours before the big dance that night.

Wednesdays quickly became the most thrilling day of the week. To line up for popcorn and dessert, and then consume such delights with all of my 350 "brothers and sisters" while watching a PG (no violence, sex, or drugs) movie? Seriously? It was about as close to *nirvāṇa* as many residents got. Of course, food combining was an issue, especially the next day in early morning practice. On Thursday mornings, the blending of certain yoga poses with the overindulgences of the night before often created some loud, vaporous classrooms. But those days were often fasting days for many of us –Wednesday night gluttony followed by forbearance on Thursday. A wise practice, no doubt put in place consciously by the Kripalu administration.

Was it scarcity consciousness, like being in a large family and wanting to make sure you got yours? Or was it the widespread deprivation of almost all physical pleasure?

Visiting guests at Kripalu generally had no major hang-ups about dessert, since they could partake whenever they wanted. But for the ashram residents, the obsession with dessert night became almost pathological.

Whatever the reason, on Wednesday nights the residents arrived early for dinner, lining up like twitchy horses at Pimlico before the starting bell. Ignoring our impatience, the cooks quieted everyone down and launched into an epic blessing of the meal that started with long, deep breaths to let go of the stress from the day. This was followed by a slow, mindful guided prayer to bless the food, a thoughtful spiritual poem, and finally, the methodical chanting of *om*. We were so jacked up by the prospect and proximity of the dessert table that we simply could not hold it together. We punctuated the beautiful meditation with obnoxious noises and muttered jokes – all the way up to the sound of the dinner bell. At that, we broke free and charged the dessert table, dodging and weaving through the unsuspecting guests interspersed in the line with us, bypassing the salads and grains and other healthful dinner offerings. The guests never knew what hit them.

The residents became so infatuated with the desserts – a rotating selection of donuts, cake, pie, strawberry shortcake, brownies, ice cream, cookies, and the like – that the dessert table was completely decimated within 15 minutes of the dinner bell, leaving nothing for the guests. I may still hold the ashram record for the number of donuts eaten on dessert night – 14! Not something I'm particularly proud of now. But back then, I was seen by my purchasing buddies as a hero of decadence. And these were not 14 of your light and fluffy Dunkin' Donuts variety; these were whole wheat, leaden hockey pucks saturated with soybean oil and sugar. I was bloated for days.

I wasn't the only one who ate more than one dessert. Most residents did. Eventually, the ashram instituted a one-dessert-per-person-before-6:15pm policy, but still the desserts flew off the table and there weren't enough for the guests. We were irrepressible. We had a shocking lack of regard for the guests, who, after all, were paying our bills.

REBEL... THE GREAT DESSERT HEIST

The ashram got serious. Off to the side, in the corner of the dining hall, they stationed a video surveillance camera and operator. Designed for deterrence, and ahead of its time, the camera was trained on the dessert table at dinnertime on Wednesdays to catch those who took more than their share. Objectively, I could appreciate the radical innovation of this solution. But on one particular Wednesday I polished off my one brownie at 5:30pm, stared at the sea of individual brownies resting comfortably on their little plates on the table, and glanced over at the camera with contempt. *Just one, huh? We'll see about that.*

There was a large in-house program that week, so the dining room was packed. I enlisted a few buddies, and together we cased the joint. The dessert table was unusually crowded, and of course, the video camera was trained directly on it. Carrying two containers we had "borrowed" from the kitchen, a friend and I sidled a little closer to the table, but still out of camera view, contemplating our options. I spied past my buddy's shoulder to examine the sight line from the table to the camera and determined that if we stayed low enough, we could remain undetected amongst the throng.

Looking all around us, we got down on all fours and crawled through the crowd and under the table. (They don't call it "table pose" for nothing!) Once there, I reached my hand out from underneath, groped around on the table until I landed on a brownie, and carefully lifted it, plate and all, off and under the table, where my partner in crime transferred the goods into the container. Moving swiftly, we successfully grabbed enough brownies to fill both containers. Either no one saw us doing this, or no one cared enough to say anything, and we slithered out from under the table, leaving nothing behind but a stack of empty plates with crumbs. Clutching our booty, we disappeared into the crowd and slid out the side door of the dining room, then bounded triumphantly down to the auditorium, armed with enough desserts to last the entire movie and then some. We ate to our heart's content.

The next day, when the administration rolled back the video footage to identify the culprits, all they saw were hands and no faces. It is with both pride and chagrin that I tell you: we never got caught.

OPPORTUNITY KNOCKS

Except for the isolated episode of rebellion here and there, I was generally a paragon of monkhood. I followed the rules, dove into *tapas* with unswerving dedication, and performed my *seva* with uncomplaining diligence. After a few years of working in the Purchasing Department, I heard a knock on the door of the department's office just as I was going over a list of recent deliveries with Balaram. Sam, my beloved teacher and the Programs Administrator, walked in. "Manu?" he asked, "can I speak with you?"

Confused and surprised, I looked to Balaram, who nodded, looking suspiciously well-informed. "Sure," I said, and we stepped into the hall.

Sam didn't waste any time. "You're being transferred to the Programs Department to teach workshops," he said, and before I could ask when, he continued, "starting immediately."

I was thrilled. Although I had made a lot of close friends in Purchasing and we always made it fun, there was very little to engage or challenge me. I thanked Sam profusely, and returned to my co-workers to tell them the news.

But Balaram had already done it.

"We'll miss you, Manu," "This is so perfect for you," and "Way to go!" filled my ears, as tears filled my eyes. You'd have thought I was leaving the ashram. Bharat high-fived me, joking, "You're gonna miss my singing," and I laughed. "You know it, man," I declared, and I meant it. Balaram pulled me into a big bear hug, and I hugged him hard back. I wanted him to know how grateful I was that he had made this happen. As sad as it was to leave them, the joy I felt at moving to Programs told me I was headed in the right direction.

I had the highest respect for the teachers at Kripalu. The memory of crying my eyes out in Sam's arms during the Quest for the Limitless You course was still fresh. I credited him, and the rest of my teachers during those 10 days, with helping me unburden myself of layers of limitation. I felt so esteemed and appreciated by this offer; it was a true honor to join the ranks of the teachers.

There was no way I could have known how this new direction would challenge my capacity to embrace my greatest fears and deepest wounds.

NOTES

[1] Quote is attributed to Sally Kempton. Exact source unknown. To learn more about Sally Kempton's amazing work see: https://www.sallykempton.com.

[2] Find out more about the Bates Method at: https://seeing.org

[3] Swami Rajarshi Muni. *Divine Body Through Yoga.* Mumbai, India: Life Mission. 2007. Print.

[4] For more information on The Laws of Manu see: http://www.duhaime.org/LawMuseum/LawArticle-297/200-BC–Laws-of-Manu.aspx and https://en.wikipedia.org/wiki/Manusmriti. Be careful about sites offering a free download of the full text.

CHAPTER NINE

The Teaching Appears

The way you unbind yourself is by binding yourself.

Douglas Brooks[1]

IS THIS ON?

As a member of the Programs staff, I began teaching more and more resident and guest yoga classes, and soon I was directing weekend programs. Some of these classes were huge – as many as 120 students – and they required that I use a microphone. While there were times that I managed to teach the entire class without a hitch, often the presence of the microphone set off some kind of psychological chain reaction in me – one that took me back to my early performance disasters at the St. Cecilia Center.

Sitting in front of the group, shaking, I would hold the microphone and freeze. I couldn't speak; my mind literally could not find any words to utter. Then, in an unwelcome deviation from my childhood piano competition days, the tears would start flowing. I would sit there, quaking and sobbing, in front of an entire room of what must have been very surprised people. In some ways, this was a step forward for me. Rather than pushing away my fear, I certainly was embracing it. Still, I felt embarrassed by this seemingly inexplicable display of emotion.

I can't know for sure what all of the students thought or felt, but I do know that some kind souls tried to take care of me and mother me, while others felt that my tears gave them permission to cry and become vulnerable. Still others saw me as courageous to just let myself shake and quake with fear and then let the tears gush out; some individuals told me that moment in the entire program was the most powerful for them. I imagine there were some people who thought I was just a crybaby. For me, my very public display of tears broadcast to the world my internal conviction: *I am a major failure.* I was mortified.

Teaching thus became my own personal, psychic battleground. Every course I taught threw me to the wolves of my inner demons of shame. I battled deep self-rejection; I was my own worst critic and didn't know how to soften it. Nothing I did made me feel good about my teaching. During those times when I was bathed in praise after successfully teaching a workshop and had no right to feel anything but uplifted, I still

177

found a way to diminish myself, find something to criticize, and make myself wrong. I was compulsive in my self-abnegation.

As strange as it seems, I was more comfortable living in shame than in standing tall in my goodness. Until one evening, when I found myself recounting to Sam the sordid details from the latest scene of degradation: "…and *three* people rushed over to me with boxes of Kleenex…"

Sam was trained to not interrupt, as we all were, but he couldn't help himself, probably because it was so clear that I needed to make a change. Soon.

"Manu, are you willing to have an experience?"

That may sound odd, but I knew immediately what he meant.

As part of the Programs team, we were trained in various yoga, teaching, and psychological skills – the ashram version of continuing education. Methods we studied combined several different approaches to psychotherapy, including body-centered gestalt therapy and other yogic practices. Often during our free time and at some program meetings, we took time to practice guiding each other through these experiences, and sometimes, when an issue came up spontaneously, another Programs teacher would ask if you wanted to go into a process.

There was no one I trusted more than Sam to help me with this gripping, crippling self-doubt. I nodded and felt the prick of tears beginning to well up. I was ready to get to the bottom of this.

UNCOVERING

The "experience" took hours, and I don't remember all of it. Here is what I do remember:

I am lying down on a yoga mat with Sam at my side. "Close your eyes," he says gently, "and take a few deep breaths."

178

I do, and soon I'm awash in anxiety. It's a familiar feeling: scared and stuck, like a small animal caught suddenly in a trap.

"What do you feel?" he asks.

"Fear." My voice sounds strangled. There is no air.

"It's all right," he murmurs, "Keep breathing. The fear is still part of you. It's okay to feel it." His voice soothes me. "Now, I'd like you to locate the fear. Where does it live in your body?"

I scan internally. "My belly."

"Okay, good. Good. Go ahead and place your hands on your belly, and breathe into it." I do. Sam pauses while I regain control of my breath.

He asks me to describe the nature of the fear. "What color is it? What shape is it? What size is it?" I don't remember my answers. He asks, "If your fear could speak to you what would it say?"

Words fly out of my mouth: "You're bad. You're awful. You're a total loser. You can't do anything right. You should just quit and give up."

He takes it all in, then rubs my arm. I feel his compassion.

"How old are you?" he asks.

"About two."
"Whose voice is this?"

"I don't know." I think it's a voice from my family, but I just can't place it.

"Is it true, what your fear is telling you?"
I don't know. I tell him.

179

"That's okay," he says, and then he falls silent. He seems to be considering something, and time passes. When he speaks again, his tone has shifted. It is even more nurturing.

"Would you like to speak as your younger self?"

Yes. "I feel a heavy burden all around me," I respond. "I'm paralyzed with fear. It's like I'm covered with earth... or something. Something thick."

Sam pats my arm. "I'm going to get something. I'm not leaving you. Hold on." I feel him move away, then return. He says, "Draw your knees into your chest and roll to your side. Curl up into a little ball." I do. Then I feel a heavy wool blanket draped over me, intentionally being pulled tighter and tighter, until it is uncomfortable.

In that constricted state, I implode. Suddenly, everything is dark and I am shrinking, diminishing under the pressure I feel all around me. I panic. I can't move or breathe. I feel like I'm going to die.

For the first time since my terrifying episode in the hotel room with my father, my childhood nightmare overtakes me again. *Don't hit me!* But this time, it is different. I am awake. I am conscious. I have the support of Sam, and I am doing this for a deeper purpose. I feel the fear, but I can separate myself enough from it to view it with an element of curiosity this time. As tempted as I am to throw off this blanket and run away, I don't. *I am so tired of living in shame. I will do almost anything to free myself of it.* I trust Sam, and I continue.

He leads me through my discomfort, keeping me under the blanket. He asks me to describe the space I'm in, and I speak from my fear: "This is how I feel when my shame kicks in. The fear in my belly makes me feel all contracted and cramped up, like I'm going to die."

At this point, I realize I have a choice. On one hand, I have a belly full of fear that insists on convincing me that I am not enough, a loser – which I suspect may be false. On the other hand, to heal myself fully

180

means I may have to love even my belly, as fear-filled as it might be. Do I continue to live bound by my rejection of fear, smallness, and shame? Or do I face my fear by *actually moving closer* to the voice of shame, by choosing to embrace it with love?

With Sam's support, I do something I've never done before. I choose the latter.

And as I do so, I begin to soften. I cradle my belly and talk to my fear. In soft, loving tones I tell it, "I'm here for you now. I'm listening now. How can I love you now? What do you need from me?" Then I hear the fear's response, and I know I'm on the right path. Fear says, "I need you to hear me. I need you to reassure me that I'm okay. I need to feel your love and I need you to not leave me. I need you to let me learn at my own pace and in my own way." I repeat back those words. I reassure my fear. I tell it that I will listen more and not be so critical.

But the thing that I most need to hear myself say, and to this day I think what my fear needed to hear, was this: "I allow myself to learn as I grow."

As I said those words, Sam removed the blanket that was covering me. With my eyes still closed, I felt the heaviness of the blanket lift, and with it, the grip of fear. Cool air rushed across my skin. I felt lighter. When I opened my eyes, all I saw was his loving gaze. His eyes were so full and bright and proud, and they told me he knew me. They told me that he understood the deep significance of what had just happened, and they held me transfixed for some time until I recognized for myself the power of my accomplishment. *I did it.* I broke into wracking sobs and he hugged me close. It was as if that blanket absorbed and then lifted away all the shame from my life. Tears of relief poured out of me, releasing years of shaming myself and being shamed, from parents, sister, friends, teachers, older school kids, everyone.

Most of all, the deepest lesson of that process was to love and accept myself just as I am, fear and all. I didn't abolish fear; I made friends with it. In doing so, I took away its power to stop me from fulfilling my dreams. As I like to say, I put my fear in the back seat and kept driving. The affirmation, "I allow myself to learn as I grow" continues to support me today. Whenever I get frustrated with myself, or if I clamp down with rejection and self-judgment, I repeat this phrase. It brings me much peace.

TRIAL BY FIRE

Soon after, I moved into Sam's office as an understudy. As my main mentor over the following year, he trained me to be a yoga teacher, sitting in on my classes and offering valuable feedback. With his compassionate guidance, I slowly became more comfortable in that role, eventually assisting him in the month-long 200-hour Kripalu teacher training. It was during one of those trainings in 1986 that I was asked to put my affirmation to the test.

He and I were just beginning to teach the students how to teach *trikoṇāsana*, triangle pose, when the door to the room opened suddenly. A member of the communication staff beckoned.

"Samadarshan, you have an urgent phone call," she said. He closed his director's manual, and she held the door for him as he hurried out.

Temporarily left alone with the class, I asked the students to send some peaceful thoughts to Sam, then continued where we left off. We finished going over the basic form of the pose, and I broke the class up into their practice groups to teach it to one another. Soon the room was filled with movement and laughter. The door opened again, and this time it was Sam. He looked stricken. I rushed over, and as I drew closer I could see the grief and panic that enshrouded him. His eyes were red.

"What is it?"

"My father. He's…" Sam struggled to find words. "He died, suddenly…" There was nothing more he could say.

I was stunned. I reached out to embrace him, and he let himself be hugged. When we separated, he held onto my arm and looked at me with purposeful intent.

"I want you to take over the teacher training in my absence. You're the director now."

My heart sank into my belly. I heard what my fear wanted me to say: *But wait! I can't do this. I'm not ready. I don't have what it takes. I'll screw it up.* Instead, I said nothing. I just looked at him and took a deep breath.

He knew me so well. Even in his grief, he found the strength to support me. He stared deep into my eyes, instilling the light of *śakti* within me, the light of my own self-confidence.

"I know you can do this, Manu," he stated. "You're ready. I have faith in you." With that faith spoken, not just *to* me but *into* me, he handed me the director's manual and left the room.

SPEAKING FAITH

I'm not an avid TV watcher. I don't even own a television. Of course, I watch enough video and streamed episodes to make up for not having a TV. Occasionally when I travel, I turn the TV on, which reminds me why I don't own one – it's so easy to get sucked into watching, and there is so little positive programming.

Once, while teaching in Martha's Vineyard in September, I stayed at a lovely cottage with a TV. On Sunday morning, while I was eating breakfast before leaving to teach for the day, I surfed to a televangelist station. On the screen suddenly was Joel Osteen of Lakewood Church in Houston, TX, giving a sermon in front of what seemed like a million parishioners. I became transfixed. He had me laughing, crying, then almost taking the vow at the end as a born-again follower.

What impressed me the most, however, was his invitation during a certain point in the service to all those who were in need of healing. He encouraged anyone who had recently lost a loved one or who was grieving or going through a hard time, to step into the aisles to receive a blessing. Then a mass of people like angels swooped in and surrounded them. One on one, these angels seemed to be whispering something into their ears. The music playing in the background drowned out what they were saying, but it looked as though they were speaking love: words of encouragement, words of promise, words of support, words of hope. They were using their agency to speak faith into the hearts of those who needed it. In that moment, I saw how we, as human beings, can become an instrument of the divine, a conduit of compassion for each other.

This is what Sam did for me that day when he put me in charge of the teacher training program. After he left the room, I stood holding the manual, my mouth agape. But his certainty rang through my being, and in its presence the negative voice from my belly fell silent. I looked at the manual, then at the students, who I realized were quietly staring at me. *Yes, I will do this.* In that leap to "yes" was an eternity of being. I entered the unknown, where my own safety was grace.

Sure enough, Sam was right. From somewhere, I do not know where, I felt an upsurge of confidence and courage. With that, and with a lot of support from the staff, I was able to complete the rest of the training successfully. By "successfully," I don't just mean that the students learned and grew, or that all of the participants had nice things to say about their experience and about me. I also mean that this was the first time I finished a program without the harsh voices of self-criticism screaming in my ears.

Something bigger than what others experienced was blossoming within me. It was my own approval, my own appreciation. This trial by fire gave me the confidence to be a teacher, not just to support others in their awakening, but for my own heart to transform and expand. I understood in that moment that teaching could be the crucible for my own spiritual evolution.

Bapuji said, "The highest spiritual practice is self-observation without judgment." Throughout my years teaching at Kripalu, I came to appreciate a corollary teaching, one to which I return again and again: "Self-love is the highest satisfaction."Self-love heals shame, perfectionism, and all the other variations of suffering that have their gnarly roots in shame. But how to get there? Acceptance and compassion, also known as: empathy.

Empathy is a quality we often extend to others, even as we overlook our own need for it. It's the one virtue that's needed to go deeper into the path of the heart; it is instrumental to the deepest listening. Empathy allows you to make space for the less evolved parts of yourself to exist, space to not have all of the answers, space to learn as you grow. It was my willingness to empathize with all of myself, including my fear, that moved me forward. I allowed myself to learn as I grew.

"PARENT SANDWICH"

Sam's experience losing his father brought my own relationship with my parents into sharper focus. During the first few years of my residence at Kripalu, I had little contact with them. When I had a spare moment, which was rare, I called them from one of the pay phone booths in the hallway, and often they expressed concern for my well-being. Fortunately, there were "family visit days," times when we could leave the ashram and spend some time with relatives. Over the course of several visits to see my parents in California – separately, of course, since their divorce – they saw that I was healthy and happy.

They, however, weren't tremendously joyful – at least, not with each other. Since the divorce, they had stopped speaking with each other altogether. Thus, I became the go-between, the impartial intermediary through whom they communicated. When I visited, I always had to negotiate the drop-off point halfway between Palm Springs and Mission Viejo, usually the parking lot of a Holiday Inn or some other hotel. There, my dad "handed me off" to my mom or visa versa. The location of the drop-off was always grounds for dispute; my dad sometimes chose a point closer to him, which inevitably infuriated my mom.

185

Their animosity was so great, and their connection so completely severed, that my dad would pull into the parking lot and maneuver to a spot far away from my mom's car. They gave each other only a minimal sign of acknowledgement – a wave or occasionally a hello. I would get out of my dad's car, hug him goodbye, and then walk over to meet my mom, who stood by her car, waiting for me. Every year, as I delved deeper and deeper into processing my relationship with my parents (and let go more and more of my desire that they change), I found this display of dysfunction intolerable.

Eventually, I couldn't handle it. Soon after Sam's father passed, I flew out to CA for a visit, and my dad dropped me off in the parking lot as usual. I hugged him, but this time I didn't let go and walk away. Some impulse possessed me, and I grabbed his arm tightly. Without thinking, I started dragging him through the parking lot toward my Mom.

"Hey! What's going on?" my dad exclaimed, but I said nothing. I simply waved to my mom to walk toward us, which she did. Once she got within arms-reach of us, I pulled her toward me and hugged them both into me. I began to shake, and tears began to flow. I hadn't taken the time to feel what their divorce did to me. I knew I was sad, but I didn't realize the schism it had caused inside me, and the pain of that separation.

A kind of cellular longing existed within me to hold them both at the same time. Because of the love they had felt for each other, their cells had joined to create me. And now their cells were separated by resentment and hatred. That couldn't be what the universe intended.

So I held them tightly as I continued to shake and simply feel. Their embrace felt incredibly healing, warm, and secure. My soul was soothed, if only for a moment. I was fulfilled in my need to feel loved by them and to feel their primordial love for each other, even if that love was gone now. As we stood there embraced in a "parent sandwich" – Mom on one side, Dad on the other, me in the middle – I spontaneously poured out the following:

186

"I'm your son. You are the cells that made me with your love. You can't stay separate like this! It hurts me. I miss you and I need you to be my parents." And then I burst into tears again.

Whether it was the words I uttered, the emotion flowing underneath and through them, or just being in close proximity to each other after so long, the result was immediate and beautiful. Tears erupted from them both.

"You're right," said my mom, and my dad chimed in, "I agree." We stood in that parking lot, crying together as one, for as long as we needed.

With my head buried in his shoulder, I heard my dad say, "I love you, Butch." My mom nodded, and her voice was muffled when she added, "I love you so much. I'm sorry you've had to feel our pain."

And with that, the healing began.

I still don't know what made me do it, though I suspect that something bigger than myself was directing my actions. I just felt that, as their son, I had a right to bring back together the ones who made me, even if only for a moment.

I sensed that they so wanted to be able to love each other, but that they were too bound up with resentment to be able to feel love. After years of blame, they lived in a continuous state of denial – a condition that cut them off from each other, from life, and even from themselves. Their avoidance of pain shut them into solitude. But from that moment of connection, acceptance, and forgiveness found in a parent sandwich, an incredible healing began to happen.

It took twenty years, and some serious health crises for both of them, but eventually my mom forgave my dad for leaving her. The real reconciliation came when my sister Sherri went through a painful, messy divorce and needed support; they set aside their mutual animosities in order to counsel her. They didn't want her to go through the same resentment and denial that they had experienced when they split up.

Years later, Sherri remarried, and the wedding was held outside at a beautiful resort in southern California, high up on a plateau looking out over an endless meadow. It was July and the ceremony took place in the late afternoon, under a wide blue sky. We were surrounded by soft, deep green grass and trees, and the smell of fresh blossoming flowers wafted through the still air. As violin and cello music began, I looked back and saw my sister adorned in a gorgeous white wedding dress flanked by my mom and dad on either side. Looking at them, I had a little moment of heaven, where I felt the perfection of the universe drop into place. I saw, perhaps for the first time, my original family: the beings that lived together and raised me for 19 years and have been in one another's lives for over five decades. I saw love. I felt love. I saw unity and harmony. I saw how proud my parents were to be there to support my sister into the next phase of her life. I felt a wave of gratitude rush up within me, and every cell of my body said, "This is the family I've always wanted and needed. I have the perfect family."

> *We all have relationships, and if you can complete your relationship with your parents, you can have incredible relationships, magical relationships, miraculous relationships. Your relationship with your parents is the source of your relationship with others. Our entire function as human beings is related to how we relate to our parents. If you're afraid of your parents for whatever reason, that fear will be in the way in all of your relationships. Until you complete your relationship with your parents, your issues with your parents will affect every other relationship unconsciously.*
>
> Werner Erhard (founder of EST)[2]

If you haven't worked out your relationship with your parents, get started. Our relationship with our parents is primary; it's the one that affects every other relationship we have – throughout the rest of our lives. Once you get clear with your parents, it's like dominoes: every other relationship begins to work out. In truth, it's a perfect set-up. Because they're the strongest human bond – a tie that cannot be broken

– we are forced to face our issues with them. Why? Because you can't get rid of them. They're your family.

Time is the great tenderizer of the heart. At some point in your life, you must eventually come back to your heart, though some wait until their last breath. Only on their deathbed do some parents or their children finally see who they've been. At that moment, remorse, apologies, and forgiveness can all make an appearance, and so much healing can happen. Dying in peace is good, but how much better to live in peace? Do your best to mend your relationships while you still have time to enjoy them.

FATE & DESTINY: THE NOSE

Yoga has opened up an important distinction for me: the difference between fate and destiny. Pastor Michael Beckwith says, "Fate is what's given to you. Destiny is what you do with it."[3] My large nose was my fate, thanks to my ancestors. My father and grandfather shared my fate, and we often joked that whenever the three of us were in the same room, everyone else risked oxygen deprivation.

Throughout my childhood, I considered having my nose "fixed"; it was the cause of much pain and embarrassment. But nose jobs were not common back then, nor was there even the slightest chance that my parents would opt for one, so I just tolerated it, unhappily. It wasn't until well into my yoga studies, around age 26, that I finally accepted my nose as a beautiful beacon of my individuality. Now I claim that I was born nose first and it took 10 more years for my face to grow into it.

Fate is *what is*. It's what was given to you. If you believe, as I do, that the universe doesn't make mistakes, then fate is *what was meant to be*. Where you were born, your parents, the religion you were brought up in, the year you were born – all products of fate. But here's the deal: as an empowered being, *you get to decide what is fate and what is destiny for you.*

Yes, fate is what's given to you. I think we can all agree that being born into the physical gender of your body is fate. However, if you identify with the opposite sex or somewhere in between, then you probably consider that to be your fate too. Here's where free will comes into play. If you wish to change your nose, or any other part of your body, you have the right to change it. That's your destiny: your choice for how you want to live your life. You create your destiny every day with your thoughts, words, and actions. Yoga is the process of creating a destiny of discovery, a destiny of fulfillment and love.

Looking through an old photo album recently, I saw several vacation photos of my dad and me. Whenever we drove through scenic mountainous areas, invariably we would stop along the side of the road, stand side by side, and pose for a photo – with our heads in profile, tilted back so that our prodigious noses could blend in with the other high peaks behind us! Fate created me *and* my nose, and fate brought me to Kripalu where the guru's nose, among other factors, would persuade me to stay and change my destiny. The nose knows.

FAMILY DAYS

Eventually, my mom visited me at the ashram to take a program or two. She dove right into the yoga and was able to at least entertain the concept that her son was a yogi. She even participated in an "Inner Quest Intensive," a long weekend course specifically designed to make you face your life and relationships, and explore where you're stuck. I was the staff musician and one of the facilitators for the course, which helped set her more at ease. She had an amazing transformation of spirit.

Dad took a little longer to come around, but his new wife Celia helped him get there. When they visited, all three of us had lengthy, in-depth conversations which offered opportunities to hear one another. Many times, Sam joined us for these talks and facilitated deep understandings among us. Over time these talks built trust and gave my father and Celia more faith in the value of the life I had chosen.

So much faith, in fact, that when Dad and Celia came to visit me during a Teacher Training intensive, they told me they wanted to sit in on a session to experience my teaching.

I was wary.

"Well," I started, trying to be honest but diplomatic, "it's going to be pretty intense. We're doing something called 'rebirthing.'" I thought that word would give them pause, but they were unfazed. They just nodded, waiting for more.

"I mean, some people might cry or have a catharsis," I added. "There will be lots of... emoting."

Dad spoke up right away. "I can handle it," he said courageously in self-defense.

Okay, we'll see, I thought, but all I said was, "Great!"

That afternoon, when I looked out at almost 90 students in the room, I saw Dad and Celia off to the side, listening closely. I guided the group into the process, so intent on the experience that I forgot they were there. When we moved into the rebirthing, I remembered them, and glanced over to where they sat. They were absorbed in the process. Later, during the integration phase near the end of the experience, I saw them wrapped in each other's arms, crying.

At the end of the session, I was about to lead the group in a closing when my dad stood up. I stopped speaking into the microphone and watched, dumbfounded, as he strode purposefully over to the raised platform in the middle of the room where I stood surrounded by a sea of students. Without a word, he grabbed the mic out of my hand, cleared his throat, and spoke.

"Hello. My name is Sandy Norian and I'm Todd's dad. I may not understand or agree with the way of life my son has chosen. But I recognize a master teacher when I see one. I'm so proud of you. I love you, Butch."

I dissolved into tears. I embraced my dad, at which point he began to weep as well. Then everyone in the room broke down, too. Earlier, when I had told him there would be lots of emoting, I did not imagine *this*.

I also didn't realize how much I still longed for Dad's approval. It wasn't until that moment, when I finally had it, that I could see its shadowy presence during my entire life. Later, when Dad and I discussed this, he told me that he had approved of me from the very beginning – whether or not he understood or agreed with my choices. What a revelation, and a turning point for me! I took this as yet another sign from the universe telling me I was on the right path, in the right place, at the right time. Had I not followed my heart, I might not have had this gestalt with Dad, or the most empowering and loving relationship with my parents.

I was grateful then, and I'm grateful now, to my parents for giving me space to be myself and for loving me through all the joys and challenges of this journey. I feel so lucky. Fate gave me just what I needed to create my destiny.

THE PATHLESS PATH

When I first began practicing yoga with Bobbi and Sam in 1980, I thought yoga was only about physical postures. Then I read *How To Know God*, [4] Swami Prabhavananda and Christopher Isherwood's commentary on Patañjali's *Yoga Sūtra*. Their book expanded my vision of yoga and I began to see its implications in my way of thinking and my life. In the early years of my practice, having had no prior knowledge or training in philosophy or religion – aside from my disastrous Hebrew school performance – I thought there was only one yoga philosophy that also included Buddhism. I was so wrong.

Even after almost a decade of living and practicing at the ashram, I still hadn't learned any distinctions between types of philosophies. For a few years in a row, Kripalu hosted a "Yoga and Buddhism" conference, founded and skillfully facilitated by my dear friend and author, Stephen Cope. Even though I attended it every year, I still only heard one philosophy taught for both yoga and Buddhism. There were no discernable distinctions brought to light within that conference or taught to us by our regular teachers.

This makes sense, given Kripalu's lineage. Bapuji, the guru of Desai Desai, was a *kuṇḍalinī śaktipāta yoga master*, one who was adept at awakening the primordial, transformational energy at the base of the spine. He was a swami or renunciate and his highest goal was surrender to the life force. In so doing, he accessed deep states of meditation where his body moved spontaneously into *āsanas, prāṇāyāma*s, *kriyā*s, and mantras, all guided by *śakti*. (For more detail about Bapuji and his path, read *Pilgrim of Love*[5] by Atma Jo Ann Levitt.)

Sahaja yoga, as Bapuji practiced it, is the path of spontaneous yoga. *Sahaja* means what's natural or inborn, and this type of yoga calls for deep surrender, one that enables the natural vibrations of the universe to flow through you. When you trust this energy completely, it is believed, the energy will purify your channels, such that the creative spirit of the divine can move through you more freely. Kripalu followed this philosophy, emphasizing surrender: to the guru, and to the process of purification.

Because the method and philosophy of Kripalu were somewhat vague, the path it laid out was sometimes confusing. In terms of bringing skillful awareness to my emotions and opening energy channels in the body to become a clear vessel of universal grace, it was profound for me. But without discernment, I remained in a kind of fog around the philosophy and practices that were given. A happy fog, no doubt, but a fog nevertheless.

The big teaching at the ashram was, "Understanding is the booby prize," which meant that whether or not you understood what was happening to you, the *śakti* was being transmitted and received. We were told, "Don't let your lack of understanding get in the way of receiving the *śakti*." There is wisdom in this, for sure. A fearful, insecure, or constantly doubting mind cannot become still enough to receive the *śakti*. Yet I also became aware that de-emphasizing understanding was another way the guru could stay powerful; residents who ceded their discriminating intellect were far easier to control, especially if they were generally content – which we were.

DON'T WORRY, BE HAPPY

Guests often questioned our sincerity, accusing us of pasting on fake smiles. How could our happiness be real? I always felt my smile was authentic, because I lived in a near-constant state of appreciation for all that the ashram provided. I had few responsibilities, healthy lifestyle practices, and a community who loved me. I didn't have to cook, shop, or clean very often; my car needs were taken care of, including car maintenance; all finances, taxes, accounting, personal budgets, and insurance were handled. I didn't even have to buy stamps. On top of all that, we had guru *śakti* almost every day. I smiled a lot because I was virtually stress-free.

Yes, we worked hard and practiced *tapas*, but we had fun, too. Every September, after the ashram closed its doors to the public for a week to do much-needed *seva* projects – renovations on the building, landscaping, painting, clearing the woods, etc. – there was always "Fun Day." The whole community celebrated with games (potato sack races, a huge tug of war, mud wrestling) arts and crafts, special food, and entertainment in the evening.

One year, in keeping with a "country western" theme, at breakfast they offered foods not normally served, like ranchero-style eggs, home fries, pancakes, tofu sausages, and muffins. While we ate, a guy dressed like a cowboy sauntered into the dining room, wearing a bandana over his nose and mouth and a 10-gallon hat pulled low over his eyes. Music played – some kind of twangy country western number – as he climbed up on one of the tables and started dancing, thumbs in his belt buckle, kicking his heels. We gathered around, clapping and stomping in time to the music, encouraging the joyful display and also thinking this guy had totally lost it.

The song came to an end and the dancing cowboy took a bow, then took off his hat and bandana to reveal… the guru! Stunned momentarily, the crowd erupted in laughter and cheers. To see our guru, an Eastern Indian, dress up like a cowboy dude was just too perfect. I laughed myself silly with the rest of the residents, and I also found his gag to be completely endearing. The guru's sense of humor and his attempt to relate to us uplifted me, and I interpreted his cowboy act as a deep expression of love – as well as a message to not take life too seriously. As he once said, "Seriousness is the highest crime in the court of God." Yes.

KARMA & LĪLĀ

So far, our discussion of *karma* has been quite serious, as it's mostly been limited to the Classical understanding of the word: *karma* as action due to laws of cause and effect, or as an obstacle you need to overcome. In the Classical tradition, *karma* is seen as a kind of punishment, a negative feature of embodied life.

The spiritual journey is defined by the urgent need to get off the karmic wheel of *saṃsāra* (the cycle of birth, death, and rebirth) in order to transcend or cure the curse of *karma*. During my time at Kripalu, I thought that my whole life and spiritual journey were governed solely by the laws of *karma*. But thanks to my teacher Brooks, I now see karma in a different light.

Karma is only part of the equation. The other part, from the Tantric perspective, is *Līlā*. "Li" means play, sport, or game: to do an activity for its own sake. One way to think of *karma* is to think of it as work. Work is conditional. We do it for reasons outside itself – for money, or advancement. Play, *līlā*, is unconditional and self-fulfilling. Kids play games for no other reason than the joy of the game itself.

The warp and weft of the universe are *karma* and *līlā*, creating the fabric of consciousness that we experience as our world, our existence, and ourselves. The weft, on the horizontal axis, is *karma,* which gives you structure and pulls things together. Warp, on the vertical axis, is *līlā,* which takes away structure. *Karma* and *līlā*, reason and no reason, have always been and will always be connected. Here are some defining characteristics of *karma* and *līlā*:

Karma:

- Causality: Physics teaches us that "cause and effect" is real. Because of that, you can use *karma* to predict certain experiences and align with them more easily. When you establish clear relationships between cause and effect, you enhance certainty and the conviction of truth.

- Probability: This is more complex than causality. Since the universe is constantly changing, nature becomes less predictable. Not everything stays the same. Variables continuously fluctuate, loosening your grasp of *karma*. Bottom line? "It depends."

- Consequences: As the universe expands by unraveling itself, you live with the consequences of your experience.

Karma explains the universe... until it doesn't. That's where *līlā* comes in.

Līlā:

- Entanglement: Everything in the universe is connected just by the way you experience life, *without* any causal connection. Since consciousness connects all of us already, my experience alone changes and affects something else without the necessity of causality.

- Randomness: *Karma* tells us that everything happens within the realm of probability, no matter how complex the variables. Things don't just happen; there are always reasons. *Līlā*, on the other hand, tells us that things *do* just happen and that there need not be reasons. According to *līlā*, randomness is also part of the way the universe works.

196

- Luck: *Karma* mandates that the world is entropic (it moves from greater to lesser order) and that you live in a reality in which causal effects and consequences matter. But *līlā* shows you that you are not captive to any particular or fixed consequences. Outcomes are not certain, no matter how certain they appear. *Karma* makes the world *appear* orderly, but *līlā* demonstrates that consciousness is not required to possess order. *Līlā* is free to follow, break, ignore, or create whatever it pleases... because it can.

Brooks uses this anecdote to illustrate the *karma-līlā* phenomenon. I paraphrase:

> *When the winner of the Tour de France several years ago was asked after the race how he did it, he responded by saying that he trained hard during the season. He rested the day before the race and slept well the night before. His bike was maintained well, and he felt at the top of his game. The interviewer asked again, "Well then, how did you win the race?" The biker said that last year he was in the same position near the end of the race. Just as he commenced his sprint to the finish line he flatted. This year he had "the lucky." The interviewer said, "The what?" He said, "The lucky. I did everything I could to prepare for the win. But this year I had the lucky. Life was in my favor." Everything he did to prepare for the race was karma. But what won him the race was līlā – luck.*

In Classical Yoga, *karma* is the obstacle you need to overcome, whereas in Tantra, *karma* is the gift of embodiment. It's the unique blueprint of infrastructure – everything that has made you "you" – that creates every experience you encounter in life. Everything about you is perfect: the life you've had and are currently living, your parents, siblings, partners, talents, interests, jobs, temperament, nationality, race, and body type – they are all perfect and precisely designed to give you what you need to fulfill your life-destiny path. The universe designed your *karma* specifically for your awakening. How do you awaken? You do it by learning how to weave together both *karma* and *līlā,* in order to launch a greater freedom.

Brooks' teacher from India, Gopala Aiyar Sundaramoorthy,[6] whom he calls Appa (beloved father), says:

> *You are the point the universe was trying to make. You don't live to achieve some other reality. We are not born to transcend our humanity. How could that be? Is that how our lives are in reality? The universe has made its decision: it has become you. In this way, the universe has chosen its form and that form is you, with all of your mortal terms, with your karma, and in your experience of līlā.*

If only *karma* ruled the universe, then naturally the model of transcending or extricating ourselves from *karma* would be our best choice. But because *līlā* also exists in the world, we are no longer compelled to "solve" the "problem" of *karma*; rather, we are invited to taste another kind of reality, one that doesn't hold us captive to an unforgiving process. *Līlā* confers the possibility that we *are* free rather than that we must *become* free.

Karma is certainty; *līlā* is uncertainty. We need both to thrive. A life with too much certainty has no fun, no spontaneity, no space for grace. On the flip side, a life with too much uncertainty causes us to lose control, lose focus, and forget our purpose. As the winner of the Tour de France showed us, success lies in the balance: Work towards accomplishment and proficiency, then step back and allow creativity (*līlā*) to work its magic.

I mentioned earlier that I learned from my jazz studies that sometimes the best technicians are not always the best improvisers. Yes, they've spent years working to perfect their craft. But somewhere along the way, they get stuck in the technique itself and lose their connection to fun; they lose their *līlā*.

At Kripalu one year, my band *Shakti Fusion* was asked to play for the last night celebration of the yoga teachers' conference. I was always concerned with practicing before a performance, and this time was no different. Although it wasn't always possible to get all eight players together on a regular basis, in the weeks leading up to the concert we somehow managed to practice a lot, rehearsing some new songs and grooves (we played mostly original music).

When it came time for the concert, we were solid. As we took our places, we all noticed something special in the air, a kind of electricity. Fully open to the excitement in the room, we played our first note. Immediately, some bigger energy took over. I still don't know what happened, but everything we practiced came out perfectly. Actually, it was better than perfect. We played with more sensitivity, accuracy, and creativity than ever before. No matter how much we had rehearsed, there was no way we could have planned for the beauty that came through each of us. This was *līlā* – the play of the divine flowing through all of us for no good reason. We had the lucky!

How do we dance in a broken world? *Karma* says there's only one way: the karmic way. But *līlā*, evocative rather than declarative, suggests there isn't just one way; there are many ways. *Līlā* says that it's a creative world of empowerment, one that you improvise as your own invention. If you want to engage *līlā*, you must learn how to evoke it. What triggers *līlā*? Touch, music, love, and passion.

To live with *līlā* is to play more deeply while staying connected to source, to bring play into your work, and to make your work your play.

THE BUBBLE

At the ashram breakfast, our dancing guru in the cowboy hat was demonstrating *līlā*, though none of us understood this concept on a conscious level. We were just happy to see him play, and to play ourselves when the opportunities arose. We trained to always be happy, to always see the good. There is wisdom in this, and "looking for the good first" is still part of my practice. Yet as happy as most of us

199

residents were, the accusation of "fake smiles" was not without some truth. The bubble in which we lived, and the shadow-less teachings of the guru, did not provide space for our "less evolved" selves and emotions, such as anger, fear, or grief, so we had little experience dealing with them.

I've since learned that any emotion not fully experienced becomes a tool of self-sabotage; it is unintentionally shoved into the subconscious mind where it controls your interactions subversively – which partially explains why some people fly off the handle for no apparent reason in a moment of stress. When the stressor unconsciously reminds them of unacknowledged hurt, pain, or anger that is buried deep inside them – they explode.

Since the ashram did not provide an outlet for negative emotions, I found my own way of dealing with them. My purchasing department *seva* buddies Balaram, Bharat, and Indra, plus a few others, took to running in the woods as their main form of aerobic exercise. I began running with them, and although it took me a while to build up to their speed and endurance, I fell in love with it. I started running more frequently in the woods, keeping a steady, quick pace as I traversed hills and uneven terrain. Most times I moved with freedom and lightness, jumping over logs and creeks, stepping on stones to cross larger streams, and scaling rocky ledges effortlessly. The sense of oneness with nature and my environment was so great that I often felt embodied by the distinct presence of a deer or gazelle. On those days, I wasn't just running; I *was* the run.

Other times, on days when I felt angry or frustrated – at something someone said, or a regulation at the ashram I didn't like – I used the woods to channel my emotions. I don't recommend doing this in public or where other joggers or hikers can hear you, but when I knew I was alone, I carried a stick and pretended it was a spear, which somehow activated my inner primal savage self. I brought my awareness back to the incident that triggered my anger, and allowed the emotion to build inside, higher and higher, until the bitterness boiled up and over. Then I gave that emotion a voice by formulating just the right "release mantra," a string of words in English that usually incorporated some choice profanity, the raunchier the better.

Rather than relying on Nature's willingness to compost unwanted emotion and energy, I asked permission from the trees to express my anger. Thus sanctioned, I took off down the trail, hollering the mantra while intermittently hitting the stick against trees and rocks until the "spear" was obliterated, then picking up another stick and continuing on my smashing, yelling spree. Without hurting anyone, including myself, I created my own private temper tantrum release ritual – and it always worked.

I believe it was the synergistic combination of fresh mountain air, the "weapon" in my hand, unfettered vulgarity, and the sheer unabashed thrashing of stick on tree that released whatever I was feeling, leaving me completely free and at peace, ready to rejoin my blissful-seeming brothers and sisters.

Kripalu's emphasis on experience rather than knowledge was a path of the heart, full of great teachings and practices. It was primarily an experiential, devotional, service-oriented, guru-focused, and heart-based form of yoga. It was not a path of strict mental discipline or a highly intellectual path of yoga; scholarship was not emphasized. Kripalu offered a beautiful approach that was perfect for me for a time. It wasn't until years later, when I began studying with Tantric scholars, that I was able to understand why I eventually hungered for more. The following teaching put it into perspective for me.

JÑĀNA & *VIJÑĀNA*

Jñāna is the Sanskrit word for knowledge, which comes from the root *jñā*, to know. *Jñā* is also cognate to the Greek word gnosis, or knowledge. *Vijñāna* means applied knowledge, the kind of understanding that comes from direct experience with the world around you. *Jñāna* and *Vijñāna*, knowledge and experience, go hand in hand. They are like two sides of a coin.

201

Have you ever tried to explain to someone what something tastes like? You might describe a mango, for example, as tasting like an exotic tropical fruit, or like a strawberry crossed with a cantaloupe but with a kind of lemony, twangy flavor. You can say it's juicy and slippery and dissolves in your mouth, but no matter how eloquent and detailed the description, until you actually eat a mango, you won't really know what it tastes like. The experience itself gives you knowledge.

Similarly, when you experience something personally, you gain knowledge by being aware and observant of outside teachings while having the experience. For example, to learn how to cross-country ski, once you've been skiing and your body has *felt* the actions of gliding and pushing, breathing and reaching, it's even more helpful to hear your instructor talk about technique – where to put your weight, perhaps, or how it's similar to ice skating. But without going out on the trails, you'll never learn how to ski. That practical experience, combined with your teacher's technique tips, creates true learning. Advancement becomes circular: the more you practice, the more adept you become at the technique; the more you study the technique, the better you become at doing it.

When applied to spiritual practices, according to Tantric teachings, both are equally important. When you have a deep spiritual experience, knowledge about that experience helps integrate it fully. Knowing why the experience happened, how to contain it, what possible meaning it has, and which point of view about it is supportive – deepens the experience. It might even allow you to repeat the experience if desired or understand precautions or signs that the experience is unbalanced or unsupportive.

If all you have is knowledge of a practice, without the experience of it, your knowledge remains void of potency. It's all in your head. You need a combination of both *jñāna* and *vijñāna*, head and heart, for integration to happen and for true spiritual growth to take place.

202

METHOD FOLLOWS PHILOSOPHY

At Kripalu, experience was everything, including the way *āsanas* were taught and practiced. This made sense. Given the Kripalu philosophy of surrender, the essence of the Kripalu practice was simply to offer yourself to divine spirit and allow that energy to guide you. Your breath and body sensations created any and all impulses to move, change postures, adjust, or even stop movement completely.

To inspire us in our own practice, the guru often demonstrated "the posture flow, or meditation in motion," which was a mesmerizing flow of meditative postures guided from *prāṇa,* the life force energy. Sitting in a circle surrounding him, we watched the guru enter into this meditative flow. His eyes were closed; as his breath deepened and his poses began flowing, we could sense a distinct and palpable *śakti* energy. I'll never forget the feeling of divine bliss I experienced every time I observed his flow.

While I was in the Programs Department, the other directors of teacher training and I always offered a similar meditation in motion while the students observed. But unlike the guru, we always invited the students to enter into their own meditative flow after watching ours. I have vivid memories of the beauty of the *śakti* moving through each student in his or her own unique flow of poses. Each pose, each movement, and each breath was offered in devotion to the life force energy within us all.

What's wonderful about allowing your spirit to guide your *āsanas* – aside from the obvious inherent benefit of divine connection – is that it teaches you to be sensitive to your body and to back off if there's pain. But it doesn't help to reshape poor postural habits, strengthen weak muscles in the body, or release tight ones. Unless you have the expert coaching of a qualified teacher, you are left to your own devices and may reinforce habits that could ultimately cause injury. There are principles of alignment and good physical therapy, along with medical science, that assist the body in healing optimally. Ideally, in the spirit of *jñāna* and *vijñāna* working together toward true wisdom, the combination of meditative body-awareness and good physical alignment is the start of a balanced *āsana* practice.

For years, I embraced the Kripalu methodology, letting *prāṇa* flow through my body while I was in a deep meditative state. As a moving meditation, it was magnificent. However, I never learned how to take care of my joints or why my knees kept hurting. My original yoga teachers, Sam and Bobbi, had impressed upon me the importance of good alignment, and I did the best I could to incorporate what they taught me with what I was told at the ashram. Without their continued guidance, however, I found the level of alignment difficult to sustain.

As I grew more trusted as a teacher trainer for Kripalu yoga, I was invited to do yoga with the guru as part of his yoga team. During those sessions, I tried to give him alignment instructions. He agreed that alignment was important, and he tried to do it, but he was very loose-jointed, and could hardly engage his muscles at all. I was surprised by his lack of proprioception (knowing where your body is in space). It's as if he wasn't really in his body. He couldn't maintain awareness of the alignment, like keeping his feet parallel in *tadāsana* (mountain pose) or maintaining the alignment of the back foot in a standing pose. I concluded that it was too hard for him to change such ingrained physical patterns – especially because his *āsana* practices, like any practices associated with a particular lineage, aligned with his forebears' worldview and philosophy.

THE MORE THINGS STAY THE SAME...

By 1990, I had lived at Kripalu as a full-time resident for seven years. I couldn't quite put my finger on it, but I did recognize that there was a kind of boredom that had set in, brought on by the predictability of my daily life. I had gotten comfortable with the routine, and now each day slid into the next with not much to distinguish them: practice, teach, rinse, repeat. I was forced to ask myself: was I too comfortable?

When is discomfort really a comfort and when is comfort really a discomfort?

In the practice of *āsana,* almost everyone feels the discomfort of *Ekapāda Rajakapotāsana Prep Pose* (One-legged King Pigeon Prep Pose) since most people's hips are tight. But that discomfort is a good thing; it lets you know you are moving toward growth. A good yoga teacher will encourage you to breathe into the discomfort while also monitoring it, so that the discomfort doesn't become an injury. Discomfort is a comfort, then, when you do something good for your health that is difficult in the beginning.

Conversely, an example of a comfort that is actually a discomfort is sitting on the sofa all day long, binge-watching television while eating ice cream, day after day. Sitting on the sofa is comfortable, but eventually it will turn into real, health-threatening discomfort if not balanced with getting outside and exercising.

The trick is being able to discern whether a discomfort (or comfort) is real. Sometimes we fool ourselves into thinking that the intense pain we feel is good for us, even when it's not. Or we tell ourselves that we "deserve" to do nothing, even when we've reached an unhealthy point of stagnation. In yoga, over time, you get to know your body well enough that you can recognize what level of discomfort is okay to hold and breathe into, and what level means it's time to shift out of it.

This fine line is where I found myself after seven years of ashram living. What initially had felt like a challenge – *I will purify myself to become eternal* – started to feel more and more like an endless slog toward an impossible goal. I couldn't tell if my restlessness was just a difficult time that I needed to push through, to get to the other side, or if I needed something different – though what that looked like I had no idea.

Although for years I had loved the predictability and safety of the ashram's emphasis on surrender, the mindless obedience no longer served me. I was chafing under its tight leash, internally questioning its validity and its presuppositions – even questioning the guru himself. Was turning away from the world really a higher, "better" way? Why were we here on earth if our purpose was to transcend it? Is it truly healthy to shame away desires and hold unattainable goals that keep me feeling permanently deficient?

I started to feel an inner itch to expand my freedom and make my own choices. I found myself longing for a healthy balance between the natural world and a rich, full spiritual practice. I wanted to make my whole life – including my relationships, my body and its natural drives and cycles, and my intellect – the spiritual practice. As comfortable as I was with the community and the routine of Kripalu, I recognized that the seeker within me had never focused on comfort; it had always pursued challenge. So I created a different sort of challenge for myself.

NOTES

[1] Quote is attributed to Dr. Douglas Brooks. Original source is unknown.

[2] Quote is attributed to Werner Erhard. Original source is unknown.

[3] From "The Answer is You" with Michael Beckwith. Aired on PBS September 2009. https://www.youtube.com/watch?v=UEkE77itolM Accessed May 5, 2021.

[4] Swami Prabhavananda and Christopher Isherwood Translation & Commentary. *How to Know God: The Yoga Aphorisms of Patanjali*. Hollywood, CA: Vedanta Society. 1981. Print

[5] Levitt, Atma Jo Sara. *Pilgrim of Love: The Life and Teachings of Swami Kripalu*. Rhinebeck, New York. Monkfish. 2004. Print.

[6] Gopala Aiyar Sundaramoorthy (Appa) is Douglas Brooks' teacher with whom he studied India. For more information, Dr. Brooks suggests this blog: https://rajanaka.blogspot.com/2010/03/dust-into-gold.html?fbclid=IwAR3ovReGJxQynsAgsutnxS0YMEHjSBo2qTSjhAt-UC1NyonN4EWq59Q7CUk. Accessed 8 May 2020.

CHAPTER TEN

A Different Path

Humanity is transforming. The time is shifting and changing. Within that, our individual life is being called to grow in unprecedented ways, in ways that powerfully draw forth aspects and dimensions of our life that had previously remained unexpressed!

Paul E. Muller-Ortega[1]

BEEF BOYS: FROM PATAÑJALI TO SCHWARZENEGGER

There had always been a few brothers at the ashram dedicated to weight training and sports. Bharat was one of them. Kripalu had a weight room gym, and during any break in the day you were almost guaranteed to find Bharat there. He loved to work out and it showed; he was buff and built like a tank, which was partially why his spontaneous musical outbursts in the purchasing office were so hilarious. Bharat taught me how to run in the woods and cross-country ski; he also bought my first road bike for me, pulled it out of the box, and put it together for me.

Another brother who taught me a lot about sports was Haridas (Steve Bankert). A skilled builder, carpenter, electrician, and plumber, he perfected whatever he set out to do – including all sports. Not only was he an enthusiast, he was an experienced trainer, as well. He taught me how to cross country skate-ski, reintroduced me to downhill skiing (which I had done since age five, but had given up after high school), and got me interested in Triathlon racing. He was an excellent teacher and a role model for me; I looked up to him and honored him.

One year at Fun Day, Haridas, Bharat, and a few other athletes set up a short-course triathlon race for the residents. It was so much fun, they offered the race every Fun Day for several years in a row. It caught on ashram-wide, even with residents who weren't necessarily serious about the sport. I got involved and found that I loved it. Pushing the envelope of pain in the physical body to expand endurance gave me enthusiasm for a new challenge.

I took training seriously, working out five days a week, joining the local U.S. Masters swim team, even mapping out elaborate weight-lifting sequences and reps according to Arnold Schwarzenegger's book, *Arnold's Bodybuilding For Men.*[2] I was committed, right down to taking supplements to build muscle mass. After paying so much attention to the spiritual, I loved the feeling of being fully embodied.

208

The more intensely I worked out, the more I craved heavier foods and more protein. We all did. Our muscles were begging for it. Other than my brief stint years ago of eating ashram-sanctioned fish, I (and the rest of the group) followed the strict prohibition against eating animal protein. We were desperate to have some, but we all knew the risks of being seen eating meat at the local pub: reprimands and suspension from privileges at best, expulsion from the ashram at worst. We were all conditioned to fear breaking the rules; shame is a powerful manipulator.

One of the teachings from the guru was, "Company is stronger than will power." How true that turned out to be! His words were supposed to help us practice the teachings of yoga diligently and keep us on the straight and narrow, but instead, they gave us the courage to flout the rules, together. We formed a covert club called "The Beef Boys," and swore ourselves to secrecy.

Our mission was simple: to eat meat and not get caught. We bought organic, grass-fed beef burgers at a local (but not too local) grocery store, then smuggled the contraband into one of the condominium apartments at Fox Hollow, a second property Kripalu had purchased a few years prior for long-term residents and married couples. There, we cooked the burgers in someone's mini-kitchen, a long way from the noses in the main building. My first bite into the burger was bliss; every cell of my being melted and expanded into a resounding "yes!" and I felt my body absorb the nourishment like the dry desert earth absorbs rain. I came alive.

When we returned to the campus, sated and happy, no one was the wiser. Mission accomplished! Our secret club continued to meet once or twice a month, strengthened by our increased protein consumption *and* our successful evasion of the rules. In fact, we were so emboldened that we occasionally had a beer with our burgers – another taboo. But with the support of the group, I felt safe. The guru was right: when there are two or more gathered, the energy is stronger. Years later, Brooks reminded me, "You become the company you keep. So keep good company."

GO BIFF, GO!

Fortified by the increasing fervor of our regular workouts, the Beef Boys lined up for the Fun Day race primed and ready to compete. Several of us buzzed our hair to take seconds off our time, though my short hair meant more than that. I believed the act of cutting my hair was symbolic; it was not quite the shaved head of a renunciate, but it was still a way to honor my deeper commitment to a life of spirit and service. With my well-carved muscles and buzzed hair, I was given a new nickname by Bharat. "Biff" was born. All I could think of was "Butch," my father's nickname for me. As I look back now, I can see the strands of grace interwoven throughout my journey from child to adult. It makes me wonder and appreciate how grace works, how it threads its way through life, waiting for you to recognize it.

We took off from the starting line, and I took an early lead. Cheerleaders, a.k.a. enthusiastic sisters offering their support, lined the route, waving flags and holding big banners that read, "Go Biff Go! We love you!" This outward expression of support by the women towards a brother was unprecedented. I felt like a hero, particularly since I had a crush on several of the sisters cheering me on. Somehow sports opened a door for me that I had closed off in order to remain on the renunciate path: the ability to give and receive love. I don't remember if I won the race or not – a marked difference from the 2nd grade loss that shattered my self-worth. I only remember feeling uplifted and supported.

After that, I *really* threw myself into working out. My muscles grew bigger and bigger, and my Body Mass Index shrank to about 5.9% fat, which is super-low. My resting heart rate slowed to a low of 32 beats per minute, which matched Lance Armstrong's and that of other elite athletes. I enjoyed both the appearance of my growing physique and the feeling of being strong and steady. From all of the yoga stretching I continued to do during this workout phase, I maintained flexibility even with the added strength. I felt healthier, stronger, clearer, more vital, and more confident.

The Beef Boys competed in triathlons in our region, each race giving me the opportunity to focus on the yoga of endurance. I learned how to maximize my heart rate during both intense sprints and distances, while still staying connected to my breath and body. I loved the feeling of pushing myself to the limit and then expanding beyond it while staying relaxed, using the tools of yogic breathing and mind over matter. It was exciting, challenging, and invigorating. I built myself up eventually to do a half Iron Man – a race with 1.5-mile swim, 56-mile bike, and a 13-mile run – and performed well, but soon I started to feel strain in my foot, then my knee. I backed off racing but continued the workouts. I was clearly still training, but for what?

THE FALSE MOTIVATOR

It may have been the buildup of strength, the ingestion of more concentrated protein, an increase in my testosterone level, or all three, but I felt myself changing. Dictums of ashram life that I had unquestioningly followed, I now saw in a different light – the most fundamental of which was my desire to be a monk. Even though I thought of myself as a nonjudgmental person, I began judging the monks-in-training as nerdy, introverted, and socially awkward. What I saw as the "jet setters" – the ones doing workouts – were always laughing, taking things lightly, and enjoying life. I felt I resonated more with them than with the serious, dour-looking monks. I told myself that even though the Beef Boys had a wild side and weren't afraid to express it, they were still pious, which was true. They were also way more fun. I dropped out of the monk study group and continued my workouts.

Though I didn't see it at the time, my judgment of the monks and their path fit into a pattern that I now recognize: making someone or something *wrong* as motivation to make a change. I've since learned that I don't have to denigrate the old in order for the new to rise up, but at that stage of my life, I had to label the renunciate path as "bad," to ease my shift into something new. I was in the midst of a huge transition that involved a change of desires, life patterns, and goals. I was unsure of what was ahead of me.

Freedom is not always comfortable, because true freedom means the freedom to make mistakes. It requires a kind of fearlessness, a faith in the unknown and a deep trust in your own heart to guide you. I call it "being between trapeze bars." When you let go of the bar that got you there and reach for the bar ahead of you, there's a moment where you are between bars – free – with nothing but the sheer momentum of your heart's desire to carry you through the space of not knowing.

All I knew then was that I needed some reason to let go of the bar that got me there. It wasn't enough to simply give myself permission to change, based on my own evolution, because I hadn't yet learned how to respect myself in times of uncertainty or insecurity. Instead, judgment took the place of permission. I realize judgment was a false motivator, a strategy I used to give myself permission to follow my heart. It was effective, but ultimately unnecessary and kept my world small. It wasn't until much later that I was able to turn away from the bar, any bar, with gratitude, and embrace both paths as honorable and beautiful without the need to make anything or anyone wrong, including myself.

CONTACT

For nine years, as part of my commitment to renunciation, I had devotedly practiced celibacy at Kripalu. I had believed in its intention, on focusing on one's spiritual path rather than engaging in romantic entanglements. The guru taught that if you followed the path of celibacy, you eventually stopped seeking love and validation through external relationships and instead, learned how to love yourself. Fair enough. But unless you're willing and able to do the deep inner work of healing your "core wounded identities" from childhood, celibacy alone may not help you stop seeking love outside yourself.

Nine years into it, though I had made real progress in my quest for self-love and acceptance, I realized that I had reached an impasse. No longer did I feel that celibacy was healthy for me; rather, I found it to be against the natural rhythms of bodily life and impossible to sustain. I also suspected that it was reinforcing the childhood shame I still had around my sexuality. By avoiding sex in the name of spirituality, I had a good excuse to avoid facing my issues around it, which was ultimately delaying my inner growth in this area. I believed now that there was a different road for me: relationship as the path to consciousness.

My renewed interest in women was sparked, in part, by participating in triathlon races and a running marathon outside the ashram. This was a whole new world – of men and women competing side-by-side in tight-fitting athletic gear. During the races, I caught myself occasionally getting distracted by all of the beautiful women around me before I would snap out of it and return to the race. These races spurred me to take a daring first step: I no longer avoided making eye contact with the sisters at the ashram. It seemed that after nine years of sublimation, I was supremely ready to explore that world.

THE THREE-STAGE CONSCIOUS RELATIONSHIP COURSE

I was not the only one seeking something different. Kripalu had recently created a "Conscious Relationship" study course for residents like me who were beginning to move away from the renunciate path and use relationship as a mode of transformation. The program had three stages, each of which consisted of approximately six months of group meetings once a week with a married mentor, various books to read, journal exercises and contemplations, and sharing circles.

The mentor I was given happened to be one of my triathlon workout buddies, Taponidhi (Joel Feldman, or Tap for short), whom I knew fairly well from our training together. In stage one, we discussed the general concept of relationship; in stage two, we explored the concept of relationship with the opposite sex.

As an aside: this was the mid-1980s, when there wasn't much public acknowledgement of the LGBTQ community in the mainstream. In the ashram, there was none, as the guru did not have any experience of alternative sexual orientation and identities. I do remember a few gay brothers in the community who always smiled when at the beginning of each new work-study semester, roommates were assigned. Same-sex roommates were mandatory!

As part of our stage two readings, we studied John Gray's books, including *Men Are From Mars, Women Are From Venus*. Although by today's standards these books could be considered sexist in some ways, at the time they fascinated me. I saw myself in the descriptions of men who would rather fix problems than simply listen and hold space for the feelings and emotions of others. I also identified with the stereotypical descriptions of males as being action and results oriented, and being more comfortable processing feelings by themselves. It was certainly true for me that I wanted to "go to my cave" to sort things out. Reading these characteristics helped me understand what I believed to be my male needs and drives, and it fostered more self-acceptance.

Stage three was the "considering marriage" stage, which was another six months of exploring marriage with a participant of the opposite sex to whom you were attracted, who had also completed stage two. This was a much deeper level of dialogue exercises and self-discovery contemplations with coaching and supervision from the mentor. If by the end of this stage the two of you wanted to get married, you could marry in the ashram and receive more mentoring and support.

BREAKING THE RULES... AGAIN

After completion of stage one and two, I carefully evaluated all of the women in the stage two program and found myself attracted to exactly none of them. *Great. Now what?*

There was a marathon in Albany coming up soon, so during a 12-mile practice run with Joel, I began peppering him with questions:

"How does it work after stage two? What should I do if I'm not attracted to anyone in the group? Is there a contingency plan?"

I fired question after question at him during the run. Up and down hills, past cornfields and dense wooded green, he answered each one patiently as the miles stacked up and we both breathed harder and harder. Nearing the end of the run, huffing up a steep incline, I threw out my last one:

"Basically, how do you fall in love here at the ashram?"

I'm not sure, but I think he was getting annoyed with me. He glanced over and then exclaimed, a little loudly, "You'll just have to lose control."

"What does that mean?"

"Just lose control."

Does that mean what I think it means? We chugged along, huffing and puffing, and then I just had to clarify: "You mean I need to step outside the rules?"

He stopped abruptly, so I did too, and he bent over and put his hands on his knees. Chest heaving, he said breathlessly, "Well. What do you think?"

We looked at each other for a long moment, still breathing hard, and I said nothing in response. Then we started running again, an understanding having passed between us. I was ecstatic. I flew through the last mile with ease, high on adrenaline-fueled liberation. "Break the rules" was what I had heard, and my inner rebel was ready to GO. It was ready to stage a revolt.

NOTES

---

[1] Quote from Paul Muller-Ortega's website: Blue Throat Yoga at: https://bluethroatyoga.com. Accessed 11 May 2020.

[2] Schwarzenegger, Arnold. *Arnold's Bodybuilding For Men.* New York: Simon & Schuster. Reprint ed. 2012. Print.

CHAPTER ELEVEN

Grace Notes

The minute I heard my first love story,
I started looking for you, not knowing
how blind that was.
Lovers don't finally meet somewhere.
They're in each other all along.

Rumi

FALLING IN LOVE, AN ACT OF GRACE

I am a planner. I like being organized and in control, and I especially like staging things to happen. Often when I'm at home in the winter and want to light my wood stove, I won't light it all in one step. Earlier in the day I'll empty out the ashes from the last fire, sweep up around the foot of the stove, and occasionally clean the glass on the front door. Later, I might split some kindling out back. When I'm ready to have the fire, I'll set it up and strike the match. I derive almost as much joy from the preparation as I do from the actual event.

No matter how much you can plan for some things, falling in love is beyond planning. It's an act of grace. And what is grace? I've used the term throughout this book, but what, exactly, is it? I never thought about the notion of grace before I came to yoga. My idea of grace was what my friend's family said before dinner; I don't remember the word grace ever being used in our home. We had words like blessing, miracle, mitzvah, or celebration. Grace is the state of the universe. Grace is what makes everything happen the way it's happening.

It's grace that breathes you, gets you up in the morning, and directs your thoughts and actions. It's grace that is behind your reading this book at this time. I believe that grace is always present whether you believe in it or not, but if you want to access grace in your life, then you have to believe. I don't mean having blind faith in grace; I mean experiencing it. When you *experience* grace, you will know it. Then there's no need to believe or not.

> *The winds of grace are always blowing, but you have*
> *to raise the sail.*
> ~Swami RamaKrishna[1]

I've learned that to believe in grace, I need to surrender the part of myself that constantly seeks evidence and proof. A subtle but persistent fear that acts like a finely woven fishing net pulled tightly around my heart, the incessant need for proof constricts my heart and keeps me closed to grace. When I surrender and relax deeply, as I've done many times through yoga, I come back to my heart where I feel the presence of love again. For me, this is how I know grace is undeniably real, because I've experienced it.

With grace there is unlimited acceptance, compassion, and forgiveness. Grace is like the sun, always shining, ready to warm you when you turn around to receive its rays. Grace is like the presence of a loving and nurturing mother, one who loves you so much that she allows you to go against nature. She allows you to misalign, hurt yourself, and even hurt others. She is always there to catch you when you fall, but she can't prevent *karma* from happening.

Trusting grace is trusting the natural perfection and timing of the unfolding of everything and everyone. It's the experience of *śraddhā*. Grace reveals the perfection of the universe and your life within the universal orchestration of everything that brought you to where you are now, to this moment of awareness.

GRACE & TANTRA

In Tantra, grace includes all of the above, but takes it further. Grace is described as the revelatory power of the universe that reveals your true nature.

As I've mentioned before, the whole universe exists within you in seed form. Then what is the power that reveals that universe? Grace. Like the potential of the oak tree in the acorn, grace opens you to your potential, to your divine potential – that is, to your greatness. As Brooks says, "Greatness is knowing that you are greater than yourself." Grace brings insight and clarity to who you are in the larger scheme of life.

Grace's fundamental attribute is revelation. Grace reveals that all things which appear separate, are intrinsically connected to a bigger energy. You are grace with a brain, grace with eyes: a two-way mirror that allows the universe to see itself through you as you see it. Grace is the power behind the hide and seek game of the universe, the energy that ensures that everything happens in exactly the way it does.

218

But in my zeal to fall in love, I didn't know about any of that.

LISTS

The next day I laid out a strategy to figure out whom I wanted to marry. I made a list of all of the eligible women – "eligible" meaning they were currently in the relationships course or had finished stage two. Then I came up with a list of all the qualities I wanted in a partner, an extensive list that included: having a yoga and meditation practice; being athletic (enjoying running, biking, swimming, and skiing); intelligence; heart-centered kindness; and a high level of integrity. When I cross-referenced the eligible list with those qualities, just like the first time around, I found I wasn't attracted to any of them.

Undaunted, I made another list. This time, I wrote down the names of all of the *in*eligible candidates that I was attracted to. These were women not in the relationships course or women who hadn't made it all the way through stage two. It was a small list, but once I determined which ones possessed at least some of the requisite qualities, the list shrank even more. Only five women were left. With those five names in my head, I set out to "find love."

In retrospect, it must have looked like I was shopping for a toaster oven. I watched each one from a distance, taking note of their interactions with others and pondering their compatibility and spiritual values. I tried to strike up casual conversations with them, to notice how they responded and how I felt. I even went so far as to interview their coordinators.

I asked one of my friends, recently married at the ashram, to take a walk with me to talk about relationship and about one of his workers. He and I took off along a path on the Kripalu grounds, and after exchanging a few pleasantries, I launched into my due diligence:

"I'm thinking of getting into a relationship and I'm interested in one of your staff, Saraswati. Can you tell me about her and what she's like to coordinate?"

He erupted into a full belly laugh. My face flushed. *Was I saying something wrong?*

"What?" I asked.

"She'll give you a run for your money."

"What do you mean by that?"

"She's feisty, outgoing, and an independent thinker," he said, and then added, "And she's argumentative."

I was undeterred. In fact, this revelation made me more intrigued. I liked the fact that she wasn't a pushover and that she spoke up for what she needed.

The more "research" I did, the more Saraswati, or Sara for short, kept rising to the top of my list. The other four didn't seem right for me. Either they whined a lot, or their temperament was right but they weren't athletic and didn't like yoga, or I just wasn't interested in them energetically. Sara, on the other hand, loved doing yoga and always stayed in the back of the yoga room after morning practice, all covered up with a blanket taking a few extra minutes in *śavāsana*. She was beautiful, with her bright blue eyes and her long, curly mane, and she was as quick to offer her opinion as she was to smile.

She was all that, and more. But she was ineligible! She was only in stage one of the relationship course, and I would be breaking the rules if I asked her to be in relationship with me before she finished stage two. *Bummer.* After a nanosecond of contemplation, I reminded myself of my conversation with Joel. *Well, I guess I just need to lose control and break the rules!*

I decided it was time to work outside of the system.

GRACE ON THE CUSHION

Sara was Reservations Manager and I was one of the managers of the Programs Department. Every week, we met with all of the other managers at Kripalu, in a meeting room that was always set up with the exact number of cushions on the floor to accommodate all 35 of us.

On the day before the meeting, my heart thumping wildly, I called her. She picked up right away.

"Hello, this is Sara."

Hoping my voice sounded casual, I cleared my throat and then spoke: "Hi! Sara, this is Manu."

"Oh, hi Manu, how are you." *She remembers me!*

"Good! Really good!" I said, probably a bit too enthusiastically. "You?"

"Yep. Me too. What can I do for you?"

I took a deep breath. "Um, could you meet with me tomorrow after the manager's meeting?" Then I threw in, as nonchalantly as possible, "In my office?"

"Sure," she said warmly, "What's the meeting about?"

We had been working together on an extra-curricular project to invite a friend of Sara's, a professional triathlete trainer, to do a workshop for the residents and program teachers on fitness. Even though I did have some details to discuss with her regarding setting up the workshop, I also needed an excuse to get her into my office so we could be alone.

"It's about… two things. One is… I'd like to discuss setting up the workshop with your friend, and the other, uh, is, uh… something personal." I knew that sounded weird, but I wanted to be honest and I didn't know how else to put it.

221

Her energy instantly shifted.

"Of course," she said, all the warmth gone. "That's fine. I'll... I'll see you tomorrow, then."

"Great. Thanks."

We hung up, and I was totally wrung out. I hardly slept that night.

By the time I showed up for the meeting the next day, I was in quite a state. I took my shoes off in the hallway, entered the room, and sat down on one of the cushions in the circle. As each spot filled, I grew more and more anxious. *Where is she?* The meeting was about to start. Every cushion was taken except the one immediately to my left. I looked around the circle once again: no Sara. All of my nervous excitement drained away, leaving me hollow and forlorn. *Maybe she got sick or something...*

The meetings always began with a meditation and the chanting of "om." I closed my eyes to meditate and sighed heavily, resigning myself to her absence. Just then, I heard a soft click as the door to the room opened. Someone sat down right beside me. I squinted through my eyelids just enough to see...Sara! My heart began to race, so much so that it felt like it was beating in my head. I thought my cranium would burst.

The wall that I had created between me and all women, to honor my strict practice of *brahmacarya*, came crashing down around my ears, leaving me free and open to all of the energy of that moment. I heard and felt her breath. I sensed a deep connection between us. It felt as though a gentle, warm stream of light flowed directly from my heart to hers and from hers back to mine.

After the beginning "om," I went brain-dead. I have no idea what the meeting was about. I couldn't concentrate. My mind was filled with one thought only: *I am going to ask Sara to be in relationship with me after this meeting.* The sentence looped again and again as I stared out at the participants like a zombie, nodding when others nodded, watching their

222

mouths form words that never reached my ears. After what was probably close to an hour, the meeting ended, and I got up from my cushion and turned to face Sara.

"So, my office. It's down the hall…" I reminded her.

"Right."

I headed there; she followed me. In that small space was a desk and two comfortable, white padded Ikea chairs I had set up to face each other. We sat down and I briefly brought up the shared business we had in arranging the fitness workshop. It didn't take long.

There was a pause, and then the words just spilled out of me: "I have something personal I want to share with you, Sara. I'm in the relationship program and was wondering… if you'd like to explore relationship with me?"

She didn't say yes or no. She didn't even smile. Her face instantly turned a bright shade of crimson. I found out later that Sara had come to this meeting assuming she had done something wrong, and that she had been bracing herself for a reprimand. My question, a complete 180° turnaround from her expectations, threw her into a state of shock, and her face radiated with the impact.

But all I saw was her silence and what looked to me like embarrassment. I didn't know what to do or say. *How can I make this better somehow?* I searched my mind for options, but nothing seemed right. I had just come to the conclusion that perhaps I should leave the room to give her more space, when finally, she spoke.

"What do you mean by 'exploring relationship'?"

I wanted to say something profound, something that would make it seem like I had all the answers. But I didn't. I had no clue how to navigate a relationship outside the system, so I gave her the most honest answer I had.

"Well, actually, I don't know. We'll just have to make it up as we go."

Sara told me later that my answer sealed the deal for her, but at that moment, she sure didn't let on. She smiled, and her face lost some of its redness, but she didn't say a word.

Then she asked,

"Are you exploring with anyone else?"

"No," I said, relieved that she was asking questions rather than turning on her heel and leaving.

After that, she got up out of the chair and started walking toward the door. I stopped her.

"Is that a yes?"

She looked at me with sparkling eyes. "Yes!" she said, and I swooned.

How could it have been orchestrated that of the 35 managers, only Sara was late for the meeting and there was only one cushion available – next to me? How could it be that the one woman I vetted and had my heart set on, said "yes" to exploring relationship with me? I'm not particularly superstitious, but the day I asked her was November 11, '92, which can be seen as 11-11-11 (9 + 2). Looking back, I choose to believe that these "coincidences" meant our relationship was divinely inspired.

LOVE IS THE DRUG

No matter how extensively I had interviewed Sara's coordinators and friends, no matter how much "research" I had done to determine who Sara was, I couldn't begin to know her magnificence. Of course, she was so much greater than any data I could collect! The real miracle, however, was the perfection and ease of love we felt for each other. Our connection was so strong that we postponed telling anyone that we were together, because we knew that our mentors would put restrictions on our ability to see each other – something we couldn't endure in our current state of excitement.

So, for the next few weeks, Sara and I carried on a completely clandestine love affair, making those weeks one of the most joyful and passionate periods of my life. Drunk on that unique falling-in-love magic, I found I was happy all the time, like bodysurfing on a rolling wave of grace. My step had a spring in it, and I experienced grace and gratitude everywhere. In Sara's eyes, I was enough – and this "enoughness" opened a new sense of self-love and self-acceptance within me. I was easier on myself, less critical. In fact, I liked myself more than ever before. I was living my dream.

During this time, my heart burst open regularly whenever I thought about Sara, particularly when music was involved. Brimming with energy, I increased my workout schedule and rode my trainer bike for hours in my little nine-by-nine personal room, blasting Pat Metheny in my headphones. Many times I was completely overcome with the beauty of the music, the flow of energy streaming through me, the unfulfilled longing to be with (or at least see) Sara, and the sheer excitement of being in love. Tears of joy flowed down my cheeks. I had to keep a box of tissues within arm's reach near my bike to wipe away the tears – and keep me from falling off my bike.

In a flurry of ardor-fueled creativity, I composed and arranged a collection of love songs and chants, including one called "Crystal Blue Eyes" specifically for Sara. I asked Rupani, one of the former lead singers of *Shakti Fusion*, to sing some of the vocals on the recording. I blew my cover by telling her it was a surprise Christmas gift for Sara, but Rupani, having gone through her own secretive marriage process a few years earlier, promised not to say a word. Ranjan, the guitar player for *Shakti Fusion*, offered his off-campus studio to record the music, and after some emotional sessions, I finished it in time to present it to Sara over the holidays.

Ranjan invited me to Pat Metheny's concert, the debut of his 1992 album, "Secret Story." This music has a gorgeously uplifting tone of love and inspiration. As I watched how Pat poured his heart and soul into the music, I felt a stirring deep inside. Pat's performance, combined with my already love-soaked heart, made me exquisitely sensitive to the music. I not only heard the music, I became it.

Halfway through the concert, I became so absorbed in the experience of the music that my heart cracked open even more. I didn't think it could open more, but it did. I felt the rocket of *śakti* explode from the base of my spine, up through my spine, and out through the top of my head. It took over my entire body. It's a good thing that the music was loud because I couldn't hold back my tears. This wasn't just a covert cry; this was a massive *kuṇḍalinī* experience. I began to wail. My spine was on fire. I sweated profusely, and the sobs poured out of me uncontrollably. From the outside, I must have looked grief-stricken, but all I felt was total joy and grace.

Then the music itself stepped inside me and talked to me. I don't know any other way to describe it! It was as if the notes being played were words that offered wisdom. Insight streamed through my mind and heart. I remembered my earlier experience at the ashram, when the guru *śakti* soared through me. This rush was almost as intense, but this time I felt like I was the experience *and* the witness of the experience, simultaneously. This time I had no fear at all. In fact, I enjoyed the release, the feeling of totally letting go. It felt as though my body was integrating, on a cellular level, my change-of-life trajectory, moving from renunciation to relationship. After about 20 minutes of this intensity, the experience shifted. I seemed to glide and soar on the music like an eagle soaring on the updraft of the wind rising up over a cliff, completely free. I believe the concert was a transformative event, one that allowed my body to catch up with my heart. To this day, I love listening to "Secret Story" because it brings me back to that experience of love and grace.

BEHIND CLOSED DOORS

Saraswati, as the manager of reservations, had the overview of all of the guest stays throughout the entire building, an angle that proved to be highly advantageous to our burgeoning relationship. Living within a closely-knit community of 350 brothers and sisters, with an additional 250 guests, made being alone nearly impossible. We had to get clever about ways to find privacy. It helped that I had my own office which we regularly employed after hours, cautiously. But the real help came from Sara's privileged vantage point.

She would look at the reservations chart, and from the rooms that were vacant but hadn't yet been cleaned, she would choose a room at the end of a hallway, out of the flow of the public traffic. Then she would visit the room to make sure the guests were truly gone. Having worked on household duty before her current job, she knew where the supplies were kept and could easily strip the bed of the old sheets, put new ones on, and generally make the room nice again. Then she would call me on my office phone from a hall phone. I'll never forget my excitement when I heard her soft murmur on the other end of the phone: "Hey, it's me. Go to room 330. Love you. Bye." Click.

Once, she spoke so softly I couldn't quite hear the room number. Since she was using the hall payphone, I couldn't call her back. I paced in my office, staring at the phone as though I could will it to ring. Twenty minutes later, it did. Cautiously, I answered.

"Hello?"

"You're still in your office?" she demanded in a whisper.

"I couldn't hear you! I knew it was you, but I didn't get the number."

"Oh!" She giggled quietly, and then said, "332."

"Three, three, two," I repeated carefully. "Yes?"

"Yes," she said, laughing again under her breath, "that's it. See you soon."

Another time, I brought candles to create romantic mood lighting. The mood was broken, however, by the smell of smoke – I turned my head to see the lampshade ablaze. Springing out of bed, I grabbed a towel, soaked it, and smothered the flame before the smoke caused the fire alarm to go off. Such a close call made us nervous; what if we had been found out? But the "forbidden love" we shared was all the more exciting, too; it heightened our feelings for each other.

SEX ACCORDING TO TANTRA

When you taste the rasa of life, you drink from a well that is never dry.

~Ramachandra Gandhi[2]

Finally! The subchapter you thought you'd never see in this book. As I touched on briefly in the Introduction, sex is only a tiny portion of the vast philosophical teachings of Tantra – but that's not how popular culture views it. The media distort sex's significance to Tantra, so much so that sex and Tantra are almost always conflated. Since there are literally thousands of guides to "Tantric sex," I'll be brief.

Nondual Śaiva-Śākta Tantra and quantum physics agree that there's one universal energy that is everywhere and infuses everything, seen and unseen. Tantra sees that energy as a sacred life force, and sex as an extension or manifestation of that life force. Therefore, sex is considered sacred. When practiced with the right partner, at the right time, in a way that's loving, respectful, and empathic, sex is simply part of the one energy that nourishes everything.

In the circle of nine *rasas* discussed in Chapter 5, *śṛṅgāra* is the experience of *eros* and passion. Eros is a part of life, a part of being human and fully alive, yet many people are not able to access it, often due to shameful or traumatic experiences around sex during their childhood. Eros is also difficult or impossible to experience when you

228

are unhealthy or suffering from an illness. But when you have good health, a sound mind, and a loving partner, sex can be something you cherish your entire lifetime.

The *rasas* immediately to the left and right of any *rasa* in the *Rasa Maṇḍala* (Appendix C) are related positively to that *rasa* and can enhance it. Conversely, the *rasas* located opposite, or near opposite, negatively influence the *rasa*. To the left of *śṛṅgāra* is *śanta*, peace. You need to have peace in order to have *eros*. As in sex, it's difficult if not impossible to have an enjoyable experience of sex while experiencing high anxiety, fear, or disgust – which happen to be the *rasas* across from *śṛṅgāra* on the circle. The *rasa* to the right of *śṛṅgāra* is *hāsya*, lightheartedness or humor, which also supports eros as it fosters an environment that is carefree, nonjudgmental, and open – all of which are conducive to connected, passionate sex.

As in other spiritual traditions, Tantric sex is not goal-oriented toward orgasm, but rather embraces all aspects of the experience equally. It places a high value on connection, harmony, communication, feelings, emotions, tenderness, and the capacity to give and receive energy between the partners. Sex, practiced in this way, is a restorative, rejuvenating, and fulfilling experience that brings deep inner healing.

I've not done extensive research in this area, other than attending Diana and Michael Richardson's couples' retreat in Switzerland, which I found beautifully helpful. I'm aware there are more esoteric practices that open the couple up to in-depth meditative experiences of absorption that can trigger deep states of consciousness and further healing. Those practices are, as you surely know by now, not within the scope of this book.

However, before we finish with this topic, let's take another look at the word "*saṃsāra*." Remember that Classical Yoga defines *saṃsāra* as being held back by the flow? In that paradigm, being human means having to participate in the endless cycle of reincarnation – a state considered to be "imprisonment." Tantra defines the word differently, based on its radically distinct worldview.

Tantra defines *samsāra* as being held by the flow, nourished by the flow, supported by the essence of spirit. *"Sam"* here is defined as a *boundary that protects, supports, and nourishes*, rather than a *boundary that binds* you. In the Tantra, *samsāra* doesn't block *nirvana*; it *is nirvana*.

The material world, just as it is, is the expression of spirit. The fulfillment of your spiritual life occurs in the world and exists not separate from it, but within it. You need to embrace the material world in order to "get to" the spiritual world. Instead of life being a problem to solve, life is a gift meant to be savored. All of it, including sex. This is the notion again of freedom *through* the body, not freedom *from* the body. The body is not seen as the epitome of *samsāra* (a desire machine), but as a temple of the divine, a conduit, a vessel of spiritual energy worthy of your love and care. When you honor your body, when you honor the body of your partner, you are honoring the divine.

Furthermore, *Samsāra* in the Tantric view, *as it relates to* reincarnation and *karma,* is that souls tend to reincarnate; that's just what they do. So stop trying to buck the current of nature. Stop trying to be perfect enough so that you don't ever have to come back. Stop trying to sublimate your natural human desires. Is it possible to pursue a fully embodied spiritual life for no reason at all other than it brings you joy and uplifts others? Yes!

In Tantra, we see ourselves as the crystallization of divinity's wish to experience itself. We are like wrapped gifts, concealed intentionally. Life then is the process of unwrapping this gift slowly over time, savoring each moment as we come to know ourselves more deeply. Birth is no longer a penance to endure; we choose birth to experience our divine nature. Instead of trying to get out of life, the Tantrika dives more deeply into it.

COMING CLEAN

After our few weeks of courtship in total secrecy, guilt crept in. If we wanted this relationship to culminate in an ashram-sanctioned marriage, we knew we had to make it legitimate. We agreed to tell "the authorities": my mentor Tap, and his wife Jyoti (Katrina Feldman), who was Sara's relationship mentor. We met with them both in Tap's office.

"So, Sara and I are… well, we're together, sort of," I stammered, looking at Sara. Her crystal blue eyes were locked on mine. *What will our mentors say?* "I mean, we love each other." Sara's eyes shone. "And we want to be together, but we're not sure how to do that…" I trailed off, hoping someone else would pick up the ball.

Tap and Jyoti both smiled in a way that made Sara and me think they already knew, and Tap said, "We'll have to work things out." I breathed a little easier.

"How wonderful," said Jyoti, "that you've found each other. I can feel a beautiful energy between you."

Sara and I beamed.

"Reminds me of us when we first got together," said Tap. "Crazy happy."

We all basked in that truth for a moment. Then the gears shifted.

"I'm not going to lie to you both," he said. "It's not easy to be in relationship and still fit within the ashram."

"That's for sure," Jyoti agreed.

There was a pause. *Of course. They are fundamentally incompatible.* Tap cleared his throat.

"So… if marriage is the plan–" he started, then stopped himself. "Is marriage the plan?"

Sara and I had never actually said that word yet. Our eyes met and we both blushed. "We're not…" I said, and Sara chimed in. "We haven't…" she faltered. "We're just… exploring." Then she reached over and took my hand. I squeezed it.

"That's okay," said Tap. "Just so you know… you don't have to stay in the ashram. You can leave the ashram and get married whenever you want. If you want to stay, though, then you have to wait until Sara is in stage three…"

Jyoti turned to Sara. "Which is when? How many months of stage two do you have left?"

"Six or seven," said Sara.

"So like Taponidhi said, either you leave the ashram, or have six months of separation… and then go public."

We had talked about this earlier. Sara looked at me for confirmation, then said resolutely, "We don't want to leave the ashram."

They both nodded, and Jyoti said, "I'm so glad!"

"Okay," Tap said, leaning forward and resting his palms on his thighs, "then here's what the next six months will look like. You're going to have to keep your relationship completely secret. Completely. No public conversations, no eye contact. If you talk on the phone, you have to make absolutely sure you're alone. The last six weeks will be *total* separation, no communication whatsoever. Then if you're still in love and you want to get married, you can be married at the ashram and have our blessing. Is that all clear?"

We nodded vigorously.

"And I'm sure I don't have to say this, but… no sex."

We nodded again, this time slightly less vigorously.

Jyoti jumped in. "I know it's hard to be totally discreet, but you know how this works. We want to maintain the peace among those in the relationship program and to keep it fair."

"At least Sara's not in stage one," Tap joked, "If you'd gone public then, there would have been riots." We all chuckled. Riots at Kripalu. Ha!

232

Before we left, they reminded us that the individual mentoring would continue and they gave us the study materials for stage three: a booklet of exercises, reflection questions, and deep conversations we were supposed to have to get to know each other better, explore what our preferences were, and clearly define who we were as individuals. We thanked them, and left the office, wistfully letting go of each other's hands and heading in separate directions.

BASHERT

I was invited to my cousin's wedding in Philadelphia. Sara and I still weren't public with our relationship yet; in fact, I hadn't even told my parents yet. During the ceremony, I paid particular attention to the vows, fantasizing about whether or not I would one day marry Sara. I became absorbed in the whole ritual, almost as though I was the one getting married! I felt everything so deeply and cried several times; the love was so palpable and real.

Before the celebration dinner started, my wonderful Aunt Eileen, whom I hadn't seen in years, waltzed over to me. Elegantly attired, silver hair magnificently in place, and smelling like a dozen fully opened roses, Aunt Eileen was one of the kindest and most beautiful relatives I had. In her late 60's, she was also probably the most open-minded and non-judgmental of my choice to live in a yoga ashram, even though she didn't fully understand what it meant, always asking me about my life, yoga, and relationships.

"Toddy! Hello, my dear, how *are* you?" she gushed, hugging me close and then pulling my face close to her smooth powdered one so that she could smooch my cheek.
"Aunt Eileen! I'm great, how are you?" I responded, as she thumbed away the bright red lipstick on my cheek.

Instead of answering, she took hold of both my shoulders, furrowed her perfectly shaped eyebrows, and gazed at me directly. Then her face changed, from inquisitive doubt to enlightened revelation, as though someone had just imparted the hidden secret to the universe.

"Toddy, you're in love!"

"*What?*"

"You're in love, aren't you," she said. She looked perfectly smug. I was dumbfounded.

"How did you know?"

"I can see it in your face. I can feel it in your energy," she said, matter-of-factly, leaning in to whisper, "And not only that, Toddy, your newfound love is bashert."

Bashert? What is that? I knew it was a Yiddish word, but I didn't know what it meant. Aunt Eileen saw my confusion and explained, "Bashert means destiny or 'meant to be.' It means that your love is perfect and it's what's supposed to happen."

I blushed, and she knew she was right. No more words were necessary; we just laughed and embraced. Surrounded by the freshness of her fragrance, I felt blessed by my aunt. She somehow was able to get inside me and speak from my own heart as a reflection of the universe outside of me saying, "Yep. This is meant to be. You are in love."

NOTES

[1] Quote is attributed to Swami Ramakṛiṣhṇa; original source is unknown.

[2] Ramachandra Gandhi, grandson of Mohandas Gandhi (more commonly known as Mahatma Gandhi) was an Indian philosopher. Read a short bio and information about his books at https://penguin.co.in/author/ramachandra-gandhi-ed-raghuramaraju/. Accessed 14 May 2020.

CHAPTER TWELVE

Union

God and man/woman, the Divine and human
Are like a boy and a girl at play in love.
They run and hide from each other
So, they can delight in chasing, glimpsing,
And eventually capturing each other.

Sri Aurobindo[1]

As you know by now, Tantra teaches that everything in material reality is composed of spirit. Everything: light and dark, good and bad. Patañjali's yoga, on the other hand, advocates moving away from the world of dark *prakṛti* toward the higher vibratory state of light: *puruṣa*. *Puruṣa* is seen as better than *prakṛti*.

This is one of the greatest distinctions between Tantra and Classical Yoga. In Tantra, *prakṛti* is seen as the agent, the embodiment of *puruṣa*. *Prakṛti* is not less than or inferior to *puruṣa*, but rather the outward expression of the spirit. Could this fit with the scientific belief that everything in the physical universe is composed of one energy? I think so. If I go out on a limb and say that energy *is* spirit, and if you join me out on that limb, then quantum physics confirms that everything is made of spirit, since even those things that seem solid are pulsing in and out of manifestation simultaneously.

Therefore, *prakṛti* is made of *puruṣa*. Within the finite exists the infinite. They are simultaneously one and the same, in each other, while also being separate. Take ocean waves as an example.

A wave on the ocean has both the individual characteristics of the wave and those of the ocean as a whole. The wave is in the ocean as much as the ocean is in the wave; both aspects exist simultaneously and are inseparable. Yet as human "waves," most of the time we act as though we are "ocean-less" – separate from the vastness of our being, separate from the energy that created us.

It's crazy, isn't it? That as humans we can forget that we are connected to the infinite, oceanic, blissful energy of the universe? But this is how we behave, especially when we feel threatened, in danger, or just stressed out. We can get nasty and disrespectful, or judge others and ourselves in a harsh manner. This forgetfulness is part of our nature. It's that cosmic game of hide and seek I keep talking about, the universe hiding itself from itself in order to delight in finding itself.

In the same way, we all pulsate with the light of the universal even though we are individuals. In 2012, when asked what is the most astounding fact of the universe, astrophysicist Neil deGrasse Tyson[2] answered:

> *When I look up at the night sky and I know that yes we are a part of this universe, we are in this universe, but perhaps more important than both of those facts is that the universe is in us. When I reflect on that fact, I look up – many people feel small 'cause they're small and the universe is big, but I feel big because my atoms came from those stars. There's a level of connectivity.*

The singular light that shines forth from the Absolute passes through a prism of sorts and refracts into the individual, varied colors of the rainbow. From the one comes the many; from the universe comes the multiverse; from the one song comes the many melodies that orchestrate themselves into the world we experience.

The wave is in the ocean is in the wave. They are one, and they are separate. That is true union.

INDIA

Back at Kripalu, during the six months of secretly "exploring relationship" with Sara, I also spent a considerable amount of time with the guru. I was his *āsana* coach, as well as one of his personal masseurs, workout buddies, and swim buddies. One night, after *satsaṅga*, I walked him back to his house. Seemingly out of nowhere, he stopped, turned to me, and said, "You feel like my very own son, my spiritual son." I felt myself melt. I was devoted to him, and in complete alignment with his yogic vision of creating a peaceful world. So when I was invited to travel with him and a few other teachers to India, I felt I had to go.

Newly in love and at the height of my triathlon training, I didn't want to leave. But as one of the lead teachers, I had no choice; our team of teachers was going to trade training sessions with the staff of Bapuji's

Indian ashram, which was run by his disciple Rajarshi Muni. The trip was set: two and a half weeks in January of 1993, in Kayavarohan of Gujarat Province, in the middle of India. Before we left, I told my close friend, fellow yogi, and co-teacher Devanand, whom I called Devas for short, about Sara. I couldn't keep the secret to myself.

Travel to India was a mini-hell. It took us 40 hours to get there, with an overnight in Mumbai (Bombay at that time), and 12-hour layovers in hot, chaotic train stations. Once we finally arrived at the ashram, Devas and I settled into our simple digs: concrete floors and walls, futon mattresses on the floor. The accommodations and the yoga room formed a square around an open courtyard of trees and plants, and all of the windows opened into the courtyard, giving the rooms a spacious, airy feel. I flopped down on the futon, fell asleep immediately, and woke up refreshed.

One of the first things we did was go on a shopping spree to get the right clothes for the ashram. The whole group of us, brothers and sisters, took a cab to the nearby town of Baroda where there were several shops and open markets filled with wonderful items – everything from fresh food to clothing to gifts of all kinds.

A few us, Devas included, went into a sari shop. The tables and shelves were piled high with the most beautiful fabrics, with jewel-toned colors and rich textures. There were all kinds of saris for women and dhotis for men. Tears sprang to my eyes. All I could think of was Sara, how much I loved her, missed her, and hated being separate from her. Devas caught a glimpse of me wiping away my tears. He knew.

"How about a sari for her?" he whispered in a low voice so no one else could hear. I perked up.

"Yes…" I said, "but which one? It's overwhelming."

"Let's look."

Not only was Devas an artist and architect by trade, with a great sense of color and style, but he also knew Sara and what colors would complement her. Soon he had helped me choose a beautiful turquoise, green, red, and orange sari for Sara, along with several other handbags, purses, and a few shawls for meditation.

"This is perfect, Devas," I said, gratefully. I was feeling better. Clearly, buying presents for Sara at least partially satisfied my longing to be with her.

The rest of the party looked at me strangely. "Wow, Todd. Who are you buying all this for?" I swallowed hard and blurted out the first thing that came to my mind.

"This? Oh, this is for my cousins back home. They love Indian clothing."

Devas caught my eye and winked.

CULTURE SHOCK

The town of Kayavarohan, where the ashram was located, was a traditional small rural Indian town. People there had very little in terms of material wealth, but they seemed so happy with their families, friends, customs, and religion. I'll never forget the beauty of their eyes as they smiled. No matter where we went, the townspeople always invited us in for tea and offered food. They were a most generous people. Caucasians were fairly uncommon in such rural areas, so we were treated almost like celebrities whenever we ventured into town.

When we had left Massachusetts for this journey, I was right in the middle of triathlon training. I was desperate to work out, having been packed into planes and trains for the past few days, so I donned my fluorescent short shorts, tank top, sleek Oakley sunglasses, and bright yellow Walkman with headphones to head out for a 10-mile run. I knew I looked nothing like your average ashram disciple, but I was so in love that I didn't care that I didn't fit in. *This is who I am.*

I took off down the dusty path, listening to high-energy workout music in my headphones, glorying in my breath and the perspiration that was beginning to form. Before long, children ran up alongside me, hailing me to stop and let them try on my sunglasses or listen to my Walkman. I couldn't ignore them, or their astonished parents who didn't quite know what to make of me. They kept asking, "Why are you running? Slow down. Where are you going? Come and have tea." No doubt I was causing some serious culture shock, though I was also experiencing plenty of my own. Running was helping me cope.

I continued for miles through the dry and dusty countryside, running past villages and fields, where workers carried water or were laboring in the intense heat. I loved feeling the scorching hot sun, feeling sweat pour off me, and feeling a union with Sara, even in this faraway land. My heart pounded with love, and tears of joy mingled with the sweat on my face. I returned to the ashram exhausted and exhilarated, and chalked this run up as one of the best of my life.

GAUZE & PROTRACTORS

In the weeks that followed, the Indian teachers at the ashram trained us in the various techniques they used – many of them traditional to Indian ashrams but totally foreign to us Westerners. Our first class was based on the *Ṣaṭkarma*s (or *Ṣaṭkriyās*) described in the *Haṭha Yoga Pradīpikā*, the first scripture written about the practice of Haṭha Yoga in 1350 CE. These are six (*ṣat*) groupings of cleansing exercises or actions (*karmas*) employed to purify the body: *neti* (much like dental flossing the nostrils – cleansing your nostrils and sinuses first with a smooth rubber catheter and then using twine – ouch!); *dhauti* (swallowing three to five feet of cotton gauze to cleanse your stomach and esophagus); *naulī* (undulations of the abdominal viscera); *basti* (a natural enema to empty and cleanse the colon); *kapālabhāti* (powerful breath exercises meant to accomplish "skull polishing"); and *trāṭak* (as mentioned earlier, an open-eye meditation that purifies your vision and creates a one-pointed focus of the mind).

We didn't do all of them, thank God; we skipped *basti*. I found the most challenging to be *dhauti*, by far. The Indian teachers gave us each a long piece of cotton gauze and instructed us to swallow it, little by little. The gauze would cleanse the entire esophagus down into the stomach, they told us. Devas and I stared at our lengths of gauze, then back at the teachers, incredulous. *Five feet of gauze? Really?*

Shaking our heads, we fed the end of the gauze into our mouths, intentionally relaxing our gag reflexes as best we could. We both laughed as we sputtered and coughed and joked about our miserable failed attempts. The teachers didn't seem to find any humor at all in the process or in our goofy behavior, and they gave almost no instruction. They were adamant: just swallow it. Obediently, but irreverently, we kept trying.

Eventually, we started to make some progress; we were getting the hang of this. Inch after inch disappeared into our gullets. As Devas swallowed his third foot, I walked around behind him and mimed pulling the end out of his rear, as if the gauze passed all the way through. Even with gauze sticking out of our mouths, we laughed so hard tears came to our eyes. Just then I looked across the courtyard and saw our guru receiving a private lesson on how to swallow the gauze. Much as he tried, he couldn't get even an inch down. He just kept gagging and choking. I held back my laughter because I didn't want to appear disrespectful, but it was hilarious to see him struggling so much while the rest of us were able to swallow several feet of gauze.

Once we had all of the gauze down (yes, all five feet!) it was time to pull it back up. There is a real technique to this; the moment you tense up or resist the gauze, it gets stuck. Yet the sensation of it coming up is also decidedly uncomfortable. Unfortunately, my gauze got stuck and I couldn't get it to release. I panicked, imagining walking around for the rest of my life with gauze protruding from my mouth, or digesting the gauze and sending it out the other end – the real-life version of my earlier pantomime.

Mildly hysterical, I called the Indian instructor over. Calmly and directly, he gave my gauze a firm yank. Somehow, that did the trick, and it quickly disgorged itself, coiling itself up on the ground in front of me in a slippery, slimy tangle. The amount of yellow and green gook that came out with the gauze was disgusting, to say the least. A perfect example of the *rasa bībhatsa*! For the next 24 hours after that experience, all of us were incredibly emotional and sensitive. We agreed: *Śatkarma* brings up a lot more than gook.

Another "highlight" of the Indian training came toward the end of our time there: the measurement of our *āsanas* with a giant protractor. As part of a flexibility test we were expected to pass, they measured us to the centimeter. To our complete humiliation, no one in our group passed the *āsana* segment of their training. Whether the Indian body is naturally more flexible, or the lifestyle encourages more pliancy, their standards were simply not attainable for us. Even those of us who had practiced yoga for decades were not even close. It seemed as though you had to be either double-jointed or in Cirque du Soleil to make the grade.

By this time, I was utterly done with the training. I realized I had checked out mentally before it even began. I just wanted to be with Sara. Whether I was swallowing gauze, flossing my nostrils with twine, or jogging through the countryside of rural India in inappropriate attire, I was lovesick and wanted to go home. I was tired of feeling like I wasn't flexible enough, or pure enough, or something enough. Enough was enough.

After what seemed like months, I finally made it back to the States and to Kripalu. Seeing Sara, hugging her after our time apart, was *pūrṇa* – the feeling of utter fullness and completion. Sara welcomed me home with a little sadness; apparently, she thought for sure that my trip to India would convince me to become a renunciate. Quite the contrary! I felt more like a prince or an explorer returning from the Far East, bringing back riches and gifts for his beloved. I couldn't wait to lavish them all on her and dispel any notion of my waning interest. Covertly, we had a beautiful re-union and reconfirmed our love for each other.

242

SEPARATION

Sara was raised Irish Catholic, but she didn't resonate with her family's religion. When she and I first got together, Sara told her mother all about me, including that I was Jewish. Her concerned response was, "Is he as Jewish as you are Catholic?" When Sara replied in the affirmative, that was the end of her concern. Her mom simply said, "Oh, okay."

In March, after a snow storm had laid down a few inches of fresh snow, Sara decided it was time for me to meet her parents, who at that time lived in Boston. Driving was not an issue; the roads were clear, and the ashram had a fleet of about 60 cars that we could sign out for work-related or personal reasons, like a family visit. Her parents agreed to meet us for lunch at the Marriott Hotel in Springfield, MA. The only problem remaining: getting into a car together...without being seen.

Then it hit me. The Berkshire County Day Care Center was the property next door to Kripalu, and its parking lot was about a half mile away. I knew the trail that led to the parking lot; I had run on it just months before. It was a short, windy, 10-minute sprint including a killer downhill. I could cross-country ski there!

At the appointed time, Sara checked out a car while I donned a backpack with a change of clothes and laced up my cross-country skis, fingers fumbling in excited anticipation. I set off into the woods, wildly in love, feeling like I was on a secret mission to escape the enemy and steal off with my beloved into the sunset. I flew down the hill, skiing fast and recklessly, checking my watch every few minutes to ensure an on-time rendezvous with Sara. Sure enough, I glided to a stop, panting, just as she pulled into the day care parking lot. I threw my skis into the back of the car, hopped in, and slunk down in my seat while she drove off. It was the perfect getaway.

Over the next few months, we refined our technique of disappearing together on the sly, culminating in the ultimate challenge: in July, Sara was invited to go camping with some college friends in Vermont, and we wanted to go together. But we would need a van, bikes, and camping gear. Could we pull it off?

Early in the morning, Sara checked out the van and left it unlocked in the parking lot. A few hours later, I came and loaded my bike in the back. A few hours after that, Sara loaded *her* bike into the back of the van. We heard later that our friend had seen the whole thing but didn't put two and two together; he just thought it was odd. He was a good friend, so he wouldn't have ratted on us, but there were others who were growing suspicious.

When I signed out the camping gear, the manager questioned me, "Why do you need a four-person tent if you are going by yourself?" *Gulp*. My mind seized on my recent successful dodge in India, and I found myself saying, "I'm going camping with my cousins. My three cousins." That seemed to satisfy her. "Oh, okay." she said. "No problem." *Thank* God *for my cousins.* I took the tent and hustled out of there.

With our gear and bags loaded into the van, we were all set. Later that afternoon, I "went for a jog" near Tanglewood, which was diagonally across the street from Kripalu. Once I got to the designated place where I could hide behind some trees, I saw Sara swing by in the van. She slowed to a stop near me and I looked both ways, then jumped in.

I ducked down until we were completely out of town, just as we had on our way to meet her parents. We were completely paranoid that someone driving from the ashram might see us. Once the coast was clear, we high-fived. We were getting good at this! Our vacation in Sara's friend's backyard was exquisite. I hate to say it, but we got away with heaps. I never lied so much in the name of love!

As hard as it was, the "keep the relationship secret" dictum was nothing compared to the challenge our mentors laid down for us next. In order for us to get married at the ashram and receive support and continued mentoring, we had to practice abstinence and total separation for six weeks. Total. No talking – public or private – and no eye contact.

Nothing. Then, after six weeks, if we still wanted to get married, they would set a date for us.

We bravely took up the challenge. In the first few days, there were a few instances when passing each other in the hallway was unavoidable. I was walking down the hall one morning when I felt a little buzz of vibration in my heart. Like a bat using echolocation, I sensed her presence before I saw her. When I looked up, I saw the distinctive outline of her hair at the far end of the hall and my pulse took off. I kept walking and so did she.

As we neared each other, I could feel the *śakti* flowing between us, like a "tractor beam" from Star Trek pulling us closer and closer. It was palpable. We couldn't make eye contact, so we both looked down. It was all I could do to not look up, to not catch a glimpse of her crystal blue eyes. My skin tingled all over and I broke out into a sweat. I remember hoping that no one walked anywhere near the invisible line between us; I was convinced that any interloper would fry from the shocking current of our magnetism.

As if by telepathy, I slowed down just as she slowed down. Everything was in slow motion. As we approached each other, I felt her energy body: warm, soothing, nurturing, and so comforting. It was as though she was moving through me, not around me. At the moment of passing each other, our energy bodies merged – if only for a nanosecond.

Eyes glued to the carpet, I felt a wave of love like a rip tide in the ocean, causing heat and bliss to ripple through my body. Time stood still. The imprint of her energetic gift seemed to say to me, "I miss you, too. But we're doing this for a bigger reason. I'm committed to playing this out. Even though I can't look at you, I am with you." Once past, barely keeping my balance, I picked up my pace in a daze, blessed by her love and savoring the connection for as long as I could.

That turned out to be only a few days, at best. The first week fast became a torture. *How am I going to do this? This will surely rip my heart out with grief.* Rather than endure this self-imposed separation, I decided to try to spend as many days as possible away from the ashram.

I devised a scheme, within the Kripalu guidelines, that lumped all of my vacation days, family visit days, and continuing education days together. In doing so, I managed to eke out almost six weeks of being away. I thought this would make it easier for me, and for us. It did, but barely. In those days before I left, Sara and I had to refrain from any contact whatsoever. It was excruciating! Living and working in the same building – while keeping separate and silent about our growing love and attraction for each other – proved to be one of the most difficult (and, I'll admit, romantic) experiences of my life.

THE STILL OF THE NIGHT

I did a 10-day *Vipassana* (insight meditation) retreat, which was marginally successful in temporarily taking my mind off Sara, and then I returned to the ashram for one day before I headed off again to visit family in California. My plan was to stay overnight at Kripalu, do laundry, repack, and fly out the next day. But my longing to be with Sara was so strong that I brainstormed a crazy idea to surprise her.

At Kripalu during those years, the men and women ate on different sides of the dining room and slept on opposite sides of the building, in the east and west wings, to discourage socializing. In the first few days of my relationship with Sara, I realized that she and I shared the exact same room but on opposite sides of the building: #329 on the brothers' side, and #379 on the sisters'. When I looked out my window I could almost see her, but there were some tree branches and vines growing around her window that partially obscured the view. Once we knew where each other's windows were, we made several attempts to communicate or signal to each other, but the distance between the windows was too great.

On that night before leaving for California, I waited until after 10pm, when most of the residents went to sleep. I looked out my window and saw that her light was off. I crept down the stairs, all the way to the basement, then snuck over to the women's side of the building. Slowly and carefully, I made my way up the sisters' stairway to the third floor, hearing only the sound of my heart thumping in my chest. Nobody saw me. *So far so good.*

Sara's room was directly across from the door to the stairwell, so I knew I only needed to become invisible for about four feet: the distance from the stairwell door jamb to the door of her room. Fortunately for me, there were no locks on any doors in the ashram. I craned my head out into the hallway and looked both ways. The halls were quiet. *Now is my moment.* I slipped quickly into the hallway and darted straight into Sara's room, closing the door softly behind me.

Sara sat up suddenly as I whispered, "It's me!" As startled and scared as she was, fortunately for both of us, she didn't scream. I dove onto her bed and crawled inside the covers with her. We snuggled up close together, body to body, and hugged. It was the most secure, warm, loving feeling. We both trembled, crying tears of joy in each other's arms. I had been a little unsure that she felt about me the way I felt about her, but at that moment, I knew that she did. Aunt Eileen was right: we were meant to be together.

This day marked the halfway point in our six weeks of silence. We talked quietly about the whole experience and how each of us was handling it. We agreed that this six-week silence was only strengthening our conviction and love for each other. I set my alarm for 3:30 a.m. so I could easily escape without being seen by early morning yoga practitioners, and then we spent the next four hours whispering, laughing, and sharing the joy of each other's company. I was beginning to trust that our connection, our union, was deeper than being in each other's physical presence.

When we said our goodbyes, we knew it was for another three weeks. I felt such a sweet sadness in my heart, but I knew that our love could withstand a few more weeks apart.

Before the sun came up, I was back in my room without getting caught.

247

Although I knew that seeing Sara during our six-week "hiatus" was cheating, I felt completely aligned with my heart. I sat on the plane to California and mused: *I'm getting good at breaking the rules, not getting caught, and being respectful of the process – all at the same time.* I knew that during this trip we wouldn't have any contact, but when I returned, we would have "served our time apart" and could get back together, in public.

On the west coast, I stayed with my mom first. We took a drive to have lunch at the lake near her house, and I talked non-stop about the experience of love and how my heart was opening more and more. Like most lovestruck puppies, I was obsessed with any songs about falling in love, and I recited a few song lyrics to her – which then led into a lengthy conversation about what love actually *is*. By the time I told her I had met Sara, she was fairly clued in that her son was completely smitten.

When I returned from California in August of 1993, the long period of secrecy finally came to an end. I found I was even more in love with Sara than before I left. I still find it ironic that the most passionate love affair we had was the year and a half of secrecy at the ashram.

As we were now officially in stage three, the "considering marriage" program, our mentors allowed us to disclose our relationship to the community. An ashram-wide announcement was made at the next *satsaṅga,* to enthusiastic applause. All of the married couples offered their support, letting us know we could always talk with them if issues came up. But not everyone was thrilled; there was a bittersweet feeling in the air that was real.

Marriage announcements in the ashram essentially proclaimed that there were two fewer people in the relationship lottery, and in Sara's and my case, our union evidently caused quite a bit of unhappiness. I was surprised to hear several of my male friends tell me how heartbroken they were that Sara was no longer available as a potential marriage partner. Sara got similar feedback from a group of sisters vying for my attention. All the more reason to abide by the ashram rule: now that we were official, we could be seen together in public, as long as there was no public display of affection.

FEBRUARY 6, 1994

Our wedding date was set for us. Ashram weddings were ceremonial and Hindu-inspired, though only intended for the marrying couple, the guru, and the other married couples at the ashram, who were invited to renew their vows. Single residents were prohibited from attending a wedding, to reduce the likelihood of their being lured away from the renunciate path.

Parents were not invited. This did not go over well with my dad when I called him.

"Not invited? That's ridiculous. You're my only son. I'm coming," he stated.

"Dad, it's February in New England. It's not Palm Springs."

"I'll bring a jacket."

I laid it all out for him: "You'll have to sit on the floor. *And* wear all white. *And* the ceremony starts at 6:00am."

He persisted. "Look, Butch, I'm your father. I want to celebrate you in your tradition. I can take it," he said, and then added quietly, "Please let us come."

I took his request to heart. "I'll see what I can do."

By some stroke of grace, I got permission for him and his wife to attend. Of course, when my mom found out that Dad and Celia were coming, she insisted on coming, too. It didn't take long for word to spread to Sara's parents. "If Todd's parents are coming, then we're coming too. There's no two ways about it," they said to Sara. Somehow, they all showed up at Kripalu, along with Sara's sisters as well.

The night before the wedding, the ashram held a *homa hotra* (burning of dried cow dung and ghee), a ceremony intended to give all of the single people an opportunity to say goodbye and bless us, thus honoring the transition from being single to getting married. It was guided by Sam, my friend and most admired mentor, who had recently taken his renunciate vows. The room was filled with electricity: the fire blazed; musicians chanted kirtan with wild drumming; everyone whirled and danced.

When the time came to do the *hotra*, Sam, with his shaved head and saffron robe, invited my father to help officiate. Dad lit up. He came forward eagerly, picked up the piece of cow dung (considered sacred in India), brushed ghee onto it, and happily offered it to the fire while mantras were chanted. He was like a little kid. Sara and I sat by the fire and silently received the blessings from each of our single friends, thanking them through our eyes, and then witnessed the blessing they offered to the fire as well. We were deeply moved.

All the while, the drums pounded and the chants rang out, loud and energizing. Throughout the wild beauty of the ceremony, I saw my father's focus. He showed true respect for the tradition, so different from his own, and he turned out to be the perfect *pujari* (one who officiates the ceremony). He was a natural. I felt so loved by him, and so impressed that he embraced all of it: the hardship of the cold weather, the foreign ceremonies and mantras, even handling the cow dung! I felt he was beginning to accept me fully for who I was.

The next morning at dawn, our families assembled in the sanctuary, along with the other married ashram residents (like Tanner, my friend who had introduced me to Kripalu, and his wife), our relationship coaches, significant mentors, and the ashram directors. I entered first, wearing a beige kurta, and when I quickly scanned the room, my eyes fell on Haridas: the perfect one, my "manliness role model," the one who could take an entire bike apart and put it back together. Our eyes met, and I felt his very real friendship. More than that, I felt a soulful brotherhood. His heart, normally hidden underneath his persona of mastery, revealed itself and joined with mine...and I lost it. As the tears welled up and out, I saw Haridas cry, too – which I had never seen before. In that moment of shared vulnerability, I felt the love of the entire community radiating through him.

250

As the clear voice of a vocalist floated above the sanctuary, Sara entered, looking absolutely radiant in a traditional red sari. She joined me in front of the directors (not the guru, who had recently discontinued doing wedding ceremonies) and took my hand. We were lost in each other and in the beauty of the entire event. We sang songs and chanted; we read our vows to each other; we drank from the same glass of water and fed each other a date; and we ritually honored our parents by bowing at their feet.

It's not common in the West that a child thanks his or her parents in this way, with so much devotion and humility, and I found it to be one of the most meaningful rituals of the marriage ceremony. Sara and I handed them each a red rose, then together bowed at all four parents' feet, one parent at a time. Doing so expressed the deep gratitude I carried in my heart for how my parents raised me, and it marked two rites of passage for me as well: from childhood to adult, and from being single to becoming a man in relationship with a life partner. In the Jewish tradition, the Bar Mitzvah is supposed to mark the transition from boyhood to manhood, but at age 13, I had had no real concept of what manhood even meant. Instead, it was at that moment, with my forehead pressed to the floor, that I made the transition, releasing my need for my parents' care, and stepping into my own power to take care of myself and my wife. When I lifted my head off the ground, I sensed the emotion in the room; this ritual clearly had meaning for us all.

Our parents were invited to speak. Sara's parents declined, my mother sweetly said a few things, but my dad leapt to his feet and launched into his composed speech – all four pages of it. He spoke with wisdom and confidence about being in relationship, that it required first being your individual self, then coming together to complete each other. It was beautiful, but as it went on and on, I started to squirm. *Okay, Dad. That's enough. You're starting to embarrass me. Wrap it up, please...cut! You're done! Stop now!* Just as I was contemplating all the ways I could politely intervene and was coming up with exactly none, he finished. Such relief! "I pronounce you husband and wife," said the ashram director, and with great joy, we kissed to seal the deal.

251

All of us – our ashram friends, our parents, and Sara's sisters – left the sanctuary and squeezed ourselves into a tiny room for our "reception": a breakfast of bagels, soy cream cheese, fruit, and granola. The menu was humble, but no one seemed to care. We ate voraciously, and everyone was happy, particularly my parents. Both of them were delighted for me. They loved Sara. Outgoing and genuinely kind, she was the kind of person who always offered to help, no matter what the situation. I believe that her presence in my life helped them accept the "strange" choices I had made, like being a yogi and living at an ashram If I could get married, especially to such a wonderful person, then perhaps my life was more normal than they had previously thought. Though I could never have anticipated it, marrying Sara brought me closer to my own family.

FOLLOWING MY HEART

As I look back, I can see that every decision I made with my heart brought me unanticipated beauty. Switching from classical to jazz, joining the ashram, releasing my commitment to celibacy, marrying Saraswati ...because I was so connected to the longing to follow my heart, every experience brought me the lessons I needed to have. Every experience helped me discover a deeper meaning and a spiritual purpose in life. The key here is believing that everything in life is for my awakening.

With this belief, there are no mistakes, no wrong way, and no wrong timing. Regret over the past is burned clean in the moment. Even the years of celibacy, which some might assume I regret, gave me lessons I needed. It didn't prepare me for how to be in the world, how to communicate, and how to be empowered in relationship, but it was part of my path. That path led me to Sara and to the lessons I needed that I couldn't get through celibacy. Marriage has been the clearest and most intense mirror I could ever have imagined.

NOTES

---

[1] Attributed to Sri Aurobindo but original source is unknown.

[2] Flock, Elisabeth. "Neil DeGrasse Tyson on the most astounding fact in the universe (video)" *The Washington Post.* 2012. https://www.washingtonpost.com/blogs/blogpost/post/neil-degrasse-tyson-on-the-most-astounding-fact-in-the-universe-video/2012/03/05/gIQAZwv6sR_blog.html. Accessed 15 May 2020.

CHAPTER THIRTEEN

Compromise

Cosmically speaking, the Tantras say that without the dynamism of Śakti – the feminine, the masculine, Śiva, is inert. Yet without the awareness and stability of Śiva, Śakti is uncontrollably wild.

Sally Kempton[1]

Before the wedding, I had gone for a run with Tap, to talk about my desire to marry Sara. We jogged along in the crisp air as he asked me questions about my feelings toward her – all of which I answered easily. As the conversation progressed, I grew more and more confident that marriage was the right next step. Before we left the topic, however, Tap asked me one more question.

"In preparation for marriage, are you willing to not get what you want?"

The strangeness of his question threw me, and I stopped running. My breath became visible as I asked, "What do you mean?"

He answered, "In marriage you can't always get what you want. You have to be willing to not have it your way. It's called compromise."

"Huh," I said. I hadn't thought about that part of marriage. I nodded, and we kept running. I contemplated this idea for the rest of the run and for days to come. It proved to be sage advice that has come in handy many times since.

SPONGE THEORY & SCUZ FACTOR

After the wedding, Sara moved into my small condo in Fox Hollow. Within a few months, a duplex on the Fox Hollow property became available and we moved there, thrilled that we now had a kitchen, bathroom, living room, and master bedroom, all rent-free. A few purchases – a couch, a bed, and a kitchen table – completed our first home.

On the fourth day of living there, I had my first opportunity to practice "I can't have it my way." I'm not sure if all recently married individuals learn this lesson so immediately, but I sure did.

While Sara was unpacking boxes in another room, I was cleaning the kitchen. Thinking I was exhibiting "model husband" behavior, I got down on all fours and began scrubbing the kitchen floor with gusto. I had only finished about three square feet when I saw Sara's feet and heard a sharp intake of breath. I looked up.

With a sternness I had never thought possible from my beloved, she uttered, "That sponge is not for the FLOOR."

I gulped. "No?"

"NO," she continued, and brought it down a notch, no doubt seeing my wide-eyed alarm. "I've been meaning to tell you this for a few days. There are different sponges for different uses. The dish sponge is only for dishes. The countertop sponge is only for countertops. When something spills on the floor, you use the floor sponge. Don't use the dish sponge for the floor and don't use the floor sponge for the countertop. In addition, each sponge had its own storage place."

I nodded, paying close attention, but it didn't sit right with me. I had a completely different concept, and I thought she should see my side.

"Well, that's not how I do it," I said. "To me, a mess is a mess – on the floor, on a countertop, on a dish – they're all the same. And you just clean it with whatever sponge is in your hand."

She narrowed her eyes at me and thundered, "That is *disgusting*. That is *not how we're going to do it*." Her fiery righteousness blasted my face and almost made my nose bleed. I nodded meekly.

"Okay," I said, and at that, she turned and strode out of the kitchen, eyes still aflame. Discussion over.

I got it, loud and clear: there are three levels of sponges in the kitchen. David Allen, organization guru and author of *Getting Things Done*,[2] says that everyone has a different toleration level for messes, disorganization, chaos, and dirt, which he has aptly termed the "scuz factor." We all have different scuz factors for different situations. Take teeth brushing, for example. When I have traveled to teach in Asia, sometimes I couldn't brush my teeth for almost 24 hours, and it really disturbed me. My dental hygiene scuz factor is about 12 hours since I like to brush at least twice a day.

Regarding the kitchen, Sara clearly had a higher scuz factor than I. This difference, just one of many we have as a couple, is why "the householder path" does not impede spiritual development. Quite the contrary. Being married deepened my ability to relate to the world around me and gave me opportunities, over and over, to put into practice some lofty ideals: humility, unconditional love, compromise.

The big one I learned in the kitchen? Surrender! At that moment, on my knees next to the stove, I recalled the advice from my mentor on how to quickly resolve an argument with your spouse: just say "Yes, dear!" I call this the marriage mantra, and it has helped my heart expand, purify, and grow.

The idea that renunciation is a higher path is simply not true. In 1893, when Swami Vivekananda was invited to speak in Chicago at the Parliament of the World's Religions, it was one of the first times a yogi spoke publicly in the United States. Vivekananda happened to be a Swami from a renunciate order. The householder path of Tantra was fully functioning in India at that time, but no yogi from that tradition received air time in the Western media. Thus, the image of what yoga is – and who a yogi can be – was limited to renunciation. After 27 years of marriage and 13 of celibacy, I can honestly say that, for me, relationship is a more difficult path than renunciation.

However, I fully honor the renunciates who sincerely feel called to renounce the world to go to God. I get it. I think it works. It's just not the *only* path to God, and it's not for everyone. The key to knowing which path is right for you is knowing your motivation. If you choose renunciation because you can't deal with the world, or to avoid facing yourself, then renunciation won't work for you. Conversely, if you choose the householder path because you've given up on spirituality and you lack the discipline needed to walk the straight and narrow, then the householder path won't do you much good either. More than the path you choose, your motivation for your path determines your spiritual success. It all boils down to intention.

There is another facet to this as well: your paradigm for evolution and how you view the world. If you believe that life is purely suffering and you need to renounce your desires to reach God, then you'll be led down the renunciate path. But if you believe that spirit resides in everything and that the body is the vehicle for the divine, not an obstacle to it, then the householder path will make more sense to you.

NO-EXIT DECISION

Why does marriage work so well as a tool for personal and spiritual growth? For me, it's that marriage is based on vows that are legally and publicly sealed. In all relationships other than marriage, you can walk away when you have a disagreement. Not getting your way becomes the perfect excuse to escape from the other person. In marriage, the person with whom you're vociferously disagreeing, the person who won't let you have your way, is the one you're sleeping with at night. Guess who's there in the morning, the afternoon, and again the next evening? Marriage forces you to face yourself.

Counselor and author Harville Hendrix, Ph.D. coined the term "no-exit decision"[3] to describe a mutual commitment to stay together, even during difficult times – an agreement that supersedes even the marriage contract, which is not ultimately binding.

Sara and I agreed to practice it early on in our marriage to afford us the fullest possibility for personal and spiritual growth. We saw it as an addition to the marriage contract, and we credited it with saving our relationship more than a couple of times. We discovered that no matter how difficult it got, even if one of us had to take a "time out" for a few days, we always came back because of the no-exit agreement. And it worked for us... until it didn't.

Tantra teaches that there are no ultimate rules. To embrace Tantra is to embrace the concept that there are always exceptions to the rule, that the answer to any question is, "it depends." Every answer depends on the situation and circumstances of the question, but I didn't have any context for this concept until 24 years into the marriage. For now, Sara and I were committed to the no-exit decision.

IMAGO

Dr. Hendrix also created a form of marriage therapy, called Imago Therapy, that Sara and I embraced. One of its central tenets is that we are all drawn romantically to individuals who embody our parents' positive characteristics, who become the "image" of our parents. This familiarity hooks us. It's not until much later that we find out that we chose a partner who embodies our parents' negative characteristics, too. That's when the power struggle ensues. Nature, in its remarkable intelligence, conceals the negative stuff in the beginning so that we keep perpetuating the species. According to Hendrix, it also provides the perfect environment in which to heal childhood wounds. As we work on the relationship with our spouse, both of us are helping each other heal our relationships with our parents.

A prime example of this mutual healing involved the role of anger in both of our lives. Even though by the time I met Sara her father had been sober for years, her childhood included episodes of his drunken, angry outbursts. Unable to trust him, she grew up seeking safety, which for her meant getting as far away as possible from the source of anger. Her strategy in those circumstances was to freeze or flee.

Meanwhile, I grew up feeling that my anger was not acceptable, and that I was unlovable when I was angry. What I needed when I got angry was for someone to love me and move toward me. I needed connection. I wanted Sara to put a hand on my shoulder and tell me, "I see that you're angry and it's okay. It makes sense to me that you would be angry about that. I still love you."

You can see where this is going.

One night in July, a few months after the Sponge Incident, we had a silly dispute about keeping the duplex clean. The argument shifted, and soon it wasn't about the cleanliness of our home anymore. It was about not feeling heard. As our emotions escalated, our voices grew louder and louder, until I hit the edge of my frustration and I shouted. All of the color immediately drained from her face and she made a fast dash into the bathroom, locking the door. She was petrified. She needed to feel safe. I, on the other hand, needed connection, acceptance, and love, which is the opposite of what I was getting from Sara. But we didn't know any of that then. We were still young as a couple, and our abilities to identify the underlying causes for our behavior were undeveloped.

It also didn't occur to me that we were recreating the scene from my childhood when Sherri escaped my father's anger by locking herself in her room. Like my sister, Sara just disappeared, cowering silently in the bathroom for a long time. At first, I felt frustrated, then as the minutes ticked by, sad and raw. I stood there, staring at the bathroom door, not knowing how in the world to fix the situation. Eventually, still feeling sad but not as raw, I grabbed my coat and went out for a walk.

When I came back hours later, she had come out of the bathroom and was curled up on the couch. I apologized immediately and so did she. Sara walked straight into my outstretched arms, and as soon as I felt her near me, I broke down in tears. These were heart-wrenching sobs, the kind where you hold your breath out while your body convulses for the longest time, and you wonder if you'll ever take another breath in. She guided me to sit, allowing me to fall apart in her lap. Even as it was happening, I knew I was healing my deeper-than-tears childhood wound of not feeling loved in my time of need when I was angry. Sara just held me. No words.

She stroked my head lightly until I was able to open my eyes and gaze into hers. I saw how much she loved me. I saw so much compassion. I saw the joint recognition of how tender it is to be in relationship and face our childhood wounds, together.

We talked for a long time, practicing "listening for the need." Often, what we say doesn't truly express what's in our heart. "Listening for the need" means listening for what's not being said, the deeper need that exists beneath the words. Of course, you can't always do this; appropriate societal behavior doesn't often allow for that kind of truth-spilling. In a close relationship, however, it's essential.

FEELINGS, NEEDS, & EMOTIONS

Marshall Rosenberg, author of *Nonviolent Communication, A Language of Life*, [4] maintains that all issues in communication and relationship stem from lack of awareness – we don't really know what we're feeling or what we're needing, let alone what the other person is feeling and needing. Sometimes that's a result of suppression – an unconscious habit of not allowing emotions to move freely – and sometimes it's just the opposite; the emotions run rampant and we have no idea what to do with them or what they mean.

I've found the concept of "e-motion as energy-in-motion," to be helpful. Emotions are energy signals that stream through your body and charge your nervous system. They don't arise to confuse or diminish you; they are the body's intelligence system, your guidance system for navigating your life and your relationships with deeper meaningfulness and success. When fully felt, emotions draw you back into your heart where the Self abides, and where you have access to a much broader perspective: wisdom, insight, and resolution.

Esther Hicks provides an "Emotional Guidance Scale" in *Ask and It Is Given*[5] that I have also found to be a useful, practical tool to understand how emotions can shift and change – for better and for worse. If you want to become skillful with your emotions, begin by feeling them fully, learning what they are trying to tell you, and following them back to the source.

Of all the emotions, anger is the most perplexing. It's the one that has offered me the most opportunities to grow (a.k.a. I have struggled with the most), and the one that many of my students want to understand and work with. I offer what I've learned, not as the definitive guide to dealing with anger, but as a jumping-off point.

CONSTRUCTIVE & DESTRUCTIVE ANGER

Like all of the emotions, anger is natural, and it has a purpose in our lives. But because it is one of the more volatile emotions when left unchecked, we need consciousness to discern its appropriateness and expression. Understanding the difference between constructive and destructive anger is a good place to start.

Constructive anger is anger that we feel in the presence of injustice. Seeing someone being bullied or being taken advantage of can provoke this kind of anger; you want to help. Getting angry in this circumstance can be the appropriate first response to try to prevent harm and scare off the predator, since it marshals extra energy and supersedes any fear that might be present. This is righteous anger, an emotion that arises out of a strong feeling of alignment with what you know to be true blended with morality and human decency. Constructive anger integrates into determination and passion.

Destructive anger is an unconscious discharge of pent-up energy, a volatile and often hard-to-control energy that is powerful and often elicits a psycho-physical response in the body (as does constructive anger) including increased blood pressure, contracted muscles, red eyes, and a flushed face. This anger is unrestrained and instinctive, as it is closely linked to our deepest fears of survival. On one hand, it is a healthy reaction to feeling threatened or wrongly treated, yet most of the time, it is out of proportion to the actual offense; someone cutting ahead of us in line is probably not a true threat to our survival. This kind of anger can also be deeply harmful emotionally if it's directed at someone. Without conscious discernment of appropriate time and appropriate place, the discharge of this emotion usually does more harm than good.

Destructive anger is the type that requires management skills, not only because of the damage it can inflict on others, but because suppressing anger carries its own hazards. Unexpressed anger can create both psychological and physical problems; anger carries a strong voltage or "electro-emotional" charge that our nervous system is not designed to hold on to for long periods of time. We need to find appropriate and healthy ways of expressing our emotion so that we are not either letting our anger eat away at us from the inside, or wantonly discharging it on others.

Rosenberg suggests that anger is just a cover for hurt, and that destructive anger is a "suicidal attempt to get our needs met." If your need isn't being met, anger is generally the emotion of unconscious choice, and most of the time, it will have the opposite effect: It will take you further from getting your needs met.

Now whenever I feel anger arise, or I see others expressing their anger, instead of reacting angrily myself or feeling scared, I ask myself, "What need do I have – or they have – that's not being met?" This allows me to soften and come closer to the true source of the anger. Once I can acknowledge the source, I begin to calm down and make better choices. For me, it's often about noticing the early detection signs so that I can catch the urge to lash out before it happens; once I let anger out of the gate, it's hard to corral it back home. There are always early detection signs. We simply need to pay closer attention.

Sitting on the couch together that night, what I learned about Sara was that she needs space when she's confronted with a certain level of anger. She needs permission to run away to find safety. It's not personal; it's instinct. She reaffirmed her intention to try to remain close to me when I get angry – to help me heal my wound – but there will be times when she can't, when the situation triggers her own deep issues. She promised she would always come back into connection when she felt safe.

What I learned about myself was that I no longer needed to subscribe to the childhood belief that when I'm angry, I'm undeserving of love. I'm acceptable and lovable when I express my anger; in fact, it's even *more* important during those times to give myself love. My work is to become aware of that emotion building *before* it gets to the tipping point – that point of no return – so I can pause, take some breaths, leave the room, or do whatever I need to soothe myself. As I'm more able to accept and embrace my anger, I'm more able to be with it in the moment without judging myself as bad or wrong. I've found that simply being present with my anger has made it easier to feel, contain, and gain the insight of the underlying need.

That night in July, after hours of listening, talking, and understanding each other, we spontaneously began to laugh. A lot. It seemed crazy; how could we be so effervescent after such a deep, painful episode together? More than once we stopped and stared at each other in disbelief, and then burst out laughing again. I've since recognized that laughter of this kind denotes integration and healing. There's a kind of inner joy that bubbles up inside when you feel completely loved for who you are – anger and fear and all. We certainly felt loved that night.

Through hours and hours of processing, studying relationship books, taking workshops, and doing the Hendrix work, we learned how to listen to each other, validate, and give empathy, while also being a container for the other to have a total meltdown, be it a temper tantrum or an unworthiness attack. It was hard work, but when it came time to put into practice what we had learned, we had the tools to help each other. This challenge sometimes felt overwhelming, and we made plenty of mistakes along the way, but we got better and better at it.

Within the Tantric tradition, there is the path of renunciation and the householder path, both of which are acceptable. One is not superior to the other, and you don't get to "heaven" any quicker being a renunciate. They are simply different trails up the mountain of spiritual attainment, with different views along the way.

As you're starting to see, choosing the householder path – the path of relationship – gave me countless opportunities to learn some of the great Tantric truths, including one of the most primary: our limits will lead us to portals of transformation, but it's up to us to go through them.

I found that being in relationship, living with the reflection it provides daily, lends itself to more "portals." When you face your challenges with courage and *self-compassion* – that is essential! – you will experience the Tantric ideal: freedom with boundaries.

Classical Yoga tells us our job is to try to get off the karmic wheel of life. From the Tantric perspective, no matter if you choose the renunciate or householder path, your task is to learn to surf the waves, to balance and stand strong in your heart even when the waves of life try to throw you off your board.

A tidal wave was on its way.

NOTES

[1] Attributed to Sally Kempton but original source is unknown.

[2] Allen, David. *Getting Things Done : the Art of Stress-Free Productivity*. New York: Viking, 2001. Print.

[3] Hendrix, Harville. *Getting the Love You Want: A Guide for Couples*. New York: Perennial Library, 1990. Print.

[4] Rosenberg, Marshall B. *Nonviolent Communication: A Language of Life*. Encinitas, CA: PuddleDancer Press, 2003. Print.

[5] Hicks, Esther and Hicks, Jerry. *Ask and It Is Given: Learning to Manifest Your Desires (Law of Attraction Book 7)*. Carlsbad, CA: Hay House. 2004. Print.

CHAPTER FOURTEEN

The Fall, Part I

Between stimulus and response there is a space. In that space is our power to choose our response. In our response lies our growth and our freedom.

Attribution Varies[1]

RUMORS

$\mathbf{M}$any months before we married, there had been a rumor about the guru having an affair with one of the long-term female disciples.[2] He had denied it, and the whispers had died down for a year. Soon after our wedding, though, Sara and I started hearing the rumors again. It seemed impossible. Our guru? The one who was married with three kids, and taught strict *brahmacarya*? The one who kicked out of the ashram anyone who was caught "falling in love?" We had all heard of guru scandals elsewhere, but surely Kripalu was above such sordid behavior…

Every time a rumor began circulating, you could feel the unrest. But then the guru and his lead assistant would publicly deny the rumor, and the community would breathe a collective sigh of relief. This went on for months. The rumors intensified, until finally, in October of 1994, in the middle of *satsaṅga*, the topic came up again. The guru and his assistant started up with their now-familiar denial rhetoric, when right in the middle of their repudiation, a female disciple stood up.

"Wait. Stop."

All heads turned in her direction.

"It's true. It happened to me."

The entire ashram burst into an uproar. Everyone spoke at once, and I didn't know what to believe. *Could this be true?* Until I heard her speak, I had been willing to dismiss the rumors; my devotion blinded me to any of the guru's faults. *Please, let this be a false accusation.* I so wanted to believe it wasn't true.

The guru called a special *satsaṅga* to address the allegation, during which he admitted that yes, he had engaged in sexual misconduct with the one woman – but only one. This revelation was met with shock and disappointment, but over the course of the following week, as he continued to maintain that there were no others, the community adjusted

267

to this new reality. There were discussions and healing circles, meetings and conversations, all designed to stitch back together the trust that had been rent.

Then, a few days later, other women stood up.

How could he?

At this news, all chaos broke out – yelling and screaming, destruction, violence. One resident took a knife from the kitchen and stabbed a large picture of the guru that hung on the wall in the reception area, the same image that was often placed on his chair and had come to life under my gaze. Another resident, in a frenzy, tore apart the altar, the guru chair, and the side tables. It was complete and utter mayhem. I felt unsafe, yet miraculously, there were no injuries.

Fearing for his own safety, Desai retreated to his home. Almost immediately, he made no statements without a lawyer present and was never seen in public without bodyguards. I'll never forget how small and shameful the guru looked, flanked on all sides by four imposing over-six-foot-tall Sikhs from the Kuṇḍalinī tradition, all dressed in white with huge long beards and white turbans. They looked ominous and carried an attitude of "*Sat Nam*. Don't f#$% with us." I couldn't believe it. I tried to be accepting, but when my judgmental mind got the better of me, I figured Desai must have called some emergency hotline for gurus about to get their ass kicked, or the hotline for cases of threat of guru-bashing where they deploy giant Sikh bodyguards for protection.

The human fortress surrounded Desai day and night. The tensions in the ashram were so high and anger so out-of-control, I wouldn't be surprised if the guru received death threats. That would explain the bodyguards, but it still seemed like cowardice to me, based in fear and shame. Like the Wizard in "The Wizard of Oz," he hid behind his bodyguards, all that was left of the "curtain" of the guru's title. I actually felt sorry for him; he was, after all, just a human being with all of his gifts and flaws. Yet at the same time, I was disgusted, too – not just with his actions that were selfish and hurtful, but with all of the disappointment, denial, years of lying, and unwillingness to own what he'd done and come clean. That irked me the most.

More details surfaced. We learned that Desai exploited his elevated position of spiritual authority, telling these women that sex with the guru was a special blessing that would benefit their spiritual growth. We learned that the sex wasn't just consensual, though that would have been bad enough. It was coerced sex. We learned that Desai had been having a long-standing affair with the main administrator who ran most of the activities at the ashram, and that all of these affairs had been going on since the 80's. Then we learned that all of this had been kept secret, all those years, by a few who had known all along.

The pain was immense. Like most of the Kripalu residents, I was disoriented and disillusioned by the truth that had come to light. I immediately gave up Kripalu Yoga from that point on; in fact, I stopped practicing any yoga at all for a few months. I gave up chanting for a year. I doubted the legitimacy of everything that I had once believed in: yoga, *prāṇāyāma*, even spirituality. I became anti-guru. I was full of rage, sadness, fear, and grief at the loss of my guru, all at the same time.

Unable to make any emotional sense of it, I and many other residents looked to the ashram board of directors for some guidance – at least in the arena of procedure and justice. I was proud of the way they handled the situation. After summarily firing Desai, they stipulated that if he didn't make the necessary reparations to the victims and seek psychological help, he would not be admitted back onto the property. As it turns out, he did give some retribution to the victims, but refused any treatment. This further angered many of us.

BURIED

In response, the administration spent the next year or two seeking ways to help the community heal. They brought in psychologists to help us process our emotions, teaching us how to feel all of our intense feelings – anger and rage, as well as grief, loss, and confusion – without causing harm to ourselves, others, or property. The psychologists met with us in small groups and did mini-facilitations, where individuals could express their rage. When one person got in touch with their anger, it opened up the space for many of us to feel our own. Ultimately, it was healing, though at times it was also scary and retriggering. Because I had so many feelings pouring out of me in such a short time, and I was surrounded by so many others emoting around me, I never knew if I was feeling my own feelings or picking up on those around me. It was probably a bit of both.

Some of the interventions that Kripalu provided were helpful; others were well-intentioned but may have caused more harm than good. One of the most helpful rituals stands out in my mind for its almost macabre method.

"Is that everything?" Sara asked me. I nodded. "You?" I asked in return. "Yes," she said, so quietly I could barely hear her. I picked up the cardboard box, heavy with all the contents we had gathered from the dismantling of our personal altars (dozens of photos of the guru, the guru's guru, and the guru's guru's guru within the Kripalu lineage, my *mālā* beads that I received at initiation, the statues and tokens that had adorned my altar) as well as anything else that reminded me of the ashram, including my white kurta shirts and *satsaṅga* clothes, all of Desai's booklets, my notes about his teachings, and heaps and heaps of guru lectures on cassette tapes: everything.

Together, we made our way to the darkened chapel, where a circle of residents sat together around a makeshift wooden box shaped like a coffin. Sara and I transferred all of our belongings into the coffin, then watched as a few more residents did the same. Once the coffin was full, we lit some candles and closed our eyes in meditation. Tears began to flow. No words were needed. I keenly felt the silence, the absence of our usual chanting of *om* to show our connection and respect. None of us seemed able to make a sound. The simple, powerful sound of om, once the most unifying and aligning force of grace within the ashram, was now silenced in darkness and suffering.

A leader said a few simple words about releasing the past, then led us in a prayer for guidance. We watched in silence as a group of brothers sealed the lid to the coffin, lifted it to their shoulders, and carried it out of the building to bury it. I was in such despair that I couldn't bear to follow them. To this day I have no idea what happened to the coffin or where it was buried.

I looked at Sara, whose face was impassive. "How are you doing?" I asked, and she just stared at me in return. I knew full well how she was; we were both in shock and grieving. Food was the only thing either one of us could think of, so we took each other out to dinner at the Panda Restaurant in Pittsfield. We hardly said a word to each other as we shoveled in General Tso's Chicken and rice.

Later, however, we talked about the ritual. We agreed: as grim and stark as it had been, it helped. Symbolically burying the past through ritual helped us take one step into the future with finality. It was over, all of it: the guru, the rituals, the teachings, the yoga, and everything else that had even the slightest smell of the ashram, including my incense. Everything that went into the coffin was now gone.

As part of their mission to further the community's healing, the new administration brought in Arnie and Amy Mindell to do their "Process Work" with the residents. This conflict resolution workshop, which did bring some insight and help move the community forward, also elicited some agonizing realizations that seemed to backfire and make everything worse.

The Mindell's method, as I understood it, was to trust "the Process." They posited that nature would bring about a resolution if you allowed both sides of any conflict to express themselves. During their workshop, over 500 residents and local community members packed the room to participate, giving full voice to their opinions and deep frustrations.

At one point, an argument broke out between those who still loved the guru, wanted to forgive him, and were intent on keeping the ashram going, and those who wanted to destroy the ashram and burn the place down. The volume and tempers rose until the Mindells seemed to lose control of the room. It was almost unbearable to stay amidst the din and chaos. In fact, a friend of mine did leave, a co-teacher who was quite adept in process work herself. Looking panicked, as though she was narrowly escaping the jaws of a beast, she caught my eye as she fled the room. She never came back.

Mindell's workshop was a tipping point for many residents. Their sessions unleashed a fury of truth-telling that threatened to scuttle the entire organization. During one meeting, a resident accused one of the senior teachers who had lived at the ashram several years before but left to start his own yoga method, of having an affair with a student while teaching on the road. The senior teacher's wife was in the room and this accusation lit her fuse. She leaped to her feet indignantly and screamed at the resident, defending her husband, as her husband stood up and denied it.

This tongue-lashing continued until a soft-spoken brother, known to be a respectful, quiet, and super-nice guy stood up in the back of the room, and said, "It's true. He had an affair. I know this because the woman he had the affair with is my blood sister." You could almost see the air fill up with crimson rage. The accused's wife wilted in front of the entire crowd and began to sob, while her humiliated husband stood there, turning all shades of purple.

The public indignities didn't stop there. More and more people came forward to divulge the raunchiest secrets about themselves and other people. It was as if the lid of light that had smothered the ashram in superficial goodness was now lifted, revealing all of the darkness, shadow, and rot that was festering underneath. I remember leaving the workshop feeling re-traumatized, raw, and even more disillusioned than I was before. It took me weeks to recover from the Mindells, who I'm sure had the purest intentions. They just didn't know the depth of pain and suffering they were dealing with on a community level. Perhaps they helped some people, but for me, everything got worse after that.

Fortunately, Kripalu also brought in specialized trauma psychologists who had experience with sexual abuse within religious communities to speak with us. These professionals helped me understand the magnitude of our trauma and gave me new perspectives to consider. One that stays with me even today is that when your spiritual teacher or a guru betrays you, it's as if God has betrayed you.

Because I was so close to Desai and was such a devoted and dedicated disciple – I'd say a particularly gullible one – I was even more susceptible to that feeling of world-ending betrayal and disillusionment. They also said that because the ashram was like a family system with the guru as the father, his sexual misconduct could feel to us like incest. Certainly, the victims were the guru's spiritual daughters, so when you add in the role of "guru as God," it's as if it were divine incest: not just your dad having sex with your sister, but God having sex with her. These concepts helped me understand why, after the fall, I felt as though I didn't know what to believe anymore, about anything.

For the 11 years prior, my experiences living in the ashram – following the guru, doing the practices he gave me, believing in his mission – had been almost entirely positive, uplifting, and heart-expanding. Yet all of this was the backdrop for the most suffering I had ever felt. On one hand, I was tormented with intense betrayal and disbelief, while on the other, I worshipped the ground on which the guru walked. This vast dichotomy is known, in psychological terms, as cognitive dissonance – the pain felt when attempting to hold two opposing or contradictory experiences in the mind at the same time.

This dissonance was causing me great confusion and distress. In desperation, I decided I had to somehow hold the good with the bad in order to heal. Without realizing it, I was engaging in a Tantric concept! While venting my rage, I had to make space for the beauty, the learning, the depth of being, and all of the life-enhancing experiences I had because of the guru. It took months, but I made progress every day.

Slowly, Sara and I inched our way back to a reconciliation with our former lives at Kripalu. We stayed on, continuing in our jobs as

Programs Manager and Reservations Manager. But teaching yoga now proved difficult for me; I struggled with what form to teach. I couldn't tolerate or even think of continuing to teach Kripalu Yoga as it was created by a guru without a sense of morality, so I substituted other forms. I began moonlighting on the weekends, teaching outside the ashram – which had always been strictly forbidden, as we weren't supposed to earn money outside of Kripalu.

One day, while walking with a friend, I found myself saying out loud what had been brewing in my head for weeks:

"I could never make a living teaching yoga."

My friend laughed. "Your humility is not serving you," he said.

I was taken aback. "What do you mean?"

He looked at me, puzzled. "You've trained over 1000 Kripalu teachers over the last 13 years."

"Yeah… so?"

"So, you could call your graduates and see if any of them would like to host you at their studios. You're like a grandfather to their students! I think you would draw a lot of participants."
The proverbial light bulb clicked on. *Of course! Why didn't I think of that?*

I thanked my friend for his wisdom, and later, went back to my room to embark on this new path. It turned out my friend was totally right. I was lacking self-esteem, and it was *not* serving me. In one weekend of calls, I booked a full year of workshops.

THE "REAL WORLD"

In 1996, Kripalu was still in the midst of redefining itself. In addition to the sexual misconduct, information had surfaced about abuse of power,

274

abuse of finances, and other malfeasances. In its quest for stability and accountability, the organization changed management teams multiple times and established a new model for itself, as a business with salaries. At this point, I was done with Kripalu and so was Sara. What was once a community of trusting individuals seeking spiritual evolution had evaporated, and with it, went our enthusiasm. I had no idea what I wanted my life to look like, but I knew one thing: I no longer wanted to participate in building Kripalu's new identity.

After 13 years, I moved out of the ashram with Sara, whom I now called by her "real" name, Theresa, or Tess for short. We found an apartment in Lenox, above a jewelry store on Church Street, and moved all of the furniture – which wasn't much – from our Fox Hollow condo into it, thus beginning our new life together in the "real world." I was still in shock over the fall of Kripalu, and as nice as our little apartment on Church Street was, I felt almost as though I was put out on the street.

I was woefully unprepared, having gone from college, where I lived in a dorm for part of the time and my parents took care of tuition, to living at the ashram, where almost all of our expenses were covered. The last time I had rented an apartment was during my college years, and even then, it wasn't for long. I was disoriented and dismayed by the "real world." Which brings me to a bigger question: What, exactly, is it?

MĀYĀ

The reality we see, as defined by *Advaita Vedānta*, is an illusion called *māyā*: the veiling of the true Self. This definition holds that any difference you see between one object and another, or yourself and any other person, is unreal. Why? Because the only reality is oneness. All differences are an illusion, created by our ignorant belief that there is anything more than the one. *Māyā*, then, is everything that you see around you; it's the illusory world that surrounds us.

Two metaphors help explain the *Advaita* concept of *māyā*. The first is that of a boy who, while walking down a path, sees what looks like a coiled-up snake. He feels a chill run through his spine and his hair stands on end. As he gets closer, he immediately sighs with relief: it's only a jump rope. The boy's so-called ignorance caused *māyā*. He lacked data, and that deficiency created illusion. Our perception of reality is the same. The truth is that there exists only oneness; everything else, any difference, is an illusion we falsely believe is true.

A more modern metaphor for *māyā* comes from the act of watching movies. A good movie draws you in, such that you get completely absorbed in the story line and identify with one or more of the characters. You can even lose yourself entirely in the event and believe, temporarily, that the movie is real. In *Advaita Vedānta*, life is like a movie. What you see happening on the screen of your life you think is real, but it's only the projection of the movie of your mind. The movie is *māyā*. What's real is what's behind the movie: the pure light that illumines the movie. That is the nondual. That light is behind everything in the physical universe.

In Tantra, however, *māyā* is not seen as an illusion that has no substance. It's real, in the way that if you accidentally stub your toe on the sidewalk, the pain you feel is real. There's no illusion about that. However, *māyā* is not the highest reality. In Tantra, *māyā* is the "magical mirror" that *Śiva* creates within his own being. It's the Supreme's power to cloak and veil itself.

When a magician pulls a rabbit out of a hat, is that real or an illusion? It looks real, but you know it's a magic trick. A truly skilled magician can convince you it was real. And isn't it more enjoyable to take delight in being fooled? When you gasp, laugh, and applaud good magic, you appreciate the value of the experience. The magic trick has served its purpose – to delight. It's your choice to be amused by life's magic trick of *māyā*, or not.

Māyā also means meter, or to measure. *Māyā*, then, is your capacity to take the measure of things, to see and understand things, and then to make choices. If *māyā* is the magical mirror, the power of the universal to color your entire life in a particular way, and you can only live in *māyā*, then your life will reflect your personal goals, desires, and

276

intentions; how you live your whole life is *māyā*. Bottom line? Since the illusion of *māyā* is real, choose which "illusion" you want to live in. In fact, if you have no choice but to live in the illusion of *māyā*, then choose the kind of *māyā* that delights you and is good for you.

Māyā is the power that makes the immeasurable measurable, the infinite finite, the unlimited limited, and the free bound. It's what makes everything in the universe possible.

ADJUSTMENT

Leaving Kripalu was my effort to choose a *māyā* that was better for me. The first thing I did when we moved out of the ashram was set up the kitchen. My macrobiotic stint in Miami had instilled in me a love of cooking, and I was excited to stock my kitchen with all of the foods that Kripalu had in bulk, like grain, beans, and spices. Since money was tight, we either ate at home or we availed ourselves of the free meal pass that Kripalu provided residents who had recently moved out. That was a true godsend. Tess and I both still worked at Kripalu, and we relied on that pass for a year or two.

Luckily, Tess's parents in Boston were close by in case we needed anything; her father gave us a spare computer and his old Mazda. But I still found it a challenge to live in the world. No one ever explained to me that I'd have to pay rent every month on time. Or that I couldn't just sign a car out and drop it off when I was done with it; I actually had to maintain it! For the last 13 years, the ashram mechanics had taken care of the fleet so I never once thought about changing the oil.

Tess and I happily shared the Mazda for a while, but at some point, it became clear to both of us that if I was going to travel and teach on weekends, I needed my own car. Now that Kripalu was no longer an ashram, they were selling some of their cars. Much as I liked the cost savings of buying a Kripalu car, I couldn't stomach the history that each of those cars carried. So I went to the local car dealer in town and bought a Toyota Tercel, which was the same make and model of the ashram fleet, without the "*karma*" (no pun intended).

Slowly but surely, we adjusted. We both missed the time we previously had available for spiritual practices, since now so much of our lives was taken up with basic life-survival responsibilities, like food shopping, cooking, house cleaning, car maintenance, solving computer glitches, and shoveling snow in the winter. What we missed from the ashram was more than outweighed by the freedom we felt: to walk to local stores and the library; to do whatever we wanted whenever we wanted; and to create our own holiday traditions.

As it turned out, since our family holiday gatherings with her side of the family were so enjoyable, and the early memory of my neighbor's Christmas bounty still echoed, I made us get a Christmas tree and lights. Meanwhile, Tess found that she loved lighting the menorah candles. She insisted I teach her the prayers over the candles, words that I had to dig up out of my childhood memory bank. Soon, our Winter Solstice ritual meant celebrating both Christmas for me and Hanukkah for her, and I found deep meaning behind both traditions and holidays.

As Tess and I learned how to live together, practicing empathy and forgiveness as a couple, I noticed that I was more and more willing to find forgiveness in my heart for others... including Desai. The anger I had initially felt at his actions was gradually subsiding, so when I heard he was making attempts to heal relationships, by holding group meetings with former disciples who were willing to participate, I decided to accept his open invitation. A few of my resident friends had done this and they seemed calmer somehow; maybe I would find some peace, too.

However, the notion of meeting him in a group setting reeked of "old school" guru power dynamics, where I inevitably lost my sense of self within the juggernaut of groupthink. *No. This time it will be different.* The day before the meeting, I called the coordinator of the event and demanded that I meet with Desai one-on-one, with no one else in the room. The coordinator demurred, saying he would have to check with Desai. I got a call back; Desai had agreed.

This seemingly small prerequisite was, in fact, the end result of a long process of self-reflection. I spent many, many hours trying to understand why I had so willingly given over all of my sovereignty to the guru, and more importantly, to the community.

RECONCILIATION

It's possible to surrender too much, or to surrender in an unhealthy way. Certainly, surrender in the form of submission can lead to being taken advantage of. Placing all of your faith in God – or a guru – is like the joke about the religious man and the flood:

> *A religious man is on top of a roof during a great flood. Someone comes by in a boat and says, "Get in. Get in!" The religious man replies, "No. I have faith in God. He will grant me a miracle."*

> *Later, the water is up to his waist when another boat comes by. Its driver tells him to get in. He responds that he has faith in God and that God will give him a miracle. With the water at about chest high, another boat comes to rescue him. But he turns down the offer again because God will grant him a miracle.*

> *With the water at chin high, a helicopter throws down a ladder and the rescuers tell him to get in. Mumbling with the water in his mouth, he again turns down the request for help in favor of the faith in God. He arrives at the gates of heaven, his faith broken, and says to Peter, "I thought God would grant me a miracle and I have been let down." St. Peter chuckles and responds, "I don't know what you're complaining about; we sent you three boats and a helicopter."*

Too much surrender can lead to becoming ungrounded, aloof, or disconnected, as well as complacent. Tantra invites you to step out of complacency and into agency and participation. Unless you are engaging with life, co-participating with it, you are not doing the yoga. The metaphor of the sailboat is apt here: in order to catch the winds of grace, you have to raise your sail. Can you refuse engagement? Yes. You

279

are always free to leave your sail right where it lies. But for "miracles" to happen, your effort is needed.

Why had I let others make all of the decisions for me? Why did I clam up in group events? (Which was essentially all the events at the ashram.) What made me feel so small and invisible? The answer was clear: unworthiness. Since I felt I didn't really matter, I embodied my own insignificance in all contexts, but particularly in groups, where my lack of worth seemed to stand out even more. Rather than risk the judgment of others, it was better to hide in the corner. It was certainly safer there.

But something had changed since then. I had been living with Tess for almost two years now, and I was now the sole creator of my daily destiny. I got up when I felt like it, ate what I wanted to, and spent each day under no one's power but my own. I cobbled together a living that was uniquely mine, and it felt *good.* So did my decision to meet with Desai on my terms, not his. Upon hearing his agreement to my demand, I rose up inside. Perhaps it was my inborn sense of worthiness, or a recognition that my needs matter. Whatever it was, I was elated.

Empowered by my choice, I arrived at the local house where he was staying, a beautiful place owned by one of the disciples. The coordinator, an old friend of mine, ushered me in to where Desai was waiting. I followed with a strange mixture of eagerness and dread. *What would this be like?* Then I saw him, standing in the doorway of a room. My heart opened and clutched at the same time. *Do I open my heart to him? Forgive him? Surrender? Or protect myself and keep the door locked?*

I immediately noticed his clothes. It was odd to see him in regular Indian street clothes rather than his customary guru robe. The image of Clark Kent flashed through my mind. Was it his attire that made him look deflated and less powerful? Or *was* he less powerful now?

"Welcome, Manu," he said, and then he seemed to remember that I wanted to meet privately with him. "Let's go upstairs." I was surprised and relieved that he respected my wishes and accommodated me immediately. Once upstairs, we went into a bedroom and he closed the door behind us. There was one cushion on the floor. He gestured to it.

"Please, sit," he said, then sat down on the floor.

I was deeply surprised. For the first time ever, he was offering me the cushion while he sat on the floor. This went against all tradition – the guru always sits higher than the disciples, to signify that the guru's consciousness is higher than that of his disciples. Bowing to the guru was part of that same tradition of offering humility and devotion, and I had always appreciated the meaning behind both gestures; I had been taught that we were honoring not just the guru, but who the guru symbolized within ourselves. Bowing to the guru always meant bowing to life, bowing to nature, bowing to the *śakti*, and bowing to my potential for living a fulfilled and happy life, blessed with the divine.

"Thank you," I said, and sat down gingerly on the cushion, unaccustomed to this new arrangement. We sat for a few moments, reading each other's faces. Our eyes met, and I saw his humanity. I also thought I saw sincere shame in his eyes. Then he began:

"Manu, I'm sorry for all of the pain I must have caused you. It must have been so difficult for you."

My jaw dropped. His statement caught me off guard and I was completely disarmed. He was making amends and it seemed sincere, though polished – I suppose it might have been rehearsed. As I remembered how much I loved him, thirteen years of deep devotion and joy flooded my mind, starting with that fateful *satsaṅga* in 1982 when Desai took on the warm presence of a Jewish grandfather.

Any defense I had melted away, and I couldn't help but respond by opening my heart. As natural as an overflowing lake, forgiveness streamed through my heart. I began to weep. He put his arm around me and held me for a while, until I composed myself.

I don't remember exactly what I said, but I know that I tried in vain to express how difficult it was for me. I wasn't being clear. I talked about being confused, sad, angry, and hurt, but I couldn't articulate my feelings; they were a jumbled mess and my thoughts were scattered, too. As I struggled to speak my truth, I kept looking to him to help somehow – to draw me out, or even encourage me to keep trying. He listened politely for a few minutes, and then, because he couldn't help but respond the way he always had, he interrupted me and started lecturing. *Really?*

He actually began teaching to me, about forgiveness and the heart's resiliency. Even seated on the ground, even dressed in street clothes, he was still the one with the answers. He was still "the guru." His words were tinged with defensiveness as he said things like, "It's not how it seems" or "I'm not all bad." And just like that, like a castle shutting down under siege, I felt my heart close down. I became quiet. He taught, the gates closed, and the drawbridge lifted.

Desai finished his teaching; as was customary, I thanked him. We hugged, and I left.

YOU HOLD THE KEY

It took months for me to understand what had happened that day. Ultimately, I realized that what I wanted from him, he couldn't give. I wanted him to just sit there and give me space to speak. I wanted him to draw me out, to say things like, "Tell me more about that." I wanted him to mirror what I said and express empathy: "That makes sense that you would feel that way. Are there other feelings?"

I wanted him to be my therapist.

But he couldn't be that, for me or anyone else. He was a guru who was raised in India, with different values, different customs, different communication skills, and different parameters of relationship in marriage. He followed different cultural norms in regard to having extra-marital affairs. It's even possible that his training at the feet of his own guru established a pattern of being the authority on everything, such that it was his automatic response to any situation. I wanted him to meet me on my terms and listen to me the way I needed, but that was about as likely as getting blood from a stone. Desai was just Desai, and he could not treat me the way I wanted.

Which led me to another realization: there I was, giving my power over to the guru again! I thought he was the one who could heal me, solve all of my problems, and be my champion. I thought he could ask the right questions and listen in the right way, to take away my pain and suffering. I wanted from him what I was unwilling to give myself. It hit me like a two-by-four: *I don't need anything from him at all. I hold the key to my own healing. Perhaps I just don't know how to love myself fully... yet.*

I took back the responsibility to heal myself. I saw how my "tentacles of powerlessness and unworthiness" were rooted in Desai's heart, how I made my healing about him rather than about me. By casting my own expectations on to him, I relinquished the power buried deep in my own heart to heal my heart. Once I recognized this, I retracted my psychic threads and drew them back into myself. I affirmed to myself: *I am already whole and complete.*

Meeting with the guru taught me something about forgiveness, too. I noticed that when I sat in his presence and his apology opened my heart, I felt wonderful: light, warm, joyful. Later, after he started teaching again, I shut myself off – which felt lousy. Aha! *Forgiveness is for me, not him.* I needed to release the burden of resentment from my shoulders so that my heart could open up again and be free.

A contracted view of life causes us to barricade our heart for protection, thinking that the veil will keep us safe from the emotional harm that others can inflict. It's normal, and those who've been hurt in relationship can become quite skilled at it. But whenever you close your heart, no matter the reason, even if the reason is to protect yourself and survive – which we all have to do sometimes – you will also close your heart *to yourself*. Bravo that you are successful in keeping out the bad guys, but in shutting down, you also cut off your contact with yourself, with your heart, and ultimately with grace.

It's tempting to close down and stay that way, frozen in a pattern that carries a heavy cost – whether you realize it or not. Here's the deal: there's pain either way. Either you close your heart to another and then can't help but feel the pain of a closed heart, or you choose to live with an open heart and feel the pain of a heart that feels everything fully. *However*, living with a closed heart is the pain that creates more pain. Living with an open heart is *the pain that heals the pain*. Tantra teaches us to engage fully with life, all of it, even the dark, painful, sad, shadowy parts, because those are grace, too. Rumi's famous poem says it beautifully:

The Guest House

This being human is a guest house.
Every morning a new arrival.

A joy, a depression, a meanness,
some momentary awareness comes
as an unexpected visitor.

Welcome and entertain them all!
Even if they're a crowd of sorrows,
who violently sweep your house
empty of its furniture,
still, treat each guest honorably.
He may be clearing you out
for some new delight.

The dark thought, the shame, the malice,
meet them at the door laughing,
and invite them in.

Be grateful for whoever comes,
because each has been sent
as a guide from beyond.

~Jalaluddin Rumi, translated by Coleman Barks[3]

You heal your pain when you allow yourself the gift of feeling your hurt and not rejecting it or acting out in a negative way. You heal your pain when you feel hurt and embrace yourself with self-acceptance, self-compassion, and wisdom. I promise you, you will heal what you can feel. Call it the "fringe benefit" of living with an open heart.

The heart is also the place where all polarities are embraced, where pure acceptance is the "stuff" of the environment of the heart, where compassion and forgiveness are freely offered, and where healthy self-boundaries are necessary. Within the Tantric tradition, at the Absolute level, love is unconditional. But at the relative level or physical level, love is necessarily conditional. In any love relationship, conditions exist – whether they are consciously created, as in speaking wedding vows, or whether they are implicit. We all have limits to the behaviors we will accept from our partners, conditions that make up the boundaries that build trust, and ultimately, bring you closer to your beloved. When these are breached, they are powerful enough to break off the relationship forever.

You could say then that intimacy is how you create appropriate boundaries. Within intimacy, you allow some people to come closer to you and others to stay away. Intimacy is a dance of permission and prohibition. If love is intimacy, and intimacy is created by establishing boundaries, then love without boundaries is not love.

It's paradoxical for sure, as you have no doubt by now come to expect from the Tantric philosophy, because boundaries would seem to negate the idea of unconditional love. But true love is unconditional *within* a set of boundaries or agreements.

Until my experience with Desai, I had operated under the belief that if I forgave someone who hurt me, I would be giving that person permission to hurt me again. No! Forgiveness is the practice of self-empowerment, of trusting yourself fully. You're not trusting that the other person won't screw up again, you're trusting that you will know what to do and how to handle it if it happens again. So, with love, I forgave Desai, and I set myself free. I decided that I never want to close my heart to anyone. That doesn't mean that I'll invite him over for dinner; it means that it's possible to let others into your heart while also holding a healthy self-boundary.

Desai moved on, eventually opening another center in Florida and taking the seat of guru once again. In the meantime, I rebounded. I went back to my practice of yoga and chanting, and a new love for yoga blossomed in me. Ultimately, I realized that by acknowledging both Desai's courage to sit face-to-face with me *and* his inability to convey empathy in the way I needed it, I could heal fully and completely. I could accept who Desai was without needing him to be different, honor his sincere attempt to make amends, and then truly let go. And that is what I did.

Ultimately, no one is perfect. As a recovering perfectionist, that is my primary lesson in relationship, in life, in this spiritual journey. The guru taught me that, and I am a better person for it. But who, in truth, is the guru here? If it's up to you to assign meaning to your experience, and the one who assigns the meaning is the guru, then you are both yourself *and* the guru. The paradox of this ultimate realization lives within the guru acronym: G-U-R-U! Gee, you are you!

There is a teaching: "The guru keeps on teaching." Perhaps it is really true.

NOTES

[1] This quote is often attributed to Viktor Frankl but researchers have not been able to find this quote in his work. It is probably a revision of a quote from Rollo May in 1963. To learn more: https://quoteinvestigator.com/2018/02/18/response/. Retrieved 8 May 2020.

[2] Speers, W. "After Sexual Indiscretions, A Yoga Master Resigns," *Philadelphia Inquirer*, 2 November 1994, p. H02. https://nl.newsbank.com/nl-search/we/Archives?p_multi=PI%7C&p_product=PHNP&p_theme=phnp&p_action=search&p_maxdocs=200&s_trackval=PHNP&s_dispstring=A%20Yoga%20Master%20Resigns%20AND%20date(all)&p_field_advanced-0=&p_text_advanced-0=(A%20Yoga%20Master%20Resigns)&xcal_numdocs=20&p_perpage=10&p_sort=_rank_:D&xcal_ranksort=4&xcal_useweights=yes#nBasdiv625. Accessed 8 May 2020.

[3] Barks, Coleman with John Moyne, translators. *The Essential Rumi*. New York: Harper Collins. 1995. Print.

CHAPTER FIFTEEN

Śrī

*When you align with Śrī, you align with
the highest intention of the universe.*

Douglas Brooks[1]

Tess and I started taking a summer vacation in Wellfleet, MA, on Cape Cod. The natural sunlight on the Cape is unlike any other I've seen. It's almost magical. The way the early morning light of sunrise illuminates the ocean and sand dunes is exquisite; it's rivaled only by the beauty of the sunsets. One warm August evening, Tess and I went to Duck Harbor, one of the places we most loved to sit and watch the sunset. By the time we arrived, the clouds had rolled in, obscuring the sun and smearing the sky with thick grey cover.

Disappointed by the dreariness of it all, I turned to Tess and proclaimed, "This sunset isn't that beautiful."

"Yes," she said, and I got up to go. Then she continued, "but do you see the subtle tones of blue, grey, and purple? Do you feel how soft the light is and how subdued the tone of the beach is?"

I paused and sat back down. I looked again, this time through the lens she had given me. *Wow.*

There was beauty there already. I had allowed a preconceived notion of beauty to cancel out any experience of the actual sunset. What I saw did not match my expectation, so I judged it as bad.

For not the first time in our relationship, Tess helped me see the world differently. I nodded, and she squeezed my hand. "How could any sunset be anything less than beautiful?" she asked. Indeed.

DIVINE BEAUTY & AUSPICIOUSNESS

The concept of *Śrī*, (divine beauty, goodness, or auspiciousness) is one of the philosophical building blocks that shapes my life perspective. Tess's wisdom at the harbor guided me toward remembering one of its central tenets: beauty is an experience that happens from the inside. You recognize beauty when it moves your heart or touches you in a certain way. When you label something beautiful, something big has opened up inside your heart: a recognition of the order and perfection of the universe. You have to conceive it on the inside before you receive it on the outside. Beauty, like happiness, is an "inside job."

The perfect example of this is the Pat Metheny concert I attended soon after Tess and I fell in love. Because my heart was already romantically expanded, my experience of the depth of the music was transformed. I've always thought Metheny's music was beautiful, but that time, I was able to experience the raw, primal, essence of the music. My sensitivity to beauty was heightened and refined, and there were no barriers to my merging with the divine source of the music itself. Metheny's music became beautiful on a whole new level.

Śrī loves order. Beauty is what happens when all parts come together in a harmonious way to serve something bigger, when there's a certain organization of elements or a pattern that is pleasing to your senses.

An orchestra, for example, creates true beauty when all of its players do their part; even just one musician with an out-of-tune instrument affects the whole. You know the music is beautiful – or the painting, or the story – by the way you feel in its presence. And everyone has a different idea about what beauty is, because everyone has a unique perspective and identity. This is why Plato was correct when he said, "Beauty lies in the eyes of the beholder," though I might add that it lies in the heart of the beholder, too.

Śrī is not glamour. It's not movie stars, or airbrushing, or photoshop. It's not about comparison to the "perfection" we see in the images that are sold to us daily. It's about the authentic beauty that comes from the inside out.

KNOWLEDGE ENHANCES *ŚRĪ*

When I took an art history course in college, I found that the more I learned about a particular artist, his struggles, the culture and time in which he painted, and all of the little intricacies of story and symbolism behind the painting, the more I appreciated the beauty of the work. The same was true with studying certain jazz masterpieces. In one of my jazz

289

composition classes, my professor played a dense, obscure jazz piece for us, and my initial reaction was: *Meh.* All I heard was chaos and noise; I couldn't make out what the bass player – or any of the musicians, for that matter – was playing.

Dutifully, we listened to the same piece for a week, and each day the professor pointed out a quirky little characteristic or organizing principle. Without even realizing it, the music slowly came alive for me. The real turning point was when the teacher scored the actual notes the bass player was playing onto the chalkboard. It's hard to describe, but seeing that the notes the bass was playing were, in fact, *the inverse* of the notes in the melody, opened up the entire composition to me. Once I understood technically what was going on, I could hear the music. It became beautiful to me.

Knowledge enhances *śrī*. The more you know about something, the more you recognize the beauty within it. This is also true about people. When you really get to know someone – their victories, their struggles, their interests – their greatness starts to shine out. It's for this reason that I've never met an uninteresting person.

Śrī also evolves over time. From what I gather, any parent can attest to that. Witness the following exchange:

"Mommy! Daddy! Look what I drew!" says the little girl, bursting with pride.

"Oh, honey, that's a beautiful flower."

Her face falls. "It's a person," she says, and Mom and Dad scramble to re-group. Can they prevent permanent damage to her self-esteem? "Yes! Right! Oh, of course it is," they reassure. "And what a beautiful person, too."

She smiles. The parents breathe again. Crisis averted.

Over time, these embarrassing parental faux pas diminish as the child gains experience, knowledge of the craft, and understanding of line, color and shape. *Śrī* evolves through experience, giving every child the potential to become another Rembrandt.

THE NATURE OF *ŚRĪ*

The more you look for *śrī*, the more you'll see it. Meanwhile, the more you look for what's broken and wrong, the more you'll see that – and you'll miss the good. What is *Śrī*'s answer to the classic optimism vs. pessimism question? The glass is half full, of course. *Śrī* is an inner attitude (what you believe) that shapes your outlook (what you see) in life. With an attitude of *śrī*, you see the goodness in something first, rather than the limitation. Not that we want to gloss over imperfection and pretend we live in a Pollyanna world; it's more subtle than that. *Śrī* asks you to see the good while also acknowledging what's broken.

When the genius painter, sculptor, architect, and poet Michelangelo created David, his 17-foot-tall marble masterpiece, he was asked by an admirer, "How did you carve such a beautiful and lifelike figure out of a clump of stone?" Michelangelo replied, "The true work of art is but a shadow of the divine perfection. I saw the angel in the marble and carved until I set him free." The spirit was already in the stone. He just removed what wasn't necessary.

Śrī is an aspect of the divine that lives inside everyone and everything. Our job is to view the world at just the right angle: the beautiful one. To understand more about the nature of *śrī*, there are three aspects to consider: abundance, value, and beneficence.

Abundance is the notion that there is always more. One evening, I was having dinner with a good friend of mine who was married with one child. He seemed distracted and somehow "off," so much so that I finally asked him what was on his mind. He said, "My wife is pregnant. I don't know how I'm ever going to love my second child as much as my first. It feels impossible for my heart to grow any bigger." I didn't say anything. I just listened.

Several months later, after his second child was born, we got together again. "So?" I asked, "What did you discover? Are you able to love your second child as much?" He laughed and said, "I didn't think I could. But as soon as my second child was born, my heart immediately burst open wider. It's actually effortless to love both children equally."

Śrī expands and operates within a natural blueprint of abundance – there's always more. When your attitude is full of *śrī*, you will continue to grow yourself. It is a choice, however. You are free to stunt your own growth with an attitude of lack. Just as science confirms that the universe is expanding and accelerating, so can your consciousness grow and expand throughout your entire life when you decide to align with *śrī*. Life just keeps getting better.

Everything has value in its own way, depending where you place it. One of the many things that attracted me to Tess is her luxurious, long, wavy hair. It's thick and healthy, a beautiful chestnut color now streaked with silver, and she wears it well. Soon after we moved in together, we were eating breakfast one morning: oatmeal with cinnamon and apples. As I was savoring a spoonful of its flavor and warmth, I felt something in my mouth. It took me a moment, but then I knew exactly what it was. "Oh, yuck," I mumbled through my oatmeal. "It's a hair!" All enjoyment stopped.

I took hold of it between my thumb and forefinger, then pulled and pulled and pulled, but it just didn't end. The strand twisted and twirled inside my mouth and kept getting caught on my tongue, and then on my teeth as I snaked it out. Like some heinous magician's trick, it just kept coming out, covered with sticky blobs of oatmeal goo. I began to panic like I was going to die. Finally, I got to the end of it. I delivered it unceremoniously to the trash, then immediately washed my hands. "Yuck," I spewed, "it was in my *oatmeal*! I hate your hair. That was disgusting." It took me a while, but once I recovered, we both started laughing and we agreed: Tess's hair is *śrī*, but only when it's on her head.

Within the Tantric paradigm, everything belongs. Everything that is here

292

is *meant* to be here. *Śrī* aligns with this, saying yes, everything belongs. But it's where you place it that matters. Soil inside the house is called dirt. Outside, where it belongs, it's soil. It's the same stuff, but the value of dirt outside the house increases, as soil is essential to plant life. Placement matters. When you sweep your floors and remove the dirt, there is *śrī* in that, because your clean house is more beautiful when it shines. *Śrī* also increases because the dirt from inside the house has been returned to where it truly belongs.

Beneficence is the idea that the universe is life-affirming. Given any chance at all, things will grow and thrive. Like a tender green blade of grass growing up through the tiniest of gaps in a sea of concrete, life is unstoppable. It is indomitable in its continuous search to perpetuate itself. *Śrī* is the practice of radical affirmation, of holding strong to an inner vision of something wonderful.

John Lennon and Yoko Ono's song, "Imagine" captures the sentiment I've held deep in my heart since the beginning of my spiritual journey: a vision of bringing heaven on earth, a vision of living in a world where beauty, kindness, respect, support, abundance, unity, and love are present. Without a vision like that, how can any of us improve this world?

Take the natural intelligence of the body. The body will automatically try to heal itself when it's out of harmony. Some time ago, I injured my neck, and consulted with an orthopedic surgeon, who I told me I had a bone spur and needed surgery. Feeling a bit scared, but wanting relief from the sharp, throbbing neck pain that traveled all the way down my arm, I scheduled a surgery appointment for ten days later. During those ten days, I sought a second opinion from a team of doctors at a teaching hospital outside Boston. After a thorough review of my MRI, one of the doctors spent over 90 minutes explaining the most minute details of what he saw, telling me that the team felt the MRI was inconclusive. They thought it was behaving more like a bulging disc than a bone spur.

As a side note, this is how I believe grace signaled me to forgo surgery. The doctor's name who said I needed surgery was Dr. Kahlia, which sounds a lot like "Kali." As you'll recall, the goddess Kali inspires awe and fright. The doctor's name who told me not to worry about it and to avoid surgery? Dr. Ramachandra, which means "preserver of the moon." Rama is an incarnation of *Viṣṇu*, the God who preserves and maintains the universe. He's pictured reclining on a couch while he dreams his vision of a harmonious life into reality. The team of doctors gave me confidence in my decision, but it didn't hurt to have grace's signature.

AN ANGEL OF *ŚRĪ*

My bulging disc was so painful I couldn't sleep at night. One night in desperation, I got out of bed and began pacing in the dark, moving from room to room in our small house, moaning and whimpering. Soon, I saw the outline of Tess coming toward me. I stopped.

"Why are you up?" I asked through gritted teeth.

"You're in pain. I'll walk with you."

"It's okay. You don't have to—"

She cut me off. "I know I don't have to. I want to." Tess's supervisor at Kripalu had warned me, and he was right. Tess was an independent thinker, and I loved her all the more for it.

She gently took my arm and we started off together in silence. A few minutes in, however, Tess began speaking to me in a soft, soothing tone.

"You'll get through this," she murmured. "Your body knows how to heal itself. The pain is melting away."

Yes, I thought, *she's right.*

She continued, "Your breath is full and is making space for your pain. You are a powerful yogi. You are a warrior. You've gotten through worse situations. You are in touch with the healing powers of the universe."

294

We walked, and I nodded, not wanting to interrupt the beautiful flow of her words.

"Grace loves you. God loves you," she whispered. And then, "I love you."

At that, the hard shell of stoicism dissolved. For the first time during the injury, I relaxed, opening myself to a bigger energy and allowing the pain. I wept uncontrollably. I felt so loved and accepted and held.

We slowly walked together back to my side of the bed. Tess helped me slide in, then she tucked me in, kissing me on the forehead. I sank into a deep sleep.

When I woke up the next morning, my neck was pain-free. Why? I believe it's because Tess helped me release my resistance. I didn't want to be injured and I didn't want to experience the pain, but my reality at that moment was that I *was* hurt. Only by letting go of my resistance to the injury could I tap into the natural healing energy of my body and allow grace, as *śrī,* to flow again.

I was so grateful. Tess helped me remember that the healing energy of *śrī* already exists inside me, and all I had to do was align with it. With Tess's love, some pretty heavy-duty anti-inflammatory meds, yoga therapy, really good physical therapy, and rest, I avoided surgery and was able to heal. It took me seven months before I was able to do Downward Dog Pose, but today I have no effects of the bulging disc. I've since learned that 90% of all discs heal through natural means: the *śrī* of the body. When you align yourself with *śrī,* you align with the deepest intention of the universe to heal and make whole.

Life is beneficent.

THE PERFECT REBOUND

I see *śrī* all around me, and I certainly saw it in early 1997, when I reconnected with my student and friend, Karen Hasskarl, who, after taking her Kripalu teacher training with me in 1988, teamed up with Michael Lee, founder of Phoenix Rising Yoga Therapy (PRYT). Karen was a gifted teacher with a heart as big as the ocean. She knew I was having a hard time transitioning out of Kripalu and connecting back into yoga, so she invited me to study with her.

Michael Lee had co-taught the Yoga Therapy course with Samadarshan back in the early 80's, when Kripalu was still at Summit Station. Once Kripalu moved to the Berkshires, he left the ashram and started his own method, building on the philosophical teaching points from Kripalu and combining them with attuning to a higher power within and learning how to trust in the guidance. That combination of heart-centricity and inner guidance resonated hugely with me; it was the perfect path during this time of upheaval.

I loved the teachings, and I respected the rigor of the curriculum. In fact, I resonated with PRYT so much that Karen asked me to become a teacher. I was delighted. We co-taught until I was ready to teach on my own, which I subsequently did. I was nervous at first, because the method required me to step into the unknown and source my creativity while I simultaneously listened intently to the needs of my students. By learning how to trust myself and rely on my deeper intention to show me the way, I found I could facilitate a large number of students into their deeper emotions in such a way that they could access their own inner guidance.

Like the perfect rebound relationship, PRYT helped me get over the ashram. I taught PRYT for the next few years, letting go more and more of my teaching responsibilities at Kripalu until I was no longer leading the teacher trainings. Finally, I was free from Kripalu, both physically, psychically, and financially. The only thing Tess and I both missed, was grass.

We were still living in the noisy apartment above a jewelry store in Lenox. As yogis, we had a way of finding comfort wherever we were; the external spaces didn't matter as much as the inner space. Yet we were ready for a more permanent home, and both of us missed the green of Kripalu: the mature trees, foliage, and especially, the acres and acres of lawns. In our current apartment, our backyard was a parking lot.

For months, we spent hours compiling our wish list, complete with the style of home, location, and yard. We wrote down on our list in bold font, "We want a yard with grass. We want grass. We want grass!!!"

We set out to find it.

EXERCISE: *Śrī*, Divine Beauty

Go to a quiet place with your journal and pen. Reflect on the following questions, then write your answers.

1. What is beauty?
2. How do you recognize beauty?
3. Make a list of 10 things in general that are beautiful to you.
4. Name 10 things within your life right now that are beautiful.
5. What is beautiful about you? Consider your own beauty on a physical, mental, emotional, and spiritual level.
6. How would your life be enhanced if you looked for what's beautiful first?
7. What are some ways you could bring more beauty into your life and align more with *śrī*?
8.

NOTES

---

[1] Quote attributed to Dr. Douglas Brooks; original source unknown.

CHAPTER SIXTEEN

Hello, Tantra

Why did we come here? Why did we receive this body? This is not a question that can be casually, superficially or only intellectually answered. It is one of the great mysteries of existence. In fact, it is only in the fulfillment of our most authentic and highest sādhanā, our spiritual journey, that we individually, each of us, discern and see the secret purpose, the truest profound meaning and value of our own individual existence. The Śaiva Tantric Tradition urges us to understand that we are important. There is something of great value, depth, purpose and transcendental importance going on.

Paul E. Muller-Ortega[1]

We searched tirelessly for a house for over seven months. I should say, Tess searched tirelessly for a house for over seven months. I was busy teaching and traveling, so Tess took on the task of researching and looking at anything that seemed remotely possible. She knew my preferences and would call me to check out the ones she thought we could both appreciate. Months passed, and we still hadn't found "the one."

Around this time, I bumped into a friend and colleague of mine, Suzie Hurley, from Kripalu. I hadn't seen her in a few years since she stopped coming to the ashram. We hugged and exchanged warm greetings.

"Where have you been?" I immediately asked, which was always the first question any of us asked each other. It was reassuring to know that our fellow ashram brothers and sisters had landed safely somewhere.

"I've been with my new teacher," she said, looking excited.

"Who's that?"

"John Friend."

The name was familiar; I had seen his advertisement in the Yoga Journal magazine. I thought back to the picture of him. With his thick, fuzzy beard, he reminded me of a lumberjack.

"John Friend? How's that going?"

Suzie glowed. "He's wonderful. You should check him out."

Her words stayed with me. The next time I taught at the Yoga Journal Conference at Estes Park, during a free hour I decided to sit in on his class. I was blown away. Friend brought it all together: joy, light-heartedness, and humor, along with refined alignment and the heart-centered teachings of Tantra, the philosophy I still resonate with today. The technique he taught was right out of the Iyengar method, so I was

299

familiar with his alignment cues and enjoyed them a lot. But what the Iyengar method lacked – heart and humor – Friend supplied through Tantra and his own comedic timing. I laughed non-stop throughout the class.

There was a moment in the class when Friend turned our attention to the statue of *Śiva Naṭarāja*, Lord of the Dance, saying, "Life is a dance, not a dirge."

Those words struck me with deep import; it was as though something inside woke up and said, *Yes*. Without my knowing it, I was still carrying some of the heavy emotional baggage from the guru scandal. I hadn't realized how dark I had become, how joyless. It took Friend's light to show me.

ŚIVA NAṬARĀJA, LORD OF THE COSMIC DANCE

In Tantra, yoga is the virtuosity of being yourself, the point the universe has been trying to make. The whole secret to the universe is hidden within the *mūrti* (statue) of *Śiva Naṭarāja*, an artful transmutation of spiritual truth into material beauty. The dancing *Śiva* emerged in Southern India during the Cholas Dynasty sometime between the 9th to the 13th centuries. This sacred murti has come to represent many of the Tantric teachings and, more specifically, teachings from the *Nondual Śaiva-Śākta Tantra* tradition. Let's take a closer look.

WHY DOES *ŚIVA* DANCE?

This is the first question you have to ask. The answer: *for the play of it*. As we saw earlier in the definition of *līlā*, play is for its own sake. The dance represents the big bang, when the infinite singular universe burst into form, becoming the infinite finitude of form. Before the big bang, before materiality, the universe was existence itself without attributes or differentiation. It was all just one soup of pure potentiality. Then one day, out of its own delight, for the play of it, the big bang happened, and

300

the undifferentiated universe of oneness became differentiated and diverse. Unity concealed itself, while diversity revealed itself. As I mentioned at the beginning of Chapter 11, the universe (the one song) became the multiverse (the many songs).

CIRCLE OF FIRE

Śiva dances inside of a circle of fire known by many names: *agni maṇḍala* (circle of fire), *akhaṇḍa maṇḍala* (unbroken, unbounded circle without parts), and *prakāśa maṇḍala* (circle of light). This circle represents the presence of grace in a halo of light that is both illuminative and transformative. The circle is typically composed of 50 flames, representing the number of letters in the Sanskrit alphabet. Because the Sanskrit alphabet encompasses all possible vibrations and utterable sounds, the circle of fire represents all possibilities. We dance in the realm of the eternal. All possibilities exist at all times.

BRAHMA, VIṢṆU, & ŚIVA

Śiva also embodies the triune godhead of Hinduism: *Brahma, Viṣṇu*, and *Śiva* (the creator, the sustainer, and the transformer or destroyer). Brahma, the creator, is represented by *Śiva*'s upper right hand, which holds the *ḍamaru*, a two-sided drum. The drum makes a "tick tock, tick tock" sound, denoting the beginning of time and the beginning pulse of life. The *ḍamaru* symbolizes the throb or pulsation (*spanda*) of life and the infinite cycle of time in the form of vibration. *Śiva* is dancing the eternal rhythms of the universe into existence.

Viṣṇu, the sustainer, is symbolized by *Śiva*'s hair. He's spinning his head side-to-side so fast due to the ecstatic joy of the dance, that his dreadlocks lift to horizontal and he appears still. (Think of the wagon-wheel effect: a wheel appears stationary when it rotates fast enough.) Dynamic stillness is one of the many paradoxes of the *Naṭarāja*. Within movement there's stillness, and within stillness there's movement.

301

My takeaway here is that our work (or play) in life is to let the wildness rip, even as we root ourselves in stability. We remain in the eye of the storm, allowing everything else around us to move as it must. Wildness without steadiness is chaotic, yet steadiness without a little wildness is boring. *Viṣṇu* maintains the balance of both.

There is more to the symbol of *Śiva*'s hair. As the myth goes, *Śiva* was called upon by the Gods to save the world from the monsoon rains that threatened to flood and destroy the world. *Śiva* used his hair to filter the flood waters and moderate the downpour until the rains abated. In saving the world he is considered the sustainer of life, and his hair thus represents both *Śiva*'s ability to maintain harmony and balance, and the goddess Ganga, which with *Śiva*'s grace becomes the Ganges River, considered the holiest river in India.

Śiva as transformer or destroyer is symbolized by the flame of dissolution held in *Śiva*'s upper left hand. Fire has the power to change your state from gross to subtle. It burns away what's no longer needed and dissolves any obstacle to being your highest self, delivering you to the next level of freedom in your life. That purifying flame also signals the end of a cycle. Since ending always gives way to another beginning, there really is no ending – just a change, a transformation.

ŚIVA'S CONSOLING *MUDRĀ*

In *Śiva*'s lower right hand, he offers the *abhaya mudrā*, a gesture which means "have no fear." It's as though he's saying to us, "Even though things pass away, it's all okay. Chill out. It's all part of the dance. Everything that's born must eventually die. There's nothing wrong here; that's simply the way it works. Don't deny it, don't avoid or reject it. Embrace it. Engage with it."

The path of the heart is not about getting rid of fear. It's about dealing with it, managing it, and not letting it stop us from following our heart's deepest desire. *Abhaya* has another definition: "never without fear" which tells us that fear is real. It's here to stay. It's part of the dance.

NIGRAHA, ARM OF CONCEALMENT

Nigraha, meaning "keeping back, withholding, or restraining" is the name given to *Śiva*'s lower left arm, which crosses and conceals his heart. *Nigraha* signifies that we all have a shadow, blind spots, and weaknesses we can't see. We also lack knowledge, with much of life concealed from us. Life is hardly ever what it seems. Much is concealed. In fact, I've heard Brooks teach that we can only know 25% of anything. There is always 75% unknown to us. As we age, we gain more knowledge, but the universe keeps expanding and accelerating, ensuring that we'll never catch up on the 75% we can't know. I don't view this as a bad thing; instead, I'm inspired to know that learning is endless.

Related to *nigraha* is *rahāsya,* which means "secret." Remember the description of concealment in Chapter 2? Secreting is the way the universe reveals itself. The universe conceals itself for the sheer delight of having a revelatory experience; without concealment, there would never be a revelation. The limitation is divine and intentional. It serves a grand purpose.

The concept of *rahāsya* is quite simple: the universe hides itself in plain sight. The oak tree has roots we cannot see; the earth is round even though it looks and feels flat, and its core has gravity invisible to the naked eye. The flower is concealed in the bud. The butterfly is concealed as the caterpillar.

In music, the notes don't happen all at once. Some notes are played while others are concealed. If you play the notes all at the same time, you get noise. In Tantra, enlightenment is a process that reveals itself little by little over time. If it were revealed all at once, we probably wouldn't be able to handle it.

In Chapter 10 of the *Bhagavad Gītā, Kṛṣṇa* (a stand-in for our highest self, or God) is the chariot driver for Arjuna, a warrior prince. Arjuna pesters *Kṛṣṇa* to reveal his true nature as the divine, but when *Kṛṣṇa* finally opens his mouth to show himself in all his awesome, gruesome

303

magnificence, Arjuna practically wets his dhoti. Shaken, Arjuna realizes that it's too much. He demands that *Kṛṣṇa* close his mouth, tone it down, and return to his human, more familiar form.

In the statue, *Śiva* himself is withholding himself. Why? Because he must, so that the world in all its diversity and ordinary brokenness can appear. But notice: even as this concealment is going on, *Naṭarāja's* lower right hand is still in *abhaya mudrā*, the consoling gesture. *Śiva* is telling us, "Yes, you will be afraid; you will be confused and concealed; your heart will close. But relax. Be fearless and remember grace. It's all part of the dance! It's supposed to be that way."

Why? Again, because *Śiva*, out of his own delight, self-conceals (*sva-pracodana*) and self-limits in order to self-reveal (*sva-prakāśa*), to have a revelation of his true nature.

Concealment and limitation become a vital part of the dance, for without forgetting who we are, we would never have the joy of remembering again. This interpretation of the *Śiva Naṭarāja* marks a significant departure from other traditions; in Tantra, limitation is considered part of the means of awakening. I see this again and again in Tantric teachings, and it's a deeply significant distinction. Instead of our forgetfulness, limitations, and contracted states of consciousness being mistakes or failures of character, they play a vital role in the journey of awakening.

LIFTED FOOT OF GRACE

Anugraha is the name given to the lifted leg and means "favor, amiability, bestowing benefits, or promoting a good cause." *Anugraha* also means "that which follows (*anu*) when grace grasps (*graha*) hold of you." One leg stabilizes the entire dance while the other leg dances wildly in a lifted position. The foot of the lifted leg is the *kuñcitapāda*: *kuñcita* (curved, bent, or twisted) and *pāda* (foot). It is also known as the lifted foot of grace.

IMP OF FORGETFULNESS

The little creature all curled up underneath the standing leg of *Śiva* is called *Apasmāra Puruṣa*, or the "imp of forgetfulness." *Apasmāra Puruṣa* (*apas* means "away from," and *māra* means "to remember") is defined as "forgetting *puruṣa*, or spirit." The imp is the ego, our individual nature, or that part of ourselves that is blinded by the shadow.

Naṭarāja does not kill the ego. He allows it to live, but keeps it at bay, pressed under his standing foot. Within the Tantric tradition, we're not supposed to obliterate the ego, or dissolve our individual life-wave. Like fear and all of the other contracted states, we're here to manage the ego and keep it pointed in the direction of our heart.

Apasmāra Puruṣa is also known as "the blessing of forgetfulness." As explained above, without forgetting, we would never experience the joy of remembering. I can think of other instances where forgetting would certainly be a blessing. For our veterans with PTSD, and anyone else suffering from insomnia due to trauma, forgetting the events of the past, at least during sleep, would be a healing blessing and a welcomed relief to the nervous system.

Apasmāra Puruṣa gazes upward at the *Kuñcitapāda* (lifted foot of grace), signifying that the ego, when it has its eyes cast on grace – or is connected to an energy bigger than itself that serves grace in some way – is absolutely necessary for the dance. In fact, the ego holds up the entire dance of life! Life is a co-creation between ego and grace. Your decisions and choices matter. You affect the entire dance based on your capacity to forget and remember, over and over again.

DOLA MUDRĀ

The *dola mudrā* is the hand gesture at the end of the concealing arm, and it points directly *at the lifted foot of grace*. Even though we are all concealed, the answer to concealment is... grace. The solution to concealment is... grace. In fact, grace is the reason for concealment.

Through grace, we remember and awaken to our true nature. Grace is the current that dispels concealment and carries us along the trajectory of our soul's quest to understand ourselves.

> *Concealment is the reason grace exists. Grace is the solution to concealment. By means of grace, Śiva ends the concealment he has imposed on himself. He comes to the recognition that his own Consciousness penetrates the cycles of the universe. Grace resolves or dissolves the illusion of duality inherent in the individual's universe.*
>
> ~from *The Splendor of Recognition*
> by Swami Shantananda and Peggy Bendet[2]

Śiva Naṭarāja's dance is referred to as the dance of resplendent consciousness and ecstatic joy, and it holds a central place in the *Nondual Śaiva-Śākta Tantra* cosmology. (See Appendix D for the Five Divine Acts of *Śiva*.) Although Friend only touched on the Tantric teachings in my first class with him, those teachings opened the shades and let in the sun. After 13 years of attempting to transcend myself at Kripalu, and the subsequent trauma of betrayal, I was in dire need of some light.

When Friend finished teaching, I went up to thank him and give him my music CD, "Deep Peace." He met me with great compassion and joy, and I experienced an instant brother-bond; we recognized in each other a shared devotion to yoga and to the great gift of being alive. As we shook hands, he encouraged me to come to another session, and I went on my way.

Later that year, Kripalu hosted a Yoga Journal Conference and again, Friend was there. Tess and I followed him around the whole time with our clipboards, trying to learn his method and take down notes on the Tantric philosophy, which he taught with clarity and passion. During a break, I asked him if Anusara Yoga could heal my shins, as I was quite bow-legged. He said it could, and then spent a few minutes showing me how. I was so impressed with his ability to connect with me and touched by the generous gift of his time. I felt totally seen.

306

Suzie was assisting Friend at the conference and invited both Tess and me to a private practice with Friend and his wife at the time. Because we were so accustomed to watching the guru do his posture flow at Kripalu, we showed up in our street clothes. As soon as we entered, Friend said, "Hey! Where are your yoga clothes? Where's your mat?" I suddenly understood that we had been invited to practice "with" Friend. I started to explain, but he didn't seem to need an explanation.

"It's fine!" he exclaimed, "You can practice with your street clothes." He produced two more mats, saying, "Here are some extras. Just join in." Once again, his generosity was striking. For 90 minutes, he led us all through a complete class, and although he did some of the poses himself, he really focused on teaching Tess and me the technique.

At that time, I was still immersed in the Kripalu and PRYT technique of surrender, so Friend taught me the importance of engaging my muscles, and how to incorporate that engagement into the *āsanas* – but not in a dogmatic way. He put us all at ease with his good humor; partway through the practice he said something that made us all crack up. It was through laughter that he was able to convey the deepest teachings and poses. I discovered that in order to let go and loosen up, I first needed to engage and become more stable – that greater flexibility came with increased stability. I remember spending a significant amount of time in *trikoṇāsana* (Triangle Pose). Friend broke it all down and helped us both achieve what felt like the most fully realized *trikoṇāsana* we had ever done.

I took up study with him. After years of being told that "understanding was the booby prize," I was hungry for the kind of knowledge that Friend was dispensing. The Tantric path was rich, complex, diverse, and intellectually demanding, and it required both my mind and my heart. It required *engagement* – not just muscular, though that was necessary for the style of yoga *āsanas* he taught.

PHILOSOPHY INFORMS PRACTICE

In Chapter 2, I gave a brief explanation of the word "Tantra," describing it as a weaver's loom, yet there are other, more nuanced interpretations of the word. Christopher Wallis, author of *Tantra Illuminated*, says: "Modern teachers like to mention that the verbal root *tan* means 'stretch, expand,' saying that Tantra is so called because it stretches our awareness and expands our capacity for joy." Although Wallis appreciates the spirit of that definition, he takes it a step further, dissecting the etymology of the word more fully. He explains that the word can be broken down into the verbal roots "*tan* and *tra*, the former meaning 'propagate, elaborate on, expand on,' and the latter, 'save, protect.'" In his analysis, then, "Tantra spreads (*tan*) wisdom that saves (*tra*)." He views following the Tantra as not only a path to spiritual fulfillment, but also as a way to protect oneself.

People who hyperextend their knees (or have bow legs, as I did) usually are unaware they are doing it. Only when it's pointed out to them do they take steps to change the pattern, which is usually one they've had all their lives. Joints that are too loose will eventually cause injury, as will joints that are too tight. Change comes from finding the balance between strengthening the muscles that are too weak and relaxing those that are too strong, to find that optimal place in the middle, the place that lives between stability and freedom. That is where peak function resides.

This way of thinking aligns with Tantric philosophy in two fundamental ways. First, you have a role to play. You have agency, and how much effort you expend is what determines the outcome. Second, too much freedom renders you powerless. The goal of Tantra and this type of yoga is to find the place in the middle, which aligns with the conundrum of being both human and divine.

Ultimately, everyone has to surrender to death. But all events leading up to that final letting go require both effort and surrender, as well as a continuous exploration of the balance between the two.

Engagement became paramount within my life philosophy. It expanded my notion of how to relate to the world around me, and the universe within me. I came to see that in order to experience true freedom I first had to get stable. Years later, I came to see this way of thinking as a practical illustration of Wallis's definition of Tantra as "wisdom that saves."

Studying with Friend, I transitioned from the paradigm of surrender into the Tantric paradigm of co-participation with the Divine – from *surrendering* my will *to* divine will, to *aligning* my will *with* divine will. This shift was reminiscent of my "pact" with the universe upon my return to the ashram after hospitalization, when I was no longer willing to simply surrender: *I agree to go with you again. But I have to do it on my terms.* I came to that understanding spontaneously, not knowing that it was related to the Tantric path of the householder. All I knew was that I had a say in allowing grace to flow through me. I had agency.

EFFORT, ENGAGEMENT, & AGENCY

In *sūtra* 2.1 of the *Yoga Sūtras*, Patañjali defines his yoga (*kriyā* yoga) as consisting of *tapas* (austerity), *svadhyāya* (self-study), and *īśvara praṇidhāna* (surrender to God), which are the last three *niyamas*. As I've pointed out previously, *tapas* from the Classical view is defined as austerity and discipline, whereas Tantra interprets *tapas* as meaning the intense longing for God or the burning desire for freedom. Both yogic worldviews agree, however, that you can't touch the Absolute without a considerable amount of self-effort. Patañjali teaches that liberation on the path of yoga takes fire, while Tantra sees it as fire of a different sort: the willingness to walk through the fires of your life and hold fast to your heart's purest vision. You have to apply yourself. You need agency.

This is a distinct shift between the renunciatory path and the Tantra path. Within Classical Yoga and *Advaita Vedānta*, there is the notion of "witness consciousness," the part of your awareness that is unattached to any results, likes or dislikes, or biases. Both schools of yogic thought hold witness consciousness or "clear seeing" as the highest form of perception. It's a way of seeing a pure, untainted vision of reality that is

309

beyond the ego, beyond selfish needs or desires. Most of us rarely get there; we generally rely on the foggy glasses of our limited perceptions – which are shaped by our *saṃskāras* or need for comfort. It's rare that we can get to that place where we perceive the world through true witness consciousness, yet the goal of Classical Yoga and *Advaita Vedānta* is to not only get there, but also stay there.

Yet, witness consciousness alone is without agency. This part of your awareness is withdrawn from any identification with the individual self, and as such, it doesn't act. It can't. One of Tantra's most influential teachings for me is that of co-participation – another term for agency. In Tantra, you are totally identified with your actions in a way that gives you power to take full responsibility for the world in which you live. There's nothing separating you from what you see. There's nothing – and no one – sitting up "on high" somewhere, untouched by life. Just the contrary. Tantra teaches that you are here, fully, taking responsibility for your actions even as you co-participate with the Absolute.

The goal in the householder Tantra path is not to stand with both feet in *puruṣa* (pure spirit) to "witness" life as a way of existing apart from it, but to stand with both feet on the earth, and from the perspective of the broader Absolute consciousness, to deal with life as it expresses itself through you, in you, as you. The goal is to engage deeply with life and with all of your relationships, individual feelings, needs, and desires, while still holding the wider, broader perspective of the Absolute.

It's not easy; holding the perspective of the Absolute while living the full catastrophe of your life, takes consistent practice over a long period of time. Why bother? Because your agency comes straight from the source of consciousness itself. The vast Absolute *engaged with life by becoming you.* You are the embodiment of the divine, acting out the drama of life that you are co-creating with grace.

The gift of our embodiment, our life here on earth, is that we have the opportunity to intervene. We can intervene with life and change our patterns, habitual thinking, relationships, and environment in ways that can shift our destiny.

310

It's all possible in the here-and-now earth plane. Because we are co-participators with life, with the Absolute, there's no predetermined script or plan from God that we simply fulfill. No. We are co-creating life with grace in each moment – by interacting with all the forces around us: past, present, future, and nature. All our thoughts, words, desires, and actions cut grooves in the playdough of time/space reality. Yoga, then, is about intervening in a way that shapes your destiny, that makes a positive difference in your life or in the lives of others.

Grace is effulgent and overflowing with abundance, and she is seeking an open heart or vessel into which she may pour out her blessings. When you have hope, when you believe in the goodness of life and the goodness in the depth of every human heart, you become an open conduit for grace to shower her blessings upon you. But if you don't participate – if you don't take action by asking – then grace can't give you its abundance. You have to ask for it in order for it to be given. No asking, no agency. No desire, no fulfillment.

If we never take the risk to ask for what we want, then grace won't have the chance to deliver. When you align with your heart and offer an intention or innocent desire without being attached to the outcome, you become a worthy vessel of grace's compassion and abundance. When you extend your hand first, with an intention or a desire free of attachment, the universe will automatically respond. This never became more apparent to me than when Tess and I tried to find our dream house.

THE HOUSE

After seven months of searching – which to us seemed like an eternity – we walked through a small house that checked off most of the boxes on our wish list. It wasn't exactly what we had hoped for, but we were both getting tired of the whole house-hunting process. We decided we were prepared to put a down payment on it.

As we drove away from the house, Tess glanced over her shoulder out the window.

311

"Wait!" she exclaimed. I hit the brakes.

"Did you forget something? I'm late for teaching..." I started to say, but she interrupted me, staring out the window at a non-descript house just down the road.

"Is that a 'For Sale by Owner' sign? I didn't see that before. They must have just put it up!" Her excitement was palpable.

"I guess... but I can't look at the house now."

"I can. Let's go home so you can get your car."

We pulled into the parking lot of our apartment building. No sooner had my second foot landed on the asphalt than she peeled out. I jumped to the side to avoid getting run over, my words "Let me know how it goes" lost in her exhaust.

About two hours later, I had just finished my class when Tess called. "Todd, you have to come over here right away. I think this is the one."

"But... what about the smaller house down the road? The one we decided on?"

"Forget that house," she said, sounding like a mob boss. "I'm telling you, Bunna (the nickname we used for each other), this is the house! It's perfect. I think you're going to love it."

As I advanced up the driveway, the house looked small and dull, like it needed a shot of espresso. Frankly, I was underwhelmed. But Tess's enthusiasm still rang in my ears (*you're going to love it)*, so I set aside my doubt.

An hour later, I was smiling uncontrollably ear to ear.

This *was* our "dream house." Tess was right. It was perfect for our needs: close to a dirt road so we could go for a run right out our front door; a

312

mile from the nearest town; close to Kripalu; fairly close to the airport. It was small enough to be cozy, but large enough to have a yoga room and two offices. The house had great potential. We imagined adding a deck, renovating the basement, and landscaping.

I could see that Tess had become quick friends with the owners, a couple in their thirties. Tess and they had a kind of chemistry I couldn't explain. The husband told us that he had built this house a few years ago, but that *his* dream house – way out in the woods a few towns over, on 70 acres of forest – recently became available. You could tell he was thrilled about moving. He went on to say that he and his wife had already signed a Purchase and Sale agreement with someone who wanted this house as a second home, but that they very much wanted to sell it to a full-time resident.

I pulled Tess aside and said privately to her, "Do you really want this house?"

Eyes gleaming, she replied instantaneously, "Yes."

"Is it worth an extra $2000 to you?"

"Yes!"

"Okay then." I knew what I had to do.

Even though I had never negotiated for a house before, I strode over to the owner and said, "Would you give it to us for an extra $2K?"

Without missing a beat, he said, "Yours."

I said, "Deal." He said "Deal."

Then we all jumped up and down like little kids.

Weeks passed, and we packed up our apartment with gleeful anticipation. The night before the closing, I called the owner to thank him again for the house. When he picked up the phone, I was shocked to realize he was in tears.

"What's wrong?"

He blew his nose, then said, "The owner of my dream house backed out of the deal. We have no home to live in." At the time, they were living with his wife's grandmother who was somewhat disabled. They were taking care of her and needed a larger house, in part, to make more room for all three of them.

"What are you going to do?

"I don't know," he responded quietly. "We don't have a plan."

Again, I knew what I had to do. Without missing a beat, I said, "Well, we'll give you back your house. You don't need to sell it to us."

He refused. "That's very kind of you. But I couldn't do that. We'll see you at the bank tomorrow as planned."

Tess and I arrived at the bank in the morning with our minds made up. When I had told her what happened, she agreed completely that we couldn't buy his house now. As heartbroken as we were, we were also clear: it would be selfish and unethical.

Before the meeting started, we pulled our lawyer aside to tell him our decision, but we were interrupted. It was time to begin.

We sat down in comfortable chairs around the enormous oak table with the lawyers, the owners, and assorted assistants. It was a sizable group. My throat was dry. I swallowed hard and was about to speak, when the owner beat me to it.

"We regret to tell you that our dream house fell through," he said. "We have no place to live. But we still want to go forward with selling you

314

our house. I don't want to do to you what the owner of our dream house did to us. It wouldn't be right."

Tess spoke up right away. "No. We can't buy your house. You will have nowhere to go. Where will your grandmother go? You have to keep your house."

"No, we couldn't do that to you two. We'll make do in our old farmhouse next door. There's enough space for us to live there until we find another home."

Both Tess and I pleaded with him, but his loyalty to his word was valiant. He kept insisting on keeping the deal we made. He was clearly torn inside, due to the loss of his dream house, yet he stood with unflinching virtue, as clear, strong, and true as the great oak tree that gave its life to become the table at which we were sitting.

"Please," he said, with a finality we all sensed could not be shaken. "Let's sign the papers and make it official."

One by one, the lawyers began to tear up. One of them began to sob. I couldn't keep it together and I began sobbing along with Tess. Before we knew it, everyone in the room was crying. Mascara ran down cheeks and people reached for their handkerchiefs and tissues. We were having a Kripalu moment right there in the bank.

So Tess and I signed, the owners signed, and everyone hugged. Then we all started to giggle a little, probably because we all reflected on what had just happened and how rare it is for lawyers to cry at a closing.

The next day, with mixed emotions, we showed up at the house with the first load of belongings. The former owner was very generous in helping us move in and showing us around the house. Over time, we became good friends with him and his family staying in the farmhouse next door. He even cut our grass for us free until we could buy our first rider mower.

On that first day in our new home, as I stood in what would become our yoga room, I reflected on that moment in the bank. I wanted to understand why I was crying. I decided it was because there was so much kindness in the room, so much consideration and empathy for the other person.

Then it hit me.

This is grace. This is the hand of providence. No matter what I said, I couldn't change the will of the owner.

He had made up his mind and he wouldn't accept anything else. This was so outside my ability to control, I simply had to let go and allow the hand of the divine to intervene and give me my dream house. It felt like grace was leading and I was following: a beautiful, glorious dance.

Here Tess and I were seven months later, as if by magic, standing in the exact home we'd imagined. Well, almost…

The property was just over an acre and the house was fairly small. It wasn't until we had finally moved in that we realized we'd forgotten to specify *how much* grass we wanted. It was as though we were living on a grass farm. All of a sudden we needed equipment: riding mower, small push mower, weed whacker, and a host of other supporting gadgets. But the kicker? It turned out I was *allergic to grass.*

Now whenever I create a wish list for anything, I try to remember to be highly specific. Lesson? Watch out for what you ask for. You're probably going to get it, particularly if you employ *sankalpa.*

Sankalpa is a Sanskrit word that means volition, intention, or to bring into existence. The word is derived from the root "*klp*" to imagine, to think, or to conceive. It also means to compose, form, or create by giving a concrete shape to an abstract thought or concept. The word *sankalpa* goes all the way back to the Vedas, which stipulates that the whole world evolved through *sankalpa* or thought.

In essence, it's an idea formed in the mind or heart that is infused with resolve, determination, or conviction. *Saṅkalpa*, the power of your will to bring forth your ideas, is also the kind of willpower that is flexible and pliable enough to be able to change with the circumstances. Yet it is strong enough to overcome self-doubt or other negative thoughts that arise that could sabotage your intention. *Saṅkalpa* remains flexible yet rooted.

> *Aspire to your greatness and have a great intention. We imprint our intention from the heart into the fabric of the body and mind. As we imprint our hopes we become steadfast in our purpose. Saṅkalpa imprints our inner intention.*
>
> ~Douglas Brooks[3]

EFFORT & GRACE: TWO WINGS

It was a combination of both effort and grace that allowed us to find the house of our dreams. Isn't that often the case? Like a bird that needs both wings to fly, we need both effort and grace to soar. With effort alone, it's like flapping one wing: you just go around in a circle, tiring yourself out and getting nowhere. With grace alone – or in other words, by surrendering only and giving over your power – you again go around in an opposite circle. Over-surrendering renders you impotent to make anything happen; it's like lots of wind blowing with no sail to catch it.

I've learned through direct experience that too much grace can cause you to become ungrounded and spacey, which then leaves you vulnerable to being taken advantage of. *Svadhyāya* (mindfulness, self-study) is the awareness to know the difference between effort and grace, to help maintain a sense of balance. That is, it takes awareness to know when we are over-efforting and not opening to a bigger energy, or the contrary, when we are surrendering too much and lacking agency.

I think we all know what it's like to over-effort in our lives. My humbling experience with overdoing it happened when I joined the local US Masters Swim Team several years ago. I'd never been an avid

317

swimmer since my low body fat generally sent me straight to the bottom of the pool – causing me to work extra hard to keep afloat.

During our workout one day, the coach taught us about relaxing into the stroke and feeling the water. He said, "When you over-effort, your technique tends to get sloppy and you lose speed. In addition, when you resist the water or fight the water, your muscles contract and you build up more water resistance. The key to this workout is to relax." I listened carefully, but after a few laps of my usual churning through the water, I found myself getting more and more exhausted.

Halfway through practice, I heard this huge voice, booming out over all of the other swimmers, "Yogi, relax! Relax, Yogi!" The irony of this statement was not entirely lost on me, or I'm sure on the other swimmers who heard it. I laughed, and bubbles escaped to the surface. Then I took a deep breath and let go. My head tilted down a bit and released strain in the back of my neck. I felt the water more, and for the first time, my body began floating on the surface of the water. Suddenly, swimming was a pleasure, not a chore. I had been over-efforting, over-participating.

That night at home I asked myself, "How often in my life do I over-participate?" The answer was, "Most, if not all of the time." It was a revelation: I'd been striving too hard in general and spinning my wheels more than I needed. I decided I only need to do 50% of the effort; grace can do the other 50%. That percentage can shift a little more or less depending on the circumstance, but half and half is generally good for all of us.

When effort and grace are balanced, you soar like an eagle – or float to the surface and swim like a dolphin.

Yes, effort helps you accomplish external goals. But at what cost? Our entire society is paying the price of doing too much: fatigue, stress, even illness. And it's not only classically "high stress" jobs that cause us to overdo. Even as a yoga teacher I've had years where I gave and gave and gave, until burnout forced me to take time off to recalibrate. Clearly, effort alone is not the answer. You might get a lot done, but it's at the

318

expense of spaciousness, joy, and a healthy life. It's not worth it, and in the long term, it's unsustainable.

ŚIVA & *ŚAKTI* ON WHEELS

Once we settled into our new home, Tess and I did a lot of road biking in the surrounding Berkshire Mountains. During my bike racing years at the ashram, I had adopted a highly detailed and structured biking workout, using a bike computer to record the mileage, average speed, and fastest speed of every ride. Even though I wasn't competing anymore, I still biked with focused effort and loved the data component of it. Tess, on the other hand, biked with a totally different intention. She loved to take in the scenery and allow her breath to dictate the pace, without pushing herself. She didn't care how far or fast she went, or what kind of route she took. Needless to say, our biking styles couldn't have been more dissimilar.

When we rode together, I generally had my eyes glued to my computer, tracking my data, while she looked around, paying special attention to any "Open House" signs posted in the passing yards. When she spotted one, she'd make an immediate U-turn, often dragging us both down dirt roads and into the house for sale, where we would unclip our biking shoes and take the tour in our socks. We weren't even in the market for a new house; Tess just loved to see homes – a holdover from our house-hunting days. The whole purpose of biking for her was to delight in real estate.

As frustrating as this was for me, I still enjoyed having a biking companion. In order to compensate for her riding style, I would sprint ahead by a mile or so, then turn around, loop around her and begin again. For every mile she rode, I probably rode another one. I didn't mind; this was just how we rode together. She often requested that I ride at her speed so we could go together – an idea I always resisted.

Until her birthday one year, when I declared at breakfast, "Since it's your big day, on this ride, I'll ride with you wherever you want to go for however long. I won't look down at my computer and we can have conversations and take rests."

She looked at me with surprise. "Really?"

"Really," I said, feeling quite magnanimous, "and we can even find the best bathrooms along the way if you have to go."

She loved the idea. So we embarked on the ride to "wherever." For the first few miles, we rolled along at her leisurely pace, which to me felt like *crawling*. Following behind her, I had to remind myself that this was my birthday gift to Tess, to keep me from just blasting past her. Partway through the ride, she slowed down even further and called over her shoulder to me:

"Todd? I need to make a pit stop."

I answered, "Do you want me to hold your bike so you can go in the woods?"

"No," she said, "I'd like to find a nice bathroom somewhere where I could sit down."

We were just passing the entrance to Simon's Rock College. "There!" she said, "I want to go there."

We turned into the campus and rode from building to building, looking for a bathroom she could access. Nothing. Finally, at the end of a long driveway, we found the athletic center. Surely there must be a bathroom there! I stayed with the bikes as she disappeared into the building. When she emerged after several minutes, she bounced down the steps, grinning broadly.

"Why are you smiling?"

"Because I feel so loved and supported that you are going at my pace," she said, "Thanks for that."

We kissed. Feeling like I had scored a point, we took the road again. In my enthusiasm, I bolted ahead about a mile before I realized I was back at my own pace and had left Tess in the dust. I turned around sheepishly and returned to bike behind her.

We pedaled along pine trees and fields, until we came upon a river near the road. Tess slowed to a stop.

"Can we sit for a while?"

"Sure," I said. We parked the bikes and walked down to the pebbly edge. I looked for a suitable place to sit, but Tess had other ideas. She started taking off her shoes and socks.

"Let's go sit on that island!" she chirped, pointing at a little island in the middle of the river. "The water doesn't look that deep."

I shook my head. "No, thanks." I was fine giving Tess what she wanted: going at her pace, making several stops, noticing the scenery. But I wasn't going to take off my shoes and wade through a stream!

She forged ahead, wading into the water. "Ooh, it's chilly," she gasped, "but nice!"

I stayed on the bank and watched her. Arms outstretched, navigating the slippery bottom and laughing when she lost her balance, she looked like she was having so much fun. She looked back at me and beckoned, and that did it. How could I resist?

Minutes later, I found myself on the island with the river flowing on either side of us. It felt like we were in the center of nature itself. We closed our eyes, mesmerized by the sound of the gently rushing water. I felt her hand touch mine. Together, we dropped into a deep meditation, holding hands. My heart slowed and softened. I wasn't in any kind of rush or race to finish. I wasn't concerned about my timing, the mileage, or average speed. I was just present with Tess, with myself, in the flow.

321

At some point, I felt her hand slip away. When I opened my eyes, Tess was standing, looking mischievous. "I dare you to go skinny dipping," she challenged.

"Skinny dipping?" I spluttered. *Now, that's just taking it too far.* "First of all, we'll get all wet and we don't have a towel..."

"We'll get WET? Oh no!" she teased.

"And it's broad daylight! And the river is right next to the road!" I could see I was getting nowhere. "It's probably illegal to go skinny dipping here!"

"Hmm..." She looked down the river, to where it made a curve away from the road. "Follow me."

We waded over to the bend and a little beyond. There was a secluded area hidden from the road. I had no more excuses. We threw off our clothes, squealing with glee like little kids, and swam around for a while in the buff. I was Adam, once again! But this time, I was with Eve. We enjoyed the freedom and exhilaration of our dip, then got dressed and hopped back on our bikes to finish the ride. That night, as we shared a wonderful dinner out to complete our celebration of Tess's birthday, we agreed: it was one of our most memorable days, ever.

When I look back on that experience, I see it through the lens of effort and grace, as well as the lens of *Śiva* and *Śakti*. In biking and in most other things, I'm more *Śiva* -related. I thrive on the steadiness of the Absolute. I like predictability, certainty, and control, and I feel good when I maintain my focus on one thing and accomplish it. Tess, on the other hand, is more like *Śakti*. She's creative, unpredictable, and loves to make it up in the moment. She loves the adventure of life and thrives on the thrill of uncertainty and passion. We make a good couple because we complement each other; she brings me the creative improvisation that opens new horizons for me, and I offer her the focus and certainty that allow her to stay grounded.

322

The yogic sages...anticipated quantum physics by pointing out that a subtle vibratory energy is the substratum of everything we know. Unlike physicists, however, yogic seers experienced this energy not simply as an abstract vibration but as the expression of the divine feminine power called Shakti.

~Sally Kempton, *Awakening Shakti*[4]

BALANCE IN DIVINE UNION

In the *Nondual Śaiva-Śākta Tantra* tradition, *Śakti* is as important as *Śiva*. Most of the *Śaiva* scriptures begin with *Śakti* asking *Śiva*, "What is the secret of the universe?" *Śiva*'s response is always, "You are. The secret is you. Everything you need to know is already hidden within you." *Śakti* is the student within all of us who seeks knowledge and freedom, and *Śiva* is the teacher who lifts the student up to the level of brilliance and greatness that already exists within her, empowering her to see that she is already free.

Śiva is Absolute consciousness, the essence of all that is, but *Śakti* is the power of that consciousness, the embodiment of the formless. As *Śiva* is the sun, *Śakti* is the rays of the sun; as *Śiva* is the stream, *Śakti* is the current of the stream. They are different from each other, and yet paradoxically, they are one and the same. One can't exist without the other; you can't have the sun without its rays!

Śakti is the individual; *Śiva* is the universal. *Śakti*, as the face of *Śiva*, is both human and divine and therefore, she reflects the humanity within us all. She is the individual expression of universal light. On another level, *Śakti* represents the very human part of us that doubts, feels unworthy, or carries some form of limitation. This is the intentionally forgetful nature I've described of the great Absolute *Śiva* himself, who finds joy in remembering, through *Śakti*.

There is no real polarity between them, even though they are encoded differently. The masculine encoding of *Śiva* and feminine encoding of

323

Śakti both need to exist in order to create the universe, just as sperm and egg are both needed to create human life. In our earlier depiction of the Absolute, we learned that one of its qualities is *spanda*: pulsation, vibration, the throb of life. Everything in the universe expands and contracts in some way. From our own heartbeats, to the quantum level flashing in and out of reality, to the breathing in and out of our lungs, to the post-Big-Bang expansion and contraction, pulsation is a universal principle. Tenth-century Kashmiri philosopher Acharya Abhinavagupta defines *spanda* as "the pulsation of the ecstasy of the divine consciousness." This subtle pulsation is the source of all creation, and it plays out in the balance between *Śiva* and *Śakti*.

The symbols of *Śiva* and *Śakti* are represented within the fourth cakra, the *Anāhata*. In Chapter 1, we learned that the symbol of the heart cakra is two interlocking triangles, one pointing up toward liberation (*Śiva*), and one pointing down toward embodiment (*Śakti*). The two energies intersect there, representing their ultimate consummation and balance of Absolute and Relative, divine and human, *puruṣa* and *prakṛti*, in the form of a six-pointed star.

Śiva and *Śakti* are conjoined and inseparable. One of my favorite teachings about *Śiva* and *Śakti* is that you have to go through her in order to get to him. It takes the mortal to experience the immortal, the individual to know the universal. In scientific terms, *Śiva* could be considered potential energy, and *Śakti*, kinetic energy. In any object that is in motion, both energies exist simultaneously.

TRAINING

I completed my Anusara teacher training in 1999, yet I still taught PRYT for the next two years. During this time, I continued studying with Friend – who introduced me to Brooks and several other brilliant Tantric scholars. I quickly found the Tantric path, with its compassionate ideology, to be a total relief to me. It was so much more forgiving! It was about aligning with nature rather than trying to outrun it, about living life fully rather than avoiding death. Tantra was a complete shift of motivation, and I found it wonderfully inspiring.

Its concept of perfection that I mentioned in Chapter 2 (the universe doesn't make mistakes, because it's incapable of doing so) was revolutionary to me. The idea that my flaws, my idiosyncrasies, are what make me uniquely me, turned my whole life philosophy upside down. Now, instead of trying to change myself to remove a flaw, I started to embrace my shortcomings, accept them, and have compassion for myself as I continued to practice.

For the first time, I saw myself as moving from a state of perfection to a state of *more* perfection. I realized that I could make changes without criticizing myself or making myself wrong. What a radical idea: *improve yourself through love!* With this shift, I was more able to accept my limitations and the limitations of others. A lot of my perfectionistic and self-critical tendencies began to drop away, uncovering a happier person and a more accepting teacher.

I began to focus on the joy of life, rather than on my difficulties, and to my great delight, my difficulties started working themselves out. I was learning how to see the sacredness of spirit everywhere, in everything, and in everyone – including myself. And my body opened up more in those two years of study with Friend than in all 17 years prior! Clearly, Tantra was bringing me *Śrī*, in myriad ways.

One piece was missing, however: the joy of training yoga teachers. When Michael Lee approached me about offering a 200-hour teacher training for PRYT, I said yes. At that time, the PRYT headquarters was only a mile away from my house, and it seemed like the perfect opportunity.

Since I was now deeply into Anusara Yoga, I decided to teach them the Anusara method of alignment and all of its philosophy, along with the heart-centered components I learned from my years of training teachers at Kripalu. The course was a behemoth. In three 10-day intensives, we had sessions from 6:00 a.m. to 9:00 p.m. every day, with only an hour break for meals. I probably taught over 300 hours. Plus, I gave the students another 100 hours of at-home study. My first training was so

325

successful that PRYT invited me to do four more trainings over the next four years.

I had been seizing every opportunity I could to study with Friend. I had traveled all over the country to attend his workshops and trainings, and, although officially certified in 2002, had been teaching Anusara Yoga since 1999 and offering Anusara teacher trainings since 2001. I had found my new identity. This time it wasn't with a guru, but with a great teacher with whom I felt a deep affinity. We were both American, we were the same age, and we shared a deep passion for yoga and personal transformation. Friend respected me, and I'm grateful that he permitted me to train teachers in his method before I was officially certified.

ŚIVA & ŚAKTI ON THE MAT

I led trainings for two years on my own, and then Tess joined me in 2006 to team-teach. We had done this for years at Kripalu, teaching workshops, partner yoga, and teacher trainings with our familiar *Śiva* - *Śakti* dynamic. Coming to class with a set plan, I would deliver my agenda – whether it was the best thing for the students that day or not. The curriculum needed to be followed, and I could usually sway the group to go with me. But Tess would always arrive agenda-free, tune into the group by asking them, "What do you want to do today?" and then skillfully and spontaneously create a brilliant class.

When we had co-taught courses that had a lot of curriculum, like teacher trainings, our divergent styles proved challenging – and teaching Anusara together was no different. As usual, she saw how I could improve the course and gave me a lot of feedback. I wanted to follow her suggestions, but I realized that what she was asking me to do – reduce the quantity of personal growth and cathartic material, increase the technical instruction – was against my nature. She was brilliant at breaking down the technique into bite-sized, understandable pieces, and she could do it totally in the moment. It just flowed out of her. I, on the other hand, could do it if I had gone over it enough times to feel comfortable with the steps. Meanwhile, the personal growth aspect was my sweet spot; I was completely comfortable in that realm. So I took her notes as best I could, and we kept going.

At some point, however, Tess said that she had no interest in continuing to co-teach the trainings as I was leading them, and that if I wanted her participation, I had to let her take over and be the director. I agreed. In retrospect, I can see a number of factors that led to that dubious decision. Primarily, I allowed her criticism to make me feel undervalued, but there was a secondary reason: I wanted to placate her.

In the past, when we had gotten into co-teaching skirmishes, we had always worked it out by appreciating and dovetailing each other's gifts. I figured we would do that again, but unfortunately, that strategy proved unworkable. I let her redesign the training, and we attempted to teach it together, taking turns. But there was little dovetailing; she made up curriculum in the moment and I had no way of following her. She interrupted my teaching with criticism, which totally pushed my unworthiness button. The situation became unmanageable.

We finally came up with a system: when I taught, rather than interrupt me if she didn't like what I was doing, she left the room and wrote down her feedback; I did the same when she taught. Then, after the session, we reconciled our differing opinions. This game plan worked well enough, but the trainings were wearing us down. At some point, we both realized that the stress on our marriage simply wasn't worth it. Our students loved learning from both of our styles, telling us how much they enjoyed how "real" we were with each other, but we felt it didn't make sense to continue to teach together. I went on alone.

EXERCISE: Five Steps to Setting a Powerful Intention

1. Take a comfortable seat in a quiet place either on a meditation pillow or in a chair where you can sit with your spine straight in the vertical axis.

2. Take a few deep conscious breaths in and out. Breathe all the way down to your sitting bones. Relax your belly, your palms, and your face. When you exhale, allow your hips to settle and become heavy. On your inhalation, allow the light of the universe to fill you. Lengthen your side ribs from your hips to your armpits. Let your collarbones "smile" upward. With each exhalation, let go of stress, anxiety, and fear, or whatever might be obstructing the light within. Soften your skin and let yourself just be.

3. Breathe from your mind into your heart and notice what you feel. Is your heart closed, tight, or hardened? Or is it soft and open? Without any judgment, simply notice. Make space for who you are in this moment and offer acceptance and space. Allow your mind to soften and to come into harmony with your heart and your breath.

4. With the least amount of effort, a kind of effortless effort, ask yourself, "What do I most deeply desire? What is my intention deep down?" Don't be in a big rush to answer the question. Wait to hear the answer from within. When you receive the answer or a sense of something, (which may come to you in a word, phrase, or as an image or color), give thanks to the universe.

5. Now offer your intention out to the universe and let go of any attachment to the result. Ask the universe to give you a sign, at the most unexpected time and in a way that surprises you, such that you have no doubt that the universe heard you and received your intention.

NOTES

[1] Quote from Paul Muller-Ortega's website: Blue Throat Yoga at: https://bluethroatyoga.com. Accessed 11 May 2020.

[2] Swami Shantananda & Peggy Bendet. *The Splendor of Recognition: An Exploration of the Pratyabhijñā-hṛdayam, a Text on the Ancient Science of the Soul.* Location Unknown: Siddha Yoga Publications. 2003. Print.

[3] Brooks, Douglas. *Currents of Grace: The Philosophical Foundations Of Anusara Yoga Volume I. Anusara.* 2001, Audiobook.

[4] Kempton, Sally. *Awakening Shakti: The Transformative Power of the Goddesses of Yoga.* Louisville, Colorado: Sounds True. 2013. Print.

CHAPTER SEVENTEEN

The Fall, Part II

Learn to fail or fail to learn.

Tal Ben Shahar, *The Pursuit of Perfect*

For 15 years, I dedicated myself to the vision of Anusara, eventually serving on committees and curriculum teams, donating countless hours, days, weeks, and months to the organization because I believed so fervently in its purpose. I also committed myself more and more fully to the study of *Nondual Śaiva-Śākta Tantra*. In 2011, I was initiated into a deep, esoteric meditation practice, *Neelakantha* Meditation, by the world-renowned *Nondual Śaiva-Śākta Tantra* scholar and professor Paul Muller-Ortega. Learning from Paul was like standing under a waterfall of bliss. More than just a meditation practice, the teachings pulled together all of my previous studies of Kripalu and Anusara and organized them historically within a rational framework that I could understand.

The timing of this initiation couldn't have been better. The *Neelakantha* Meditation practice proved to be a lifeline to me as the events of the next year unfolded. By 2011, Anusara had become a thriving movement of approximately 400 teachers and 600,000 students. Its popularity was growing and Friend's name with it. It was then that I began to see some behaviors in him that I didn't understand, such as drinking alcohol during evening social gatherings and an unexplained three-month sickness. Then, rumors began to spread about bizarre sexual rituals and relationships, none of which seemed believable to me.

He began dating one of his employees, which was a bit of a taboo, but their relationship wasn't hidden; it was made public by both of them. Around this time, I was teaching an Anusara Teacher Training in Canada. The group convened after lunch, and together we started reading through the ethics chapter of the circa-2008 Anusara manual. We got to the part about yoga teachers not dating students, and I made a point of reading the guideline aloud to the group, to establish its importance. The guideline clearly distinguished the power differential between teacher and student, and laid out the rule: if the teacher acknowledges an attraction for the student, the teacher should ask the student to forego coming to class for six months.

One of the students raised her hand.

"Um, Todd? That's not what my manual says," she said. I was confused. I read through the protocol again to myself, checking it for accuracy.

"Huh," I said. "What does yours say?"

She scanned it, then looked up. "Basically, it says that teachers are allowed to date students as long as it doesn't disturb the class."

What? "Can I see it?"

She nodded and brought it over to me. Sure enough, she was right. I checked the date on the front; hers was a new edition, one that I had never seen and didn't even know existed. I was slightly embarrassed.

"Okay, well… let's jump forward for now, and I'll look into it." We moved on.

After our training session that day, I checked in with one of the other teacher trainers. They had no idea what was going on. It became clear that Friend had rewritten the ethics section of his manual without notifying any of his trainers.

That was a red flag for me. Although I was bothered by the surreptitious manner in which the changes were made, I was most disturbed by the new guideline itself. It was a big change from the previous one, clearly reflecting Friend's new relationship with his employee – who was also his student. He was in violation of the guidelines we had all agreed upon, but because he was the founder of the method and author of his manual, he apparently felt he had the right to change the ethics without communication or input.

This event turned out to be the first in a slide toward authoritarian rule. Following my pattern of the disempowered student, I did not raise my concerns or speak up in any way. Friend used to brag about his management style for the organization, calling it a monarchy, and I had always laughed it off. Now, it seemed highly accurate: he truly *was* the king and we were his subjects. *Gulp.*

332

Then, in February of 2012, it happened. I may not have all of the details correct, but my understanding is that a disgruntled employee of Friend's created a special website that revealed his sexual misconduct, abuse of power, and financial wrongdoings. I, along with the entire Anusara community, was stunned. And angry. As part of Friend's inner circle and a member of the governing council, I agreed with the group's decision to ask him to own his mistakes, step down from teaching, and seek psychological help. But he refused. He continued to teach, and while teaching, continued to deny the allegations. The anonymous website provided plenty of proof (emails, photos, etc.) that Friend had acted inappropriately, yet he immediately went on the defensive – another red flag. After his staunch denials, he then made up another excuse: he was a sex therapist helping his student overcome sexual problems.

Friend's inability to admit that his actions were hurtful, not only to those with whom he engaged in sexual misconduct, but to the whole community, caused even deeper wounds. Yes, his actions were in direct violation of the teachings he espoused. Yet had he stepped down, admitted his mistakes, and sought the help he needed, I don't think the community would have broken apart.

For me, I was desperate to avoid a second betrayal. I called him on the phone, hoping against hope that he might be the person I had thought he was, the person I wanted him to be. I asked him if what I had heard was true, and he replied by telling me it was all rumor, that none of it was true. For a split second, I felt relieved. I so wanted him to continue being my hero: the one who lifted me out of my despair over losing Kripalu; the one who introduced me to life-changing teachings and Tantric scholars. But my relief was short-lived. The more we talked, the more convinced I became that he was lying. Bald-faced, point-blank. I hung up, devastated. Soon after that, Friend publicly refused to step down from the Anusara organization, and it was then that I fully accepted the hard truth: I had invested my trust in someone who didn't deserve it. Again.

Having gone through the dissolution of another spiritual community, I was painfully aware of the impending pitfalls – the community would fracture and choose sides, I would lose close friends, and we would all go through grief, anger, sadness, fear, and confusion. Fortunately, knowing that those experiences were imminent lessened their intensity; I suffered, but not as much as I did during Kripalu's debacle. This time, I had just enough insight and detachment to be able to coach and counsel other Anusara teachers, which I did for hours on the phone each day.

It seemed like I had to resign, but I was ambivalent and confused. The Anusara method, the practice I loved that had become my life, was still good, just as Kripalu yoga was still true even though the teacher chose poorly. What was different about this guru scandal was that my livelihood now depended on its outcome, as almost my entire yoga business was plugged into the Anusara matrix. Resigning meant not only turning away from another scandalous leader and community, but also setting a torch to my career of 15 years.

Tess resigned her license immediately and wanted me to resign as well, but in the days that passed, I held out for the possibility of saving the method. Tess and I were sitting in the living room when the phone rang. We looked at each other, and I nodded resignedly. *Yet another wrenching phone call.*

"Hello?" I answered. An unfamiliar voice on the other end came to life.

"Is this Todd Norian?"

"Yes," I said cautiously, "who's this?"
"I'm Sarah Jenkins [not her real name] from *The Washington Post*," [2] she said briskly. "I'd like to talk to you about John Friend and the Anusara scandal."

My heart took off racing. "Um, no thanks," I said with an attempt at finality that probably sounded wishy-washy. She saw the opening and kept going.

"Aren't you willing to answer one or two questions?"

"No, I'm not," I stated, and this time I meant it. "Goodbye." I hung up. Tess had been listening. "Who was that?"

"*The Washington Post.*"

"Oh my God!"

Tess sprang off the couch like a startled cat and started pacing. I could see her trembling.

"This is terrible, terrible," she intoned. I worried that she was seriously going to lose it.

"Tess, it's okay—" I started in what I thought was a soothing voice, but she cut me off, her voice shrill and rising with panic.

"No, it's not! It's not okay! Don't you know what this means? It means we, both of us, are associated with John! He's toxic, you know that, Todd. He's going down and he's going to take us both down with him!"

I just listened. I knew she couldn't hear me now.

"You can't wait anymore! You have to resign, Todd. You just have to. Please, please, please just resign. Immediately." Her eyes were wide with fright.

"Okay, Tess. Okay."

The state that Tess was in, the agitated panic, had become more and more frequent in the past few months. During the last Partner Yoga Program she had taught at Kripalu, her assistants had finished teaching the course for her; her anxiety had been so intense that she couldn't find her words. I had supported her decision to discontinue leading programs, thinking that perhaps she just needed a break from that kind of pressure.

335

Seeing the terror in her eyes again now, I did what I thought would calm her. I drafted a letter of resignation and made it public. But a week later, I was still wrestling with that decision. I knew I hadn't walked away from Anusara on my own accord. A few of us committee members who shared an idealistic vision of somehow saving the method without its founder met as a group to try to figure out how to do it. In a state of confused heroism, I reinstated my license, and for the following week, our group discussed, brainstormed, argued and strategized. It was heart-rending to see the Anusara community splinter as Kripalu's had, dividing into warring factions and cliques where once there was unity.

The conflict soon grew even more acrimonious when Friend's lawyers got involved. At that point, it seemed hopeless. I wasn't willing to try to keep the ship afloat. In my mind, if Anusara continued, it would forever be tarnished by the memory of the founder's disavowed abuses. I couldn't align myself with that. A few days later, I re-resigned, this time for good.

The timing of my resignation couldn't have been more awkward. I was in Canada, finishing up an Anusara training. It made me almost physically ill to have to explain to these eager, motivated, brand-new Anusara students that I was done – and more nauseatingly, *why* I was done. I walked them through the whole thing: the sexual misconduct, the resignations, the internecine battles. The students were stunned and distraught, and many of them were overwhelmed by their conflicting emotions. I spent a great deal of time processing until some stability returned; eventually they were able to accept the situation and make their own decisions about Anusara.

For me, this second betrayal re-traumatized me and sent me into a tailspin. I over-cleaned the house. I ate to distract and numb. I procrastinated. I tried to design a workshop but soon found myself staring out the window, wondering: *Who am I now? What is my purpose?* I had been so sure of my identity – I was an Anusara teacher. If that was no longer true... *now what?*

All alone at the kitchen table one day, I suddenly felt an inferno of emotion smoldering within my chest. It rose like hot lava until I couldn't contain it. I roared with tears and deep sobs, grieving the loss of another beloved teacher. *Why did this have to happen again? I am totally lost. I just want to be with God.* It was reminiscent of my first Kripalu awakening experience when Don facilitated my emotional catharsis; I knew that allowing my emotions to flow would be gut-wrenching but ultimately healing. I cried and cried, until I couldn't squeeze out one more tear.

I flashed back to the Kripalu scandal and how lost I was during the weeks and months afterward. I had struggled to practice yoga, meditate, or teach. But I remembered that over time, as I touched the pain inside, encouraged it to flow and then let it go, I had once again come home to myself. I had found my way back to my heart of hearts, to the me that loved yoga. Just then, a deep conviction landed: it was all okay. Yes, I had lost my teacher, my community, and my ease of livelihood. But I was still me. *I am okay.*

That conviction didn't stop me from incessant questioning, however: *How could I have let myself be sucked into another scandal?* True to form, I blamed myself more than anyone else, including Friend. It took me some time to get over the fact that whatever part I played in the whole sordid drama, I was not the one who acted inappropriately. Friend was the cause; I was the effect. Once I fully accepted that, *then* I was free to look for the ways in which this experience might have happened for my awakening. That's where grace comes in, again.

GRACE PERMITS EVERYTHING

I've talked about grace before, but to understand the relationship between the heart and grace, we need to broaden the definition of grace a bit more. For traditional religions, grace is described as a divine intervention, a blessing born of faith. The words to the popular gospel song, "Amazing Grace," describe that kind of grace – a power that saves your soul, brings relief, and pardons – in the first four lines:

337

Amazing grace how sweet the sound
That saved a wretch like me.
I once was lost but now I'm found.
Was blind but now I see.

~John Newton[3]

In this view, we think of grace as a surprise gift. We might say, "Wow. I really wanted that job and I didn't think I would get it. That's grace." Or, "I'm so grateful I got home safely. The roads were so icy and there were reports of several accidents." Grace, then, becomes associated with luck. On the flip side, if something bad happens to us, we feel like we lack grace: "I'm so tired of being sick. I wonder what I did to deserve this. Life sucks." But in yoga and especially in Tantra, the view is that grace is constantly happening. Grace is what permits *everything* to happen as it does, both good and bad. Check out the next two lines of the song:

'Twas grace that taught my heart to fear
And grace my fears relieved.

This is Tantra in action! Grace is on both sides of the equation: allowing fear *and* relieving it. To see grace at work in your life, you have to trust that grace is present in every moment, that even the most challenging burdens are there to provide you with exactly what you need. During those dark times, it's sometimes beyond difficult to see the light of grace working within that darkness. But it is there. If you can choose to see that light, that active choice automatically harnesses the power of meaning to change the course of your life.

And the final Tantric concept:

How precious did that grace appear
The hour I first believed.

Grace shows up in your life *when you believe in it*. It's an inside job, born of empowerment. If you believe grace exists and is playing an active role in your daily life, then it does. If you don't believe grace exists, or that you need to see it before you believe it, then it doesn't exist for you. The key is your belief.

As I've touched on before, your thoughts and beliefs infect the quantum field. In Tantra there is the notion of nonduality or oneness, the belief that there is a unified field of awareness or consciousness that permeates everything. When you harbor negativity in your heart – when you take on "victim consciousness" and repeat thoughts of doom or failure – it's as though you are sending out a GPS signal into the universe for negativity. The universe picks up on your signal, locates you, and begins to respond by orchestrating your life and the external universe (people and things) to deliver more of what you're thinking. Fortunately, the opposite is true, too. When you focus on positive beliefs like love and abundance, it's more likely you will experience more positivity in your life.

Your beliefs are the lenses of contact between your inner and outer reality, and they are governed by the heart. Reliance on the physical senses is perfect in a court of law, but it's disempowering to the spirit. This is where the real work of yoga happens: over and over, choosing to see with the heart rather than just the five senses. This takes practice but being open to another possibility – that there is more to reality than what you can see – is the first step in this journey of the heart.

After this second betrayal by my teacher, I was in a prime position to apply all of these teachings – everything I had learned and subsequently believed in – to my own situation. As tempting as it was to sink into victimhood, or to see this event as some random, excruciating slap in the face by the universe, I just couldn't do that. It was the perfect time to heed the advice I had been doling out to students for years: life has your back, always. I knew I had to embrace everything, including this betrayal, as the gift of grace it was meant to be.

EVERYONE HAS A SHADOW

After so many years of deep personal work at Kripalu, I had found that deeply rooted patterns tend to repeat themselves in life until the lesson is learned, so I persisted in digging. After a few months, an insight came, and it had to do with "shadows."

The "shadow" is a term first coined by psychoanalyst Carl Jung[4] to describe the disowned parts of ourselves, parts that reside in a kind of "blind spot" in our own psychology. Shadows can be positive or negative traits, but everyone has them – they are those parts of ourselves we don't like to acknowledge or reveal in public. When you fail to identify and address your shadow, it gets swept under the proverbial carpet of the subconscious mind and wreaks havoc on your conscious mind: what you think, what you say, and how you act. I discovered that there are two psychological terms that employ shadows: "shadow hugging," and "shadow boxing."

SHADOW HUGGING

When I first heard the definition of shadow hugging, I knew it applied perfectly to me: a repressed positive trait that is projected onto others. I realized that all along – from my first encounter with Desai until Friend toppled from his pedestal – I had been giving away my power, in the form of "shadow hugging."

In the case of both Desai and Friend, I over-appreciated them, being overly devotional and complimentary as a smokescreen for my own lack of self-esteem. I transferred all of my self-appreciation, self-honor, self-respect, and self-love onto them, which left my own heart empty and disempowered. The positive virtues I saw in Friend were the same that existed in me, but I was unable to acknowledge them. I projected goodness onto him instead of honoring my own goodness, seeing his brilliance instead of seeing my own.

For obvious reasons, this phenomenon is also called the "guru syndrome." You make the guru higher, more magical, more powerful, and more gifted than he really is. Out of your own self-rejection, you project onto him or her a higher IQ, a higher consciousness, a special gift that you don't have. It's a way of disrespecting yourself by worshipping someone else. In focusing only on the guru's gifts, I missed seeing my own – even when others tried to point them out.

I was completely incapable of receiving a compliment, and I'd been guilty of this my whole life. When someone complimented me, I often shrank and looked away, or turned red and looked down, shrugging it off and deflecting it in some way. It fit with my deep-down denial of my own divinity: "I'm not good enough to deserve this compliment. I'm not smart enough, brilliant enough, loving enough to be divine."

I also couldn't see how my deflection of compliments affected the givers, how it was diminishing their gifts. Without some acknowledgment and reception of the compliment, the givers may have felt they came across somehow as insincere. If I didn't believe the truth of the compliments, what did that make the givers? Liars?

Once, after I taught a 200-hour teacher training, a student told me how much she enjoyed the course. She said that I had a gift for teaching and for creating authentic community like no one she's ever seen before. Even though I could see how sincere she was, I winced inside and felt my heart contract. I said thanks, but I looked down in doubt and embarrassment.

Later that day, I reflected on our exchange. Why couldn't I just stand there, smile, and take it in fully? I realized that I didn't believe that what she was saying was true. I doubted myself so fully, that I prevented myself from receiving the external recognition of my deepest intention. The worst part of this for me was my utter certainty; I believed in my disbelief more than any compliment coming my way. I rejected myself. And in not being able to receive her blessing, I rejected her, too.

When someone goes out of their way to offer you a sincere, authentic expression of appreciation, how do you respond? Do you deflect it? Do you receive it graciously? Do you believe what they are saying is true? True not just for the giver, but for you – is it true about who you really are? Usually what's underneath our inability to take in a compliment is a deep-seated fear, not of failure, but of the validity of our own worth.

Later, one of my students offered me a technique to help overcome the inability to receive a compliment. It's difficult to do, but empowering for anyone with an unworthiness or perfectionist issue. When someone compliments you, practice saying these words *exactly*: "Thank you. It's true." The first time I used this phrase, my face turned bright red. I had to catch my breath and swallow hard. Yet I felt my heart unwind with relief, as if it had been longing for me to say those words and acknowledge my own goodness and value.

After a few weeks of practice, I could say it and begin to mean it. When you fully receive a compliment offered sincerely by another person, it completes the energetic loop of grace. I now see a compliment as an instance of grace trying to speak faith into me, through the words coming from the other person. As I receive their compliment and respond with a clear and humble "Thank you. It's true," I return their energy in a way that leaves me feeling recognized and leaves them validated. Their experience of me is real, they aren't crazy, and their compliment holds meaning for me. In essence, when I receive a compliment from another, I'm honoring myself and I'm honoring them. "Thank you. It's true" then becomes a beautiful, mutual blessing of our shared divinity.

> *Our deepest fear is not that we are inadequate. Our deepest fear is that we are powerful beyond measure. It is our light, not our darkness that most frightens us. We ask ourselves, 'Who am I to be brilliant, gorgeous, talented, fabulous?' Actually, who are you not to be? You are a child of God. Your playing small does not serve the world. There is nothing enlightened about shrinking so that other people won't feel insecure around you. We are all meant to shine, as children do. We were born to make manifest the glory of God that is within us. It's not just in some of us; it's in everyone. And as we let our own light shine, we unconsciously give other people permission to do the same. As we are liberated from our own fear, our presence automatically liberates others.*

~Marianne Williamson, *A Return to Love*[5]

342

SHADOW BOXING

If shadow hugging is the act of projecting your disowned *positive* qualities onto other people, "shadow boxing" is the opposite: projecting your disowned *negative* qualities onto others. When you feel a strong negative reaction towards someone, it can be a signal that they mirror to you some unintegrated shadow of your own.

I used to dread visiting my dad. I knew I loved him, but anticipating our get-togethers filled me with gloom. His judgment of others always sent me into a spiral of negativity – and I had no idea why. As he ranted on and on, criticizing family members and others, I experienced more and more discomfort, retreating into myself further and further – until I felt entirely vulnerable and disempowered.

After the Anusara incident, I realized that *his* judgmental nature mirrored *my own* judgmental tendency, my shadow. I resolved to integrate that disowned aspect of myself. For one year, I took on the practice of letting go of any judgments of others. Whenever I caught myself thinking or speaking negatively about someone, I reframed it in a more positive light, or I simply stopped talking. It didn't take long for me to see just how judgmental I was!

Over months, with a lot of self-compassion, I began to accept that part of myself that had opinions. It dawned on me that embracing my opinions and standing tall in who I am, were, in fact, healthy changes to make. Honoring my opinions seemed to counteract my tendency to diminish myself or go silent; perhaps if I accepted and valued myself more, I might have been less susceptible to the hero-worship I engaged in. So I made a commitment to love myself, opinions and all.

I visited my dad again after that year of committed shadow work and noticed a huge change in myself. I no longer felt offended when my dad launched into one of his judgmental tirades. I saw it for what it was: his words, his choice to speak harshly about others, not mine. I had much more compassion for and tolerance of my dad's judgments, and I stopped trying to change him. I simply accepted him.

343

But here's the really beautiful part. I noticed that without my usual reaction to his judgments, he shifted more quickly away from negativity. Near the end of my visit, we talked about it candidly. He told me that he was aware of his judgmental nature and that he had recently taken on the practice of judging less, because he himself was becoming sick and tired of listening to his rants! We both laughed.

LIGHT AND DARK

I admit that for the majority of my ashram years, I was a light chaser. There's nothing wrong with being a light chaser; after all, enlightenment and transcendence are the carrots that lure us forward on the path. However, light is only part of the equation, and ignoring the need for balance can result in a big wake-up call somewhere in your life journey. If you don't own your shadow, then when a crisis occurs, as it always does, sooner or later, for all of us – a life-threatening illness, a job loss, or the end of a relationship – you'll be much less able to learn and grow as you move through that event. If you don't actively look for your shadow, your shadow will eventually find you. Shadows tend to repeat themselves with more and more intensity until, at last, you choose to embrace them and learn from them.

I love the title of Debbie Ford's book, *"The Dark Side of the Light Chasers,"*[6] because she says it like it is: there's always a dark side to the light. Buddhist nun and spiritual teacher Pema Chödrön[7] teaches that compassion for another is dependent on your ability to sit with your own darkness. And I always laugh when I hear Deepak Chopra's[8] wise words, *"If you think you don't have a shadow, then you must not be standing in the light!"*

I am so moved and touched by all of the students in my recent courses who've had the courage to explore their shadow with me. Like rich, deep, dark soil, the shadow is fertile ground where seeds of light are planted. It is through the integration of the dark, that your authentic light grows brighter. Often, you can learn more from your darkness than from your light. But I always caution: be careful of becoming stuck in your shadow.

Remember the definition of guru from chapter 5? *Gu* means "dark" and *ru* means "light." Too much "gu" becomes "gooey": it will swallow you whole. Likewise, be careful of "ru-ing" too much, too: going for the light only. In your enthusiasm to embrace the light, be careful not to disassociate from the dark.

Yoga is about embracing the full spectrum of who you are, both light and dark. If you don't acknowledge and work with your shadow, if you ignore it and sweep it under the rug, it will be forced to malinger in the subconscious, dreaming up ways to finally get your attention. In short, your shadow will come back to bite you in the butt! Embracing both light and dark is the road to true fulfillment and happiness.

GURUTVA: THE GURU PRINCIPLE DEFINED

As I stated earlier, one definition of guru is the one who reveals the light and leads you out of darkness. But the guru does not have to be a teacher in the form of a human. Guru comes from the Sanskrit term, *gurutva*, which means "the guru principle." In a broader sense, *gurutva* describes the process of learning from everything – not just a teacher. Everything in life has the potential to teach: your relationships, your work, nature, your environment, and your daily life experience. A friend who is able to authentically be there for you during your darkest hour is, in fact, a guru for you at that time. If you can be open and receptive to life, you'll learn from everyone and everything.

As I've mentioned before, if you adopt the attitude of the yogi, "Everything in life is for my awakening," you become the victor rather than the victim. Before I discovered yoga, I used to believe that everything and everyone was against me. Life was an uphill battle. I lived in "victim consciousness" most of the time. Through the teachings and practice of yoga, over many years, my attitude began to change to one of "victory consciousness." I made the shift from "life is happening *to* me," to "life is happening *for* me."

In this state of victory consciousness, the yogi knows that challenges arise in order to bring change. Stumbling blocks become stepping-stones of possibility, and obstacles become opportunities. *When the student is ready, the teaching appears.* When you are open and receptive, the lesson of life will be given and received.

Which brings us back again, to grace. If *gurutva* is the process by which we are led from darkness to light, from ignorance to knowledge, and from the limited to the unlimited, then guru is actually synonymous with grace. Grace is the power of the universe that reveals your true nature – which is bliss.

THE NEW GURU

I have had years now to reflect on the events that led to the Anusara scandal. In my opinion, I don't think Friend had bad intentions. His message was good, and his delivery of it was delightful and uplifting. I think the Anusara method focused too exclusively on the body and spirit, ignoring the mind and emotions. There was no exploration of the shadow, the vulnerability of the heart, or any psychological work. It was all about strength, positivity, humor, and performance, which are all wonderful qualities. But the deeper underbelly of our core-wounded identities, our shortcomings, and our vulnerability was completely ignored and swept under the rug. Feelings of sadness, grief, doubt, fear, and anger were pushed aside. I believe that like all of us, Friend had a shadow, but his inability to see it meant he could not accept any responsibility for what he did or take the advice of his closest circle of friends and colleagues to step down and get help.

Just as children inherit both the strengths and weaknesses of their parents, the community takes on the strengths and weaknesses of its leader. With conscious awareness and a little bit of luck, children can grow from the situation and go beyond their parents' limitations. The same is true for a community. Isn't this the goal of evolution? To grow yourself through whatever family situation you grew up with and go further? In that spirit, I offer this affirmation from Louise Hay – "I willingly go beyond my parents' limitations" – and I honor the work that the Anusara School for Hatha Yoga (the successor to Friend's movement) has done to learn and grow from its history.

Scandals within large organizations and movements seem to emerge almost daily. The Catholic Church, Hollywood, corporations, media: Like all human systems that involve leadership and power, they are prone to the abuses of power. You might ask the question, "Is the guru dead?" In my opinion, not at all. If you define guru as the process of awakening, then the guru is here to stay. But "guru" in the form of a spiritual teacher who abuses their power and their students? That needs to change.

Anyone in a position of power, be it a spiritual teacher, therapist, schoolteacher, professor, priest, supervisor, boss, parent, older sibling, politician, or friend, has the potential to abuse that power. It's not an issue specific to gurus. It's an issue of decency, morality and treating others and all of life with respect. It's about creating and honoring sacred space wherever you go.

I believe we are living at a time when students are more experienced and knowledgeable, and they demand the highest integrity from their teachers and each other. The vision for leadership and management today has evolved. Rather than being dictatorial, leadership needs to be community sourced. Decisions are made with feedback and input from the members.

Do we really need gurus today? I'm not so sure. I don't have a guru now, but I have teachers. I know we'll always need teachers, leaders, and role models who lead from the heart. But if we still need a guru, then what's needed is a "new guru." I define the "new guru" as an effective leader:

- One who walks the talk with humility, vulnerability, and admits mistakes, yet is a role model for having the strength and courage to follow their heart, face their fears, and be willing to take responsibility for their actions;

- One who prioritizes being a decent human being with kindness, compassion, and respect for others; and

- One who, to the best of their ability, honors and lives by basic human codes of morality and ethics – as outlined in all spiritual traditions and religions, i.e., Patañjali's *yamas* and *niyamas* – while also accepting their limitations and imperfections.

Our new gurus/leaders must be willing to be torchbearers of consciousness and gatherers of grace, to lead by example. They must intend to make a difference in people's lives, to instill inspiration and hope, and to offer perspectives that challenge our smallness. They must do their own deep inner work, to understand their own darkness and pain, because that is the only way anyone can authentically "be" with someone else in theirs.

One of the beautiful things to remember about gurus is that their highest purpose, and perhaps their only purpose, is to point the way to your *own* inner guru, known as the *sadguru*, (the true guru) deep in your heart. The spiritual journey, your journey, is never finished. It is an ever-evolving process of awakening. I am excited to be on this path of awakening together. May we support each other to embrace our shadows and bravely grow our light in community, with great love, acceptance, respect, and humility. I bow to the guru within you.

ĀNANDA TĀṆḌAVA

Ānanda Tāṇḍava, the dance of bliss (*Tāṇḍava* is dance, *Ānanda* is bliss), is the term used to describe Śiva Naṭarāja's dance. But *tāṇḍava* also refers to the state of being entirely saturated, infused, possessed, or wholly *in* the state of whatever it is you are feeling and experiencing. It's your capacity to experience "wildness without savagery, fury without anger, and urgency without anxiety," says Gopala Aiyar Sundaramoorthy, Brooks's teacher. "And when you feel savagery, anger, and anxiety, that's *tāṇḍava* too." In Tantra, the path of radical affirmation, *everything* is a *tāṇḍava*. Beyond the binary of good and evil, *tāṇḍava* embraces all seeming contradictions.

The fact is, we need both shadow and light to be whole. You can't have one without the other. The brighter your light, the greater the shadow you cast.

Tāṇḍava describes my experience of the guru scandals: accepting the shadow with the light. Survival in this world requires this kind of acceptance; is there anything in life that comes to us as completely good or bad? I often say that the scandals were one of the best things that ever happened to me, because they brought into clear focus the patterns in me that no longer served, patterns of self-abnegation and people-pleasing. The scandals showed me, painfully, how easily I gave away my power, and through the struggle to understand why, I found my way back to my heart.

I realized that yoga is true. The practices are true. I am true. My heart, my devotion, and my longing are all true. But bad things also happened along the way. Whom did I need to become in order to hold both the good and bad? The answer is simple, if difficult: I needed to become *tāṇḍava*. If I had seen only the bad, I could have been justified in dwelling in the negative; betrayal is a terrible thing to experience. On the other hand, if I had only seen the good that came of it, I could have left myself vulnerable to more betrayal, expecting that all people are good. They may have good intentions, but not everyone is aligned with his or her highest good.

Tāṇḍava is the path of "yes, and." *Yes*, my gurus disappointed me in the deepest way possible... *and*, they taught me the most valuable lessons in my life. Believing as I do that everything in my life is for my awakening, I bow every day to both of my teachers. Without their betrayals, I would have never found my own yoga and stepped into my own power. I'm grateful beyond measure for their final teaching to me, through the doorway of a heart broken wide open.

> *'Twas grace that taught my heart to fear*
> *And grace my fears relieved.*

349

Tāṇḍava is grace in action. It's trusting that hidden within the darkness is the light of grace. To fully experience this grace, I had to allow the pain. I had to "meet them at the door laughing, and invite them in," as Rumi counsels. Both times, I let myself fall apart. Both times, I allowed myself to feel it all. This is *tāṇḍava*. By diving deep into the grief, I was able to retrieve pearls of wisdom that were waiting for me. How else could I begin to fully understand, embrace, and eventually change my core-wounded identity of giving my power away to others and diminishing myself? I still work to heal this deep groove in my psyche, but thanks to my teachers, I took a giant step toward healing. I know that as I progress on this path, more steps will reveal themselves. More pearls will appear. But this one step is enough.

I view the guru scandal as I view all betrayals: as a rite of passage. I used to think that my betrayal was something special and unique, but in fact, we are all betrayed at one time or another. A friend lies, a committed partner cheats, you are let down by your boss, co-worker, the government, God. You name it. In my classes, if I'm teaching about forgiveness and I ask the group, "How many of you have experienced betrayal?" the younger people often don't raise their hands. To them I always say, "If you haven't been betrayed yet, just wait." Don't be afraid. Betrayal is a natural rite of passage that makes you strong. The good news is that when it comes, you'll be ready.

For our hearts to grow to their fullest, we must walk through the doorway of betrayal… and feel it all. We must begin to see betrayal in a new light and make the shift from impasse, to rite of passage. How you deal with betrayal is what makes the difference. Can you allow it to deepen your understanding of yourself? Of forgiveness? Of vulnerability and boundaries?

THE THREE LEVELS OF THE HEART

The essence of yoga is love, which is accessed in the heart. But the heart is so tender and vulnerable that it quickly protects itself against pain and closes down. Although it's safer to live with a protected heart, the protected heart isolates us from others and, more importantly, from our own self. This is the "pain that increases pain." In order to experience the flow of grace, we need to live with an open and vulnerable heart – as painful as that is. This is the "pain that heals the pain." How do we do this? By going through the three levels or stages of opening the heart.

The first stage is self-acceptance. Self-acceptance is your capacity to turn toward yourself, to look within and see what is actually happening, dispassionately. This first stage can effectively bring you out of denial, or resistance to knowing the truth, if you are able to see yourself authentically, objectively, and without criticism. Lack of self-acceptance isolates you from yourself, like standing outside the wall of your heart without the password that opens the door. Eventually, once you get tired of standing outside that door, you will accept yourself – and feel the relief and freedom that comes from that first step.

Stage two is self-compassion, your capacity to hold yourself with empathy and non-judgment. Self-compassion makes whatever you are feeling, no matter how intensely painful or dark, okay. This freedom allows you to fall apart, let go, and shed tears, thereby moving the *śakti* (life force) in such a way that it disassembles your protective wall and mental constructs of fear. After a good cry, you will often feel clearer. Tears rejuvenate, bringing insight and illumination. The water element softens and moves around obstacles, and water in any form – even tears – will carry you back to the source, the ocean of consciousness.

At the very core of your being is the third stage: self-forgiveness. When you forgive yourself, you are really saying, "I trust myself again." When you trust yourself, you give yourself permission to feel safe, to feel content just as you are. When that happens, you relax. Self-forgiveness means you are willing to release the burden of any guilt you may carry in your heart. Guilt is a corrosive agent and can leave deep scars on the heart. When you accept yourself with compassion, these scars begin to heal.

AN ASIDE: REGRET

In my experience, regret should be redefined as *"your doomed attempt to change the unchangeable."* What's unchangeable? The past and other people. Regret is the number one crusher of power and joy. Like an idealistic hamster on a wheel, you keep spinning the same thought of regret over and over, thinking that will help: *I wish it had never happened.* But it did. You only have three options in dealing with the past:

- reject it, which implies a constant, exhausting battle with reality;
- ignore it, which is denial; or
- accept it, which is true yogic wisdom.

Acceptance opens the door to learning and growth, allowing the past to reveal its lessons such that you don't repeat the same mistakes. To paraphrase Dr. Joe Dispenza, "Don't let your history get in the way of your destiny."

Regret is a natural expression of grief or sadness, but like shame, it can be used to beat yourself up. Regret statements are often followed with a second statement of condemnation, self-pity, or fear. One of the remedies for the hamster wheel of regret is to replace the word "regret" with the word "accept."

Some examples:

> I **regret** that I gave up playing jazz piano. I was given a gift and I just threw it away.
> I **accept** that I gave up playing jazz piano in favor of using music as a means for healing and for creating sacred space.

> I **regret** that I didn't have kids when I was younger. There's no one to take care of me as I age.
> I **accept** that I didn't have kids when I was younger. I have chosen a path of service and see myself as a parent to the world.

I **regret** that I had osteoarthritis in my hip. I should have been more careful in my movements growing up.

I **accept** that I had osteoarthritis in my hip. I've had a full-out, active life, and I wouldn't trade that for anything.

If you want to take the burden of a lifetime off your shoulders, let go of regret and stop trying to change the unchangeable. Accept that whatever happened, for better or for worse, has already happened. Let it go. Forgive yourself. Learn from it and move on.

We live in a universe of "cosmic forgiveness." The universe has already forgiven you, and continues to do so, constantly, instantaneously. Forgiveness is its nature. Not only that, it has already forgotten. Why do you keep remembering your past unskillful behaviors when the universe does not? The sooner you can forgive yourself and let go, the sooner you will be able to move forward in your life.

Self-acceptance, self-compassion, and self-forgiveness are the three threads of light that braid together to form self-love. And love is always the secret password that opens the door of the heart.

FORGIVENESS

It's not easy to forgive someone for hurting you. You must be willing to sift through many layers of feelings, including shame, betrayal, anger, loss, confusion, grief, and fear, before you get to authentic forgiveness. I always tell my students that if you can't forgive yet, can you forgive yourself for *not* being able to forgive right now? Forgiveness has to start somewhere, and that simple kindness toward yourself can lead the way.

Finally, when you are ready to forgive another, you generally have to let go of something tightly clutched, usually resentment. You are not alone in clinging to resentment, thinking that you are somehow protecting yourself by doing so. Similarly, it's not uncommon to think that you can "get back" at the other person by holding onto resentment, when in fact it has no effect whatsoever on anyone but yourself. It's a weight carried on your shoulders alone.

When I forgave Desai, I struggled until I found the right balance between openness and boundary. Forgiveness with boundaries sounded like this for me: "I choose to hold a healthy self-boundary even as I open my heart again." I forgave, but I didn't forget. You can do the same. Forgiveness is not about condoning poor behavior; remember that I don't have to invite Desai to dinner in order to forgive him.

I could have chosen to wall off my heart to the world, so that I didn't experience the pain of being betrayed twice, but then I would have cut off my connection to grace – and those fifteen years of practicing, learning about, and teaching Anusara were *filled* with grace. I wouldn't be the teacher or human being that I am now, without those years of open-hearted freedom.

In some ways, when this second betrayal happened, I was fortunate that I already knew how to forgive. I did choose to word my forgiveness a little differently this time, acknowledging that this was the second occurrence of betrayal: "I let this person (Friend) back into my heart, but I will never allow myself to be mistreated again." I didn't say I would trust him again; in my opinion, he's not worthy of my trust.

You can only trust others to the extent that you trust yourself. If the other person betrays your trust or makes a mistake, you may feel hurt, as well as the other surface emotions that come with that betrayal. But if you possess an inviolable trust in yourself, you won't stay hurt for long. You will tap into the resiliency of your heart to bounce back. The purpose of forgiveness is to re-establish a bond with your own heart, to be willing to trust yourself again.

Yoga is the practice of learning how to "tenderize" the heart, such that you know how to remain open to grace while maintaining your boundaries. If you recall, Tantra teaches that in order to unbind yourself, you need to bind yourself. You need to create healthy limits in order to maintain and sustain your freedom.

I no longer see betrayal as something negative. I see it as an emotional portal that invites you to the other side of being, where instead of being attached to your core-wounded identity, you step into your divine identity. What is that? It's the combination of your divine essence of freedom *and* your limitations, and it requires that you embrace and encompass both. You are an unlimited being in your essence, and you have potential far beyond yourself. To access that potential fully, to realize your divine identity, you must learn how to soften, accept, and love your less-evolved parts. That's when you truly become one with yourself and one with grace while holding the full spectrum of light and shadow, duality and nonduality. The entire journey of life, then, is the journey of consciously returning to your original state of unity, composed of duality. This is the state of the Absolute.

EXERCISE: Forgiveness Contemplations

Ultimately, the definition of forgiveness is your capacity to forgive the unforgivable. Whatever you think is unforgivable, that's probably what you need to work on. However, it can be overwhelming if you're not yet ready to forgive the unforgivable. You need to slowly work through the levels of emotion in order to get to the ultimate forgiveness. This can take time. There's no need to rush the process. Be compassionate with yourself.

During this exercise, if you find it difficult to forgive another or yourself, choose an experience that's less intense. You don't need to work with the deepest, darkest wound or resentment right away. I think you'll find that after practicing forgiveness with the smaller hurts, you'll eventually be able to tackle the larger ones.

Come into a comfortable seated position or a position lying down on your back. Take a few deep breaths and tune into your body. Now draw your awareness to your heart. In a soft and non-invasive way, look into your heart and explore any areas of your heart where you feel some harshness or areas that have closed down. Breathe into any areas that feel tight and see if you can open, soften, and let go.

ASKING TO BE FORGIVEN BY ANOTHER

Reflect on your relationships and interactions with others. Remember a time in the recent or distant past where you hurt someone either emotionally or physically, whether intentionally or unintentionally. Allow this person's face to appear in your mind's eye. Continue to breathe and soften. See the hurt and pain that you inflicted, knowingly or unknowingly, on this person. Feel their hurt and pain. See it in their eyes. Then say softly and silently to them, using their first name, "_____, I ask for your forgiveness. I ask you to forgive me whatever I may have done to you intentionally or unintentionally. I ask you to forgive me."

Now pause in the silence for a few moments. Visualize this person's face soften and their eyes swell and tear up. Then see them nod their head, yes. Hear them say, "Yes, I forgive you." Allow yourself to receive their offering of forgiveness as a gift. Take it in. Breathe it in deeply. Feel yourself being let back into their heart with compassion. Then let this person go on their way, touched by a blessing of forgiveness. Choose another person and repeat or move on to the next reflection.

FORGIVING ANOTHER

Bring into your mind's eye someone for whom you have resentment. Someone who hurt you or caused you pain intentionally or unintentionally, knowingly or unknowingly. Visualize their face, their eyes, their mouth. See them clearly. Try to hold them gently in your heart. If this is difficult, acknowledge that to yourself and let it be okay. (Consider regressing this person down to about a two- or three-year-old child in your visualization. Try to see them as their younger, less-evolved self.)

Look straight into their eyes and say their name, "_____, I forgive you. I forgive you for what you did to me. I forgive you for the hurt and pain you caused me." Give yourself the benefit of the doubt. If you're not yet ready to forgive, let that be okay. Can you forgive yourself for not being ready to forgive? It's okay not to forgive right now. Remember that forgiveness takes time. You have to be ready to forgive, which usually requires you to move through your anger, rage, fear, confusion, doubt, loss, grief, and sadness before you can forgive. Simply acknowledge that you're not ready yet and let that be okay.

If you can forgive this person, say the words again using their first name, "_____, I forgive you." See their face soften and their eyes begin to water. Sense the burden of shame they've been carrying begin to dissolve. See the light return to their face and a faint smile begin to appear. Allow your heart to open to this person again. See if you can gently let them back into your heart.

Remember that forgiveness does not mean that you condone hurtful behavior. It means that you wish not to push anyone out of your heart. You recognize that you are able to hold a space in your heart for this person that is filled with love and appropriate boundaries. See them filled with the blessing of forgiveness. Then release this person and let them go on their way touched by the blessing of forgiveness. Choose another person and repeat, or when you are ready (take your time), open your eyes. Take some time to write in your journal.

FORGIVING YOURSELF

Hold yourself in your mind's eye. Breathe into your heart and feel the vulnerability of your humanness. If this is difficult to do, imagine yourself as a small child, your younger, less-evolved self. Be with yourself fully now and acknowledge your gifts as well as your challenges. Acknowledge that you are a masterpiece of the divine, that you are talented, that you are beautiful, that you have the favor of the divine. Hold yourself tenderly inside and offer as much acceptance as you can. Imagine being with yourself right now the way the divine mother or grace is with you all of the time. Let yourself be held by the divine mother with unconditional love and acceptance.

Then turn within and reflect on any ways in the recent or distant past that you hurt yourself, judged yourself, or put yourself out of your own heart. Let your heart open, and with compassion, bring to mind a time when you doubted yourself or when you chose not to follow your heart. Keeping this memory in your heart, say to yourself, using your first name, "_____, I forgive you. I forgive you for hurting or harming

357

yourself, intentionally or unintentionally, knowingly or unknowingly. I forgive you for putting yourself out of your own heart."

Take a couple of deep breaths and hold yourself in your heart with love. See if you can let yourself be forgiven by you. Receive the warmth and compassionate acceptance from yourself. It can sometimes feel like it's coming from the universe or Goddess herself. Let the entire universe forgive you. Dwell with yourself in a warm embrace, your younger self and you, deep in your heart, free of judgment, free of rejection, free of fear, free of any trace of doubt.

NOTES

[1] Ben-Shahar, Tal. *The Pursuit of Perfect: How to Stop Chasing Perfection and Start Living a Richer, Happier Life.* New York: McGraw-Hill Education. 2009. Print.

[2] Roig-Franzia, Manuel. Scandal contorts future of John Friend, Anusara yoga. The Washington Post. 28 March 2012. https://www.washingtonpost.com/lifestyle/style/scandal-contorts-future-of-john-friend-anusara-yoga/2012/03/28/gIQAeLVThS_story.html?noredirect=on&utm_term=.863a 47fa19f2. Accessed 14 May 2020.
Also see: Broad, William J. "Yoga and Sex Scandals: No Surprise Here" The New York Times, 27 February 2012. https://www.nytimes.com/2012/02/28/health/nutrition/yoga-fans-sexual-flames-and-predictably-plenty-of-scandal.html. Accessed 14 May 2020.

[3] Newton, John. "Amazing Grace," Lyrics written 1772, hymn published 1780. *Wikipedia.* https://en.wikipedia.org/wiki/Amazing_Grace. Accessed 8 May 2020.

[4] Jung's shadow work is the inspiration for multiple books and articles for other scholars and therapists. The original reference can be found Jung, C.G. "Psychology and Religion." In CW 11: *Psychology and Religion: West and East.* p. 131. Princeton, NJ: Princeton University. 1938. Print

[5] Williamson, Marianne. *A Return to Love: Reflections on the Principles of "A Course in Miracles."* New York: Harper One. Reissue 15 March 1996. Print.

[6] Ford, Debbie. *The Dark Side of the Light Chasers: Reclaiming Your Power, Creativity, Brilliance, and Dreams.* New York: Riverhead. 2010. Print.

[7] Learn more about this amazing teacher at https://pemachodronfoundation.org. Accessed 15 May 2020.

[8] Chopra, Deepak. *Power, Freedom, and Grace: Living from the Source of Lasting Happiness.* San Rafael, CA: Amber-Allen. 2008. Print.

CHAPTER EIGHTEEN

Return to the Heart

We dive deep and soar high in the vast spaciousness, the sky of Consciousness. Here wisdom and meaning, understanding, vision, insight, and all knowledge rest. This is the extraordinary domain, the secret Heart of Reality.

Paul E. Muller-Ortega[1]

"ASHAYA"

In my recovery from this second betrayal, I called on the spiritual strength growing within me, thanks in large part to my continued *Neelakantha* Meditation practice. One of the many practices in this tradition is recitation. We learn beautiful Sanskrit mantras and recite them as *svadhyāya*, a form of study that brings a kind of mental purification through powerful vibration.

Some of the mantras are simple and short, while others are several pages long and take concerted effort to memorize. Learning these mantras one day brought me a revelation: I'm back to my childhood! Just like playing a passage of music at the piano over and over again until I could make the notes smooth and effortless for an upcoming recital, learning a Sanskrit mantra requires the same patience and mental process. There's a way of pronunciation that takes that same careful, slow practice to get my lips and tongue to move with the rhythm, which is usually quite complex.

Another flashback occurred at a *Neelakantha* Meditation retreat, as a group of us chanted in view of the *Śiva Naṭarāja* murti holding the secrets of the entire universe. In an instant, I was at the minyan with my Dad, surrounded by all of the deeply religious practitioners chanting in Hebrew. The tiny hairs on my arms and legs stood on end, and my entire body shivered. I recognized this response as a sign of *śakti* awakening, brought on by grace. I burst into tears, first of recognition, and then astonishment as a kind of subtle funnel of light opened inside me. I peered over the edge of the funnel, to see my life flash before my eyes. It was as if a tender silken thread of grace, no wider than a single filament from a spider's web, had guided me throughout my entire life through every twist and turn, only to land me right here in front of the cosmic dancer. In that moment, I finally knew what I had been longing for.

From deep within my being, I heard and felt the overwhelming and resounding message, "I'm home." I was surrounded by others who valued freedom, surrender, empowerment, deep practice, and longing

360

for knowledge. I knew deep in my heart that I was in the right place at the right time, and that this was the path I was supposed to be on.

In the summer of 2012, understanding blossomed. I loved yoga. Yoga had been and still was my life. I wasn't about to give it up just because two of my teachers messed up and didn't own it. An inner fortitude more powerful than I had ever felt before rose up within me, and I woke up one morning in August with perfect clarity: It was time for me to brand my own style of yoga.

It was a decision – or more accurately, a calling – that came from deep down in my heart; I'd say it came from my soul. Being betrayed twice was more than enough to ignite the fire in my belly to become the teacher that I'd always wanted to have. Having learned the lessons of hero-worship, I was keen to jettison it. More importantly, I was ready to make a commitment to love myself and stop giving my power away to other people.

I journaled and contemplated for a few weeks, drawing on my decades of experience to create a wonderful method, one that would combine the best of everything I had learned about surrender, engagement, alignment, and personal development. For years, I had taught that when you align with a vision and purpose greater than yourself – in line with your highest needs, the needs of others around you, and life's needs – then your light shines its brightest. Finally, I accepted that my gift was to teach, and that the world desperately needed to receive the compassionate teachings of Tantra. I was ready to offer my gift to the world, such that it could do the most good. I was on fire.

I needed a name. I explained to Brooks what I was seeking, and he came up with "*Ashaya*." He also included a page and a half of definitions of the term, including "abode of the heart, sanctuary of the heart, a safe haven of the heart," and then ended by writing, "This is you." I loved what Ashaya meant, but I didn't like the sound of it for two reasons: first, its connotation with the word "shy," made me think of my childhood shyness and disempowerment; and second, I was concerned that it sounded too much like Ashtanga and Anusara! I emailed back, saying, "I don't think I like the name, Douglas. Could you send me another?" and waited for his reply. As the days and weeks passed with no email from him, I said "Ashaya" to myself over and over every day for weeks like a mantra. The name was growing on me slowly, but I still wasn't sold. Then I remembered a visit with my grandfather.

GRANDFATHER HARRY

Harry was my father's father. A simple man, well-groomed but not nearly as fashionable as my grandfather Aaron, he was a man of few words. Harry was affectionate and loving, soft-spoken, and wise, and he always greeted me with a hug and a kiss on the cheek. Whenever he saw his grandchildren he would come alive, smiling from ear to ear, tears forming in his eyes. Especially in his older age, he talked less and less, and observed more and more, such that when he spoke, I listened.

When I was 19, I decided to fly out from Michigan to visit him in Scottsdale. He was in a hospital, recovering from recent quadruple bypass heart surgery. His first wife, my grandmother, had died of Lupus when I was six years old, and he had remarried twice, moving out to Scottsdale to be with his third wife. I know he loved his first wife so much. Though he never said it, I don't think he ever recovered from losing her.

I traversed the corridors of the hospital until I found his room. I looked in; he was lying in his hospital bed, looking frail and weak. I knocked gently as I came in.

"Hi, Grampa," I said. His eyes lit up. He reached his unsteady arms out to hug me, and I leaned in more so he could give me my kiss on the cheek.

"Todd. It is so good to see you."
"You, too, Grampa."

We gazed at each other for a long time, just enjoying the other's presence. A nurse poked her head in.

"Time for your walk, Mr. Norian. Is this your grandson?" she asked kindly. We both nodded. "How nice."

Harry viewed me with hope. "Would you walk with me?" he asked.

"Absolutely," I said. "I'd love to."

We made our way slowly along the corridors and out the revolving door into a courtyard, where we stopped for a moment, squinting in the bright light. The sun beat down hot and radiated up from the gravel pathways. We resumed walking.

As we inched along, he asked about me and what I was doing. "How is school? How is music?" He just listened as I told him about getting bad grades in music and how confused I was about what I should do with my life. I told him that I was enrolled in classical piano performance, but I wasn't doing well. "I'm not a prodigy and I can't keep up." I poured out my frustration. "I love jazz. But making a living playing jazz or any kind of music is near impossible unless you're the best."

After I complained about everything else that was wrong in my life and had nothing left to say, he stopped, and turned to me. Taking a moment to catch his breath, he stared directly into my eyes.

Harry said, "You just need to follow your heart, you know. Everything else will be taken care of."

Then he looked down at the ground. I could see he was out of breath, so we turned around and headed slowly back to his room. At the time, it didn't seem like a big deal, and I didn't realize the gravity of his soft words. I said goodbye to him, not realizing that it would be the last time I saw my grandfather. He died a year later.

Suddenly everything lined up. When I thought about Harry's simple advice, "You just need to follow your heart and everything else will be taken care of" I felt the perfect clarity of grace move through me. Brooks

363

was right: "Ashaya" *was* me. For years I didn't know if Douglas refused to respond or if he didn't receive my email; it turns out he never got it. I branded the name Ashaya and dedicated myself to a purpose greater than myself.

I could never have known that my grandfather's words would be the teaching that has guided, and continues to guide, every one of my major life decisions.

PROVIDENCE

Until one is committed, there is hesitancy, the chance to draw back, always ineffectiveness. Concerning all acts of initiative (and creation), there is one elementary truth that ignorance of which kills countless ideas and splendid plans: that the moment one definitely commits oneself, then Providence moves too. All sorts of things occur to help one that would never otherwise have occurred. A whole stream of events issues from the decision, raising in one's favor all manner of unforeseen incidents and meetings and material assistance, which no man could have dreamed would have come his way. I learned a deep respect for one of Goethe's couplets: 'Whatever you can do, or dream you can do, begin it. Boldness has genius, power, and magic in it. Begin it now.'

~William Hutchison Murray[2]

The "Providence" that Murray describes in the above quotation is a term not so commonly heard today. What is it? What value does it have in our lives?

Providence is grace, constantly being dispersed. We live in a universe of power, interconnectedness, and synchronicity. There are no coincidences. Everything happens for a reason, though Tantra recognizes that sometimes that reason is actually for līlā (divine play). As Murray suggests, it's the commitment you make that initiates the response of providence. Life is a co-participation between yourself and the divine, between *Śakti* (the individual expression of consciousness) and *Śiva* (consciousness itself).

In August of 2012, once I had founded Ashaya Yoga, I knew I needed a logo. Having no idea what I wanted, I thought I would take a stab at drawing one myself. I sat down with paper and pencil and drew a heart inside the classic image of a simple house with a chimney and a wisp of smoke curling out of it.

Abode of the heart, yes? Well, no. Although I had good intentions of creating a symbol of a heart held within a community of loving beings, Tess (who at the time was partnering with me to create Ashaya) respectfully pointed out that my drawing fell quite short of conveying what I had hoped, and added (lovingly, of course) that my drawing skills are really that of a third grader.

A few weeks later, after teaching at a studio and noticing their lotus-inspired logo, I sent the basic idea to a professional designer in California. For no small fee, she created an artistic lotus logo which we used for a short time. It was fine, but there was something not quite right about it. I found another designer, and in her hands, it became the symbol I couldn't imagine or create myself. It was still a lotus, but such a beautiful one, with "abode of the heart" as the byline. I fell in love with it. We put it on everything: our website, business cards, and eventually on our Ashaya t-shirts and tank tops. The long, painstaking process of refining the logo finally paid off… but in the most unexpected way.

Before teaching a morning session one day, I stood in front of the bathroom mirror combing my hair. I looked at the logo on my t-shirt and my mouth fell open in awe. The lotus flower she had designed was composed of five outer petals and four inner petals. The five elements (sky, earth, water, fire, and air) form the foundation of the Ashaya method, and they support The Four Essentials™ of alignment: Open, Engage, Align, Expand. It was the perfect symbolism of the four embraced by five.

There's no way I could have planned this. At the time this version of the logo was created, I hadn't officially nailed down the elements and the Essentials of the Ashaya method! It was by pure accident that this synergy happened. Or was it? There's no such thing as a "co-incidence" that isn't connected to the vast, infinite energy of grace; a coincidence is really a cosmically coordinated incident. I realized then that as hard as I work to make events in my life happen, there are some things that are way beyond my reach. How marvelous, then, to know for certain that there is a bigger energy out there, working in my best interest. I don't have to do it all.

The point here is not "this lucky thing happened to me." The point is that I chose not to ignore it and write it off as accidental, coincidental, or insignificant. I chose to see this as the simple, remarkable hand of providence. Seeing it this way, I felt the love, blessing, and encouragement from the universe, assuring me that I am following my heart and going in the right direction. The way isn't always easy, but it is true. When you follow your heart and stay open to grace, life becomes a joyous dance with the divine.

That's right, it's a dance – a dance that requires two people. In order to welcome providence, you have to extend your hand, in the form of your effort, intention, desire, and action. To dance with the divine, you have to act. In the first chapter of the *Bhagavad Gītā*, one of the most revered sacred texts of India, the warrior Arjuna becomes despondent when confronted with battling his cousins, teachers, and mentors, all lined up on the opposing side. He sits down in his chariot and chooses not to act. But the god *Kṛṣṇa*, disguised as his chariot driver, won't let Arjuna get away with that. He points out to Arjuna that even inaction is an action, saying:

> *Indeed, no one, even in the twinkling of an eye,*
> *Ever exists without performing action;*
> *Everyone is forced to perform action,*
> *even action which is against his will...*
> Bhagavad Gītā (Sargeant translation)[3]

Since we can't *not* act, it is best to act with skillfulness. Yoga is skillfulness in action, and when you act in alignment with your heart and the highest good, providence becomes your partner.

Had I not realized the connection between the logo and the Ashaya method, and had I not brought it into the light by telling my story, perhaps it would have vanished from reality, living only in a remote part of my mind. Providence is constantly happening in every moment of our lives, but you have to look for it in order to see it.

The more you look, the more you'll see it. That's part of the dance. If you choose not to believe in something bigger or you write off the notion of providence too quickly, you may never see it blossom in your life. You get what you put out. If you put out negativity, doubt, and pessimism, that is exactly what you'll get back. But if you choose to open to a bigger energy, choose to see the good, choose to believe in the hand of providence that is constantly working in every moment of your life, then you'll begin to see that hand moving in small and sometimes not-so-small ways.

What makes you more receptive to seeing and experiencing the hand of providence? Practice. Practice of yoga, meditation, mantra, prāṇāyāma. It's the daily ritual of practice that clears the screen of your mind and opens the ears of your consciousness, to deliver you to the present moment, the place where you can see and hear clearly the subtle stirrings and whispers of the divine. Practice is the "hand" you extend to receive the hand of providence.

UNIVERSE OF POWER: YOU ARE GOD

Tantra yoga teaches that a universe of power, infused with wisdom, exists deep in our own hearts. But we've lost our connection to this power. We've fallen into the deep abyss of darkness that lacks vision, lacks wisdom, and lacks fulfillment. Our core-wounded identities have taken over, to the point at which we often feel overwhelmed with doubt, fear, confusion, and a lack of purpose. It's as though we've lost the map that guides us back to the heart where the real treasure is, where we feel at peace, where we feel connected to our purpose, where we feel healthy and energized, and where we feel motivated.

> *Love yourself. Respect yourself. Meditate on*
> *yourself. For God lives in you as you.*
> ~Tantric yoga master, Swami Muktananda[4]

What would life be like if you fully recognized that the whole universe, God, lives inside of you as you? And not just recognized it in an intellectual way, but in a fully embodied, visceral way? Wouldn't that radically change the shape of your life and all human life on this planet? To come to that recognition, you must start with belief.

Beliefs form the hub of every experience you encounter in life. They are the tools of empowerment. Anodea Judith, in her book *Wheels of Life*,[5] describes our beliefs as integral to our subtle energy system and the cakras: "Our belief systems at the core of our being create the cakras which govern our lives. These are the beliefs with which we create our world." To live an empowered life begins with examining the beliefs – all of them – that you carry in your heart.

Any disempowering beliefs you carry encase the heart with a shell that prevents you from participating in the flow of this powerful universe. If you continue to live governed by your familiar, but disempowering beliefs, rather than letting them go and choosing more empowering ones, you continue to perpetuate the lie. What is the lie? That you are not God. That you are not worthy and that there truly is something wrong with you. What's not true are all of the beliefs bolstered by fear: fear of success, fear of being judged, fear of being hurt, fear of death. By now you know that fear of failure was a big one for me. Which one is big for you? Do you know?

Yoga happens on the inside. If you're not aware of the beliefs you carry, then you have some homework to do. You must come into deeper relationship with yourself and your beliefs. Yoga is the art and science of knowing how you tick, how you work, how you think, and how you feel. It's the art of understanding all of that and then letting go of those beliefs that just don't serve you. First, you must learn how to embrace and accept those beliefs. To be able to let something go, you first must be able to let it be. Can you start with that?

The Tantric view is that the power of the universe flows through all of life and through each individual. It's the force that gives life to living beings and animates all of life's creation. You, in your individual self, are a single, perfect point of light – flaws and all – along a radiant spectrum of vibration that is divine. Your finger is on the dial. You have free will and free choice to dial your light up or down, to embrace yourself and improve yourself through love, or continue to believe the lie.

YOU HAVE A UNIQUE GIFT

Everyone is born with a dream in the heart, a unique gift to give to this world. Some people discover that gift at a young age and pursue it; others take almost an entire lifetime to discover theirs. This process is not a function of time. It's a function of consciousness. For me, it was a gradual process of following my heart and trusting that each step I took would send me deeper into a purposeful, meaningful life journey. It did. Based on my own experience, I am more convinced than ever that the only way to true happiness is by recognizing that you are connected to a bigger energy, to grace, and by following your heart toward your purpose for being here – even if it takes you in a completely different direction than you ever imagined.

My life is ordinary. Most lives are. But what I want to offer is that no matter what your life experiences are, there's a way to view them such that you awaken to the vastness of spiritual power within you. Tantra's central teaching – that you are the crystallization of the divine's desire to know itself – means that your life, no matter how ordinary you think

369

it is, is extraordinary. There's no life that isn't a miracle unfolding. It's not so much about what you do in life that matters, it's how you are being. I like to say that *"It's not how far you go, but how you go far."* You have everything you already need to create happiness, fulfillment, and joy in your life. Now, I hope, you know how to tap into it.

AFTER ENLIGHTENMENT? BE LIKE A BEE

Let's assume you've already attained enlightenment. Great! What happens after that? Since Patañjali's yoga only deals with how to get you to *samādhi*, the answer to that question in Classical Yoga would probably be: "I'm outta here! There's really no reason to stick around on earth now that I've awakened." Tantra, which teaches that enlightenment is possible here and now, has a different answer.

Remember, Tantra is all about the round-trip journey: Once you've touched the most profound experiences of stillness and transcendence, you use that insight and wisdom to bring more light and love to the planet, thereby refining your embodiment and expression of the great light of consciousness in human form. Big job, right? Where to even begin? Tantra would say, "after enlightenment, be like a bee."

MĀDHURYA

The concept of *mādhurya* (from the Sanskrit word for honey: *madhu*) describes how being like a bee can lead you to post-enlightenment fulfillment. Here are the directions:

1. Honey bees gather nectar, moving from flower to flower, then return to the hive to deliver it. **Gather your experiences throughout your life and then bring them back to your *"kula."***

Kula means "family of the heart" or "community of the heart." In a general sense, it's your tribe, your friends and family. More traditionally, it refers to a group of like-minded seekers who study and practice the spiritual teachings together. They uplift one another, support one another, hold space for one another, and celebrate one another all along the journey of life. In *Nondual Śaiva-Śākta Tantra*, *kula* referred to the group of students who received the same level of initiated practice. You were permitted to share your experiences within the *kula* or with others at your level of initiation, but not with those outside the initiated class. This was a way to maintain the efficacy, privacy and sacredness of the initiated practices.

2. Inside the hive, bees mix the nectar with their saliva and enzymes. **Taste your own experiences, savor them and truly make them a part of you.**

3. After that? Brace yourself: The bees vomit. They share this concoction with the other bees in the hive, who chew it non-stop, mixing it with their own digestive juices. **Share your experiences with the *kula*. Give and receive ideas with others. Share yourself. Inspire others through conversation.**

Only then does the raw nectar become honey. Only when you share your experience with others does it truly serve, because only then do you truly integrate it. *It becomes yours through giving it away.* Bees who don't throw up their nectar die. Everyone needs to share, to listen to others, to depend on others; the psyche "dies" through isolation. We need the support of a community, where we can have, be, feel, and give love.

When you look at life from the viewpoint of *mādhurya*, you begin to see why secrets are so damaging. When you withhold authenticity, when you hold those secrets back, they eat away at you from the inside. They grow your shadow, which diminishes your light. You need to free yourself through intimacy, through conversation. Remember, you are the secret the universe is telling. So, tell your secret, share your story, and fulfill the deepest intention of the universe for you.

SAUMYA

Saumya means sweetness. It's derived from *soma,* which means moon, as well as distillation, or drink. (Think moonshine!) Soma also means nectar or wholeness and is first mentioned in the Vedas as the deity responsible for maintaining the wholeness in the Absolute. It's the wholeness that sustains the wholeness in wholeness. This might sound redundant, but bear with me.

Consider the Absolute as perfectly whole and complete within itself, all the time. Remember *pūrṇatva* in Chapter 3, the principle of fullness? The kind of wholeness that never gets depleted like a gas tank? The kind that's so full that it includes lack as part of its totality? Soma is the e*nergy* that maintains that *pūrṇatva,* that fullness in fullness, wholeness in wholeness. Because of s*oma,* everything is seen as whole or on its way to wholeness. Soma ensures that the Absolute never becomes diminished.

Saumya means having the total experience of *soma,* becoming fully intoxicated with the elixir of the immortal or divine. Everyone wants to "get high." It's what you need to flourish. Once you have found enlightenment, enjoy it! Drink to the intoxication of wellness and joy. Drink in the delight.

Saumya also includes an experience of *soma* that is more esoteric. The moon is *vimarṣa* (light that reflects in on itself) since the moon is a reflection of the sun. As I mentioned in Chapter 7, Tantra teaches that *vimarśa* is how the One universal is seen – not through direct gaze, but through its reflection. There has to be a reflection to see the One. That means that in order for you to perceive Oneness, there must be something to compare it to. There must be two: the thing itself, and its reflection.

Direct perception allows no comparison. When there's no comparison, there's no conversation to have. Without conversation, there's no sweetness. When the bees can't vomit (and share their experience), no honey is made, and the bees die.

The moral? Tell your story. Sweetness is found in the story told, and the story heard.

SAUNDARYA

The third practice is *saundarya*, from *sundarī*, which means having the experience of beauty. When you experience beauty, there's an awakening of your true nature. It's enthralling. It stirs the heart. It allows you to step into the experience of expansion, fullness, awe, and wonder. Appreciate the beauty.

Don't wait until you're enlightened to live by these three teachings. Apply them now.

Finally, in the spirit of *madhurya*, of sharing my story completely and authentically, I have one more narrative to tell.

EXERCISE: Unlock the Power of Providence

Find a quiet and comfortable place to sit with your journal. Close your eyes and take a few deep belly breaths. With every inhalation, invite the light of the universe to fill you. With every exhalation, release whatever's in the way of the light. Surrender to what is, right here and now in this moment. Open to the bigger energy and allow yourself to be held in total acceptance, love, and peace.

Now, open to the "hand of providence," the bigger energy of the universe, the power behind all of nature that's beyond what you can control. Soften your skin and surrender to all that is. Open to the possibility that everything in life is happening for you, that life has your back, and that the universe flows all around you and through you in the form of providence, goodness, and auspiciousness. Savor your breath as you savor this moment. Imagine you could dwell in the essence of providence as a radiant light.

After a few minutes, open your eyes and reflect on the questions below. Allow the wisdom of the universe within to flow through you as you write in your journal.

1. What does "the hand of providence" mean to you?
2. Reflect on your past, either recent or distant past. Write down one or two instances of providence in your life that you can remember.
3. Explain what happened? What was the situation?
4. When did you recognize that it was providence?
5. How did you feel when you understood that it was providence and what did you learn about yourself?
6. Now envision your future. What kind of future do you want to create?
7. Knowing that the hand of providence is always being extended to you, how would you like to offer your hand to the hand of providence?
8. Where in your life would you like to experience more providence, more grace?
9. What gets in your way to receiving providence?
10. What are you prepared to let go of to make room for more providence in your life?

NOTES

[1] Quote from Paul Muller-Ortega's website: Blue Throat Yoga at: https://bluethroatyoga.com. Accessed 11 May 2020.

[2] Murray, William Hutchison. *The Scottish Himalayan Expedition.* London: Dent. 1951. See *Wikipedia* for more information about W.H. Murray: https://en.wikipedia.org/wiki/W._H._Murray. Accessed 8 May 2020.

[3] Sargeant, Winthrop. *Shri Bhagavad Gītā.* Albany, NY: Suny. Chapter 3, Verse 5,1993. Print

[4] S Core teaching from Swami Muktananda (1908-1982). https://www.siddhayoga.org/teachings/essential. Accessed 8 May 2020.

[5] S Judith, Anodea. *Wheels of Life: A User's Guide to the Chakra System.* Woodbury, Minnesota: Llewellyn. 1989. Print.

CHAPTER NINETEEN

Serrated Edge

The Unbroken

*There is a brokenness
out of which comes the unbroken,
a shatteredness
out of which blooms the unshatterable.
There is a sorrow
beyond all grief which leads to joy
and a fragility
out of whose depths emerges strength.*

*There is a hollow space
too vast for words
through which we pass with each loss,
out of whose darkness
we are sanctioned into being.*

*There is a cry deeper than all sound
whose serrated edges cut the heart
as we break open to the place inside
which is unbreakable and whole,
while learning to sing.*

Rashani[1]

This is a difficult one.

Over years of deep practice and inquiry, and participating in so many psychological processes before, during, and after my first and second guru scandals, I know for certain that challenges never come to crush us. They come when we are ready to rise up higher. Yet unless we have already attained enlightenment, our initial reaction to challenges is usually not one of immediate gratitude. It usually takes us time to live into our new reality and appreciate its gifts.

I started writing this book a few years ago, when Tess was struggling with anxiety. She supported the book fully, and when she was feeling better, we talked about some of the experiences we thought would be good to include in it, and how sharing those experiences might help others. At that time, I had no idea to what extent her struggles would overtake her, and I never thought I would need to write this postscript to my story. But I do.

"WE HAVE TO GO"

Tess looked thinner, paler. Her hair unkempt, she had the expression of white terror I had come to associate with one of her episodes. I knew she hadn't slept in days. She got down on all fours and pulled me down closer to her.

"What?" I asked. I could hardly hear her.

"Shhhhh! We have to whisper!" she said urgently. "They are listening to every word we say." I knew Tess believed, with utter certainty, that we were being bugged or spied on by the CIA, IRS, or some other government agency.

"Tess, what did you say, honey?" I whispered.

"We have to leave."

I knelt down even closer to hear. I couldn't quite make out what she was saying, or maybe I couldn't believe my ears. I'm not sure which.

"What do you mean?" I asked her gently.

"We have to go."

I caught my breath. As much as I didn't want to clarify what she meant, I knew I had to.

"Do you mean... we have to leave this life?" *Please don't say yes.*

"Yes. We have to go."

Oh, god. "Do you mean both of us have to go?"

"Yes."

"You mean, you want me to commit suicide together with you?"

There was no hesitation on her part. "Yes."

My heart burst into a thousand pieces. I went cold, almost numb. I had never seen Tess this bad. She had been steadily getting worse and worse, more and more depressed. Her bouts of debilitating anxiety, sadness, doubt, and confusion had escalated. At her last psychiatric appointment, her diagnosis was not good. It seemed to be triggered by the phone call I had received in 2012 from the Washington Post wanting to interview me about the fall of Anusara. But I couldn't know for sure where it all started for her.

For the last eight years, I'd witnessed the love of my life descend into mental illness. For all of the help and healing work I suggested and she tried, she only got worse. It was all such a shock to me. No amount of psychotherapy or meds seemed to help. Six months prior to this event, her doctor had said that she needed someone with her 24/7, and we agreed. Tess could not stay at home alone. Since I had to continue teaching and traveling, she agreed to live at a friend's house until we came up with a better plan.

Her condition worsened. She suspected my new office manager of stealing from us. She wouldn't trust anyone. The day before I was to return from teaching in Asia, Tess's friend called, warning me that Tess was having an episode and wouldn't be able to pick me up at Kennedy Airport. I hired my office manager to come get me instead, and when I returned, Tess was a mess. Her paranoia had progressed from distrusting the manager, to insisting that we whisper at all times inside the house.

And so I whispered.

"Are you serious?"

She nodded her head with a little sigh. Was it a relief that I understood her? Relief that I might join her? Both? I don't know. I took her hands in mine and tried to throw her a lifeline with my words.

"Well, I can't go with you because I want to live. I love my life and I love you. I want to keep going," I uttered, my heart spilling over. "You need to keep going too. You have so much more life to live. You have people who love you. Your family loves you. I love you and I won't let you go. I don't want either of us to go."

I searched her face for any sign that I had reached her. There was none.

I immediately got up and called Tess's psychiatrist, who told me to drive Tess to the emergency room, quickly. This was the second time she had to be driven to the ER for suicidal ideation – thoughts of suicide without an active attempt. Her friends took her the first time two months ago when I was away teaching. At that time, Tess went willingly and had extensive testing done. There were no tumors, no medical reasons to explain Tess's psychosis. By all accounts, she was physically healthy.

But this time Tess resisted. "I'm not going."

"Tess. This is the best thing you can do for yourself," I responded. "Your doctor said we should get help right away."

"No," she said firmly, "I don't want to go. It won't help. They just poke me and shoot me up with meds that make me so sleepy and numb."

It was true that Tess's previous stay at the psychiatric ward hadn't helped much, if at all. But we had no other options. The more I insisted, the more she resisted. Caught between a desperate desire to get help for her and an inability to think of anything else, I simply picked her up as lovingly as I could. Some bigger energy took over, and suddenly, I had the strength of an ox. I carried her, kicking and whining, down the stairs to the garage and put her into the car. Once the engine started and we began moving, she settled down. Maybe she knew, too, that this was the only option she had.

"Okay," she said, "I'll go. But it's not going to help. Nothing can help." And then she added, "I just don't want to be here anymore."

On the ride to the ER, her eyes were a confused haze of anxiety and apathy. I didn't know what was happening to her. I had never been with anyone in such an extreme state as this, and I felt scared for her. I flashed back to my own spiritual emergency, when I was lost inside myself in a very confused and mixed-up way. *She'll find her way through this,* I thought. *I did.* Deep in my bones, I felt a sense of knowing that she would be okay. My emergency lasted a week or two and it left me better off than before the event. *She'll be all right.*

After several weeks in and out of psychiatric hospitals and halfway houses, Tess came home. More episodes persisted. Her situation was clearly different from mine: more deeply seated, more insidious, all-pervasive. Her illness was ongoing and was not getting better. I was at a loss.

Tess and I discussed the possibility of divorce, because we both knew the marriage wasn't working. When I tried to make an appointment with a couples retreat therapist, the therapist told me that until Tess was of sound mind, it would be unfair and unbalanced to enter couples therapy. In my dream of dreams, I still prayed that Tess would be able to heal, and we could put our marriage back together.

Then, a bright spot. We found a psychiatric community built on a farm, and it seemed like a good fit. She moved there, and for a few months she seemed to do better. There was community support, fresh air, outside work, and farm animals. In some ways, it was like a return to the place we met and fell in love. I was relieved and hopeful.

Early in 2018, her mother, who had been living for the previous five years in a nearby senior facility, passed away. It seemed to me as though it was this event that tipped Tess over the edge. She left the farm situation to take care of the funeral arrangements and her mom's belongings, and she didn't go back. Her depression turned into a high-intensity mania, fueled with rage and bizarre actions.

She began hanging out with the homeless, drinking alcohol, becoming overly friendly with the locals, and spending or giving away all of our money. She bought thousands of dollars of antique restaurant furniture for no reason at all that I could see and invested in local businesses and B & B's. She was vulnerable and people took advantage of her. Although I believe her intentions were good – to help the homeless, to support local businesses and local taverns – her actions were ungrounded and irresponsible.

She was off-balance in a way I had never seen before. She stopped taking her meds and became dangerous to herself and others. She dismantled almost our entire house while I was away teaching, a violation that left me feeling traumatized and distraught. For some reason, she removed everything from the cabinets everywhere – the kitchen, the office, the bedroom, the utility room, the yoga room. She even took the pictures off the walls and dragged everything in the back basement out of storage. There were piles of debris and stuff scattered about everywhere. When my administrative assistant arrived to work that day, she couldn't open the front door to the office due to all of the stuff blocking the door.

Whenever I've been away for a long period of time, I always look forward to coming home to peace and quiet: sleeping in my own bed, returning to my yoga room, and seeing my beautiful sacred altar. It's medicine for me. This time, I came home to a disaster zone. It was like a tornado had touched down inside the house. I filed a "stay away" order against her.

The next time I was away, however, she ignored the stay away order and did it again, this time moving much of the furniture out of the house into storage with a moving crew and damaging property. I came home to a half-empty house, littered with empty beer cans and dotted with altars of the goddess Kali built upon piles of my personal belongings all strewn about. (Ironically, Kali, not only the goddess of darkness and destruction, represents the fierce longing for truth and the vast mystery of possibility, transformation, and growth.) In addition to this chaos, Tess left heinous notes of hatred directed toward me. I was fearful for my life.

Ultimately, Tess was arrested for a variety of crimes, including OUI (operating under the influence) and disorderly conduct, and she was finally ordered by the courts to a state forensic hospital for several months to receive forced treatment and psychiatric care. It pains me to say that it was shortly before she was arrested that, after 25 years of being married to the woman of my dreams, I filed for divorce.

This was by far the most difficult thing I've ever done in my entire life. I know that I said earlier that life never gives you a challenge you're not totally ready to handle. But this was – and still is – devastating. The woman I was in love with, our magical ashram romance, the nearly two and a half decades of marital bliss, all of it... over.

I chose to end our marriage because I've been without a wife and partner for too long. Yet that choice is still loaded with conflicting emotions and a battery of questions. How could I leave her at the time of her greatest need? My heart floods with guilt. But I also know that grace works in mysterious ways. What supports Tess the most? Without creating a boundary, wouldn't I be enabling her? Do I sacrifice my freedom and joy for her? I've hung in there with her for such a long time. Should I give her eight more years of my life? I've circled round and round inside my head for answers.

I used to feel that divorce was the ultimate sign of failure. I never, ever wanted to get divorced, and swore I never would, because of the pain that my parents' divorce created for me. But couldn't that also be seen as a blessing? If my parents had never gotten divorced, I might not have satisfied a need for family by staying at Kripalu.

Although the notion of divorce triggered my unworthiness, big-time, I managed to rise up and tell myself that given all of the circumstances, divorce was the only thing left for me to do. I recognized that I don't have to go down with the ship; that is not required of me or of anyone. It tore me up to do this, and it still tears me up inside at times. But standing in my truth and in my center, ironically, I've never felt more fully myself than I do right now. My capacity to have compassion for the full range of feelings has never been greater. In turn, this has expanded my compassion for Tess, my family, and everyone else.

I've come to the conclusion that divorce is not a bad thing. In fact, it can be the thing that heals and makes us whole again. Even though I still feel bad for my mom, I've forgiven my dad for divorcing her. I get it now. He did what he felt he had to do. And actually, my conversations with my dad during this time were never better. He called me more often and when we talked, he listened better. He just let me vent. He was quite good at it. When I told him so, he replied, "Thanks, Butch." (Sadly, my dad passed away on Oct. 31, 2019.)

And my mom? Well, after doing a lot of soul-searching, grieving, and figuring out her life, she's happier than I've ever seen her. She lives alone, and surrounds herself with loving friends and family. Although she's retired, she never seems to have enough time to do all of the things she wants to do. In the end, both of my parents turned out okay. Time heals, and life goes on.

I've also spoken to many divorcees who remarried and found happiness again. My sister, for one, went through a horrific divorce, only to find the love of her life several years later. Even though I subscribed wholeheartedly to the idea that happiness depends on being married to one person for your entire life, I've since reconsidered.

As difficult as this has been for me to understand and integrate, through the support of my friends and community, I've stepped into the next chapter of my life. I still have bouts of grief and sadness, but under all of it, I come back to my heart where I recognize that this journey continues. I can either dwell on how traumatized I have been by the events of Tess's illness, or I can pick myself up, and with compassion, move forward. I still cherish the authentically good times we had together. I still hold the lessons I learned close to my heart, all the deep feelings of love, trust, belonging, friendship, and joy. They rest as flames aglow on the altar of my heart, indelibly etched into the fabric of my consciousness.

This is my spiritual practice:
- to embrace and accept what I didn't want to happen but did happen;
- to release all blame and guilt; and
- to allow myself to feel the depth of my very real grief while also feeling gratitude for the very real love we shared.

In short, it is a practice of strengthening the capacity we all have to hold both grief and gratitude at the same time.

My deepest prayer for Tess is that she finds her way home to herself again and that she comes to understand her illness and accept it. I believe that some mental illnesses can be healed but some can only be managed. My hope is that Tess comes back to a reality where she sees that she is worthy, gifted, talented, and beautiful; that she sees she can and does make a difference in this world; and that she knows she has the possibility to live the rest of her life in a state of grace, humility, strength, freedom, and service to others. She has been the greatest inspiration in my life (and I know, in the lives of her students and friends) and I am eternally grateful for her presence and all of the lessons she's helped me learn in this part of my journey. I wish her well.

Just as I did after the betrayals of my gurus, I choose to see that these events have molded my life and shaped me, giving me more character, experience, and wisdom. They have stretched my heart with compassion and forced me *to stand by my own side* against the greatest odds. This seems to have been a theme in my life – rising up to face my challenges. But then, isn't that what we're all doing? Is any one of us exempt from the struggles of life? No. But we do have a choice about how we respond to the challenges. That is the essence of my message.

We all have our stories full of both triumph and trauma. We can stay silent, isolate ourselves, and avoid the experience. Or we can choose to open up and share our stories with one another, with authenticity, sensitivity, honesty, and boldness. We can be like the bees and make honey. We can all tell our stories of how we rose up with courage to face our demons, and how we failed, got confused, made mistakes, or did the wrong things. Taking it out of the realm of right or wrong, in the end, it's what we are called to do. We're all just having our own experience of life.

> *Love life. You are here to love life. That's what the Tantra is offering; the opportunity to step fully, ever more deeply, every day, in every breath, into the possibility of savoring the gift of embodiment; of realizing that the universe has gone through all of this trouble to make you. That you're not here to get something, or acquire something, or achieve something; but merely to taste, to savor the gift of the conversation of the heart. And let that be enough to let this message of love in.*
> ~Gopala Aiyar Sundaramoorthy (Appa)[2]

I think Tantra's gift to us is the understanding that we're not here to get it right. We're not here to achieve anything or prove anything. We're not here to fix the problem, but to manage the paradox. We're here to savor the experience we're having. We're here to engage with life in any given moment with whatever life is presenting to us, for better or worse.

There's no wrong way and no right way. There's only your way and the meaning you assign to it. Tantra's question is, "Are you savoring?"

Are you?

NOTES

---

[1] S Rashani, *The Unbroken.* https://rashani.com/arts/poems/poems-by-rashani. Accessed 15 May 2020.

[2] Gopala Aiyar Sundaramoorthy (Appa) is Douglas Brooks' teacher with whom he studied India. For more information, Dr. Brooks suggests this blog: https://rajanaka.blogspot.com/2010/03/dust-into-gold.html?fbclid=IwAR3ovReGJxQynsAgsutnxS0YMEHjSBo2qTSjhAt-UC1NyonN4EWq59Q7CUk. Accessed 8 May 2020.

CHAPTER TWENTY

Unreasonable Happiness

Do you know what you are?
You are a manuscript of a divine letter.
You are a mirror reflecting a noble face.
This universe is not outside of you.
Look inside yourself;
everything that you want,
you are already that.

~Rumi[1]

I was utterly exhausted after a long three-day weekend of teaching in Cincinnati, OH. The flight had been late taking off from Cincinnati, so I landed late at night at Bradley International Airport in Hartford, CT. The plane's delay didn't bother me; I've flown enough over the years to know how to relax when my travel plans change. But for some reason, as we taxied from the runway to the gate, I found myself especially tired. I gathered up my belongings, wishing for one last time that I had my earbuds.

On the flight out to Cincinnati on Thursday, I had lost my earbuds. Yes, I've become one of those people who walk around, engage with the world, and still carry on a conversation on the phone. I remember when I used to think people were crazy, talking to the air. Now I'm one of them. I bring my earbuds everywhere.

All weekend, I could not find those things for the life of me. I searched everywhere, multiple times. I kept telling myself to let it go; after all, why get stressed out over something I couldn't find? *I must have taken them out at home before I left.* Still, I obsessed about not being able to find those earbuds. It's not like me to forget something. I looked and looked for them, each time gently reminding myself to let it go.

I deboarded the plane, knowing that I still had another 75-minute drive home to the Berkshires. As I entered the terminal, everything seemed typical for that time of night: it was quiet; weary travelers dotted the airport; and I passed some rumpled individuals sleeping with their arms wrapped around their carry-on luggage. I headed toward baggage claim and stepped onto the escalator going down. As I descended lower and lower, I glanced up and took in the "Welcome to Hartford, CT" sign, next to some unmemorable advertisement. It was about as ho-hum and non-eventful as a moment can get.

Just then, something unusual happened. I suddenly noticed: *I am happy. Really, really happy.* I smiled and began laughing out loud. I allowed myself to experience the sheer delight of it. I felt youthful; I felt like I was in love; I felt like I wanted to jump up and click my heels together

387

in the air! I couldn't figure out why I should feel this way. I was spent, the flight had been delayed, it was super-late, and I still had over an hour of driving ahead of me. I should have felt tired and stressed out. But I didn't. I was happy.

Then it hit me. *This must be unreasonable happiness. This is the experience of being happy for no reason at all.* The very moment I acknowledged that I was experiencing unreasonable happiness, it vanished. At that, I laughed even harder, because I'm so familiar with heightened states of consciousness vanishing when the mind intrudes. Because I found that funny, the happiness kept coming back. It seemed as though no matter whether my mind got involved or not, happiness persisted.

Then, right at that moment, I reached into my coat pocket and felt… my earbuds! OMG! I became ecstatic. I began laughing uncontrollably. I looked up, stared the universe right in the eyes and said, shaking my fist at the sky, "You!" The universe was playing with me. By hiding my earbuds from me, then revealing them at that exact moment, grace underscored and validated my experience of unreasonable happiness. It's as if grace said, "Yep! This is the experience of unreasonable happiness. Do you get it?"

Did I ever. The yogi doesn't just want accidental happiness, coincidental happiness, or temporary happiness. The yogi wants permanent happiness, the kind that transcends the normal ups and downs of life, the kind that exists as the backdrop to everything else that happens in life.

This is happiness that is independent of external causes; it's an inside job that requires, no, *demands*, that you follow your heart. When you do that, you access a deeper consciousness – and you begin living from the inside out.

Happiness like this is available to everyone. It's your birthright. According to the Tantric tradition, your true nature pulses with *ānanda*, the highest bliss possible. This doesn't mean you never experience the ups and downs in life. You do. Yet underneath sadness, states of anxiety, or self-doubt, is the constant flow of happiness, like a kind of wholeness, fullness, or serenity. With practice, you can cultivate the ability to touch that river of happiness deep within you, to know that all is well. This is yoga. This is the purpose of practice: to experience unreasonable happiness, the spark of the divine.

In that desolate airport, late at night, I felt completely seen and loved by the universe. One meaning I attached to the whole earbud incident was that grace showered me with a blessing of love, giving me confidence that I was in the right place, doing the right thing, and fulfilling my purpose in life. For me, this was an unmistakable communication.

But the other meaning is the one I most want you to take away, the jewel at the center of it all: *What you've been looking for is already hidden within you.* Remember, I had the ear buds all along! The joy of the revelation is the divine joke that life plays on us, the role of *līlā* in our lives. We ARE already what we are seeking.

Isn't this our predicament? Aren't we constantly searching for "the thing" that's going to make us happy? A job, a relationship, a purchase? A guru? It has taken me many years to finally understand that life is about being on this magnificent journey... to come home to the heart.

Home is with us all the time. Home is our deep inner self, the Self of all, the inexhaustible Absolute source place that is constantly flowing with vitality, wholeness, and possibility. Getting close to that self, or touching that self, is the essence of the journey. It's the big Why. It's the only "thing" that brings lasting happiness, unreasonable happiness.

You are already worthy, already talented, already a one-of-a-kind masterpiece. There's no one else on the planet quite like you. But you don't have to hear it from me, or anyone else, for that matter. You can hear it from yourself. Right now, grace is whispering to you. All you have to do is soften, open your heart...and listen.

EXERCISE: Letter from the Universe

1. Find a comfortable position lying on your back, with a pen and piece of paper within easy reach. Close your eyes and take three or four deep breaths. As you exhale, open to a bigger energy and relax. Release your muscles away from the bones. Allow your bones to release into the earth. Imagine your organs sinking to the back side of your body. Soften the root of your tongue and relax your jaw. Release the muscles of your face. Let your eyes sink to the back of your skull like smooth, round pebbles being tossed into a pond and sinking all the way down to the sandy bottom. Feel all tension drain from your body and bask in the vastness of your being.

2. Now place your left hand on your heart and your right hand on your belly. Take a moment to breathe into your heart and belly and let go even more. Without any expectations, open to the presence of the universal energy, to the mysterious life force that surrounds and infuses you with light. Open to grace.

3. Sense the subtle depth of presence. Listen to the silence with your inner ears. Savor it. Now allow yourself to open to receive a message from the universe. What might the universe or life be trying to tell you? What's the message the universe has for you, the message you need to hear?

4. Soften and allow your awareness to become even more subtle. No strain or effort. Sometimes the message comes in loud and clear. Other times it comes as a faint image, a phrase, a whisper, sometimes an animal totem from nature. Allow yourself to let go now. Trust something greater. If the universe surrounds you and is inside of you, doesn't it make sense that it could guide you or speak to you, that you could converse with it?

5. Once you've received a message or a sense of something, offer thanks. Then, when you're ready, slowly roll to your right side

to sit up. Take the pen and paper and simply begin writing. Allow the universe to write through you. Imagine you were a clear, open channel, a vessel for the universal energy to speak through you. Begin with the words, *"Dear (your name), What I want you to know is…"* Take five or ten minutes to write, stream of consciousness, without any editing or commentary from your mind. See what arrives. Once you've finished, be sure to add the appropriate salutation, *"Love, the Universe. P.S. …and remember, I love you."*

6. Now, fold your letter, put it in an envelope, seal it, and self-address it. The last step is very important: give it to a friend or family member and ask them to mail it to you in about four to six months without telling you when, so that one day you will receive a surprise letter from the universe/yourself. I give this experience to my teacher trainees after they graduate and I'm told that the letter always comes at the perfect time, a time they most needed to remember their connection to the universe. Try it and see what happens….

NOTES

[1] Barks, Coleman with John Moyne, translators. *The Essential Rumi*. New York: Harper Collins. 1995. Print.

Blessings of Love from Todd

Dear Heart Follower,

Thank you for reading my story and for joining me on this transformational journey of the heart. I am so grateful for the courage and vulnerability that I know it takes to look into your own heart and your own life to find fulfillment and a deeper meaning for all that has happened for you.

I ask myself often, "What is the meaning of my life? Why am I here and why do I have to go through such suffering?" The answer is always clear. I am here to learn and grow myself, to become more accepting and affirming of the grace and blessings that have carried me across this vast ocean of change.

If there's anything more I can share with you, it would be this: Become still. Listen to your inner calling and follow your heart no matter what. As long as you point your heart in the direction of your highest aspirations, you will arrive at your destination. Although it won't be anything like how you thought it would be, you'll get there just the same. And along the way, breathe, enjoy the view, fall in love again and again with people, places, and things, and grow yourself into the beautiful, strong, vulnerable, courageous being that you are. Then open your mouth and share your story with everyone you meet. Make honey.

From the depth of my heart, I thank you. Thank you for participating with me in my journey. Thanks for your support, your love, and your friendship. I hope we meet again. Maybe it will be in a yoga course? in a cafe? or simply walking down the street? Whenever that happens, I will look straight into your eyes and see the blessing of the divine staring back at me.

Namaste,

Todd

Continue Your Journey

Stay connected and deepen your learning at ashayayoga.com. Here you'll find my events schedule, monthly free teachings, my blog, and transformational online courses and training programs that I've created from the heart.

Ashaya Yoga exists to awaken hearts to their own inherent, unlimited potential. We seek to reignite the desire in others for a great life and to lead the way to deep acceptance, ecstatic joy, and true healing.

Join us at ashayayoga.com
Facebook.com/AshayaYoga

About the Co-Writer

Mary Poindexter McLaughlin believes in the transformative power of story and seeks to bring those healing stories to light. An award-winning playwright (*The Buddha's Wife*), published poet, and essayist, she holds a BA in English from Stanford University, where she was the recipient of a Golden Grant Award for playwriting, and an MA in Theatre & Performance Studies from SUNY Buffalo. In writing this book, Mary happily drew on her Ashaya Yoga teacher training, her analytic mind, and her love of metaphor to illuminate the *Nondual Śaiva-Śākta Tantra* principles and help Todd make them accessible to all. Her most recent project, a full-length play entitled *Her Own Words*, answers the question "was Shakespeare a woman?" by employing Elizabethan language and modern theatricality to amplify the indomitable feminine voice. When not writing, Mary teaches theatre arts, laughs with her family, and dances in the orchard.

Website: poindextermclaughlin.com
Blog: https://medium.com/@marypoindextermclaughlin

Nāḍīs

Nāḍīs, which means little rivers, are subtle energy channels that carry the life force, or *prāṇa*, throughout the body. According to the book *Prāṇāyāma: The Yoga of Breathing* by Andre Van Lysebeth,[1] each of us has about 72,000 of them, although some sources say that number is closer to 300,000. Suffice it to say, we have a lot of them.

Of the 72,000 *nāḍīs*, there are three most important channels: *piṅgala nāḍī* (or *surya nāḍī*, sun channel, right nostril); *ida nāḍī* (or *chandra nāḍī*, moon channel, left nostril); and *suṣumna* nāḍī (she who is most gracious), the most important and central channel along the front of the spine. The *piṅgala* and *ida nāḍīs* twine around the *suṣumna nāḍī*, which is also known as the *brahma nāḍī*, or the conduit of the divine. All of the subtle energy centers, or cakras, are sourced in the *suṣumna*.

Just as we can develop arteriosclerosis, or clogged arteries, we can also develop clogged *nāḍīs*. They can get congested with psychic debris, such as long term regret, resentment, worry, anxiety, rage, depression, blame, fear, or indecision. Certain *prāṇāyāma*s are designed to clear this debris, the most common of which is *nāḍī śodhana*, or alternate nostril breathing.

Instructions for *Nāḍī Śodhana*: (channel purification)

Take a comfortable seat. If you're sitting on the floor, elevate your hips about four inches by sitting on a folded blanket or firm cushion. Sit up tall, making sure you have a gentle lower back curve (lumbar arch).

Close your eyes and take a few deep breaths. *Nāḍī Śodhana* is done by alternating the nostrils with each breath. To close each nostril, use *Viṣṇu Mudrā* (take your right hand and fold your index and middle fingers down to your palm. Use your thumb to close your right nostril and your fourth and fifth fingers together to close the left nostril).

To begin *Nāḍī Śodhana*, breathe in through both nostrils. Close the left nostril and exhale through the right nostril. Then inhale through the right nostril. When your lungs are full, pause. Then close the right nostril and exhale through the left nostril. When the lungs are empty, pause. Inhale through the left nostril. This is one round. Then close the left nostril and exhale through the right nostril and continue. Keep your breath slow, smooth, soft, and steady. Repeat 5-10 more rounds, or until you feel a greater sense of calm.

When you are ready to complete, the next time you inhale through the right nostril (wait for the cycle), pause, then exhale through both nostrils. Exhaling through both nostrils creates evenness and balance. Exhaling through the left nostril will create more peace and calm, while exhaling through the right nostril will be more energizing.

---

[1] Andre Van Lysebeth, *Prāṇāyāma: The Yoga of Breathing.* New York: Harmony, Crown Publishing Group. 2013. Print.

36 *Tattvas* of Tantric Cosmology

As the great vast, undifferentiated universe comes into existence and moves from potentiality to manifestation, it moves through levels of materiality from the most subtle, to the subtle, to the gross. The Tantrikas expressed this transition from the unmanifest to the manifest, from the formless to form, from invisible energy to visible material, through a series of principles called *tattvas* or principles of existence. At the top of the chart is *paramśiva*, which represents the heart, where *Śiva* and *Śakti* unite. *Paramaśiva* is pure potentiality of being, it's that which simultaneously transcends and encompasses all things. It is the supreme paradox; it is the Absolute reality.

The next five *tattvas* are aspects of the Absolute that begin to organize themselves as the Absolute dives down into the relative. They are called the absolute *tattvas*, or five *śaktis* or powers: *Śiva*, or chit *śakti* (the power of consciousness); *śakti*, or *ānanda śakti* (the power of bliss); *icchā śakti* (the power of intention); *jñāna śakti* (the power of knowledge); and *kriyā śakti* (the power of action). Think of them as five phases of God's awareness, all different aspects but evenly weighted and without hierarchy.

The next *tattva*, *māyā*, separates the absolute tattvas from psychical *tattvas*, or microcosmic reality. It's the "magical mirror" that *Śiva* creates within his own being, the Supreme's power to cloak and veil itself.

It makes sense, then, that the next five *tattvas* are all *kañcukas*, or cloaks, that cover the Absolute, limiting it, shaping it, giving it form. Think of each of the Absolute *tattvas* of the five *śaktis* being cloaked. Or, as I sometimes joke in my teacher trainings when I'm trying to explain the profound and difficult concept of the *kañcukas*, it's as if the five powers jump down from the Absolute into the relative, from formless into form, and into their cloaks like jumping down into hoodie footie pajamas. *Kañcukas* are the five prerequisites for the embodied experience: *kalā* (limited agency or *kriyā śakti* cloaked); *vidya* (limited knowledge or *jñāna śakti* cloaked); *raga* (limited desire or *Icchā śakti* cloaked); *kāla* (limited power or *śakti* cloaked); and *niyati* (causality or *Śiva* cloaked). Each kañchuka is one of the five *śakti*s with pajamas on (concealed), and each one prevents us from recognizing the divine nature of the Absolute.

The rest of the *tattvas* are considered physical *tattvas*, aspects of individual consciousness and the relative world. They include *puruṣa* (spirit) and *prakṛti* (materiality), which can be further broken down into the three psychic instruments (*buddhi,* or intellect; *ahaṃkāra,* or ego; and *manas,* or mind) and twenty (four sets of five) sense organs, motor organs, subtle elements, and great elements.

The Heart
Paramaśiva: Śiva/Śakti in perfect fusion

The Absolute Tattvas
Universal Consciousness

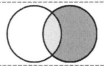

1. Śiva
Consciousness

2. Śakti
Power of
Consciousness

3. **Sadāśiva:** Icchā Śakti, power to be, will to exist
4. **Īśvara:** Jñāna Śakti, power to know
5. **Śuddhavidyā:** Kriyā Śakti, power to act
6. **Māyā:** the power to differentiate and conceal itself,
   Makes the immeasurable measurable

The Psychical Tattvas
The Five Kañcukas (cloaks)
7. **Kalā:** limited agency, capacity to act, Kriyā Śakti cloaked
8. **Vidyā:** limited knowledge, Jñāna Śakti cloaked
9. **Rāga:** limited desire, creates longing to be full, Icchā Śakti cloaked
10. **Kāla:** limited power, sequential time, Śakti cloaked
11. **Niyati:** causality, creates fabric of space, Śiva cloaked

The Physical Tattvas
Individual Consciousness, the Relative World

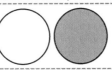

12. Puruṣa
pure spirit,
individual consciousness

13. Prakṛti
nature, materiality

The Three Psychic Instruments
14. **Buddhi:** intelligence, discrimination, decision maker
15. **Ahaṃkāra:** "I" maker, ego, personalization
16. **Manas:** mental, administrative process, memory

Jñānendriyas	Karmendriyas	Tanmātras	Mahābhūtas
sense organs	action organs	subtle elements	great elements
17. Ears: hearing	22. Mouth: speaking	27. Śabda: audibility	32. Ākāśa: space
18. Skin: touch	23. Hands: grasping	28. Sparśa: tactility	33. Vāyu: wind/air
19. Eyes: seeing	24. Feet: walking	29. Rūpa: appearance	34. Agni: fire
20. Tongue: tasting	25. Genitals: pleasure	30. Rasa: tastability	35. Ap: water
21. Nose: smelling	26. Bowels: eliminating	31. Gandha: smellability	36. Pṛthvī: earth

Adapted from *Tantra Illuminated* by Christopher D. Wallis, page 124.

Rasas: Nectar of Life, Tastes of Embodiment

Rasa means emotion, experience, flavor, feeling, taste, flow, liquid, nectar, juice, or essence – all of the ways the divine experiences its embodiment through human form via the emotions and feelings. Emotions are the sacred "divine palette of flavors" inherent within us as the gifts of life.

In the Tantric philosophy, the *rasas* provide the basis for understanding the depths of our human experience and the divine's participation in the gifts of embodiment. *Rasa* defines the core of our being and explains the qualities of life that we discern, absorb, and know by tasting or taking in our direct experience. To study the theory of *rasas* as a spiritual teaching is to enter into an entirely new, transformative, and profound experience of life's possibilities. There are few subjects more sublime or important for the evolution of one's personal yoga and for a deeper appreciation of traditions of Tantric yoga.

The Nine *Rasas* (originally there were only eight; Tantra added *śanta*, the ninth *rasa* which pervades all eight):

1. *Śṛṅgāra*: passion, love, the erotic
2. *Hāsya*: comic, light-hearted
3. *Karuṇā*: compassion, tragic
4. *Raudra*: furious, cruel, anger
5. *Vīra*: the heroic, courage
6. *Bhayānaka*: fearsome, fear
7. *Bībhatsa*: gruesome, loathsome, disgust
8. *Adbhuta*: wondrous, astonishing
9. *Śanta*: peaceful, mindful

Dhvani/Rasa Dhvani: resonance, alignment, the essence behind what's being said, the real feeling underlying all expression, the soul or deepest sense of power behind any feeling or expression

In the Tantric philosophy, the *rasas* provide the basis for understanding the very depths of our human experience and the divine's participation in the gifts of embodiment. *Rasa* defines the very core of our being and explains the qualities of life that we discern, absorb, and know by tasting or taking in our direct experience. To study the theory of rasas as a spiritual teaching is to enter into an entirely new, transformative, and profound experience of life's possibilities. There are few subjects more sublime or important for the evolution of one's personal yoga and for a deeper appreciation of traditions of Tantric yoga.

Rasa Mandala

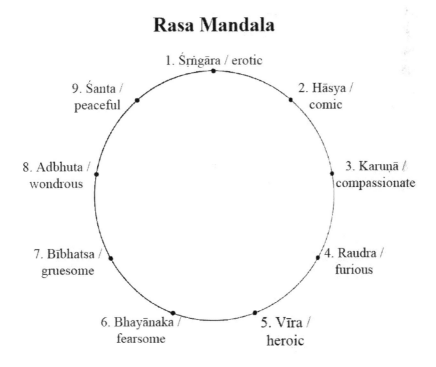

1. Śṛṅgāra / erotic
2. Hāsya / comic
3. Karuṇā / compassionate
4. Raudra / furious
5. Vīra / heroic
6. Bhayānaka / fearsome
7. Bībhatsa / gruesome
8. Adbhuta / wondrous
9. Śanta / peaceful

"Rasa is the rejuvenating juice of life that is present all around and within us if we know how to tap into its source."

~ Shiva Rea

APPENDIX D

The Five Divine Acts of *Śiva* (*Pañca Kṛtyas*)

The five acts of *Śiva* define the ways *Śiva* acts in the world, either one at a time or all at once. In Tantra, we don't just go through the motions of these actions, we become *Śiva* in all of our expressions. In other words, *Śiva* becomes us through the actions we take.

1. *Sṛṣṭi*: Creation and the beginning of a new cycle, or birth. *Sṛṣṭi* is the stepping-down in vibration from subtle into gross, from spirit into matter. This is the manifesting current of consciousness, and is exemplified by Brahma, the creator.

2. *Sthiti*: Sustenance, maintenance, and stability. This is the middle portion of the cycle of life as portrayed by *Viṣṇu*, the sustainer. *Sthiti* is the energy that holds form together and gives it the appearance of solidity.

3. *Saṃhāra*: Dissolution, death, and the end of a cycle. In the act of *saṃhāra*, the outer is dissolved back into the inner. The gross dissolves back into the subtle, difference into unity, and matter into spirit. This is the liberating current of consciousness, the power of *Śiva*, the transformer.

4. *Vilaya or Tirobhāva*: Concealment. This is the power of the universe to veil and hide itself, the power of *Śiva* to limit itself and self-shadow.

5. *Anugraha*: Revelation, grace. The act of *anugraha* employs the power of the universe to reveal itself and awaken to its true nature.

Additional Resources

MORE WORKS BY TODD NORIAN

TODD'S MUSIC

- *Deep Peace: Music for Yoga and Relaxation.* Slow and flowing, meditative.
- *Bija: Music and Mantras for Yoga and Meditation.* Slow and deeply relaxing, om and bija mantras for the chakras.
- *Shakti Fusion,* by Todd Norian and friends. Jazz/rock/Sanskrit chanting fusion.
- *Tejase: The Essence of Illumination.* Slow but rhythmic, *Shiva* mantra.
- *Ocean of the Heart.* Slow relaxation, *Shri Ram Jaya Ram* mantra.
- *Intimate Moments.* Solo piano compositions for inspiration and contemplative moods.
- *Invocation: Heart of Darkness and Light, Music and Mantras for Creating Sacred Space*

TODD'S MEDITATION AND SAVASANA CD'S

- *Ecstatic Meditations for Enhanced Living*
- *Savasana: Guided Relaxations for Enhanced Living*

Available through all major music sources, streaming services, and ashayayoga.com.

YOGA MANUALS

- *Ashaya Yoga: Align Your Body. Awaken Your Heart.* Overview of the Ashaya Yoga method and philosophy, complete Ashaya method techniques, *asana* sheets, sequences, more.

- *Introduction to Touch of Grace: Hands-On Adjustments.* How to give supportive, unforgettable hands-on adjustments.

- *Introduction to Ashaya Yoga Therapy.* Therapeutic applications of Ashaya Yoga for all of the major joints in the body.

Available through ashayayoga.com.

403

WORKS BY OTHER AUTHORS

TANTRA PHILOSOPHY

Brooks, Douglas. *Auspicious Wisdom: The Texts and Traditions of Srividya Sakta Tantrism in South India.* Albany, NY: SUNY Press. 1992. Print.

Dyczkowski, Mark (translator). *The Stanzas on Vibration.* Albany, NY: SUNY Press. 1999. Print.

Kempton, Sally. *Awakening Shakti: The Transformative Power of the Goddesses of Yoga.* Louisville, Colorado: Sounds True. 2013. Print.

Kramrisch, Stella. *The Presence of Śiva.* Philadelphia: Philadelphia Museum of Art. 1993. Print.

Lakshmanjoo (translator). *Śiva Sūtras: The Supreme Awakening.* Bloomington, Indiana: AuthorHouse. 2007. Print.

Mahony, William K. *Exquisite Love: Reflections on the Spiritual Life Based on Nārada's Bhakti Sūtra.* Location Unknown: Sarvabhava. 2014. Print.

Mishra, Kamalar. *Kashmir Śaivism: The Central Philosophy of Tantrism.* Varanasi, India: Indica Books. 2011. Print.

Muller-Ortega, Paul Eduardo. *The Triadic Heart of Śiva: Kaula Tantricism of Abhinavagupta in the Non-Dual Shaivism of Kashmir.* Albany, NY: SUNY Press. 1988. Print.

Odier, Daniel (translator). *Yoga Spandakarika: The Sacred Texts at the Origins of Tantra.* New York: Simon and Schuster. 2005. Print. Also see: https://www.danielodier.com/english/enspanda.php

Rhodes, Constantina. *Invoking Lakshmi: The Goddess of Wealth in Song and Ceremony.* Albany, NY: SUNY Press. 2010. Print.

Roche, Lorin. *The Radiance Sutras: 112 Gateways to the Yoga of Wonder and Delight.* Louisville, Colorado: Sounds True. 2014. Print.

Singh, Jaideva (translator). *Pratyabhijñāhṛdayam: The Secret of Self-Recognition.* Delhi, India: Motilal Banarsidass. 2016. Print.

Singh, Jaideva (translator). *Śiva Sutras: The Yoga of Supreme Identity.* Delhi, India: Motilal Banarsidass. 2012. Print.

Swami Muktananda. *The Play of Consciousness: A Spiritual Autobiography.* Location Unknown: Siddha Yoga. 2000. Print.

Swami Shantananda and Peggy Bendet. *The Splendor of Recognition: An Exploration of the Pratyabhijna-hrdayam, a Text on the Ancient Science of the Soul.* Location Unknown: Siddha Yoga Publications. 2003. Print.

Wallis, Christopher D. *Tantra Illuminated: The Philosophy, History, and Practice of a Timeless Tradition.* Boulder, CO: Mattamayura, 2nd edition. 2013. Print.

CAKRAS

Avalon, Arthur. *The Serpent Power: The Secrets of Tantric and Shaktic Yoga.* Mineola, NY: Dover. 1974. Print.

Judith, Anodea. *Wheels of Life: A User's Guide to the Chakra System.* Woodbury, Minnesota: Llewellyn. 1989. Print.

Judith, Anodea. *Eastern Body, Western Mind: Psychology and the Chakra System as a Path to the Self.* Berkeley, CA: Celestial Arts. 2004. Print.

Leadbeater, C.W. *The Chakras.* Wheaton, IL: Quest Books. 2013. Print.

Myss, Caroline. *Anatomy of the Spirit: The Seven Stages of Power and Healing.* New York: Harmony Books, 1996. Print.

OTHER YOGA PHILOSOPHY

Bryant, Edwin F. *Yoga Sūtras of Patañjali.* New York: North Point. 2009. Print.

Eliade, Mircea. *Yoga, Immortality, and Freedom.* Princeton, NJ: Princeton University Press. 2009. Print.

Feuerstein, Georg. *The Yoga Tradition: Its History, Literature, Philosophy, and Practice.* Prescott, Ariz: Hohm Press, 2008. Print.

Mitchell, Stephen (translator). *Bhagavad Gītā: A New Translation.* New York: Three Rivers Press, 2000. Print.

Mascaro, Juan (translator). *The Bhagavad Gītā.* New York: Penguin. 2003. Print.

Paramahansa Yogananda. *Autobiography of a Yogi.* New York: Philosophical Library. 1946. Print.

Rieker, Hans-Ulrich. *The Yoga of Light: The Classic Esoteric Handbook of Kundalini Yoga.* Lower Lake, CA: Dawn Horse. 1974. Print.

Sargeant, Winthrop. *The Bhagavad Gita.* Albany, NY: SUNY Press. 1993. Print

Swami Vishnu-Devananda (translator). *Haṭha Yoga Pradīpikā.* Varanasi, India: Om Lotus of Pilgrim Book House. 1997. Print.

Made in the USA
Middletown, DE
06 June 2021